Introduction to Political Sociology

Introduction to Political Sociology

Fourth Edition

ANTHONY M. ORUM

University of Illinois at Chicago

Upper Saddle River, New Jersey 07458

Library of Congress Cataloging-in-Publication Data

Orum, Anthony M.
Introduction to political sociology / Anthony M. Orum.—4th ed.
p. cm.
Includes index.
ISBN 0-13-927153-8 (pbk.)
1. Political sociology. I. Title.

JA76. 078 2001
306.2—dc21 00-036690

VP, Editorial Director: Laura Pearson
Publisher: Nancy Roberts
Managing Editor: Sharon Chambliss
Editorial/production supervision
and interior design: Mary Araneo
Director of Marketing: Beth Gillett Mejia
Prepress and Manufacturing Buyer: Mary Ann Gloriande
Cover Art Director: Jayne Conte
Cover Designer: Bruce Kenselaar

Credits appear on p. 284, which constitutes a continuation of this page.

This book was set in 10/12 Palatino by A & A Publishing Services, Inc., and was printed and bound by Courier Companies, Inc. The cover was printed by Phoenix Color Corp.

Printed in the United States of America

10 9 8 7 6 5 4 3 2 1

ISBN 0-13-927153-8

PRENTICE-HALL INTERNATIONAL (UK) LIMITED, *London*
PRENTICE-HALL OF AUSTRALIA PTY. LIMITED, *Sydney*
PRENTICE-HALL CANADA INC., *Toronto*
PRENTICE-HALL HISPANOAMERICANA, S.A., *Mexico*
PRENTICE-HALL OF INDIA PRIVATE LIMITED, *New Delhi*
PRENTICE-HALL OF JAPAN, INC., *Tokyo*
SIMON & SCHUSTER ASIA PTE. LTD., *Singapore*
EDITORA PRENTICE-HALL DO BRASIL, LTDA., *Rio de Janeiro*

Contents

Preface to the Fourth Edition xi

CHAPTER 1
Introduction 1

Power and Authority 2
Institutions, Networks, and Culture 4
Visions of Societies and Politics: Marx, Weber, Durkheim, and de Tocqueville 5
Pedagogical Guidelines 6

CHAPTER 2
On the Economy and Politics: Karl Marx and the Neo-Marxists 8

Karl Marx on the Economy and Politics 9
The Essential Marx 9
The Economy and Social Stratification 12
Substructure and Superstructure 13
Politics as a Reflection of the Class Struggle 15
State Power and Its Limits 16

Sustaining Capitalism and the Rule of Capitalists 17
Revolution and Change 17
The Neo-Marxists 23
V. I. Lenin 23
Antonio Gramsci 27
The Frankfurt School 29
Nicos Poulantzas 32
Conclusion 34
Notes 35

CHAPTER 3
On States and Societies: Max Weber and the Neo-Weberians 38

Max Weber on States and Politics 40
The Essential Weber 40
The State 43
The Power of the Ruler 44
Authority and Its Legitimacy 45
Political Power and Contending Social Groups 46
The Neo-Weberians 47
Reinhard Bendix 47
Charles Tilly 50
Theda Skocpol 55
Summary 61
Notes 61

CHAPTER 4
On Civil Society and Politics: Emile Durkheim and Alexis de Tocqueville 64

Emile Durkheim on Civil Society and Politics 65
The Essential Durkheim 65
Society 67
States, Politics, and Societies 70
Alexis de Tocqueville on Civil Society and Politics 72
The Essential Tocqueville 72
Equality in America 73
The Conditions (Causes) for Equality 74
Threats to Democracy in America 75

Concluding Observations 77
The Neo-Consensualists 77
Talcott Parsons 77
Seymour Martin Lipset 80
Robert Bellah 82
James S. Coleman and Robert Putnam 84
Conclusion 87
Notes 88

CHAPTER 5
Basic Forms of Political Rule: Democratic, Totalitarian, and Authoritarian Regimes in the Modern World **91**

Basic Types of Political Rule: The Classical Greek Conceptions 92
Types of Political Rule in the Modern World 95
Democracy 96
Totalitarianism 101
Authoritarianism 105
Conclusion 107
Notes 108

CHAPTER 6
Power and Equality in Modern America **112**

Prologue 113
The Power of the American State 117
The American State as a War-Making State 119
The American State as a Welfare State 124
Sociological Perspectives on the Power of the State Today 127
The Power of Business and Corporations 129
The Corporate Community 131
The Corporate Inner Circle 132
Multinational Corporations and the Growth of the Global Economy 133
Does America Possess A Ruling Class–or Even a Dominant Class? 134
Equality and Inequality in Modern America 136
Economic Inequality 136
Political Equality 138
Concluding Observations 142
Notes 143

CHAPTER 7
Power and Politics in the Modern Metropolis **147**

Theoretical Perspectives on Cities and Politics 148
Political Pluralism in the City: Civil Society and the Dispersal of Power 149
The City as a Growth Machine: The Political Economy of the City 150
City Limits 152
Regime Theory: History and Local Governance 153
Concluding Observations 155
The Metropolis in American History 155
The Rise and Fall of the Industrial Metropolis 156
The Contentious Politics of the American Metropolis: Central Cities, Suburbs, and Edge Cities 160
The Post-World War II City: Sunbelt Cities and Metropolitan Fragmentation 162
Can American Cities Make a Real Difference in the Lives of Their Residents? 164
Cities and the New Global Economy 167
Global Cities 167
Other Postindustrial Cities 168
Regional and Urban Experiments of Major Developing Nations: China, South Korea, and Taiwan 169
Conclusion 171
Notes 171

CHAPTER 8
Political Parties and Political Partisanship **175**

The Nature of Modern Political Parties 176
The Birth of Modern Political Parties 177
Variations in Modern Political Parties: Highlights of Current and Former Patterns 179
Current Patterns 179
Former Patterns: The Political Machine of Urban America 185
Power and Politics within Modern Political Parties 187
Robert Michels's Iron Law of Oligarchy 187
Political Partisanship: Contemporary Patterns and Trends in the United States 191

The Breadth of Political Partisanship 192
Values and Partisanship 195
The Social Foundations of Partisanship 196
The Past and Future of Modern Political Parties: The Case of the United States 202
Notes 205

CHAPTER 9
Citizen Participation in Politics: Conventional and Contentious Forms **210**

Conventional Politics 211
Types and Levels of Participation 211
Social Cleavages and Conventional Political Participation 213
Civil Society, Social Capital, and Conventional Political Participation 216
Contentious Politics: Politics by Other Means 218
Contentious Forms 219
The Origins of Contention 225
The Institutionalization of Contention 233
Contentious Politics and Political Victories 235
Conclusions 237
Notes 238

CHAPTER 10
Building Nation-States in the Modern World **244**

The Essential Elements of the Modern Nation-State 245
Major Building-Blocks in the Construction of the Modern Nation-State 247
Nationalism 247
Political Legitimacy and Stability 251
Citizenship and the Establishment of Common Political Identity 253
Economic Development 255
Key Social Agents in the Construction of the Modern Nation-State 259
Intellectuals 259
The Military 261
Peasants 263

Alternative Pathways to Nationhood: Democratic, Authoritarian, and Totalitarian Regimes 265

The Seeds of Democracy: Seymour Martin Lipset on the Structural Foundations of Modern Democratic Regimes 266

Barrington Moore on Democracy and Oligarchy in the Modern World 267

Dietrich Rueschemeyer, Evelyne Huber Stephens, and John Stephens on Capitalism and the Development of Democracy 270

Success and Failure in Nation-Building: The Interdependence of Nation-States 273

Globalism and Nation-Building in the Twenty-First Century 278

Notes 279

Credits **284**

Index **285**

Preface to the Fourth Edition

Several years ago I was asked by Baruch Kimmerling to write a brief essay on the field of political sociology and the course of its development in the United States. I agreed to do the essay, in part because I had not thought much about the field for some time, and I wanted the opportunity to discover where the field had come over the course of a decade or so since I had worked in it. I tried to capture some of the changes in the field by concentrating on the movement from its strong behavioral roots, in the late 1940s and early 1950s, to its greater emphasis on institutions and their development. This theme, I believe, was inspired by an article by David Brian Robertson, "The Return to History and the New Institutionalism in American Political Science," published in 1993 in the journal *Social Science History*.

I received some interesting reactions to my brief essay, most of which I had not anticipated. While some were complimentary, certainly there were defenders of the faith, such as Seymour Martin Lipset and Theda Skocpol, who read the field differently than I. This started me on the course of rethinking my own view of political sociology, which I had first put in the form of a textbook late in the 1970s. How had the field changed since then? As it happened, I had the chance to put my thoughts into some order on the matter when Nancy Roberts, Publisher at Prentice-Hall, suggested that I revise the 1989 edition of my text. I was very pleased to take her up on the offer. I also was astonished, as I began to review writings in the field, to learn how much political sociology had changed in the course of the two decades since I first drafted the original framework for the book. And I must confess that I was a tad embarrassed because of my earlier failure to revise certain sections of the 1989 edition.

After some hesitation, I decided to embark on a thorough revision of the book. I also decided not to dedicate another four years of my life to such a project, largely because I was not sure whether I had another four years to spare, in part because of other things I wanted to write. The result is the current book.

This is in many ways a much different book than the third edition. Mainly that is because the world itself has changed so dramatically, forcing sociologists to rethink many old questions and issues. I have tried to pay as much attention to the changing world as to the new ideas populating the thinking of political sociologists. At the close of my 1996 essay, I spoke of my concern that political sociology was not nearly so vital a field of endeavor as it had been two or three decades earlier. Parts of the field were still very vigorous, such as the work on social movements, but other parts, such as work on the nature of power and politics in America, seemed almost moribund.

Having now spent the past year reading and reflecting on the field of political sociology, I would say that my assessment in 1996 was not quite accurate. There is a great deal of new and energetic work being done by political sociologists, but because of the rapid pace of events in the world, this work seems quickly outstripped in its relevance by the very changes taking place. I would like to think–though others must make their own judgments on this matter–that my efforts to redo the current edition of *Introduction to Political Sociology* represent at least one scholar's serious attempt to show the persisting relevance of political sociology for the important questions of our times. What are the best forms of government now available? How can the new nations become effectively and durably transformed into democracies? What role can the state play, not only in stimulating the economy, but also in making the lives of its citizens measurably better? How can everyday citizens work to transform the large-scale political institutions that surround them? And how do the lives of cities, and their residents, provide a way for understanding the political world in which we live?

In redoing this edition, I have found that many of the questions that seemed so academic and abstruse twenty, even ten, years ago, now have assumed a much greater urgency and immediacy. Matters of how to achieve democratic governance, and how it has been secured in the past, no longer seem to be merely the musings of scholars. Today they point to real concerns, and thoughtful and lucid answers to these questions can provide the shape of social and political institutions in the years to come. I think, as Baruch Kimmerling said to me some years ago, it is time that political sociologists actively reconnect to the world.

Two critics of my 1989 book played a vital role in helping me to redo this one; I thank them for their extensive and courteous efforts to review that book. One is Diane E. Davis of the New School for Social Research. Her comments were incisive and extraordinarily helpful. I almost think of her as the anonymous coauthor to the new edition. She provided extremely useful comments, not only on particular questions and issues, but also on the reorganization of the book. She also urged me to retain the perspective of Talcott Parsons, but to repackage it. I owe her a great debt of gratitude for the time and imagination she devoted to helping me, through her review, to rethink the format for this new edition. Equally I owe a great debt to Daniel Levy of Columbia University, who, through a similar exacting review, provided me with important new ideas and help in crafting this new edition. In addition, I'd like to thank Mary L. Ertel of Central Connecticut State University for her insightful comments. I, of course, remain responsible for its failings, particularly for my inability to include all the many new writings on the changing societies and politics of today. I hope that teachers who choose to use this book will see it as a device to encourage their students to probe more deeply into some issues that I could only cover here in a limited fashion.

There were many people who played a central role in helping me to craft the three previous editions of this text. Among them, those who played the most significant part were Neil Smelser and Mayer Zald. Though each of these fine scholars takes a different approach to the social world–particularly evident in their views of collective action and social movements–each also furnishes a wonderful role model for the rest of us to imitate.

Lastly, I want to thank the members of my family for their continuing support on this project as on all my other writings and work. They have managed to tolerate my preoccupations with the sort of patient kindness usually reserved for small children and the elderly. I want to dedicate this book, in particular, to my three children–Nicholas, Hannah, and Rebekah. I hope that the world of the twenty-first century is filled with much less violence and much more social justice than that of the century just passed and, especially, that each of my children, in his or her own way, will contribute to bringing such a world into being.

Anthony M. Orum

Introduction to Political Sociology

Chapter 1

Introduction

Today we live in a time of great and rapid changes. Old nations have collapsed. New states arise from their ashes. Capitalism, and the pursuit of profit, thrives in a world no longer centrally occupied by the forces of communism. Democracy has been victorious, but older democracies still seek ways to revitalize themselves. Territorial barriers between nations have broken down, allowing tens of thousands of immigrants to travel freely across the globe. The world no longer is threatened by the great wars, but acts of terrorism by small bands of individuals lurk as an imminent danger, more ominous and potentially catastrophic than the military force of earlier times.

In this book I shall tell you about the ways that political sociologists think about these matters. Political sociology, as a subfield of the broader discipline of sociology, originated in the writings of several great nineteenth-century social theorists. All of them lived, as we do today, in a world that was undergoing vast changes and upheavals. Revolutions abounded; old regimes died; new social classes surfaced. And these thinkers tried, as we do today, to make sense of the changes.

Certain themes today dominate the work of political sociologists, making it different from other ways of studying politics. For one thing, political sociologists take a panoramic view of the world, seeking to see the connections between political institutions and other world institutions, especially economic ones. For another, political sociologists believe that while political institutions, like the state, can take on a life of their own, such institutions also are necessarily grounded in some fashion in the other institutions of the world. Democracies, to take one example, do not spring up full-blown, but depend on a set of special historical and social circumstances to emerge. Likewise, the collapse of old regimes, like authoritarian governments or totalitarian dictatorships, disappear (though often not completely or overnight) not simply because of the personal failures of their leadership, but also because of their inability to navigate the often treacherous waters of international relations. Finally, political sociologists are very interested in the temporal construction and unfolding of political institutions. Thus, time and history are important elements in their calculations, far more so than they would be in the analytical tools employed, let us say, by many modern political scientists.

I have worked in the field of political sociology on and off for about three decades. I have seen it develop a great deal over this period of time. Most of all, I have seen it mature as a field of academic endeavor. Today, more so than ever before, the vital lessons it has to teach us are lessons that must be shared and publicized among all citizens. These are lessons about the success and failure of political institutions—how, for instance, human agents can work to create new durable and responsive democracies. This book will attempt to make these fundamental lessons clear and compelling even for those among you who at this point possess only a limited background in the study of politics.

POWER AND AUTHORITY

There are two basic concepts that guide the thinking of political sociologists. These concepts are terms familiar to us from everyday life—*power* and *authority*. They provide the central direction and animate the key questions raised by political sociologists. Thus it is important to understand them at the outset of this book.

Power generally refers to the capacity of a person or, more often, a group and institution to be able to manipulate and shape the views and actions of people. When parents can make their children behave, following their orders, we say that the parents have power over their children. Likewise, when a government is able to collect taxes from its citizens, we also say that the government exercises power over its citizens.

Authority is like power except that it always refers to a set of institutions, and institutionalized arrangements, in which it operates. If a bully beats up a coward, using force and violence to subdue him, we say that the bully has been victorious because of his greater power. But the bully has no authority, no set of institutions to back up his force, no set of institutionalized arrangements that compel the coward to obey him. He wins by virtue of his sheer exercise of muscle.

A basic premise of modern sociology is that the social world would not work effectively—it would, in fact, be sheer anarchy—if obedience were simply grounded in the force, or muscle power, of people. It would be a world occupied only by bullies, and eventually one in which only the person with the biggest muscles would occupy. We know, however, that the world is filled both with bullies and cowards and with all sorts of other people as well. And it works because of the set of social arrangements and institutions that guide it, working almost behind the scenes of our everyday lives. Social institutions operate to establish the set of rules that provide guidance to our lives, and that, in the case of our illustration, permit the cowards of the world to secure compensation if they have been attacked and beaten by bullies.

These rules represent authority. They are the institutional guidelines that dictate the conditions under which one person may fairly ask another to comply with his or her wishes. If the chairman of my academic department asks me to teach certain courses, I do so, not because my chairman is stronger than I am, but because it is part of my contract with the University as a teacher. The University delegates authority to the chairman of my department, and, as chairman, he can demand that I teach courses. If I rejected his claim and disobeyed, he could fire me because of the authority he exercises over me as an official of the University.

Power and authority, then, refer to the exercise of one person or one group's ideas to shape the views and/or action of another. Authority is the routine everyday medium of such relationships in nations. It is the layered and multidimensional element that fundamentally keeps our world working. When large-scale institutions break down, such as occurred with the government of the former Soviet Union, it is their fundamental authority that collapses. Power takes over in these circumstances precisely because, in the absence of institutions, there are no rules to follow. The bullies win.

The real trick, as some political sociologists point out, is not the precise nature of the rules that are to be created when old governments collapse, but how to secure *legitimacy* in the authority of the regimes that will arise. Legitimacy becomes a key element in the further unfolding from power to authority because essentially it is the sense of trust that is the foundation for the durable and continuing construction and operation of social and political institutions. Where it exists, or can be created, then so too can institutions and the authority they exercise; where legitimacy fails, so too will authority and its various rules. Certain modern social philosophers, such as Jürgen Habermas, pay a great deal of attention to the entire process of *legitimation*, or the creation of legitimate regimes, precisely because of the importance it has for the construction of durable social institutions.

To sum up, all political sociologists come to their study of politics, and the world in general, bearing a strong awareness of matters of power and of authority. These are the common coin of their intellectual realm, playing a role similar to that of atoms (or even quarks) for physicists. They are the basic terms that guide their search of the dominant patterns of the social and political world. In the chapters that follow I shall often use the terms *power* and *authority*, relying essentially on the definitions I have provided here. At times I also will use them interchangeably, mainly because in many contexts it is more felicitous to write and speak of power rather than authority. Nevertheless, the distinctions I draw here—between power and authority, and the importance of legitimacy—are critical ones; I urge you to keep them in mind as you read this book.

INSTITUTIONS, NETWORKS, AND CULTURE

Besides the elements of power and authority there are three other concepts that are crucial to the work today of political sociologists. I have already introduced you to one of them. It is the concept of *institution*. The early sociological theorists were very attentive to the nature of social institutions. Max Weber, about whom you shall learn in Chapter 4, more or less created his understanding of sociology by his focus on the nature of social institutions and how they were created, even destroyed. For a period of time in the mid-twentieth century, sociologists tended to disregard the nature of social institutions, preferring to focus their attention on various forms of social behavior. But now the nature and form of social institutions have come back into popularity. You will find throughout this book various discussions about the nature of social institutions, such as political parties, governmental regimes, and business firms. In general, social institutions represent *the established and organized practices of a given society*. Moreover, once formed, they can exercise a profound shape and direction over the course of history and the lives of individuals.

A second major theme to the study of modern political sociology is that of *social network*. Social networks represent the social ties and bonds among people, the organized set of relationships that link individuals to one another. There is a growing awareness among sociologists that much of our everyday life can be thought of in terms of the social networks in which we are embedded. Again you will discover in the following pages that the idea of social networks recurs in different ways among the topics of political sociology. For example, students of voting behavior have looked at a voter's social networks in order to understand the process whereby he or she arrives at a decision on which political candidate to support. Or, to take another example, analysts of social movements examine the nature of various social networks in a society as a means of gaining insight into how movements originate and develop over the course of time.

The third concept on which political sociologists have come to rely is that of the *culture*, or beliefs among large groups of people. Culture, as a tool to be used for understanding the dynamics of societies, has become increasingly helpful for contemporary sociologists. I shall point to several ways in which the political dimensions of societies can be better understood by tracking the nature of their culture. One very visible way is in the form of nationalism that exists in different nations. Nationalism represents the form of culture that is peculiar to the territorial-bounded organizations of nations. In the United States, it has taken the form of a distinctive emphasis on equality and individualism, beliefs that have developed and taken root among Americans over the course of the past two centuries. Another way in which culture makes itself felt is in the manner in which modern social movements, such as feminism and environmentalism, emphasize the importance of central beliefs and the creation of new identities for their members. Such an emphasis stands in contrast to the older social movements, such as that of trade unionism or even the civil rights movement, whose main stress was on the specific benefits to be achieved by the movement in concessions gained from management and the government.

These three concepts—institution, network, and culture—provide a way for thinking about the larger issues of politics. They help sociologists to frame their discoveries and also aid in directing their search for new findings. I urge you to be aware of how these concepts are used in the following topical sections and how large a role they play in the analyses of political sociologists.

VISIONS OF SOCIETIES AND POLITICS: MARX, WEBER, DURKHEIM, AND DE TOCQUEVILLE

Four major scholars have provided an intellectual legacy that helps to shape how political sociologists think about politics today. There are ways in which contemporary political sociologists have moved beyond this legacy, but it also has left a very deep imprint on our view of the world.

Chapters 2 through 4 will introduce you to the writings of these men. Chapter 2 takes up the major themes of Karl Marx. Marx was the first of the great nineteenth-century social theorists, and his writings on social class and modern capitalism have left their mark on many political sociologists. Though he did not have much to say about the nature of politics and the state—they largely were reflections of the dominance of capitalism—his basic imagery still animates the writings of some sociologists, as you shall discover in the chapters on American politics and on the development of the modern nation-state. Chapter 3 considers the work of Max Weber. Weber is the pre-eminent political sociologist. He dealt with themes that Marx failed to treat, and put an emphasis on political institutions and ideas that Marx simply considered relatively minor themes in the grander evolution of capitalism. Weber left us with our basic understanding of the state, as well as with the intimate ties of the state to other social institutions.

Emile Durkheim, a French sociologist, and Alexis de Tocqueville, one of the most insightful analysts both of America and of the French Revolution, left a somewhat different legacy. Unlike Marx and Weber, both these scholars emphasized the common beliefs and institutions that animated societies. Durkheim turned his attention to the nature of social phenomena, in general, and created a set of ideas that help to focus our attention on what today we call civil society—that part of the social world that is neither the state nor the economy. Alexis de Tocqueville provided us with unparalleled insight into the workings of American democracy, furnishing a portrait that relies heavily on the links between democracy and the general pattern of civic associations and participation in America. In the past decade, the writings of these figures, plus others, have grown in popularity as scholars try to fathom what it is that makes for an effective democratic government.

One can understand the work of modern political sociologists, I must confess, without delving deeply into the writings of these eminent scholars. Indeed, many political sociologists proceed about their work without even taking the time to consult the writings of these figures. Yet, it is my own conviction that these writings, while in many ways now out-of-date, still provide wonderful models of how to create panoramic portraits of the world, portraits that make sense of the labyrinths of diverse facts. In this fashion they continue to inspire our work and imagination.

PEDAGOGICAL GUIDELINES

When I wrote the first edition of this textbook I concluded with a few paragraphs about my view of teaching and how it had shaped the book. Although much of this book has since been rewritten and revised, happily I remain convinced that what I wrote more than twenty years ago remains significant today. Thus, I will conclude this introduction with slightly retouched paragraphs from the earlier work.

In my effort to present a broad and accurate portrait of political sociology, I have done a couple of things in this book that are a bit different from those that might have been done by my friends and colleagues. First, I have tried to illuminate the abstract character of concepts by referring mainly to materials from the United States—its present as well as its past. Where possible, I also have tried to point out differences between the character of politics in the United States and elsewhere, particularly in Western Europe. This attempt to draw in the comparative materials still has not gone quite as far as I would have wished—though it has gone a good deal further than twenty years ago. I hope that both students and instructors might introduce as many materials from other nations as possible to highlight the special features of the American setting and to flesh out the contents of the concepts used by political sociologists. Second, I have presented the theories on a particular subject and then evaluated them in terms of available evidence and, occasionally, in terms of the requirement of a good theory. Where it has been impossible to resolve the differences between theories on the basis of known facts, or to dismiss a particular theory because it does not fit what we know about the world, I have said as much. (Pay special attention to these considerations in Chapter 6.) Thus, in addition to the general diversity of ideas that I present, you also will confront an effort to present differences among theories and unresolved issues. The world about us is not a neat and tidy place in which all our ideas are confirmed by our observations; there is no reason to sugarcoat a book about this world and, especially, its politics—such an act would demean your intelligence. The ideas in this book, just like those present in our world, demand that we think and reflect.

If there is any single lesson that I have tried to get across in this book, apart from the many substantive ones, it is this: One must approach the world in a state of curiosity and openness, be willing to arrive at conclusions about the world, be sufficiently resilient to formulate tough statements of opinion, and be persistent enough to discover whether or not those judgments are accurate. This is what politics often proves to be about; it is what the enterprise of learning must be about.

Chapter 2

On the Economy and Politics

Karl Marx and the Neo-Marxists

> One capitalist always kills many. Hand in hand with this centralisation, or this expropriation of many capitalists by the few, develop, on an ever-extending scale, the co-operative form of the labour-process, the conscious technical application of science, the methodical cultivation of the soil, . . . the entanglement of all peoples in the net of the world-market, and with this, the international character of the capitalistic regime. Along with the constantly diminishing number of the magnates of capital, who usurp and monopolise all advantages of this process of transformation, grows the mass of misery, oppression, slavery, degradation, exploitation; but with this too grows the revolt of the working-class, a class always increasing in numbers, and disciplined, united, organised by the very mechanism of the process of capitalist production itself. The monopoly of capital becomes a fetter upon the mode of production. . . . The knell of capitalist private property sounds. The expropriators are expropriated.
>
> Karl Marx, *Capital,* Volume I

How are we to explain the nature of politics to ourselves? What are the forces that will help us better understand the nature of politics and governmental institutions? Sociologists follow not one line, or point of view, but rather one of three different perspectives. In this and the following two chapters, I shall explain the nature of each one. I shall also try to provide a blend between the more classic statements about these views and recent contributions by eminent scholars.

Perhaps the most central and well-known of the arguments began more than a century ago with the writings of Karl Marx. Marx offered a very powerful and comprehensive view of the modern world. His is a view that continues to inspire the writings and political activities of many people today. Marx's main contribution, as we shall see, was to locate the forces and energies that animated politics and government in a society's economy. Many scholars continue to follow the lead of Marx today either wholly, by adopting the entire apparatus of his view of the world, or partly, by tracing the dynamics of modern society to the workings of its economy. As capitalism has spread across the world over the past two decades, and as economic inequalities between people and nations increase rather than diminish, this view has come to take on an increasing significance to many observers of politics.

KARL MARX ON THE ECONOMY AND POLITICS

The Essential Marx

Karl Marx was born in Trier, Germany, in 1818 and died in London in 1883. Jewish by birth, his father converted the family to the religion of Luther in 1817, a year before Karl was born. His father was an educated man and lawyer, but nothing exceptional. The family had several children, the most obstinate and intellectually aggressive among them being Karl. Marx matured easily. He did his academic work in the faculty of law at the University of Bonn. There he came under the influence of the neo-Hegelians, absorbing ideas that were to weave themselves in and out of his thinking over the course of his lifetime. Within a decade of his University education, he would become involved with his lifelong friend, Friedrich Engels, and the work of the newly created Communist Party. Together they would leave an indelible influence on the thinking and politics of humankind.[1]

In writing of the influence of Karl Marx, Isaiah Berlin remarks:

> If to have turned into truisms what had previously been paradoxes is a mark of genius, Marx was richly endowed with it. His achievements in this sphere are necessarily ignored in proportion as their effects have become part of the permanent background of civilized thought.[2]

Many of us, for instance, subscribe to the view that there exist some groups of which we are aware and with which we identify based on common levels of wealth and property—more succinctly, social classes. Marx helps us to appreciate the significance of this idea. Many of us believe, further, that people's ideas about politics or about religion are in some manner influenced by their wealth or property. Marx has had a major influence over our thought on this matter. Finally, there are many of us who adopt the position that there are marked inequalities of wealth and power in modern societies and that these inequalities may become the source of major ideological struggles. Again, Marx helps us to recognize this aspect of many societies.

Ironically, many people whose own intellectual heritage owes the most to the theories of Marx are also among his most vociferous detractors, mainly because his theories have been employed as programs for political parties and whole nations; Marx even became the omnipresent symbolic figurehead for many of these nations, including those of the former Soviet Union and its allies. His ideas became transformed into Marxism; people became either their strong proponents or staunch opponents, regardless of their inherent truth or insight. Such deep feelings hold true for no other figure whom we consider here.

Marx occupied a variety of roles during his lifetime. He was, on occasion, a philosopher of history, an economist, a revolutionary, a sociologist, and a historian. Rarely did he bother to reveal the role he occupied at any time, producing innumerable and interminable controversies over the content of his writings. At the outset of this discussion, therefore, it is important to make clear the exact nature of these different roles and the manner in which Marx attempted to join them creatively.

For Marx, as all scholars, there is an inherent tension between the role of a practical human being and the role of a student of society and ideas. The former calls for practical action, involves one in the immediacies of everyday life, and above all else, requires moral commitments. The latter calls for a theoretical and dispassionate stance—for an unbiased observation of things as they are, have been, and will be. Scholars such as Max Weber who recognize the tensions springing from the dilemma of occupying two seemingly contradictory roles choose to divorce one from the other explicitly; the person of action, with his or her opinions, should make those opinions known *only outside* of the academy and scientific discourse, while the person of thought, with his or her ideas, is obliged to render those ideas known *only within* the confines of the academy.

Marx chose to resolve the tension created by the seeming contradiction by wedding the roles into one. To illustrate, as a historian and sociologist, Marx believed that through the careful study of history one could discover the main principles that bring about historical change and development. Furthermore, he claimed that he and Engels had hit upon these basic principles with the theory of dialectical materialism. Certain aspects of this theory are discussed in detail later; for now it suffices to say that the theory asserts that the proletariat, or working classes, would emerge victorious from a revolutionary confrontation with the capitalists, or owners of industrial enterprises, during the modern capitalist era.

As a social philosopher, Marx believed that his theory of change was itself the product of historical development, that is, the development of society under capitalism in the nineteenth century had enabled some men, like himself and Engels, to grasp the principles of historical change. When change in society was imminent, he thought, some men would become armed with a theoretical understanding of it much as other men might become armed with weaponry.[3]

Marx believed that all of people's ideas were the product of social and historical circumstances. Most people—proletarians *and* capitalists—were so constrained by their social class interests even during eras of imminent change that they were incapable of comprehending the principles and the coming of change by themselves. A few people were capable of achieving the necessary transcendence of their own times and their own class biases, for example, he and Engels.

For Marx, it was but a small step to achieving the synthesis between his knowledge of change acquired as a theorist and his desire for change growing out of revolutionary convictions. Equipped with an understanding of change, he believed it incumbent on himself, as an advocate of revolution, to spread such understanding among the principal beneficiaries of change, the working classes, in order to enlighten them as well as to hasten change. Theory of change and action to change were married; theory and action were combined. He wrote in *Contribution to the Critique of Hegel's Philosophy of Right:* "Just as philosophy finds its *material* weapons in the proletariat, so the proletariat finds its *intellectual* weapons in philosophy."[4]

If we are aware that Marx achieved this remarkable synthesis between the demands and constraints operating on him, then many seemingly paradoxical elements of his thought and action are clarified. There are some scholars, for instance, who believe that Marx's emphasis on determinism, that is, the inevitability of historical change, and his advocacy of revolution on behalf of the working classes are contradictory; they argue that if change is inevitable in history and if the working classes are destined to come to power, then free will, in the form of man as a voluntary revolutionary, is impossible, nay futile. Yet Marx effected a marriage of the two. Lewis Feuer writes of Marx's doctrine:

> It called upon human beings for a supreme deed of free will, that of intervening in their history with a revolutionary act and creating their own society. But it did so with a necessitarian vocabulary, so that the working class in its highest moment of freedom was fulfilling historical necessity. Freedom and determinism were joined in a dialectical unity. The language of liberty always had its deterministic semantic commentary, and the mystic revolutionist became one with the scientist.[5]

Like many marriages, this was not always a happy one, and on occasion one role, such as that of the scientist, took priority over the other, such as that of the revolutionary. Yet on the whole, Marx managed to unify them as few scholars before or since have done.

Another key to understanding Marx is that certain themes preoccupied him throughout his life, despite their being cloaked in somewhat different guises. The most important was that of alienation; it drew upon the humanist and rationalist traditions of the eighteenth century and was heavily discussed in his early manuscripts as well as implicit in many of his later economic manuscripts. Humans, as social beings, are alienated—that is, estranged from their own unique creative capacities and from their capacity to empathize with one another. The principal causes of alienation are the institutions of society, in particular social classes and the division of labor; while the principal manifestation of alienation is the belief of people that social institutions are immutable—that such institutions possess a life of their own. Other sociologists have adopted somewhat similar ideas, albeit with a different slant. For example, the French sociologist Emile Durkheim maintains that the division of labor, as all social facts, represents a phenomenon of a genre or kind unto itself (see Chapter 4).

Marx's position has its own peculiar twist. In truth, he maintained, social institutions are *not* immutable but are rather continually being created by men—in the past, during the present, and into the future. Further, Marx assumed, all history, in particular the continuous unfolding and changing of social institutions, is moving toward a single goal of eliminating alienation among men and, thus, revealing to them that they are the masters and creators of their own social world. Each major stage in historical development brings with it greater progress toward this goal—an increasing capacity for societies to permit people to be freed from the constraints of alienation, to be freed from social institutions. The final attainment of this goal would come about with the collapse of capitalism and the advent of communist society. Communist society for Marx *had* to be a society without social classes, since it was classes that gave birth to the alienation of people.

The Economy and Social Stratification

Man's primary role in life is that of a producer. The products that are created and the manner in which they are created—that is, whether an agrarian system of production or an industrial one—represent the foundations of the economy. To Marx it was these foundations that were central to the operations of society. Until Marx's time the study of the economy was left at that—to understand the nature of production and the mode of production. But Marx introduced an important new wrinkle. He would maintain that out of the natural course of production social inequalities also arose, inequalities that had nothing to do with the nature of the human beings themselves. If some people were poor and others rich, it was the effect of the process of production—and in modern society the very nature of capitalism itself.

Social groups, or strata, are created as a result of the manner and mode of production in society. Such groups together represent the social stratification hierarchy of that society, and they are called specifically *social classes*. In mature capitalist society there are two such principal classes: the *capitalists*, a small minority of the population, and the *proletariat*, the large majority. The two groups differ in one essential fact—the capitalists own the means of production, that is, the technological and scientific apparatus, and the proletariat own nothing but their labor power. Ownership of property, moreover, entitles the owners to be the sole beneficiaries of the fruits of that process, profit or, technically, surplus value.

Though Marx would rely on this bifurcated conception of social class throughout the course of much of his work, it is important to acknowledge briefly some ambiguities in it. In *The Communist Manifesto*, a political manuscript written with Friedrich Engels and published in 1848, in addition to the capitalists, or industrial bourgeoisie, and the proletarians, or working classes, Marx spoke of the "lower-middle class, the small manufacturer, the shopkeeper, the artisan, the peasant . . . [the] 'dangerous class,' the social scum."[6] In *The Class Struggles in France*, a historical analysis of the regimes of Louis Philippe and Louis Bonaparte, he wrote of the "finance aristocracy . . . [the] industrial bourgeoisie . . . [the] petty bourgeoisie . . . and the peasantry."[7] There are other instances when Marx wrote of these additional classes as well, and this inevitably raises questions about what he had in mind when he wrote of social class.

Since Marx died before he was able to clear up this issue, a great deal of controversy as well as scholarship has developed around it. For didactic purposes, in my discussion I shall rely mainly on the social class division between capitalists and proletarians, but not without good reason. This is the conception employed throughout Marx's abstract analysis of the economic development of capitalism.[8] In addition, this conception figures more prominently in his political analyses of capitalism. In *The Communist Manifesto*, for instance, Marx and Engels portrayed the two final political camps of capitalism as the industrial bourgeoisie, or capitalists, and the proletariat. All additional classes, they claimed, would be incorporated into either one of these groups. Finally, this conception is the most compatible with Marx's overall definition of capitalism, namely, private ownership of the means of production. Defining social class and the foundations of capitalism in the very same terms was a deliberate ploy that allowed Marx to predict the collapse of capitalism and the capitalist class at one and the same historical instant.[9]

Substructure and Superstructure

Marx possessed an expansive vision of the social and political world. It was one that spoke not only about the present but also about the past. The economy, to Marx, represented the key to unlocking the mysterious foundations of this world; hence people's connections to the economy shaped their lives. Marx viewed the economy as having a deep and profound impact on virtually every feature and institution of the world. Thus, not only did the economic processes of a society shape its politics, for example, but they also shaped the nature of its religious ideas, its philosophical premises, its educational institutions—indeed, the full and entire range of its way of life. "The ideas of the ruling class," Marx once wrote, "are in every epoch the ruling ideas."[10] Hence, under modern capitalism, the ruling ideas of this age, and societies that are capitalist, are the ideas of the class of capitalists.

Marx's view of the precise and diverse nature of politics extended his ideas about the role and importance of the economy in any society. In general, he believed that politics represented merely a reflection of the underlying nature of the form and relations of production under modern capitalism. Thus, since capitalists represented the dominant social class under capitalism, that is, they were the owners of the means of production, they also were the dominant political force as well. By the same token, their opposite number, the proletariat, were the mere subordinates, or powerless, group under modern capitalism.

One helpful way to think of this general picture of how Marx construed the relationship between the economy and politics is in terms of a metaphor that has become common among scholars of Marx, the link between the *substructure* and *superstructure* of a society. Consider the portrait in Figure 2-1. The substructure consists entirely of the economic foundations of modern capitalism, hence the nature and form of its production. It would include both the means of production, or such elements as the material kinds of production that occur, as well as what Marx termed the relations of production, that is, the nature and form of social classes. The superstructure that is built on top of the substructure consists, among other things, of the political regimes under capitalism, as well as such specific elements as political parties. As a general rule Marx believed that the economic substructure exercised powerful limits over what could and could not be done by political institutions and leaders.

Figure 2-1 Substructure and Superstructure

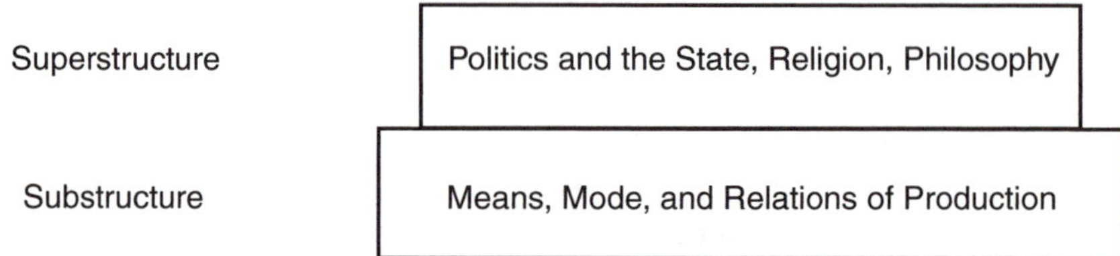

Politics as a Reflection of the Class Struggle

Politics appears to most of us as a continuing battle and struggle among different people, groups, and parties. To many observers of American politics, for example, the battle is fought in purely partisan terms, between conservatives and liberals, Republicans and Democrats, and similar groups. To understand the nature of the battle for most people means simply understanding the specific terms and issues in which the battles are fought. If Republicans and Democrats disagree on the use of the federal government's revenue surplus, in this view, it is simply a matter of understanding how they might use the federal surplus differently—Republicans to lower federal taxes, Democrats to furnish greater Social Security benefits.

To Marx, however, the differences among and between contesting political groups are really based on differences in class and/or forms of property. For example, he observed in nineteenth century France several different political factions and parties within the National Assembly that contended with one another for control of the government and manifested little unity among themselves. The absence of harmony among the political groups, Marx believed, simply reflected underlying social class differences, and the opposing political programs sprang from *different forms* of property:

> Legitimists and Orleanists, as we have said, formed the two great sections of the Party of Order. Was that which held these sections fast to their pretenders and kept them apart from one another nothing but lily and tricolour, house of Bourbon and house of Orleans, different shades of royalty, was it the confession of faith in royalty at all? . . . What kept the two sections apart . . . was not any so-called principles, it was their material conditions of existence, two different kinds of property, it was the old contrast of town and country, the rivalry between capital and landed property.[11]

Continuing in the same vein, he provided one of the clearest expositions of his theory about the connections between material conditions and political views:

> Upon different forms of property, upon the social conditions of existence rises an entire superstructure of distinct and characteristically formed sentiments, illusions, modes of thought and views of life. The entire class creates and forms them out of its material foundations and out of the corresponding social relations. . . . If Orleanists and Legitimists, if each section sought to make itself and the other believe that loyalty to their two royal houses separated them, it later proved to be the case that it was rather their divided interests which forbade the uniting of the two royal houses. And as in private life one distinguishes between what a man thinks and says of himself and what he really is and does, still more in historical struggles must one distinguish the phrases and fancies of the parties from their real organism and their real interests, their conception

> of themselves with their reality. Orleanists and Legitimists found themselves side by side in the republic with equal claims. If each side wished to effect the *restoration* of its *own* royal house against the other, that merely signifies that the *two great interests* into which the bourgeoisie is split—landed property and capital—sought each to restore its own supremacy and the subordination of the other.[12]

If the state does not clearly govern in favor of the capitalists, Marx believed, that means only that there is not yet a single dominant social class, but there are contending ones whose power derives from different forms of property and wealth.

State Power and Its Limits

The state machinery of capitalist societies is comprised of "organs of standing army, police, bureaucracy, clergy and judicature," plus the parliament.[13] This machinery develops policies that generally serve to the advantage of the capitalists; this is consistent with Marx's abstract view of the political order. In *Capital*, for instance, he claimed that the British Parliament passed many laws that were principally designed to extend the workday of the laborers and thus to increase the profits, or surplus value, of the capitalists.[14]

To Marx, as to many modern neo-Marxists, the state is a very powerful social institution. It concentrates a considerable amount of power and resources into the hands of a relatively small number of officials and institutions. Now, to all appearances it would seem that such institutions can exercise decisive power over the lives of people. The executive branch of the United States federal government, for instance, can make declarations of war, veto decisions by the Congress, and provide for a general and vigorous political leadership for the United States.

But, in Marx's view, the power and leadership of the state, and its officials, is ultimately determined and limited by the nature of capitalism itself. States and state leaders cannot make decisions that, in the long run, are counter to or undermine the interests of capitalism itself. Both the system of capitalism, which is a system of private property in which the benefits of ownership belong to private individuals and groups, and the actual class of capitalists, limit the freedom and exercise of power by the state. As Marx and Engels would write, "(t)he executive of the modern State is but a committee for managing the common affairs of the whole bourgeoisie."[15] (In subsequent writings, these general claims would be updated and made more subtle by later Marxists.)

Sustaining Capitalism and the Rule of Capitalists

What is it that sustains modern capitalism, especially in the face of deep inequalities of wealth and material well-being that exist? Many observers and scholars have written about this issue, seeking to discover the nature of its hegemony and integrity. To Marx, capitalism was sustained by two central forces: the power of its ideology and the strength of its economy, especially over the working classes. *Ideology* was one of the features of the superstructure of capitalism, and represented the ideas, or ideals, that sustained it. To Marx it also represented a form of "false consciousness" insofar as the ideas of capitalism were not those that served the best interests of the workers, but rather those that served the best interests of capitalism and modern capitalism itself. Any belief, or set of beliefs, that serve to further the interests of capitalism—for example, the dream that everyone and anyone can become rich in America—constitute capitalist ideology.

But at a deeper level of capitalism, it was the features of the system itself that were self-sustaining. Marx maintained that capitalists secured their profit, or surplus-value, simply by providing workers only subsistence wages while they reaped huge amounts of profits, like many corporate chieftains today. The effect was to prevent workers from accumulating sufficient capital to become independent of the process of production. Thus, in Marx's view, workers only possessed their own labor power, and they were forced on a daily, weekly, and monthly basis to work simply because they could not accumulate any capital themselves. "Free wage labor," a term used to describe the nature of labor under modern capitalism, was, in fact, anything but free for the laborer!

Revolution and Change

In recent years, many sociologists have turned their attention to movements for political change, in particular those that help to promote revolutions or fundamental changes in political and social institutions. The collapse of the Soviet Union and of its Eastern European allies represent just a few of the major political changes that have occurred, and which interest many political sociologists.

Marx furnished a very powerful portrait of revolutions that drew upon his general imagery of the nature of capitalist societies. He believed that the ultimate foundations for revolution were to be found in the nature of the economy and economic relations. Moreover, he believed that every society ultimately contained the materials within it that would spell its own doom. Societies were to him self-contradictions, forces that were promoted by one social class but that, in the course of development, laid the foundations for their own demise.

There were three general sets of factors that were antecedent to the rise of revolutions, according to Marx. They were: critical economic factors; social factors; and the creation of a class-consciousness among the working class. The forces that grew out of the economy were the most important to him, yet the others played a significant role as well.

Economic Antecedents. Marx expected that the lust of the capitalists for profits would eventually produce an overabundance of commodities—a surplus that exceeded the capacity of the world market to absorb it. Most of the economic antecedents of revolution stem from this central premise. The first of these are the periodic crises and falling profits of capitalists. As Marx and Engels observed in *The Communist Manifesto:*

> It is enough to mention the commercial crises that by their periodic return put on its trial, each time more threateningly, the existence of the entire bourgeois society. In these crises a great part not only of the existing products but also the previously created productive forces are periodically destroyed. In these crises there [appears] an epidemic that in all earlier epochs would have seemed an absurdity—the epidemic of over-production.[16]

Marx's second economic antecedent of revolution is the centralization of capital; a diminishing proportion of the owners of industries come to possess an increasingly greater proportion of the wealth—an exaggeration of capitalism's tendency for wealth to be controlled by a minority. "That which is now to be expropriated is no longer the labourer working for himself, but the capitalist exploiting many labourers. This expropriation is accomplished by the action of the immanent laws of capitalist production itself by the centralization of capital. One capitalist always kills many."[17] One of the effects of centralization is presumably to make the source of oppression and the fact of oppression more visible to the working classes.

Another effect of centralization is proletarization, a critical antecedent of revolution. Expropriated from the means of production formerly controlled by them, many capitalists are compelled to join the ranks of the working class in order to survive; in effect, they are downwardly mobile. "Entire sections of the ruling classes are, by advance of industry, precipitated into the proletariat, or are at least threatened in their conditions of existence. These also support the proletariat with fresh elements of enlightenment and progress."[18]

The last of the major economic antecedents of revolution is also open to the most diverse readings. According to Marx, the financial conditions of the average worker would worsen as a result of the growing numbers of economic crises and the steady displacement of workers by the introduction of technology. In particular, a large surplus population of laborers, an industrial reserve army, would be created, leading to a reduction in workers' wages and to a general burden on the working class.

The industrial reserve army, however, represents only one part of a much broader process, *Verelendung*, or increasing misery. "Accumulation of wealth at one pole is, therefore, at the same time accumulation of misery, agony of toil, slavery, ignorance, brutality, mental degradation, at the opposite pole, i.e., on the side of the class that produces its own product in the form of capital."[19] Disputes arise among scholars about whether Marx intended to argue that the *absolute* wages of the working classes would diminish, that is, that there would be a decline in the general wage level of the working class, or whether he meant to claim that there would be an absolute rise in the general wage levels throughout society but a decline in the *relative* wage level of the proletariat, that is, their share in the national income. The dispute is more than academic; if Marx meant to imply that the lot of the working class would become progressively worse in absolute terms, then he was clearly mistaken, and this might account for the absence of the revolution he predicted.

While the controversy is likely to rage for a long time, with reputable scholars giving arguments for one or the other interpretation, the most sensible statement is that of Ronald L. Meek:

> There does indeed exist, we may plausibly argue, at any rate in a kind of "pure" capitalist system, an "innate tendency" towards "increasing misery" in Marx's sense, but for various reasons this "innate tendency" has been "offset" or "counteracted" in our own times by various factors which Marx abstracted from his model. . . . If we adopt a Leninist line, we may put the blame on imperialism; or we may point, alternatively or in addition, to the great wages of technical innovation and consequent increases in productivity which have occurred since Marx's time, to the immense growth in the extent and power of trade unionism which has increased the power of the workers to press for a higher share of the growing national product, to the change in the aims of the trade union movement which has made it more interested in getting what it can out of the capitalist system than in putting an end to it, and to the growth of the socialist sector of the world which has made the capitalists more willing to grant the workers the wage increases they demand.[20]

These and similar reasons, including other defects in Marxian economic principles, are often asserted by observers of contemporary politics who wish to explain why Marx's expectations for revolution failed to materialize. Of course, the extent of trade unions in the United States and Great Britain, among other countries, are important differences from Marx's day and perhaps undercut the pivotal element in the Marxian scheme of things. Yet these arguments, after all, only consider *one* of several antecedents that Marx

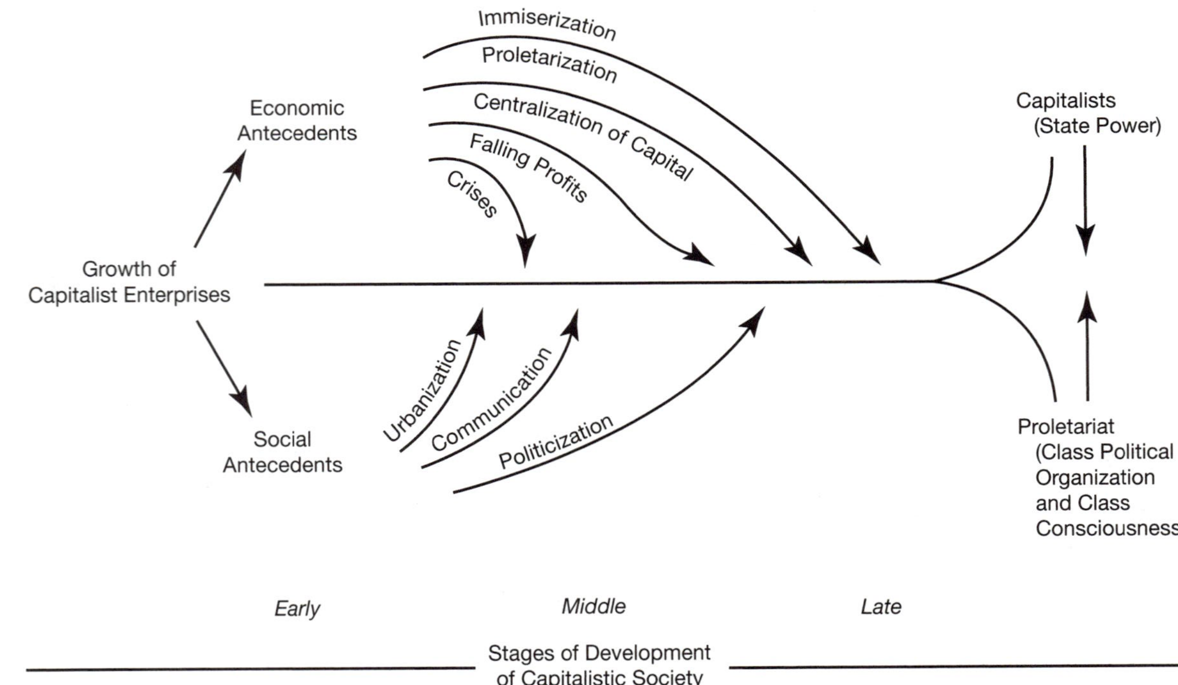

Figure 2-2 Economic and Social Antecedents of Class Conflict and Revolution in Capitalist Society

believed would produce revolution and thus provide only partial accounts for the absence of revolution.

Social Antecedents. A *leitmotif* characteristic of Marx's thought is an alleged opposition between town and countryside. The theme is evident in Marx's emphasis on urbanization in promoting revolution. The congregations of workers drawn into urban areas possess a far greater potential for revolution than the peasants and farmers in the country. There are two reasons for this: Workers in the urban centers are generally employed in factories, thus encountering the most degrading and dehumanizing forms of work, and sheer density of numbers presents a potential for the organization of revolutionary movements, a fact peculiarly characteristic of urban centers.

A second social antecedent of revolution stems from urbanization, namely communication. Communication among workers is essential to the formation of a revolutionary movement, mainly because it enables them to recognize the similarity of their experiences and to develop common beliefs:

> Now and then the workers are victorious, but only for a time. The real fruit of their battles lies not in the immediate result, but in the ever expanding union of the workers. This union is helped on by the improved means of communication that are created by modern industry and that place the workers of different localities in contact with one another.[21]

The importance of communication among the working class is that it serves to counteract the control of the capitalists over the means of communication in society as well as the general hegemony of the capitalist system of values.

The last of the major social antecedents required for the development of revolutionary movement on the part of the working classes is their politicization. There are two sources of this politicization: one that occurs almost naturally as a result of the encounters between the workers and the capitalists is trade unionism, and the other that is brought into the working classes from without is the effort by revolutionaries like Marx and his compatriots to direct the politics of the working class. Marx and Engels noted this latter process in *The Communist Manifesto:*

> Finally, in times when the class struggle nears the decisive hour, the process of dissolution going on within the ruling class, in fact within the whole range of old society, assumes such a violent, glaring character that a small section of the ruling class cuts itself adrift and joins the revolutionary class, the class that holds the future in its hands. [So] now a portion of the bourgeoisie goes over to the proletariat, and in particular a portion of the bourgeois ideologists, who have raised themselves to the level of comprehending theoretically the historical movement as a whole.[22]

The two sources, of course, are not necessarily compatible. Indeed, it is on matters of the precise form of this politicization that loyal followers of Marx's doctrines have become divided.

Class Consciousness and Political Action. Perhaps the most significant component in the Marxian scheme of revolution and, more broadly, of change is class consciousness. It is also the component least understood. In order for the working-class members to overthrow the capitalists, they have to become aware of themselves as a class. Adapting terminology from Feuerbach, who himself took over terms ultimately traceable to Kant, Marx asserted that the proletariat had to transform itself from a *Klasse an sich*, a class simply by virtue of similar economic and social conditions, to a *Klasse für sich*, a class whose members were aware of those conditions.

What precisely constitutes this phenomenon of class consciousness? Marx came closest to giving his most concise and clear conceptual exposition of it in *German Ideology*: "The separate individuals form a class only insofar as they have to carry on a common battle against another class; otherwise they are on hostile terms with each other as competitors."[23] Class consciousness consists of two elements: the shared awareness among a group of people that they are on hostile terms with another group of people, and a shared desire for united action against this group of people.[24] Class consciousness among the members of the proletariat, in particular, means that as a group they are aware that the capitalists are oppressing them and, further, that they are convinced of the need for collective action to be taken against the capitalists.

Political organization probably plays a major part in the formation of class consciousness. What precise form does such political organization assume, especially among the proletariat? Many scholars and revolutionaries believe that the trade-union movement that emerged among working-class groups worldwide represents the "false consciousness" of the workers, not a genuine class consciousness. They maintain that trade unions generally accept the standards and ethics of capitalism and thus are unprepared to overthrow the capitalists and establish a new society to benefit the majority of the citizens. In recognition of this, more militant followers of Marx, Lenin the chief one among them, argue that trade unions must be combated:

> There is a lot of talk about spontaneity, but *the spontaneous* development of the labour movement leads to its becoming subordinated to bourgeois ideology . . . for the spontaneous labour movement is pure and simple trade unionism . . . and trade unionism means the ideological subordination of the workers to the bourgeoisie. . . . [The task of the Social Democrats in Russia would be] to combat spontaneity, to divert the labour movement, with its spontaneous trade-unionist striving, from under the wing of the bourgeoisie and to bring it under the wing of revolutionary Social-Democracy.[25]

Since Marx, the best political form that would allow the working class to meet their own needs and goals has been an issue on which differences in persuasion and tactics emerge, even among the most devoted loyalists to Marx. There are those, such as the German Social Democrat Eduard Bernstein, who adopted a reformist position and argued that the chief goal should be to improve the working conditions of the working classes; if these are improved under the regime of capitalism, then there is no need for revolution. Others, including Lenin, adopted a more militant position and argued that the main goal should be to liberate the proletariat; this is an action that requires an overthrow of the entire structure of capitalist society. No doubt such intellectual struggles and differences will long persist.

THE NEO-MARXISTS

V. I. Lenin

V. I. Lenin, born Vladimir Ilich Ulyanov in Russia in 1870, furnished important additions to the stream of the Marxist legacy in terms both of the meaning of revolutionary praxis and to the body of theory itself. Above and beyond his theoretical contributions, to which we shall turn shortly, Lenin and his collaborators, including Leon Trotsky, furnished a model for all subsequent revolutionaries. By virtue of their success, they showed how a revolution could be made, particularly in a country that had skipped over the stage of capitalism, ousting the Russian autocracy largely on the strength of a peasant revolution.[26] For under the regimes of the Tsars, Russia had been a largely agricultural land, with a relatively small working class; the dominant class had not been one of capitalists but rather one of a nobility whose power lay in land, in nonproductive wealth, and in their heritage. Thus, once revolution came to this backward country, one that had not been predicted by Marx to be the first site of a major socialist revolution in the world, naturally all attention turned there. Much subsequent discussion and analysis thus came to be devoted by Communist theoreticians, both within and outside Russia, to the specific factors that contributed to the overthrow of the Tsar and later the government of Alexander Kerensky, and to the conditions required in order to bring a socialist regime to full fruition. It was precisely on these points that Lenin and Trotsky divided, and that later Stalin and Trotsky separated, leading ultimately to the latter's death at the hands of an assassin in Mexico in 1941.

On Revolution. If Lenin's chief contribution to the Marxist legacy lay in his practical political successes in Russia, so, too, therein lay his chief theoretical contributions as well. In 1903 he published a famous pamphlet,

What Is to Be Done?[27] This document was intended in part to be a polemic against his adversaries among the Social Democrats in Russia—Plekhanov, in particular—as well as against those who advocated anarchy, a style of political action that had gained much enthusiasm in Russia during the latter half of the nineteenth century, particularly among the *narodniki*, or Russian populists. Lenin in this pamphlet argues that the nature of the socialist revolution had to be carried out on several fronts—a political and theoretical as well as an economic one. One could not assume, he insists, that the trade-union efforts on behalf of the working classes would by themselves produce liberation for the workers. Such efforts, which he labels *economism*, were alone insufficient. They were especially inadequate because they failed to cope with the existence of the Tsarist autocracy—itself a political, not an economic, institution. In arguing against simple efforts on behalf of better wages, and trade unions in general, Lenin was arguing, too, against the reformist efforts that had occurred within various camps of socialists—in Germany, in particular, by Eduard Bernstein. Lenin's point was that those who sought revolution had to be prepared for it. The revolutionaries were almost compelled to help to create and to mold the sentiments of the working class, to elevate them to a true consciousness of the whole movement of history in the doctrines of Marx and Engels. Thus, he believed, revolutionaries had to work to achieve theoretical innovations and, at the same time, they had to devote themselves fully to the political effort—the effort of agitation against the government and of the preparation of a party to carry out the revolution.

For revolutionaries and for lay scholars alike, Lenin's analysis of the nature of the revolutionary party holds particular fascination. In contrast to many of his contemporaries, Lenin insists that the revolutionary party must consist of a cadre of full-time revolutionaries, people so completely devoted to the revolutionary cause that it absorbs their entire lives. Lenin's own life became an example of such dedication as he gave his energies over entirely to the revolutionary effort in Russia, even during those many years he had to spend in exile abroad. It was such full-time revolutionaries as himself who would make the revolution. They would train themselves by becoming steeped in the doctrines of Marx and Engels, by devoting their entire attention to the nature of the actual situations they confronted, and by fostering the appropriate understanding of the current historical situation among the masses of people who would constitute the revolutionary movement. Such revolutionaries, Lenin further insisted, must necessarily engage in a tireless campaign of agitation, both in an attempt to arouse the enthusiasm of the mass of supporters, but also in the difficult effort to unseat the powerful regime they confronted. The success of the Bolsheviks in Russia inevitably led many other potential revolutionaries to seek the answer to their own form of revolution in Lenin's *What Is to Be Done?*

With considerable admiration Georg Lukács described Lenin as a person who was part theoretician, one who invents and elaborates the theories necessary to the success of the revolutionary party, and part politician, one who possesses a broad grasp of which tactics are to be used, and when and how to use them most effectively. Nowhere is this delicate blend between attention to theory and to actual fact more evident than in Lenin's constant demand that revolutionaries seek to interpret the current state of affairs in light *both* of the unique historical situation and of the state of class conflict in a particular society. He condemned those so-called Marxists who blindly spoke of the working and bourgeois classes, and of class conflict in all societies, failing to take account of the special concatenation of circumstances within them. He believed that the nature of the class struggle was not everywhere the same in the modern world. Thus, he observed that "a Marxist must take cognizance of actual events, of the precise facts of *reality*, and must not cling to a theory of yesterday, which, like all theories, at best only outlines the main and general, and only *approximates* to an inclusive grasp of the complexities of life."[28] Lenin's insistence on an acknowledgment of the actual state of affairs, construed with the aid of the theory of historical materialism—rather than an unreflective application of those theories—has become recognized as yet another of his important contributions to the Marxist legacy, and has particularly influenced such scholars as Louis Althusser and Nicos Poulantzas.[29]

On the State. As with his other contributions to Marxist theory and practice, Lenin's contributions in *State and Revolution*, a document completed in August, 1917, but published after the October Revolution, took the form of political theory.[30] He explores at length the exact nature of a socialist or workers' state, something which, as we have learned, neither Marx nor Engels had been able to elaborate. It is here that Lenin seeks to discern the outlines of a revolutionary dictatorship of the proletariat, to determine how, in Engels' words, the state would ultimately "wither away." Lenin argues that in Russia the February Revolution, that which brought Alexander Kerensky to power but left the Parliament intact, was merely a preliminary step to the true socialist revolution. Indeed, he suggests, the February Revolution seemed to have all the characteristics of a bourgeois revolution, successfully overthrowing the Tsarist regime but, at the same moment, leaving the bourgeoisie in control of society. Thus, it was necessary that this regime, itself, be overthrown, and that it be overthrown in the name of the proletariat, the working classes of Russia. To do so, he further argues, required a joint effort on behalf of the peasants and the workers, the former largely outnumbering the latter save in a few urban places like Petrograd.

Once having overthrown the despised Kerensky regime, Lenin argued, the Bolsheviks then must turn to the task of constructing an appropriate workers' state in Russia. But what did it mean to say that such a state would be a revolutionary dictatorship of the proletariat? Was it not true, in the writings of Marx and Engels alike, that the state was conceived merely as an instrument for the oppression of the ruled by the ruling classes, and that with revolution it must necessarily disappear? On these issues Lenin had to struggle with the ambiguities found in the body of Marx's thought, to search for a way to remain consistent with the Marxist doctrine yet, at the same time, to develop novel principles to guide the workers' state in Russia. Hence, he came to argue that the workers' state had to take over the reins of power on behalf of the working classes, and that it had to be occupied by people who themselves came from the working classes. But such a state also had to be used as a weapon against the previously dominant ruling classes, the remnants both of the bourgeoisie and the Tsarist regime. Here Lenin went beyond that which Marx and Engels proposed. He insisted that the workers' state could become a weapon in the struggle for the emancipation of the workers, and with them the rest of society. He further suggested, again on the basis of his reading and understanding of where Russian society stood in mid-1917, that the workers' state necessarily would entail a concentration of power in the hands of the representatives of the workers—an armed movement, in other words. In contrast to those who proposed to implement a democratic republic, he claimed such a democracy would not be suitable for Russia, at least for a time, because the remnants of the past society still displayed pronounced social and economic inequities.

Lenin sought to use the Paris Commune of 1871 and, in particular, Marx's analysis of it, as a further device to furnish some sense of the socialist state. He found here support of his claim that the Russian state must be run on behalf of and entirely represent the workers rather than all citizens, as a simple reading of bourgeois democracy might suggest. And later, in the course of establishing a government on the heels of the Bolshevik Revolution of October, Lenin came to organize the new socialist regime on the basis of the soviets, the councils of workers who had helped to form the basis for the overthrow of the Kerensky government. The soviets, together with the development of the Communist Party apparatus, thus became the practical realization of the workers' state which Lenin sought to define in *State and Revolution*.

On Imperialism. Lenin made one further, some even claim his most enduring, contribution to Marxist thought in the form of an analysis of imperialism. Imperialism, he argued was the most advanced state of capitalism.[31] In his writings about mature capitalism, particularly in *Capital*, Marx seemed to have failed to keep pace with historical events much beyond the middle of the nineteenth century. Yet it was at this time, if not somewhat later, that capitalism commenced to take on a novel appearance.

Countries like Great Britain and France, for example, began to seek to extend their dominion over other parts of the world, particularly the lands of Asia and Africa. In need of ever more abundant supplies of raw materials and of cheap labor for manufacture, not to mention larger markets for their goods, these more advanced capitalist nations sought to make permanent subjects of unsuspecting inhabitants of other lands. The net effect was to commence a deep and growing division in the world at large, between the richer, capitalist countries and the poorer, colonial, or subject, nations, a division that remains vividly alive today. (See Chapter 10 on nation-building, for further discussion of these issues.)

Lenin sought to clarify and to explain these developments in his pamphlet entitled *Imperialism: The Highest State of Capitalism*. Drawing upon historical developments in the last quarter of the nineteenth and early years of the twentieth centuries, together with the pioneering analyses of J. A. Hobson and Rudolph Hilferding, Lenin argued that modern imperialism entailed the development of handfuls of monopolies within capitalist countries alongside the rise of finance capital to a place of paramount significance.[32] In search of ever greater profit, the motive force of capitalism, the great industrialists in America, France, Germany, and the few other capitalist countries of the world turned to invest their capital in enterprises in the less-developed lands, and to further secure their dominance over these countries through large loans. Ultimately, Lenin argues, by the early twentieth century the world had become divided into the nations of owners, or capitalists, and nations of owned, or subjects. The division occurred in part at the initiation of the capitalist class and in part by the cooperative efforts of government officials who sought to make lawful the control of monopoly capitalism in occupied colonies.

Lenin's analysis represented a novel twist to the Marxist legacy insofar as it emphasized the growth of monopoly capitalism as a new state of capitalist development. Moreover, it was novel as well because of the way it portrayed the growing development of ties and alliances among the various countries of the world, and of the deepening polarization between those countries that one might regard as bourgeois—including segments even of the working classes, as in Great Britain—and those countries that were largely, if not exclusively, made up of masses of laborers. This division, Lenin seemed to sense, was so powerful that it could provide the basis for the worldwide proletarian revolution earlier anticipated by Marx.

Antonio Gramsci

As with Lenin, the Italian radical Antonio Gramsci had become deeply involved with socialist politics even as a young man, but unlike Lenin, Gramsci never succeeded in participating in the overthrow of the regime on behalf of the working class. In fact, as with so many other leftist radicals in the 1920s, Gramsci came to admire the Soviet regime for its great successes. Gramsci had taken up membership in the Italian Communist Party in 1926, after many years of active political and intellectual involvement with the Italian left-wing groups. Only one year later, after flirting with capture for many years, Gramsci was seized by Benito Mussolini's police and put into prison. He remained there for the last decade of his life, subject to torture and to recurring physical ailments. This period also became the most intellectually creative of his life, a time when he attempted to deal with the possibility of proletarian revolution in Italy. In the course of his reflections he developed ideas that have had a profound influence over much subsequent Marxist thought.

On the Communist Party. One of Gramsci's principal ideas dealt with the role of the Communist Party in its efforts to oust the established powers. Departing from the seminal document of Niccolò Machiavelli, *The Prince,* composed in the sixteenth century while Machiavelli served as counselor to the House of the Medicis in Venice, Gramsci argued that in the modern world the prince actually represented not an individual person, but rather a corporate group, a collective will, to be quite specific, a party such as the Italian Communist Party.[33] If so understood, then there were many lessons that the Communists could learn from the reflections of Machiavelli. Just as the prince, the party must learn when the moment is right for the effort to take and to secure power. Just as the prince, the party must stand firm in its political convictions, committed to specific lines of action designed to acquire power for itself and for the working classes. Most important, just as the prince, the party must appear as the "centaur—half-animal and half-human."[34] That is, the party must exhibit a sympathy to the natural dialectics of the world, be able to engage in the use of force as necessary, but also be able to take advantage of the widespread convictions and sympathies of the public. It must seek, however delicately, to steer a course between imposing itself as a collective will on the people from without and regarding itself as a simple expression of the will of the people.

On the Hegemony of Class Rule. Gramsci's analysis of the role of the party displayed an unusually acute and complete grasp of the strategic problems that confronted revolutionary parties such as that of the Communists. This very same sensitivity also helps to account for the power of his insight into those conditions that sustained established regimes, an analysis of the conditions of *hegemony*.[35] Troubled by the failure of working-class parties to secure power on behalf of the working classes, particularly in Italy, Gramsci argued that no party could come to power unless such power rested upon the hegemony of their rule. As in the case of his analysis of the modern prince, this meant that the regime must be regarded by the public, not as an unsympathetic villain, but as the single, true expression of their wishes. The power of the State under its hegemony rested not on its force alone, but on a compliance more or less freely given by its subjects. Such a free and widespread public compliance, Gramsci reasoned, arose from the deep and complete entrenchment of a regime. Further this entrenchment meant that a widespread loyalty must exist among the public for the regime, a loyalty that was manufactured by the panoply of social and cultural institutions.

The hegemony in the rule of a class thus came to rest on a highly complex and very diffuse set of sentiments within the public, sentiments virtually impervious to the occasional attacks of parties. "The superstructures of civil society," Gramsci wrote, "are like the trench-systems of modern warfare. In war it would sometimes happen that a fierce artillery attack seemed to have destroyed the enemy's entire defense system, whereas in fact it had only destroyed the outer perimeter; and at the moment of their advance and attack the assailants would find themselves confronted by a line of defense which was still effective."[36] Gramsci's analysis, of course, was extremely helpful to the effort to elaborate Marx's ideas in order to grasp the historic intransigence of regimes to the attempted radical penetration of them; at the same time it bore grave witness to the pessimism that overwhelmed him as he lay isolated and alone in prison.

The Frankfurt School

Among contemporary Marxists there are few groups of scholars which can rival the influence of the Frankfurt School. Founded in 1934 in Germany by Theodor Adorno and Max Horkheimer, later temporarily transplanted to the United States during the reign of Adolf Hitler, the Frankfurt School's principals have interpreted Marx mainly as a philosopher rather than as a dedicated revolutionary thinker. In a sense, they have returned to the early, younger Marx as a means of drawing out the main insights they believe he contributed; at the same time, they have added new elements to Marxist thought, introducing ideas such as sublimation and repression from Sigmund Freud, and rationality and legitimacy from Max Weber. Drawn toward a more philosophical rendering of the writings of Marx, they have fashioned a corpus of thought that almost is intellectually impenetrable, certainly a far remove from the needs of the working classes of the world today.

Herbert Marcuse. One of the main novelties of the Frankfurt School, particularly the writings of Herbert Marcuse and Jürgen Habermas, is the blending of ideas originally emphasized by Max Weber with the critical assessment of capitalism found in Marx. No longer concerned with the proletariat itself, or even with labor as productive activity, as in the classic Marxist formulations, Marcuse achieved great success and fame in the United States with his *One-Dimensional Man*.[37] He argues that modern civilization exhibits a radical divorce between the Reason sought after by the ancient Greeks, and the reason that displays itself throughout modern society. The Reason of the ancient Greeks was associated intimately with the search for Truth, and mind, itself, was not divorced from nature but was viewed as part and parcel of it. The Greek philosophers had assumed an intimate harmony between mind and nature, the one the part of the other, and Reason represented the working of the mind as it sought, by virtue of deep reflection, to discover those principles that were essential to nature and those that merely were ephemeral. What modern capitalist civilization has done, in the eyes of Marcuse, is to create a fundamental alienation of man from nature, of reason from Reason, and it has accomplished this by suppressing all those qualities that are fundamentally and essentially human—man's need to reflect deeply on the world as well as his sensual nature, his Eros, or love. In assuming this sort of perspective, Marcuse, just as Lukács before him, reintroduces dialectics into the nature of Marxist critical thought, so much so as virtually to disguise the essential Marxist twist to the thought itself.

Marcuse's indictment of modern capitalist civilization, with America taken as the supreme instance of this civilization, draws a certain inspiration from Weber's emphasis upon the nature of rationality in the modern world.[38] Weber, as we shall learn in the next chapter, distinguished between technical rationality, that which seemed to characterize the essential element of modern capitalism, with a specific emphasis upon technique, efficiency, and calculability, and substantive rationality, that which was concerned with the ends, the goals, the values toward which action was targeted. That which is especially characteristic and, he implied, equally oppressive under modern capitalism, is that all action, in virtually every sphere of society, has become dominated by a concern with the quantitative and calculable assessment of the costs involved in reaching a particular end, any end, rather than with the substantive meaning of the end itself. Marcuse compliments Weber upon this basic insight, yet he then turns around immediately to condemn him for failing to carry through, in a true critical fashion, to ask why it is that technical and substantive rationality have become divorced.

To Marcuse, the answer lies, of course, in the fact that modern capitalist civilization displays the radical separation between the two forms of reason: technical reason becomes reason, substantive reason stands for the

Greek conception of Reason. In a fashion strongly reminiscent of Hegel as well as of Lukács, Marcuse argues that the objects created by man thus come to stand apart from, and apparently above, him at the same time as his own capacity for deep reflection, or imagination, is itself repressed. In effect, man no longer represents man, but something dehumanized; his own sense of himself is seen through the objects and bodies of thought to analyze objects he has created. Hence, man comes to think of himself simply as a technical instrument, a worker on the assembly line divorced from a sense of self, owing to the scientific principles of management in modern civilization. His language takes a form of some immediate connection between a concept and a thing rather than an imaginative connection empowered by his mind; even his sexual passions come to be reified, in the form of appeals to his prurient interests, and to his own body as a mere object of sexual passion rather than as a part of himself intimately involved in love. A good deal of this form of indictment of modern capitalism, it may be interesting to learn, found an even earlier expression in the very lucid and exceedingly insightful analysis of Antonio Gramsci.[39]

Jürgen Habermas. In perhaps his most well-known analysis, Jürgen Habermas, the current leading member of the Frankfurt School, also draws upon the work of Max Weber to critically understand the nature of modern capitalism. Taking up Weber's concern with the nature of legitimacy and legitimation, Habermas argues that the contradictions in modern society, in particular those engendered by the twin and paradoxical emphases upon social welfare and upon mass democracy, have created a crisis in the assumed rightness and propriety of the decisions taken in modern capitalist nations. Both Weber and other scholars who shared with him an emphasis upon the legalistic nature of legitimacy, Habermas claims, were misled into believing that the very nature of legal decision making in modern society was itself sufficient to secure proof of the propriety of decisions. That, in fact, is incorrect, Habermas claims—there is a deeper, or different, level upon which legitimacy rests, one of validity based upon peoples' shared normative understandings of what is to be valued in the social world. But this level of understanding is obscure both in modern society itself and in the theories about this society. Only a critical theory, he argues, one that holds as problematic the very foundations of modern capitalism, can penetrate to the truth of things in the world, and in this effort, Habermas proposes a program of "universal pragmatics," which seeks to expose the distortions and contradictions under modern capitalism through a detailed analysis for discursive language and communication.[40]

Nicos Poulantzas

The preeminent political sociologist among contemporary Marxists was Nicos Poulantzas, a theorist who died an untimely death in 1979. Poulantzas sought to extend the Marxist framework to twentieth-century capitalism, and to an understanding of the twentieth-century state. In particular, he tried to understand how the state might become an independent actor in the history and development of the class struggle, and his ideas have become enshrined in discussions among Marxists about the "relative autonomy of the state."[41]

On Structures. Poulantzas provided some unique and special ways of thinking about capitalism and modern politics. Perhaps the most unique element of his vision was one that he adopted from his French mentor, another Marxist, Louis Althusser. Like Althusser, Poulantzas thought of societies in terms of structures. Structures represent more or less coherent ensembles of elements, and they serve to maintain the integrity of a social order. They are abstract forces, somewhat parallel, for example, to the notions of superstructure or civil society that we used earlier to explain Marx's imagery. They are much more than mere concepts, however, for, though abstract, they still serve to shape how the world works. Poulantzas, following Althusser, insisted that there are several structures at work in the operations of modern capitalism. They are the ideological, or the realm of ideas; the political, or the realm of politics and the state; the economic, or the realm of production; and the juridical, or the realm of law.[42] Thus, in the ideological realm, Poulantzas included such claims as the importance of individual rights, or the representation of multiple interests as instances of liberal political ideology under modern capitalism. Moreover, like Althusser, Poulantzas maintained that each of these structures could operate independently of one another, and that in any given concrete historical society, say the United States in the twentieth century, one structure could dominate the others in the workings of the social order. For example, he maintained that in certain instances the ideological structure could prevail over the other three, whereas in other instances, the political, and in particular, the state, could achieve dominance. Of course, the implication of this claim was that Poulantzas rejected any simple, or vulgar, reading of Marx, with its emphasis on economic determinism. The notion, that the economic element determined the functioning of capitalism in the last instance, was taken by Poulantzas in a very loose and liberal fashion.

On the State. A second and related element to the unique view of Poulantzas is his claim that the state, as a structure, can independently foster the survival and growth of a capitalist society. Here his argument is twofold. He asserts that the institutions of the state may intervene in the class struggle, particularly if and when there is a stalemate between the dominant and subordinate classes. Indeed, the state may even act apparently to further the interests of the subordinate classes over and above those of the dominant capitalist class. He writes, for instance, that "the state aims precisely at the political disorganization of the dominated classes . . . [and] . . . where the political struggle of the dominated classes is possible, it is sometimes the means of maintaining the [hegemony of the dominant classes]."[43] In other words, where the state permits open competition and conflict among classes, this may simply serve to maintain the overall hegemony of capitalism in the economic, juridical, and ideological spheres of society. But there is another way that the State may serve as an independent actor in society. It does so by becoming itself a site on which the class struggle is fought. What Poulantzas means by this claim is that the state may be composed of different fractions of classes, including members of the dominant capitalist class but also members of the subordinate classes as well. Moreover, Poulantzas argues, sometimes the fate of capitalism is determined not by the hegemony of the capitalist class but by the hegemony of another class, one that more clearly unifies a capitalist society at a particular historical moment. It is in this sense that Poulantzas seeks to explain the modern welfare state, many of whose measures benefit the working class. The victory of the working class is only apparent, however. The benefits provided through the welfare state, such as Social Security, Medicare, and other measures, in Poulantzas's view simply ensure that the other fundamental components of modern capitalism will escape attack.

The Relative Autonomy of the State: Poulantzas vs. Ralph Miliband. Poulantzas's imagery of society and of the state is obviously more complicated than that of Marx. Whereas Marx had once asserted that the "state is nothing but the executive of the ruling class," Poulantzas claims that the state can represent a battleground on which the conflicts and contradictions of capitalism are fought out among different classes. While this revision of Marx seems well taken, Poulantzas's argument about states as structures, and about their relative autonomy from the economic workings of capitalism, resulted in considerable debate with other contemporary Marxists, especially Ralph Miliband.[44] Miliband argues that in twentieth-century capitalist societies the state remains the central vehicle through which capitalism will survive. How? It happens, he claims, because members of the capitalist class constitute the key policymakers in such state institutions as the judiciary, the police force, the legislature, and, especially, the executive branch of government. Miliband provides very convincing documentation for his thesis. Poulantzas, however, asserts that Miliband's version of Marx—which clearly adheres to the "executive of the ruling class" notion—is much too simple-minded. It is the state as structure, not as people, that fosters and furthers the rise of modern capitalism. To reduce the state, or even capitalism as a whole, to individual agents, Poulantzas maintains, is to trivialize the fundamental ideas of Marx and to miss Marx's emphasis on capitalism as an impersonal, working system.

The intellectual battle between Poulantzas and Miliband over the nature and operations of the state in modern capitalism became quite heated in the 1970s. It also reflected some of the ambiguity evident in the ideas of Marx himself, an ambiguity to which we alluded in our discussion of Marx. One such point has to do with the role of people, or agents, in the Marxist scheme of things. Are they merely vehicles for the realization of the workings of the capitalist system, or do they serve somehow as independent forces? Indeed, are they, in fact, real? Poulantzas would deny them a reality altogether, while Miliband, though acknowledging their reality, would suggest they still serve to implement the long-term interests of capitalism. But the implication of Miliband's view, too, is that if the state were to be occupied by agents of other classes, then it could operate contrary to the interests of capitalism itself. It might even reform capitalism. That, clearly, is not at all the implication of Poulantzas's argument. Another point of ambiguity has to do with the role of the state itself. While Poulantzas wished to emphasize how the state could achieve an autonomy in the evolution of the class struggle, becoming dominated by classes other than the capitalist class, in the end his perspective reached no clearer view of this matter than did that of Marx. For, like Marx, he insisted that while the state structures might in a given historical circumstance favor some subordinate class, as, for example, the peasants in the case of the regime of Louis Bonaparte in France, in the long run such actions continue to favor the growth of capitalism. In other words, the autonomy of the state for Poulantzas is just as much a fiction as it was for Marx; for both theorists the hegemony of the capitalist class, and with it, capitalism, escape untouched by the workings of the state.

CONCLUSION

The writings and ideas of Karl Marx continue to play a very important role today in how sociologists think about politics. They animate some rather major views of history, including the world-systems analysis of Immanuel Wallerstein (see Chapter 10). And even where much of the Marxian paraphernalia has disappeared from view—including the notions of alienation and dialectical analysis—Marx's ghost still remains a powerful force over our view of the world. Perhaps the most potent idea that remains attractive to modern analysts is that of the deep injustice and misery that exists for so many citizens of the world. Marx focused on capitalism and its inequalities as a means of revealing how the system acted to make some people very rich, while others became incredibly poor. As capitalism has spread across the world today, inequality remains, indeed the disparities between the rich and poor within nations, but especially between nations, seems to have grown.

What is it about the economic system of capitalism that promotes such disparities? What will have to be done to help the poor and the needy to overcome their difficulties? These were questions central to Marx's economic analysis and thought about the world, and they are questions that remain his enduring legacy and vision for hope in the modern world.

NOTES

1. Isaiah Berlin, *Karl Marx: His Life and Environment* (London: Oxford University Press, 1963).
2. Tom Bottomore, ed., *Karl Marx* (Englewood Cliffs, New Jersey: Prentice-Hall, Inc., 1973), 68.
3. Georg Lukàcs, *History and Class Consciousness,* translated by R. Livingstone (London: The Merlin Press, Ltd., 1971).
4. Robert C. Tucker, ed., *The Marx-Engels Reader* (New York: W.W. Norton Co., Inc., 1972), 23.
5. Lewis Feuer, ed., *Marx and Engels: Basic Writings on Politics and Philosophy* (Garden City, New York: Doubleday and Co., 1959), xi.
6. Feuer, *Marx and Engels,* 17–18.
7. Ibid., 282.
8. Since Marx, like every other sociologist, could not conduct such experiments in the real world, he conducted them in the abstract. The results, no less significant for being obtained in such a manner, indicated among other things the manner in which capitalist enterprises would grow. Defects in the actual economic principles employed by Marx, owing largely to the source of them, David Ricardo, rendered many of his predictions wrong or indeterminate. For example, see Fred M. Gottheil, *Marx's Economic Predictions* (Evanston, Illinois: Northwestern University Press, 1977). Such is the fate of many of our scientific predictions, however good they might appear for a time.
9. Even when Marx wrote of the capitalist and proletariat classes, he seemed confused about what they represented. On occasion he wrote of them as though they were real groups. However, he usually viewed them as abstract entities that were useful for conducting analyses and making predictions [Stanislaw Ossowski, *Class Structures in the Social Consciousness* (New York: Free Press, 1963)]. More important, if Marx meant to define the capitalist and proletarian classes by their relationship to property, there must be one additional social

class under capitalism, the landed aristocracy—a remnant of feudalism whose property consists, not of the technical and scientific apparatus, but of land. There then appear to be three main social classes under capitalism, not two: the capitalists, owners of the technical and scientific apparatus of production; the landed aristocracy, owners of land; the proletariat, owners of no property, simply their labor power. These, incidentally, were the three principal classes that Marx defined in the third volume of *Capital.* Nevertheless, if Marx had remained alive long enough he would probably have argued that as capitalist societies matured—and no capitalist society in the late nineteenth century could be considered mature, not even England—land would diminish in importance as a source of profit, thereby leaving only the two great classes, the capitalist and the proletariat.

10. Marx,"The German Ideology," in Tucker, *The Marx-Engels Reader,* 136.
11. Marx, "The Eighteenth Brumaire of Louis Bonaparte," in Tucker, *The Marx-Engels Reader,* 459.
12. Ibid., 459–60.
13. Marx, "The Civil War in France," in Tucker, *The Marx-Engels Reader,* 552.
14. Marx, *Capital,* I, Chapter 10.
15. Marx and Engels, "The Communist Manifesto," in Tucker, *The Marx-Engels Reader,* 337.
16. Feuer, *Marx and Engels,* 12.
17. Marx, *Capital,* I, 750.
18. Feuer, *Marx and Engels,* 19.
19. Marx, *Capital,* I, 644–45.
20. Ronald L. Meek, "Marx's Doctrine of Increasing Misery," *Science and Society,* 26 (Fall 1962), 436–37.
21. Feuer, *Marx and Engels,* 16.
22. Ibid., 17.
23. Tucker, *The Marx-Engels Reader,* 143.
24. There is one additional element that figures into class consciousness on a philosophical plane—the class of people must be aware of their coming ascendancy to power in society (Georg Lukàcs, *History and Class Consciousness: Studies in Marxist Dialectics.* Cambridge, Massachusetts: The MIT Press, 1971, 83 –222).
25. Lenin, *What Is to Be Done?* (New York: International Publishers, 1943), 41.
26. Isaac Deutscher, ed., *The Age of Permanent Revolution: A Trotsky Anthology* (New York: Dell Publishing, 1964), passim.
27. V.I. Lenin, "What Is to Be Done: Burning Questions of Our Movement," in *The Lenin Anthology,* ed. Robert C. Tucker (New York: W.W. Norton & Co., Inc., 1975), 12–114.
28. V.I. Lenin, "Letters on Tactics," in *Lenin, Marx-Engels-Marxism* (Moscow: Foreign Languages Publishing House, n.d.), 400.
29. Two works by Poulantzas which are particularly valuable are *Classes in Contemporary Capitalism* (London: Verso, 1978), and *Political Power and Social Classes*

(London: Verso, 1978). Both reveal the influence of Lenin's thought on Poulantzas' own work.

30. V.I. Lenin, "The State and Revolution," in Tucker, *The Lenin Anthology,* 311–98.
31. V.I. Lenin, "Imperialism: The Highest State of Capitalism," in Tucker, *The Lenin Anthology,* 204–274.
32. Rudoph Hilferding, *Das Finanzkapital* (Vienna: I. Brand, 1910); and J. A. Hobson, *Imperialism* (Ann Arbor, Michigan: University of Michigan Press, 1902, 1965).
33. Antonio Gramsci, "The Modern Prince," in *Selections from the Prison Notebooks,* Antonio Gramsci, edited and translated by Quintin Hoare and Geoffrey Nowell Smith (New York: International Publishers, 1971), 123–205.
34. Gramsci, *Prison Notebooks,* 170.
35. Gramsci, *Prison Notebooks,* 125 *et passim.*
36. Gramsci, *Prison Notebooks,* 235.
37. Herbert Marcuse, *One-Dimensional Man* (Boston: Beacon Press, 1964).
38. Herbert Marcuse, "Industrialization and Capitalism in the Work of Max Weber," in *Negations: Essays in Critical Theory,* Herbert Marcuse (Boston: Beacon Press, 1968), 201–26.
39. Antonio Gramsci, "Americanism and Fordism," in *Prison Notebooks,* Gramsci, 277–318.
40. See his various works, among them, Jürgen Habermas, *Legitimation Crisis* (Boston: Beacon Press, 1975); *Communication and the Evolution of Society* (Boston: Beacon Press, 1979); *Theory and Practice* (Boston: Beacon Press, 1973); and *Knowledge and Human Interests* (Boston: Beacon Press, 1971).
41. For a good introduction to the ideas of Nicos Poulantzas, read Bob Jessop, *Nicos Poulantzas: Marxist Theory and Political Strategy* (New York: St. Martin's Press, 1985). Poulantzas's own discussion of the relative autonomy of the state can be found in Poulantzas, *Political Power and Social Classes,* Part IV.
42. Poulantzas, ibid., Part I *et passim.*
43. Ibid., 191
44. For interesting highlights on the debate, see David A. Gold, Clarence Y. H. Lo, and Erik Olin Wright, "Recent Developments in Marxist Theories of the Capitalist State: I" *Monthly Review Press,* 27 (October 1975), 29–43.

Chapter 3

On States and Societies
Max Weber and the Neo-Weberians

> "Every state is founded on force," said Trotsky at Brest-Litovsk. That is indeed right . . . force is a means specific to the state. . . . Today . . . we have to claim that a state is a human community that successfully claims the monopoly of the legitimate use of physical force within a given territory. . . . The state is considered the sole source of the "right" to use violence. Hence, "politics" for us means striving to share power or striving to influence the distribution of power, either among states or among groups within a state.
>
> Max Weber, *Politics as a Vocation*

It would seem to be a virtual truism that the institutions of the state, or government, exercise control over workings of politics. Certainly that claim is an integral part of the view of all those scholars who call themselves political scientists. But sociologists, at least since the time of Karl Marx, have taken a slightly different tack on the matter. Politics, they argue, cannot simply be understood by examining the internal operations of the state itself. Instead, one must work with a broader canvas—which, for many Marxists, would include the unfolding nature of social classes and the economy as well as the international setting of countries—in seeking to explain the nature of politics.

The writer and thinker to turn our attention back to the nature of the state and its connections to other social institutions was Max Weber. Weber, it has been suggested, considered himself a kind of antithesis to Marx. He tried to correct Marx's materialist philosophy with one that also left an important, if not decisive, role for ideas and ideals in the study of history. In his famous conclusion to *The Protestant Ethic*, a work that traced the origins and consequences of the rise of ascetic Protestantism in the West, Weber observes that " . . . it is, of course, not my aim to substitute for a one-sided materialistic an equally one-sided spiritualistic causal interpretation of culture and of history. Each is equally possible, but each, if it does not serve as the preparation, but as the conclusion of an investigation, accomplishes equally little in the interest of historical truth."[1] In the realm of politics, Weber also tried to offset Marx's heavy emphasis on economic causes of social phenomena. Unlike Marx, he believed that the actual administration of politics in nations played a very significant part in shaping how power is exercised over people and other nations.

One other element that Weber brought to the study of politics is an emphasis on the role of great figures in the making of history. Most sociologists emphasize the long-term significance of fundamental organizations and social institutions, like the state, over historical outcomes. Weber, however, believed that individuals of great personal power and influence—*charismatic* personalities, he called them—could also exercise a decisive role in the shaping of modern nations. "Everywhere the development of the modern state is initiated through the action of the prince," he once wrote.[2] Figures like these often will arise under conditions of societal instability, providing the leadership necessary to take unstable institutions and to reshape them for future generations. In recent times, there are important figures like Mikhail Gorbachev in Russia and Nelson Mandela in South Africa, who furnished precisely this kind of leadership in times of social and political upheaval.

Though sociologists disagree about the extent to which such figures can play a role—beyond institutions themselves—Weber tried to have it both ways. He argued that the strength of state institutions was due to the force of their law and administrative apparatus, and yet also to the singular figures who helped to furnish their direction and leadership. Such singular figures, he insisted, not only serve to sustain ongoing institutions, but they, and their immediate allies, have the energy and vitality to create them anew. "Weber shared with Nietzsche the conviction that only the individual, as a rule only the outstanding individual, was capable of setting new goals and of imparting a new drive to society," observes Wolfgang Mommsen.[3]

MAX WEBER ON STATES AND POLITICS

The Essential Weber

Max Weber, it has been said, was one of the world's last great polymaths. An expert in any number of fields, ranging from law to economics, Weber tried to unravel a number of the mysteries about the development of the West. Unlike Marx, he never produced a grand theory. Nor did he believe such theories to be valid and important instruments for the development of the social sciences. He writes:

> Laws are important and valuable in the exact natural sciences, in the measure that those sciences are *universally valid.* For the knowledge of historical phenomena in their concreteness, the most general laws, because they are most devoid of content are also the least valuable. The more comprehensive the validity,—or scope—of a term, the more it leads us away from the richness of reality since in order to include the common elements of the largest possible number of phenomena, it must necessarily be as abstract as possible and hence *devoid* of content. In the cultural sciences, the knowledge of the universal or general is never valuable in itself.[4]

Instead, he attacked specific, but broad problems, with a kind of attention and historical rigor absent in the work of Marx. He believed that the history of human societies was such that it would be impossible to ever formulate some basic general laws or principles about such societies; at best one could offer specific explanations for particular historical events. Further, as time passed, and the world changed, even the questions posed by social scientists would change, reflecting new issues and concerns.

Because of his many pursuits, Weber was compelled to engage in a delicate balancing act, seeking to sustain his work as a scholar and to continue with his active interest in everyday politics. Eventually he shaped a strategy for himself that has since become a model for many social scientists and historians. Above all else, he advocated, an intellectual must attempt to segregate his life as a scholar from that as a man of action. The judgments involved in the two pursuits simply could not be mixed without endangering the effectiveness of each; as a scientist, in particular, one could not fairly or safely judge the proper course for the citizen. Along similar lines, the scholar, in his capacity as teacher, should not engage in polemics in the classroom, particularly if such a strategy is designed to achieve popularity rather than to educate. "The task of the teacher," he wrote, "is to serve the students with his knowledge and scientific experience and not to imprint upon them his personal political views. . . . I am ready to prove from the works of our historians that whenever the man of science introduces his personal value judgment, a full understanding of the facts ceases."[5]

As serious scholarship and science make it imperative that polemics be removed from the setting of intellectual discourse, so, too, the political arena is marked by its own special rules. Politics, in essence, represents a continuing conflict over the control of scarce material and symbolic (or ideal) resources. Any person who wishes to engage in this arena must be prepared to struggle, to compromise, but eventually to emerge either on the side of the victors or on that of the vanquished. Thus, an ethics of ultimate ends, especially that of natural law that insists on the inherent rights and equality of all men, is doomed from the beginning to failure in politics. Obviously Weber's view of politics, as of its connections to scholarship, differs greatly from that of Marx; Marx sought to achieve a unity among the seemingly independent pursuits. Nevertheless, Weber's perspective, like that of Marx, must be understood in the context of his view of Western societies.

The nature of social and economic life in the West, according to Weber, represents the pinnacle of professionalism and routine activity. Each of the many and diverse kinds of activities is defined in the form of a profession, or vocation, thereby establishing a unique career path as well as a special set of rights and obligations. This theme, in turn, is part of a much broader and pervasive trend in the development of Western civilization; the theme is the *rationalization of life*. This, for Weber, means that all life is subject to a common form of assessment, calculability—that is, the assessment of the most technically efficient means for attaining particular ends. Thus, in the marketplace the most efficient means for purchasing goods and services can be calculated with precision; in the courts the form of penalty or obligation incumbent on the lawbreaker can be made almost exactly; in war the strategy best designed to accomplish quick and efficient naval or land victories can easily be assessed.

These patterns are embodied in rational bureaucracy, the most dominant and striking feature of the West. This form of administration, Weber claimed, has both its advantages and its disadvantages. As the structural embodiment of the major themes of Western civilization, it represents major *technical* advances over all prior civilizations; it can accomplish tasks more quickly, precisely, and cheaply than any other form of organization. It also, however, invites the alienation of man; it represents the structural avenue through which modern life is administered, and the individual, lacking the ability to control this institution, is therefore unable to control the activities of his own life. Further, bureaucracy has become so pervasive an institution that the individual's options for action, and thus his freedom, have been reduced.

Although any individual's choice with regard to means has been reduced to a common measure of evaluation, it has not been similarly diminished with respect to ends. There are a finite number of values from among which men and women may choose to commit themselves. Such values represent an integral part of Weber's sociology, finding their expression as objects that could provide the basis for distinctive social groups, *status groups*, as well as sources of competition and conflict among groups in the political arena.

Weber's greatest intellectual achievement is to be found in his effort to explain the broad differences between the West and the Orient. Here he turned his attention and efforts to understanding the nature of religion. He made religion the centerpiece of much of his work, and the study of the rise of ascetic Protestantism in the West the major part of it. He argued that ascetic Protestantism was a major fact of Western life, signifying a major difference between the West and the Orient. The tenets of ascetic Protestantism—its emphasis on salvation; the unceasing vigilance of the believer over his or her life; the abstinence from self-indulgence; the single-minded devotion to one's work and life—helped in a paradoxical fashion to secure the dominion of capitalism in the West by providing a moral foundation for the shrewd and relentless accumulation of wealth.[6]

Weber's sense of the possibilities and power of politics and political officials was far more astute and developed than that of Marx. He believed that administration, in general, and the modern state, in particular, could exercise as much influence as the workings of the economy. Unlike Marx, who believed that the activities of societies were grounded fundamentally in their mode of production and economic institutions, Weber believed that the exercise of authority, or domination, was central to modern societies. A large part of his intellectual agenda was devoted to deciphering the precise nature of that authority and how it worked in modern, feudal, and ancient societies, alike.

Like Marx, Weber believed that people are alienated, but from the means of administration rather than from those of material production. Unlike Marx, however, Weber was less certain that humankind could throw off the yoke of its alienation; he believed that virtually nothing can be done to reduce the encroachment of bureaucracies over the individual's life. Moreover, unlike Marx, his work contained no teleological endpoint or purpose toward which humankind was moving. History and life moved on; at best one could understand the major themes that had constructed the past, but one could not easily discern the lineaments of the future. We are, he concluded, prisoners of the "iron cage" of the institutions of the modern world: "The Puritan wanted to work in a calling; we are forced to do so," he writes. "(The modern economic) order is now bound to the technical and economic conditions of machine production which today determine the lives of all . . . individuals. . . . In Baxter's view the care for external goods should only lie on the shoulders of the 'saint like a light cloak, which can be thrown aside at any moment.' But fate decreed that cloak should become an iron cage."[7]

The State

Weber bequeathed to his followers the outlines and main features of how to think about modern states and their operations in society. The principal feature of the modern state, according to him, is that it exercises the "monopoly of the legitimate use of physical force within a given territory."[8] Such a monopoly provides the state with a power that no other institution or agency possesses in modern society; it enables the state, and its officeholders, to wield its power in a way no other group, including large social classes or firms, could possibly exercise. On matters, then, of force and might, the state is the ultimate authority. In a sense, Weber insisted, the state in the modern world occupies the same place of prominence and centrality as the Church did in the medieval world.

For Weber there were two critical features to the organizational dimensions of the state. The first is the *state bureaucracy* itself. From his point of view, this bureaucracy is central to the organization and administration of the state. It provides the articulation and implementation of the laws and policies on behalf of the larger society. Although the parliament, or Congress, represents the elected officials, the state bureaucracy, consisting of civil servants, remains decisive because it actually carries out the law that is formulated by political officials. In nineteenth-century Germany, in fact, the state bureaucracy was far more powerful than the elected officials, and Weber held out little hope that officials, even democratically elected officials, would ever prove as effective and competent as the civil servants.[9]

The second principal dimension of power is that of particular *groups of officials* who gain ascendance over others. Such ascendance grows out of their expert knowledge and skill in the administration of politics. Since law—specifically, modern rational law—had become so important to the daily life of modern societies, those who understood the law—modern lawyers—would, Weber argued, become most central to politics and to the implementation of the force of the state.[10] Lawyers, to Weber, represented a powerful social alliance as societies modernized, far more potent perhaps than even the capitalist social class.

In a democratic society, Weber observed, the rule of law obtains. Citizens must obey the law, or suffer the penalties of disobedience. Each day moves smoothly, almost like clockwork, as people go about their routines and move in an orderly, rational fashion. Weber believed that beneath the surface of this order, however, there lay the potential for deep internal threats to society in general, and democratic society in particular. The first such threat came from the very emphasis on rational norms and their application by the state, and also by other modern institutions. Such norms placed an emphasis on efficiency and calculability at the expense of deeper issues such as justice and equality. By shifting the emphasis to efficiency, Weber believed the deeper and more powerful ends of life—and questions about such ends—were pushed aside, lost in the array of rules and bureaucratic order.

The other threat came from the bureaucratic nature of the modern state itself. Weber believed that as the state became more complex and powerful, the ability of any group of individuals to challenge the state, much less a single individual, diminished. The great threat to the future of democratic societies, in his eyes, lay not in the concentration and centralization of capital, as Marx had argued, but in the centralization of power under the state. A state without vigorous leadership, but only a smoothly working group of bureaucrats, poses as much harm to the long-term well-being of its citizens as a state ruled by a leader of ill will. "(T)here is only the choice between leadership democracy with a 'machine,'" he wrote, "and leaderless democracy, namely, the rule of professional politicians without a calling, without the inner charismatic qualities that make a leader."[11]

The Power of the Ruler

Can we really speak of a "great man" theory of history? Tension and ambivalence abound in the writings and thinking of Max Weber about the role of individual figures or leaders and the role of institutions.[12] This tension leads to vastly different readings of Weber. Some scholars will emphasize Weber's intellectual leanings toward the power of great figures, such as Bismarck in nineteenth-century Germany, emphasizing that Weber believed, along with Friedrich Nietzsche, that great personages could exercise enough power to overturn and transform the world, making institutions and customs the mere servants of the power of the individual.[13] Others will emphasize that while Weber admitted the power of individuals, he also believed that institutions did take on a life all their own (as he showed in his work on the Protestant Ethic), remaking society and life in their own outlines. It is this reading of Weber that makes much out of his emphasis on the role of the modern state and how it can reshape and remake societies.

The most judicious way to understand Weber—and to extend his view of politics—on the matter of leadership comes from the writings and interpretations of the German sociologist Wolfgang Mommsen. Mommsen argues that in Weber's thinking institutions and personal authority should not be thought of as dualities in opposition to one another, but rather as part of the actual workings of organizations and institutions. He firmly believed in democracy, but it was a democracy of institutional law and force, guided by benevolent leaders. "From a realistic perspective," writes Mommsen, "(Weber believed) democracy can at best mean domination by freely elected leaders, who are then in a position to proceed essentially at their own discretion. It can never mean the superseding of domination by a system of policy formation from the bottom up."[14] Thus, the power of the modern state lies not simply in the regular and efficient workings of the state bureaucracy, but also in the leadership and charisma given to the state by the power of individuals. In this sense, then, great figures like Winston Churchill in wartime England or Golda Meier in the fledgling state of Israel provided a kind of voice and direction to the state that it would otherwise lack.

Some very recent organizational sociologists, such as Peter Blau, completely disavow the crucial significance of rulers and singular figures of influence and power, maintaining that the work of modern society is really done by the regular and routine activities of organizations and other structures. Yet to the end Weber himself insisted that "(p)olitical action is always determined by the 'principle of small numbers.' . . . In mass states, this caesarist element is ineradicable."[15]

Authority and Its Legitimacy

In the study of politics, one of Weber's most enduring contributions lies in his effort to understand how it is that large assemblages of individuals are held together and operate. For Marx, it had been partly a matter of ideology. For Weber it became a matter of authority, or, as some sociologists put it, domination.[16]

The grounds for obeying authority are written into their very foundations. In modern societies such authority rests on the rational-legal foundations of law. Law is an instrument of universal and impersonal rule, and it furnishes many great advantages to the running of large-scale societies. For example, Weber insisted, it helped in the creation of modern democratic societies, which by their very nature must rest on universal grounds rather than particular ones. But law possesses an even deeper significance. It provides the terms in which both the officials and the citizens of modern states make a contract to agree to the nature of rule.

Law by itself does not guarantee compliance, or domination, in modern society, however. There also must be an administrative apparatus that helps to implement the law, to carry it out. Administration helps to enforce the obedience of people to the ruler by providing punishment for noncompliance with commands, by levying and collecting taxes, by carrying on war, and by attending to related matters. "Organized domination," Weber remarked, "requires the control of those material goods which in a given case are necessary for the use of physical violence . . . [as well as] control of the executive staff and the material implements of administration."[17] Administration entails its own problems because major struggles for the position of dominance always occur between the ruler and his staff. To lessen the threat of usurpation of the ruler's power, there must also be a solidarity of interest between the ruler and the staff; the burden for establishing such solidarity falls on the shoulders of the ruler. As in similar instances, such solidarity is insured through the provision of material and ideal rewards by the ruler: "The fear of losing [material reward and social honor] is the *final* and *decisive* basis for solidarity between the executive staff and the power-holder."[18]

Though Weber characterized the modern state as exercising a monopoly over the means of violence in a given territory, the legitimacy on which the rule of the state was based in the long run may have been more important to him. Rulers, Weber avowed, could not simply exercise their rule without the willing obedience of their subordinates. Power was a matter of sheer domination, but authority was grounded in the compliance of citizens. If citizens were not compliant, no amount of force could compel them to be so. The recurring dualism of Weber's thought—between the power of individuals and of institutions; between the power of ideas and of material production—surfaced even on this matter of the legitimacy of rule. State rulers can rule, of course, because they hold the means of force behind them, but unless their followers fully believed in their right to lead, no exercise of power by rulers could ever succeed.

Political Power and Contending Social Groups

Inasmuch as modern states exercise the legitimate control of force in modern societies, they are routinely considered the prize for contending social groups. Marx argued, as we recall, that such a prize was secured by the dominant class in a specific historical society, and in modern capitalism was controlled by the forces of the wealthy. To Weber the matter was not quite so simple. Indeed, to him it was a great deal more complex. Though he agreed with Marx that social classes existed, in his view they simply represented general aggregates of people who shared a similar position in the labor market. Social classes could never be organized to take decisive action because they lacked any common basis for such action. Instead Weber insisted that common and purposive action was more apt to occur for two other kinds of social alliances.

One is what he called *status groups.* Such groups consist of people who share a common occupational or professional position, like doctors, artists, or lawyers. As a result of their common position, such people can also come to share certain values and lifestyles in common. They may live in similar areas of a city, shop at similar grocery stores, work in a similar kind of manner. In the 1980s, people wrote of *yuppies,* or young urban professionals. They were people who worked in urban areas, made a good deal of money, and lived in parts of the city in similarly upscale housing. They represented a classic example of a status group.

Sometimes status groups can become the basis for political action. They are able to do so precisely because their members share similar lifestyles and values. Hunters in modern society represent something of a status group in the sense that hunting and rifles represent a major part of their leisure-time activity. Moreover, when efforts are made to control the sale of guns, such hunters, through the vehicle of organizations like the National Rifle Association, can become very effective at preventing the passage of major laws that would control the sale and use of weapons.

More often, however, it is specific *political associations* and *parties* that are the main contenders for the power of the state. The party, unlike either a social class or status group, is organized specifically to pursue political ends and the exercise of power. "Parties live in a house of 'power,'" Weber once observed. "Their action is oriented toward the acquisition of social 'power,' that is to say, toward influencing a communal action no matter what its content may be."[19] Political parties focus their energies and plan their strategies to secure power. Sometimes they have long histories and records of successful campaigns as well as winning high political office, as in the case of the Democrats and Republicans in America. Other times they serve more limited ends and purposes, even emerging as contenders for power within bureaucracies and other kinds of organizations.

In the final analysis, Weber insisted, there is much conflict in modern society, but social classes prove much too large, unwieldy and diverse to be effective at seizing the rewards of power. Status groups on occasion, but parties most often, are the prime contenders for the privilege to rule—and to wield the vast forces of the modern state.

THE NEO-WEBERIANS

Although Weber never created a large band of followers and ideologists in the same manner as Karl Marx, his writings on states and societies have proved influential for a number of sociologists in recent decades. Here we shall discuss three of the most notable ones—Reinhard Bendix, Charles Tilly, and Theda Skocpol.

Reinhard Bendix

A refugee to America from Germany in 1938, Reinhard Bendix helped introduce to American sociology a strong emphasis on comparative and historical studies. He drew upon concerns and themes from Max Weber as well as from the French scholar Alexis de Tocqueville (see Chapter 4). Bendix was interested in social and political change on a grand scale, and especially in the role that ideas played in the constitution of societies as well as in prompting such change. With the publication in 1960 of *Max Weber: An Intellectual Portrait*, he became the foremost interpreter in the world of Weber's work.[20]

On the Nature and Exercise of Authority. The central Weberian theme that Bendix helped to illuminate in his own writings was that of political authority. Authority in Weber's work played the same central role as the economy and ideology did in Marx's writings. Weber believed that differences in authority were the key differences that distinguished between different historical regimes and epochs. Moreover, he came to believe that the main innovation feature of modern society was not capitalism, *per se*, but rather the form of rational organization and the underpinnings that secured its authority over men and women. Bendix elaborated on these themes, blending them together with questions and issues raised by Tocqueville.[21]

In refashioning Weber's original concept Bendix made it clear that authority does not simply represent the simple exercise of power, even legitimate power, by rulers. Instead, the exercise of authority represents a kind of delicate balancing act, a constant tension arising from the strong desire of leaders to get their commands implemented and the reluctant willingness of followers to obey those commands. Thus, if one wished to understand the nature of a society one should not only investigate the nature of authority and who holds it, but one should also inquire into the grounds and reasons that enabled leaders to exercise their power over their followers. Authority could not simply be wielded by powerful figures with no sense of the nature or character of followers themselves. In his biography of Weber, Bendix remarks:

> Domination involves a reciprocal relationship between rulers and ruled, in which the actual frequency of compliance is only one aspect of the fact that the power of command exists. Equally important is the meaning that rulers and ruled attach to the authority relationship. In addition to the fact that they issue commands, the rulers claim that they have legitimate authority to do so. . . . In the same way, the obedience of the ruled is guided to some extent by the idea that the rulers and their commands constitute a legitimate order of authority.[22]

Indeed, to Bendix the exercise of authority said as much, if not more, about the mind-set of followers as it did about leadership.

Work and Authority in Industry. Weber had emphasized that the integrity of societies arose not simply out of the material resources commanded by the wealthy, but also and often because of the dominant ideas and ideals. Bendix extended this argument further, insisting that political struggles took place over both ideal and material interests of competing social groups.[23] Ideal interests, in fact, played as major a part in the nature of politics as material interests did, though often they had to be discovered through a more subtle and nuanced historical analysis.

Bendix's major contribution to the study of ideal interests and their role in society's conflicts took the form of his study of the changes that occurred in the ideologies of managerialism that were exercised beginning in the early part of the nineteenth century. He began his analysis from the collapse of the royal authority at the end of the eighteenth century. Once this collapse happened, a number of forces were unleashed. Bendix notes, among other things, that the lower classes now were free to pursue their own course of action, unfettered by the authority relations of the past. This created a kind of paradox in his reading of the situation: the individual was freed to pursue his interest, but in order to do so he was compelled to join with others in this pursuit.[24] A kind of tension ensued between the individualism unleashed by the collapse of the old regime and the need for workers to band together to pursue their material interests in common.

This situation of transition, from a society in which the relations between nobility and the peasants were fixed, to a society in which industry now arose and new occupations opened for the masses of people, presented a problem in the nature of labor itself. Now that the people were free, what would convince them to work in the new industries and for their new masters? Why should they even work for new masters? Bendix believed, with Weber, that ideas were the key here to the authority relationship, but what kind of ideas, or ideologies, were necessary to create the grounds for this new form of compliance by the former peasants? This was the essential Bendix question posed both in his early writings on work and authority and in his later writings on kings and rulers.

In the case of labor, Bendix insisted that the different ideologies arose both in the West and in Russia to secure the loyalty of the worker.[25] Over time the nature of the ideological justifications for work would change in both countries. In the West, in particular, there came to be an increasing emphasis on the scientific character of work, and the best way that production could be done by the laborer. This culminated in the rise of the ideas and writings of Frederick Taylor in the 1920s and 1930s, ideas that claimed there was only one right way to do work, and the trick for management was to get workers to perform in that manner. The underlying ideology of Taylorism replaced the earlier emphasis on laissez-faire capitalism, and ideas that had stressed the basic laziness and idleness of workers. Such management ideologies, in Bendix's eyes, were crucial to the nature of labor itself, far more crucial than a simple material Marxian emphasis on labor and labor power under modern capitalism.

Kings or People. Bendix's broadest attack on understanding the nature of authority took the form of his last major work, *Kings or People.*[26] In this work he sets himself the goal of seeking to understand the transition from the authority of kings and nobles to the authority of the people, or the masses in the world of the eighteenth century and beyond. He examines the problem of political authority across the wide spectrum of history and in different national/cultural contexts, ranging from that of Russia to England to France and Japan. He argues, in a way strongly reminiscent of Weber, that the spread of ideas and the mobilization of intellectuals played a significant part in the construction of modern societies:

> intellectual mobilization—the growth of a reading public and of an educated secular elite dependent on learned occupations—(is) an independent cause of social change. . . . For example, the invention of printing and the scientific revolution of the seventeenth century were part of an intellectual mobilization that was facilitated by commercialization in the early modern period, but *that also occurred well in advance of commercialization and provided a means to promote commerce and industry.*[27]

Moreover, he argues on behalf of what he calls the "demonstration effect," namely that the collapse of the old regimes and inauguration of the power of the people takes place as one nation copies the achievements of another. Thus, the English revolution and the rise of Parliament in the late seventeenth century provided a model for other countries to emulate, particularly for those groups of intellectuals who aspired to democracy. The role of such groups of people, motivated as they were by the effort to copy the successes of other regimes, for Bendix plays a major part in the creation of new states and nations.

Bendix drew especially on a certain theme in the work of Weber—that which emphasized the role of ideal forces in the making and unmaking of societies. He believed that to comprehend the social order required that one understand the deep and underlying bases of authority, in other words, the grounds for why one group of people obeyed another group. His careful analysis helped to reveal the way that such ideal forces arose and worked, both for the power of kings and for the power of workplace management. Yet his work has had limited lasting influence over contemporary political sociologists. Perhaps the main reason is that he failed to leave us with a clear, systematic and powerful model of how ideas and ideals continue to work their power in politics, a model that would serve to direct and to inspire the analyses of today's sociologists.

Charles Tilly

Charles Tilly, one of the leading historical sociologists in recent times, falls somewhere between Karl Marx and Max Weber in his theoretical style. He is not so much a direct intellectual descendant of either man as he is someone who has helped further our understanding of the same questions they raised about politics and societies.[28] In his analysis of economic circumstances and class differences, he has helped to extend our detailed understanding of how such forces play a role in history—not through broad models, but through exacting and careful historical analysis.[29] And in his copious writings on the state—both state-building and struggles over the authority of government—we find him adding to and refining the Weberian legacy.

Tilly believes that change is a major theme in the nature of societies, and he has devoted much of his body of work to its examination. Instead of taking a broad, overly theoretical view of change, his work focuses on how change comes about—especially how forces of protest and forces for change arise among the common people, whether peasants or the urban proletariat. His work always is deeply rooted in specific historical events, grounded in the vast details of agony and discontent that arise among groups of aggrieved citizens; moreover, most of it has been devoted to studying the origins of dissent and disloyalty in France and Great Britain over the past several centuries. He is one of the most prolific of contemporary sociologists, and also one whose own ideas seem to evolve and change over time. Here I shall point to several key contributions he has made to understanding the nature of the modern state as well as the forces of resistance that arise to confront established political authority.

On the Origins of the Modern State. Almost three decades ago, Tilly was a member of a team of social scientists who were asked by the Social Science Research Council in America to draw together their research and observations on how European states came into existence.[30] What emerged from this task was a series of very interesting research papers on different features of state-making and state-building. Indeed, though there were considerable differences in the method and arguments of each of the scholars, they came to agree that the central focus for their work was state-building, not nation-building.[31]

Tilly's main contribution was to orchestrate and to synthesize the diverse research programs and papers. There were four main contributions that emerged from his synthesis at the time. The first was a very clear and coherent definition of the modern state:

> The structure which became dominant in Europe after 1500, the national state, [bore these features]: (1) it controlled a well-defined, continuous territory; (2) it was relatively centralized; (3) it was differentiated from other organizations; (4) it reinforced its claims through a tendency to acquire a monopoly over the concentrated means of physical coercion within its territory.[32]

This definition clearly echoes key features of the concept of state to which Weber first drew attention. The second contribution was his effort to ask the question about the origins of the state in a way different from his fellow social scientists at the time. In particular, he insisted that any effort to understand the origins of the modern state had to inquire not only about the institution that actually emerged, but also had to inquire as to why alternative forms of the state, or government—e.g., the city-state—failed to survive.

His third contribution was the argument that origins of the modern state were closely connected to the development and success of political institutions in war. Essentially state-making was war-making: Those governments that were successful in war also had the best chance to develop a modern state. His fourth and final contribution was perhaps the most important. He insisted that other analyses had emphasized the sequence and stages of state-making—actually political development—far too much. Because modern states, he claimed, differed greatly from one another, it would be a mistake to somehow believe that one sequence, or one model, represented the way of all state-making. In fact, he suggested, there was so much variation in the nature of modern states that any sound analysis must examine the origins of states more deeply, and not be satisfied with the idea that all states moved through an identical set of stages.[33]

Tilly's 1975 statement on state-making served as a preliminary sketch for work he undertook some years later. In this later treatment, published in 1990, he argued that modern states, such as France, England, or Holland, arose from a combination of two central factors: (1) the concentration and accumulation of capital; and (2) the concentration and accumulation of coercion, or force.[34] Where political institutions were able to mobilize and to concentrate capital, there, too, they would be able to devote much of the apparatus of the modern state—in particular, the financial organization and devices for extracting resources from the population. Similarly, where political organizations were able to concentrate the means of force under a single authority, amassing both weapons and a strong military, there also would the key elements of the modern national state emerge.

Tilly argued that the variations among different modern states arose from different combinations both of the elements of capital and the elements of coercion. For example, he observes, the Dutch state arose primarily because it was able to draw on the resources of capital, and those of urban industry and financiers, to create and solidify its base of power. In contrast, the modern German state was successful because it was able to mobilize both military and administrative forces through its exercise of force and coercion over various political rulers in the diverse and various principalities like Hanover and Prussia. In general, however, state-making was always most successful and most likely because of war-making.

> A ruler's creation of armed force generated durable state structure. It did so both because an army became a significant organization within the state and because its construction and maintenance brought complementary organiza-

> tions—treasuries, supply services, mechanisms for conscription, tax bureaux, and much more—into life.[35]

War-making was particularly decisive in the late fifteenth century. It was then that a number of major and critical wars were fought. And those states that were successful in such wars tended to be larger, to control more territory, and to be better administered—in other words, to look very much like the modern state, as Tilly had identified it in his 1975 work. Those states that failed tended to be smaller, on the order of city-states, and would later become the historical residue of state-like organizations that failed in the struggle to survive competition with other territorially based organizations.

Though the mobilization of capital and the exercise of coercion represented the key factors in the making of modern states, other forces also played a role. Thus, Tilly observes, the kind and strength of social classes in a country could affect the kind of state that emerged, and the process through which the state was built. So, too, the geopolitics of a region were crucial, particularly in terms of the range of territory that was under dispute, or under the governance of different and sometimes competing political authorities.

While Tilly's arguments and evidence have helped materially to move our understanding of the origins of modern states much further along than Weber's preliminary researches, and even those of other contemporary scholars, there is one critical point he fails to clarify—one that leaves his work unsatisfying. He insists that the variation among states depends critically on the success of organizations in mobilizing both capital and coercion and that there exist a wide variety of states. But he never informs us of the nature of such variations by producing some kind of classification. How *do* states differ from one another? In what terms? And are such differences significant from one another? In what ways? In other words, how are we to classify states? In the end, Tilly says far too little about the differences among states to permit us to understand precisely how the main factors of capital and coercion, and the subsidiary ones of social classes and geopolitics, actually combine to produce such variations.

On the Politics of Contention and Mobilization. Among sociologists, the work for which Tilly is best known is his writing about social movements and revolution. His seminal work is a piece of scholarship now more than two decades old, devoted to understanding the nature of political mobilization.[36] This work is one of the more widely read and widely cited pieces of literature on social movements.

Tilly argues that sociologists must shift their attention from the grand paradigms of Marx and Weber to focus more on the dimensions of political contention itself. His life's work in the study of political protest is devoted to a proper conceptualization and empirical study of these dimensions. He introduces what he calls the "mobilization" model of collective action. There are several key elements to the model: *interests*; *organization*; *mobilization*; and *opportunity*. To understand how collective action, ranging from riots to revolutions, arise, it is necessary to understand how each of these elements operates.

Interests refers to the advantages or disadvantages a particular population is likely to have relative to other groups in the population. *Organization* refers to the common identity, and the social structure promoting such an identity. *Mobilization* refers to the resources that can be controlled by a group seeking new political advantages. And *opportunity* refers to the chances that a particular group has in mobilizing its resources and acting as a contender in the battle with the established political forces in a society.

Tilly notes a number of specific empirical features of each of these elements. For example, he notes that a population group's basic social structure can influence its ability to mobilize to challenge the authorities in a society. Thus, drawing on the pioneering work of sociologist Anthony Oberschall (1973), he notes that strong social links and connections among a group can facilitate the mobilization of that group for collective action. Opportunity is also a key factor in the ability of a group to mobilize effectively and counter established forces. If the authorities are successful in their efforts to repress challengers, then there are limited opportunities to mobilize. But if the current regime is undergoing powerful threats, or if general social conditions help to loosen the otherwise repressive forces of a regime, then the opportunity to mobilize increases significantly.

Much of Tilly's effort to think of collective action is an effort to draw up a different set of concepts and schemes from those earlier employed by the great social theorists like Weber. Moreover, what he attempts to do is to show how radical collective action is a process that occurs in a sequence of steps. In this respect, he adds considerably to the visions created both by Marx and Weber, showing in greater historical detail what specific events must take place for radical mobilization to occur. Along the way he helps to invent entirely new and important concepts.

Perhaps his most important concept—and one to which he often draws attention—is the concept of a *repertoire of collective action*. The notion of *repertoire* refers to the specific kinds of protest and discontent that emerge among common people in an historical epoch. Thus, in some periods, street demonstrations represent the mode of collective action, whereas in others, especially in the United States during the mid-twentieth century, the repertoire has included such things as sit-ins and wade-ins. In his important analysis on discontent and protest in France, for instance, he notes that the change in repertoires was a critical one. Between 1650 and 1850, collective action tended to be *parochial* and *patronized*, taking the form of local actions, such as the seizure of grains, against local, or village, authorities. Between

1850 and 1980, however, the repertoire became *national* and *autonomous*, involving strikes and demonstrations that often were nationwide and directed against the whole panoply of French political authority.[37] Collective action, in other words, can exhibit alternative forms depending on the period in which it arises.

Perhaps most of all, Tilly takes the notion of revolution and protest out of the grand mists of great history, as concocted by Marx and Weber, and makes it more amenable and accessible to the contemporary period. Collective action for him is no longer the major revolutionary events of great social classes, as in Marx, nor the charismatically or ideologically inspired movements, as he understands Weber. However, it can involve a host of different populations each engaged in different kinds of struggles. In this respect the Tillyian vision is very much in keeping both with Marx and with Weber. Grievances, he has written, exist at all times; the key is to understand how in a continuing situation in which challengers and authorities are always at odds, the challengers manage to create a situation in which their challenge can be effective. Such success depends on large causes, like opportunities provided by social openings, as well as on the strategic aims of actors that seek to mobilize for revolution. It is a canvas created both out of structural causes and out of specific strategies chosen by potential revolutionaries.

The greatest legacy of Tilly's work on collective action is his invention of certain key concepts that enable one to investigate collective action in a variety of different historical situations. Though his own main concern is with the classic issues of Marx and Weber—agrarian protests, the conflicts between peasants and nobles—the concepts he develops lend themselves to a variety of different possibilities and historical situations. This has permitted them to be used by a great many contemporary researchers. And he has directly influenced a number of the more prominent younger scholars in the study of collective action today, including Doug McAdam and Aldon Morris.

Theda Skocpol

Like Charles Tilly, Theda Skocpol is a student of Barrington Moore, Jr., a famous sociologist-historian who taught at Harvard. Moore's writings, particularly his work on dictatorships and democracies, provided a sociology that was strongly rooted in historical and comparative analyses (see Chapter 10). Skocpol has carried that emphasis forward in a number of significant writings over the past two decades.

The chief aim of Skocpol's work has been to revive the concept of the *state*, as construed by Weber and the historian, Otto Hintze, and to show how it could prove useful to understanding different historical issues.[38] The modern concepts of the state and social classes originated in the writings of the

German philosopher, Georg Hegel. It was Hegel who wrote of the nature of civil society and social classes, on the one hand, and the state, on the other.[39] Hegel's view of the world, one that later deeply influenced Marx, was that history was moving toward the emancipation of humankind, and that the highest achievements of the modern world were to be the product of the thinking of the great philosophers—like himself—and the institution of the state. Marx picked up on these same themes, but, as has often been noted, turned them upside down. Philosophy was a sham, or false consciousness, to Marx; material forces were the driving motor of history not ideas; and social classes and class emancipation lay at the end of history, not the achievements of the state.

Skocpol has drawn much from Weber and Hintze as well as from Marx. From Weber, she has taken the view that the modern state is more than simply a reflection of the dominant class. The modern state, she believes, represents an autonomous institution, one that possesses a force and energy all its own. It consists of a variety of specific organizations and actors, including the legislature and legislators, the administrative bodies of government, and, in certain historical circumstances, royal authority. Adopting one of Weber's most crucial insights, she has come to believe that the state, like other institutions, can take on a life all its own and actually direct the energies and decisions of society. Indeed, the question about which much of her work centers is the extent and circumstances under which the state furnishes the powerful directions for society itself.

There are several ways in which she has explored these themes, including her works on the origins and development of the New Deal Administration of Franklin Delano Roosevelt. Unlike some theorists, who imputed the origins of this administration to the catastrophic collapse of the American economy, she argues that many policies preceded the origins of the New Deal Administration, and that state actors and institutions were sufficiently autonomous to develop actions that were the cause of the economic resurgence. In the discussion that follows, I shall point to two major instances in which Skocpol's treatments have expanded our understanding not only of the state but of two broader questions: the nature of social revolutions and the origins of welfare policy in America.

States and Social Revolutions. Skocpol's most famous and to date most influential work deals with the role that the state and other political forces played in the major revolutions of the past two centuries—the French, Russian, and Chinese revolutions.[40] Here she takes on the themes of her mentor, Barrington Moore, Jr., who himself sought to explain why the social and political history of some countries, like Japan, produced dictatorships, while others, like England, produced democratic regimes.[41] She argues that Moore, among other things, left major factors out of consideration, the chief one being the role that the state, or protostate, forces played in the development of each of these countries.

Skocpol asserts that there are three essential points to take into account in explaining the origins of these revolutions: (1) Causes of revolutions are to be found in the structural, or objective, conditions of a society, not in the expressed intentions or wishes of revolutionaries; (2) international conditions and circumstances play a major role in promoting revolutions, prominently influencing the capacity of the reigning authorities to direct and control a particular society; and (3) the state, through its agents and institutions, is a crucial factor in the success of a revolution and, contrary to Marxist interpretations, may act in ways autonomous of social classes, or other economic forces, to impede or to promote the success of a social revolution.[42] These several claims thus set her thesis apart from many other theses about the origins of reform or revolutionary movements, and they also establish her work as unique and novel today.

Skocpol draws a careful and important distinction between the conditions that promote the vulnerability of a society, and state, to revolution, and those that, in fact, transform the existing institutions. As to the facilitating circumstances themselves, she closely examines the set of conditions in France, China, and Russia prior to the revolutionary times and finds in all instances roughly similar circumstances. The state bureaucracies all had been relatively strong; control over the peasants and other groups had been effective; and wars and other external pressures eventually made the bureaucracies vulnerable to attack. In each of these instances, wars had been long and had taxed the capacities of state rulers to govern at all. Moreover, Skocpol goes on to show, in other countries where revolutions might have taken place because of some roughly similar conditions—Prussia, for example—the international environments were very different, and the external pressures on the governments' ability to govern were not nearly so strong.[43] Likewise, she goes on to show how the economic and social conditions in each society were sufficiently encouraging to promote the organization and development of the peasantry into an effective revolutionary force. Again, in those countries that escaped revolution, such as Japan or Prussia, the peasants were unsuccessful at developing and sustaining solidarity, sometimes, as in Prussia, because the landed nobility held such a strong hand of control over the lands.[44] Ultimately, she argues, it is the peculiar historical conjunction of weakened and eviscerated state regimes coupled with the creation of strong and successful peasant organizations that promotes the imminent likelihood of revolutions.

And yet, Skocpol rightly points out, it is only the possibility of revolution that originates from such conditions. Whether the fundamental transformations so essential to creating a revolution happen depends on the capacity of the insurgent forces to engage in successful social and political changes of a country. Here, again, Skocpol wishes to direct attention not to some vague and amorphous changes, but rather to the manner in which state-building occurs. Indeed, among the very different circumstances that ensued on the heels of the revolutionary outbreaks, it was the common fact of the creation of far more powerful and successful state bureaucracies and administrations that, according to Skocpol, permit one to label the changes in China, France, and Russia as revolutionary.[45] In France, Napoleon introduced a whole range of new measures, including legal codes, more complex administrative forces, a deeper and more disciplined army, in brief, a greater centralization of political authority, that qualified as revolutionary state-building. In Russia, roughly the same thing happened, but in a more systematic and powerful fashion, aided principally through the activities and development of the Communist Party. Tougher bureaucracies, greater central authority, and more uniform codes and activities throughout the country also were the result of the victory of the Communist Party in China, Skocpol shows. Finally, in a touch of irony, she claims, in all three regimes the losers, in some sense, were the very forces that helped to topple the old regime, the peasantry.

Skocpol's analysis proves to be a very compelling, indeed brilliant, one. Nevertheless, her admirers, while legion, are not universal. Her argument can be criticized on several grounds, including the fact that she leaves little room in her perspective for the importance of ideological factors, or beliefs, and even less for the activities of human agents. Indeed, one might ask of her: How is it at all possible to have revolutionary movements, much less actual social transformations, if there are no human agents to perform the activities?

The Origins of the American Welfare State. Skocpol's other major contribution to studies of the modern state and its impact on society is her revisionist interpretation of the origins and development of welfare state policies in America. Unlike other Western industrial democracies, such as those of Germany, Scandanavia, or even Great Britain, the welfare state, with its variety of associated benefits for healthcare, pensions, and unemployment, developed much differently and somewhat later in the United States. It was not until the 1930s, in the midst of the Great Depression, that substantial aid was provided by the government to the needy. It took the form of the provision of the Social Security Act of 1935 that furnished each American with a guaranteed pension on retirement. The difference in the development of the welfare state in America and in other Western countries has led scholars to a set of explanations for the origins of the difference. Some, beginning with Werner Sombart, trace the absence of a strong welfare state in America to the absence of socialism here.[46] Others trace the absence of a welfare state to a peculiar set of American values, with their emphasis on individualism as opposed to collectivism, for example, an emphasis, scholars argue, that merely led to a different historical trajectory in America.[47]

Skocpol, in her usual fashion, takes on these previous arguments in her work *Protecting Soldiers and Mothers,* offering new evidence on welfare measures in America as well as a different interpretation of the development of the welfare state here.[48] She agrees with other scholars that the welfare state in America simply never became nearly as strong as in Western European democracies. But her interpretation for the differences takes a new tack.

Her argument is rather complicated, but, as in all her work, it is rooted in an understanding of the historical and institutional context of America. It begins with her discovery that, in fact, the United States government at the end of the nineteenth century possessed an important building block for a strong welfare state in the form of pensions and benefits provided for Civil War veterans. Here was a case in which the federal government provided aid to a needy group well before the invention of the welfare policies of the 1930s by the New Deal. Skocpol poses the question: If such a policy was in effect at the end of the nineteenth century, why did it not provide a "wedge" for the development of a full-fledged welfare state, composed of the kind of benefits and aids provided by governments like those of Sweden and Denmark?

Skocpol argues that the failure of the Civil War pensions to become the carrier for a larger social program for the needy and poor depended on several specific historical factors. One, the United States lacked a centralized and autonomous state apparatus that could become the vehicle for developing such a program. Rather, over the course of the nineteenth century the state in America consisted of a system in which the courts and political parties exercised the greatest power, not the officials of the federal and state governments. Decisions, therefore, came from the bottom up rather than the top down, as in Europe. Political parties were important not as unifying national forces but for the programs they provided in local circumstances, in cities and states to the poor. In addition, the elites and middle-classes in America failed to provide the support necessary for social programs, instead turning their wrath and anger on immigrants and the poor during the late nineteenth and early twentieth centuries. Businessmen, rather than providing support for a broad social welfare program that could be organized and implemented by the government, provided their own piecemeal efforts, thus robbing the state of an opportunity to build on the Civil War pensions. In other words, there were specific factors that discouraged welfare polices from above as happened in European states.

The other key part to Skocpol's argument is that the unique historical and institutional context in America which impeded such development was a strong *paternalist* state, one that was run by men and that benefited the male worker as the breadwinner of his family, that actually facilitated the development of a strong *maternalist* state. Whereas white men were granted suffrage in nineteenth-century America, women were not. This helped to encourage a kind of extrapolitical activity on the part of women, forcing them to undertake extramural efforts on issues they deemed important. Here Skocpol also uncovers a new set of evidence. It shows a broad and active array of voluntary associations and groups in American society among women, groups that would become vital to the success of their effort not only to gain suffrage in 1919 but to secure the passage of welfare policies that would benefit them, as mothers. and their children.

The state, in this rendering, is what Skocpol considers a "federated polity" of organizations and associations, groups consisting of women that were able to mobilize on behalf of benefits for mothers and other kinds of women's aid. In effect, American politics, by Skocpol's accounting, was organized less on the basis of classes and labor unions, as in Europe, and more on the basis of gender. And because it was so organized, and because women proved so forceful, measures here that would have benefited workers and labor failed, whereas those that benefited housewives and mothers succeeded. They succeeded, in part, because male legislators proved more sympathetic to them than they did to class-based measures that would have benefited male workers and their families. Accordingly, what would unfold in America, at least up until the 1930s, was a maternalist rather than a paternalist set of welfare policies.

Skocpol's view of the failure of a full-fledged welfare state in America to grow out of the Civil War pensions, is novel, while her argument about the development of a maternalist state draws upon recent work among American historians. It is a novel melding and merging of different bodies of evidence and insight, though in the end it makes the state appear as far less autonomous and active than in her earlier work on social revolutions. She notes, early on in this work, that the state is "any set of relatively differentiated organizations that claims sovereignty and coercive control over a territory and its population, defending and perhaps extending that claim in competition with other states," and therefore that the United States "has always had one."[49] But clearly the way the state unfolds in her story of welfare state policies in America is much different than the centralized and powerful state in so many European regimes. In fact, in her emphasis on voluntary associations and gender, she really mixes the state and civil society and invokes a kind of state that is only a short distance from the kind invoked in the writings of Alexis de Tocqueville (see Chapter 4).

Regardless, Theda Skocpol has invigorated the study of the state and political institutions both among sociologists and political scientists, drawing on a tradition of scholarship first begun in the nineteenth century by Max Weber.

SUMMARY

Max Weber started sociologists on the path to understanding the nature and complexity of modern states, and the writings of several contemporary scholars have helped us better to understand the workings of these institutions.

States are very vital to the modern world. Among other things, they remain powerful forces, and they exercise the legitimate control over the weapons of violence. Moreover, it is through states that the people have an opportunity to voice their opinions about the direction they wish societies to move, and how, among other things, the body of citizens as a whole will meet the needs of the poor and the indigent. A great issue now looms ahead of us: How much authority can states continue to exercise, and how can they regulate the power of corporations and capital? There are those who argue that the forces of globalization are such that states may ultimately become something like bit players in the arena of money and politics. But if that is so, they would have to do so with the consent of those whom they serve—the citizens.

I can think of no questions nor issues quite so significant for contemporary political sociology as those that concern the relative strength of states and of modern capitalism. Unlike Marx's early and rather crude image, states are not merely the handmaidens of great corporations. They often take actions that run counter to the interests of capitalists and the business class, especially when they engage in actions against many of their own citizens, as in the recent examples of Rwanda and Kosovo. Modern states also have provided, over the course of the past fifty years or so, important forms of welfare and other benefits to the most needy of citizens. As global capitalism increases, as more public enterprises are turned over to private sources, who will take care of the needy? Or the poor? Or the elderly?

NOTES

1. Max Weber, *The Protestant Ethic and the Spirit of Capitalism*, translated by Talcott Parsons (New York: Charles Scribner's Sons, 1958), 183.
2. Max Weber, "Politics as a Vocation," in Hans H. Gerth and C. Wright Mills, eds., *From Max Weber: Essays in Sociology* (New York: Oxford University Press), 77.
3. Wolfgang J. Mommsen, *The Political and Social Theory of Max Weber: Collected Essays* (Chicago: University of Chicago Press, 1989), 26.
4. Max Weber, *The Methodology of the Social Sciences*. Translated and edited by Edward A. Shils and Henry A. Finch. With a Foreword by Edward A. Shils. (New York: The Free Press, 1949), 80.

5. Max Weber, "Science as a Vocation," in Gerth and Mills, *From Max Weber*, 146.
6. See, for example, the section on religion in Gerth and Mills, *From Max Weber*.
7. Weber, *The Protestant Ethic and the Spirit of Capitalism*, 183.
8. Weber, "Politics as a Vocation," in Gerth and Mills, *From Max Weber*, 78.
9. Max Weber, *Economy and Society: An Outline of Interpretive Sociology*, translated by Guenther Roth and Claus Wittich (New York: Bedminster Press, 1968), Volume III, 1393 ff.
10. Weber, "Politics as a Vocation," in Gerth and Mills, *From Max Weber*, 94–5.
11. Weber, ibid., 113.
12. Arthur Mitzman, *The Iron Cage: An Historical Interpretation of Max Weber* (New York: Alfred A. Knopf, 1970).
13. Chapter 9, "The Sociology of Charismatic Authority," in Gerth and Mills, *From Max Weber*.
14. Mommsen, *The Political and Social Theory of Max Weber*, 32.
15. Weber, *Economy and Society*, III, 1414.
16. See, for example, Reinhard Bendix, *Max Weber: An Intellectual Portrait* (Garden City, New York: Doubleday & Co., 1962), Chapter 9.
17. Weber, *Economy and Society*, I, 264.
18. Weber, "Politics as a Vocation," in Gerth and Mills, *From Max Weber*, 80.
19. Weber, "Class, Status and Party," in Gerth and Mills, *From Max Weber*, 194.
20. Bendix, *Max Weber: An Intellectual Portrait*.
21. Reinhard Bendix, *Nation-Building and Citizenship: Studies of Our Changing Social Order* (Berkeley: University of California Press, 1964).
22. Bendix, *MaxWeber: An Intellectual Portrait*, 292.
23. *State and Society: A Reader in Comparative Political Sociology*, Reinhard Bendix, ed. (Boston: Little Brown, 1968).
24. Reinhard Bendix, "The Extension of Citizenship to the Lower Classes," in Bendix, ibid., 233–56.
25. Reinhard Bendix, *Work and Authority in Industry* (Berkeley: University of California Press, 1956).
26. Reinhard Bendix, *Kings or People: Power and the Mandate to Rule* (Berkeley: University of California Press, 1978).
27. Bendix, ibid., 266.
28. See, for example, Charles Tilly, *From Mobilization to Revolution* (Reading, Massachusetts: Addison-Wesley Publishing Company, 1978), Chapter 2.
29. Charles Tilly, *The Contentious French* (Cambridge, Massachusetts: The Belknap Press of Harvard University Press, 1986), and *Popular Contention in Great Britain, 1758-1834* (Cambridge, Massachusetts: Harvard University Press, 1995).
30. Charles Tilly, ed., *The Formation of National States in Western Europe* (Princeton: Princeton University Press, 1975).
31. Ibid., 6.
32. Ibid., 27.

33. Also see Charles Tilly, *Big Structures, Large Processes, Huge Comparisons* (New York: Russell Sage Foundation, 1984), Chapter 2 especially.
34. Charles Tilly, *Coercion, Capital, and European States, AD 990-1990* (Cambridge, Massachusetts: Basil Blackwell, 1990).
35. Ibid., 70.
36. *From Mobilization to Revolution.*
37. *The Contentious French*, 392–3.
38. See Otto Hintze, "The State in Historical Perspective," in Reinhard Bendix, ed., *State and Society*, pp.154–69.
39. *Hegel's Philosophy of Right*, translated by T.M. Knox (New York: Oxford University Press, 1942); also see the excellent commentary by Charles Taylor in his *Hegel* (Cambridge, Massachusetts: Cambridge University Press, 1975), Chapter XVI.
40. Theda Skocpol, *States and Social Revolutions: A Comparative Analysis of France, Russia and China* (Cambridge, Massachusetts: Cambridge University Press, 1979).
41. Barrington Moore, Jr., *Social Origins of Dictatorship and Democracy: Lord and Peasant in the Making of the Modern World* (Boston: Beacon Press, 1966).
42. Skocpol, *States and Social Revolutions*, 14–33.
43. Ibid., 104–12; 155–57.
44. Ibid., 140–47.
45. Ibid., Chapters 5–7.
46. Werner Sombart, *Why Is There No Socialism in the United States?* (White Plains, New York: International Arts and Sciences Press, 1976).
47. Louis Hartz, *The Liberal Tradition in America: An Interpretation of American Political Thought Since the Revolution* (New York: Harcourt Brace Jovanovich, Inc., 1955).
48. Theda Skocpol, *Protecting Soldiers and Mothers: The Political Origins of Social Policy in the United States* (Cambridge, Massachusetts: The Belknap Press of Harvard University Press, 1992).
49. Ibid., 43.

Chapter 4

On Civil Society and Politics

Emile Durkheim and Alexis de Tocqueville

> The system of signs I use to express my thought, the system of currency I employ to pay my debts, the instruments of credit I utilize in my commercial relations, the practices followed in my profession . . . function independently of my own use of them. . . . Here, then, is a category of facts with very distinctive characteristics: (they) consist of ways of acting, thinking, and feeling, external to the individual and endowed with a power of coercion, by reason of which they control him. . . . They constitute . . . a new variety of phenomena; and it is to them exclusively that the term 'social' ought to be applied.[1]
>
> Emile Durkheim, *The Rules of the Sociological Method*

Since the late 1950s, one of the major distinctions that writers about sociology make is that between the "conflict" and "consensus" schools of sociology.[2] Though the distinction really is one of emphasis, it helps to highlight the crucial differences among our leading theorists of society and politics. The conflict school is said to date from the writings of Karl Marx and Max Weber. It puts its emphasis on the divisions and battles in the nature of societies. The basic conception of history is as one of continuous conflict until, of course, as in the case of Marx, the working class achieves its great and lasting revolution.

The consensus school pictures the world very differently. Instead of an underlying division in the nature of societies, it presumes an underlying set of agreements, or beliefs. Permanence and stability are achieved through the daily workings of social institutions, most often through the educational institutions, the family, and religion. When politics is invoked, it is not a politics of division and exploitation, but a politics that creates and recreates the important institutions of society, through its recollection of key dates, events, and symbols. Paradoxically politics—which in everyday life we think of as a battleground pitting groups against one another—is seen by the consensual theorists as an arena of fundamental harmony and manufactured unity, not underlying division and tension.

Two nineteenth-century French writers furnish us with the sociological basis for this consensus picture of societies and politics. One, Emile Durkheim, is usually classified along with Marx and Weber as the greatest sociological theorists ever—certainly prior to the twentieth century. Durkheim's principal concern throughout his career and writing is a concern with the nature of social solidarity and how it comes about in societies. The other scholar is Alexis de Tocqueville, a great political and intellectual figure of nineteenth-century France. Tocqueville's greatest contribution to political discourse was *Democracy in America*, which, most critics agree, stands out as the most penetrating analysis ever of American politics.

In this chapter I will take up the important ideas of both scholars, using them as the basis for that picture of society and politics that begins with a set of social underpinnings and understandings, a deep and layered social infrastructure to the world. To use the terminology once again of Georg Hegel (and many other social theorists, including Jean Jacques Rousseau), Durkheim and Tocqueville emphasized *civil society* in the construction of politics, whereas Marx emphasized the economy, and Weber the state.[3] This emphasis on civil society, though in decline among sociologists from the late 1960s through the early 1990s, has lately been in ascendance, the result of powerful and fruitful research by, among others, the sociologists Robert Bellah and James Coleman and the political scientist Robert Putnam.

EMILE DURKHEIM ON CIVIL SOCIETY AND POLITICS

The Essential Durkheim

Emile Durkheim was born in 1858 in the Alsace-Lorraine region of France, an area that came under dispute during the course of World War I. He was the model of an educator. Punctual to his classes, elegant in his deliveries, committed to reforming the French educational system, he saw himself not as a revolutionary nor even as a political figure, but as someone who would transform society through the strength of his teachings and the discoveries of his research. He stood directly in the line of French scholars, dating from the writings of Jean Jacques Rousseau, whose concern was with the nature of the "general will," or that set of understandings that bound civilized human beings to one another. If there is a common thread to the life's work of Durkheim it is the effort to use scientific methods to uncover the nature of this general will and how it came to make itself felt in the thinking and beliefs of humankind.

Durkheim thought of himself as both a scientist, of the social order, and as an educator. As a scientist, he took up the call of his French intellectual predecessor, Auguste Comte. Comte had insisted on the existence of a science of society, a science of social facts that had the same permanence and force in the world as biological or physical facts. Sociology was the name of such a science, according to Comte. Durkheim became the figure in France to implement the agenda and vocation Auguste Comte had begun. Sociology, he wrote, is the study of social facts, those "collective and shared ways of thinking, feeling and acting" in the world that exist beyond both the psychology of the individual and the biological principles of humans as a species.[4] Social facts have a force and power over human beings as much as psychological or biological facts do, he insisted. They are equally external to human beings, and they influence human behavior and thinking in the same manner as psychological states or biological conditions do.

Much of Durkheim's written work over the course of his life was to provide the intellectual underpinnings for the significance of this approach. In one of his earliest writings, *Suicide*, he took great pains to show that suicide was not due to biological causes.[5] Nor was it simply a psychological fact: He demonstrated that different societies varied in the rates of their suicide across time and in different regions. In his last and greatest work, he took on, among others, the great German philosopher Immanuel Kant. Kant had insisted, in effect, that the nature of the physical universe, in terms of its causes and processes, was a product of "humankind's imagination and intelligence," shifting the emphasis in philosophy from the nature of the external world to the nature of the human being, or the subject.[6] Durkheim argued against Kant, insisting that the source of ideas about the physical universe, such as force, and about the social order, such as *mana*, was due to the very power that society held over the thinking of human beings. It was society, in general, and social institutions, in particular, that created the intelligence of human beings and that gave birth to their picture of the universe and the moral order.[7]

Unlike Marx, who believed that the ongoing order of capitalism was inherently pernicious and, therefore, had to be eliminated, Durkheim insisted that the disorder he confronted, in France in particular, was brought about by the attenuation of the moral order of society. If one could to determine both the causes and the nature of this attenuation of the moral order, one would need not to overthrow the ongoing institutions but rather amend or improve them. At the conclusion to his famous work, *The Division of Labor in Society,* he writes that profound "changes have been produced in the structure of our societies . . . (and because) certain of our duties are no longer founded on the reality of things, a breakdown has resulted. . . . (Therefore) our first duty is to make a moral code for ourselves."[8] This meant, to Durkheim, that great research effort had to be expended on discovering the fundamental character of the moral order, how it became diminished, and the directions in which society was likely to move. Durkheim's understanding of chaos and conflict was fundamentally at odds with Marx and with Weber. Whereas Marx understood the conflicts by workers in the nineteenth century to be a product of the evil exploitation by capitalists, Durkheim understood it to be a product of the failure of principle institutions of society to properly inculcuate the norms and values of society. To Durkheim, social institutions needed a kind of moral rejeuvenation; to Marx they needed to be completely levelled and entirely rebuilt from the ground up.

Durkheim thus focused his energies on discovering the nature of that moral order, particularly in France. It was, he believed, certain fundamental norms and values that held people together in society. Social change, or *modernization* as we now would term it, had eaten away at the norms that people held in common, creating a greater fragmentation among groups and, at the same time, in Anthony Giddens' apt term, a greater *individuation*—of individual differences—among human beings. Once those norms and values were discovered, and seen as the rules whereby the moral order must and should operate, then Durkheim turned his attention to how to secure reform through the educational institutions. He argued, in *Moral Education*, that the school was central to the reform of society, and that it must engage in a deliberate and careful instruction of the nature of the moral order.[9] It was less important for schools simply to teach "reading, writing and arithmetic," and much more important for them to teach the basic rules and discipline required of citizens of society. The *volonte generale* dissected by Rousseau became the "collective conscience" of society that Durkheim sought to recover and restore through educational institutions.

Society

Just as the central focus for Marx and his work is the nature of social class and class conflict, the central focus for Durkheim's writings is the nature of society. Society is the object that the science of sociology treats and seeks to understand. As it unfolded in his writings, society came to consist of several different key elements, though the overriding feature of society was its wholeness and integrity—its solidarity—as opposed to the underlying divisions and conflicts that beset the images both of Marx and Weber. Societies consist of several main features: norms and laws; institutions; symbols and rituals; and the division of labor. Each of these elements Durkheim treats at length in his several writings.

Social Norms and Laws. The basic elements of societies are their social norms and laws. Such elements act as the rules that guide the behavior and thinking of the members of societies. They are the basic social facts to which Durkheim addressed much of his attention. For any society to work properly the norms and laws must carefully govern the behavior of society's members. In smaller, more primitive societies, there are fewer such norms and laws, and they are meted out with a force that compels all to obey them on pain of death. In larger societies, such laws become more fragmented, and their hold over all the members of society also becomes more tenuous.

Moreover, the nature of punishment or sanctions differ between the two forms of society. In smaller, primitive societies the laws seek retribution on behalf of the entire society, whereas in larger, more complex societies the laws seek to compensate the individual party. The more limited punishments of laws in more modern societies correspond with the increasing complexity and differences of such societies, and the increasing "individualism" that also occurs. The differences are evident between penal law, on the one hand, and civil and corporate law, on the other. Penal law, characteristic of smaller, more inclusive societies, exacts harsh punishments from the offender, whereas civil law simply seeks restitution on behalf of the victim, restoring things, as Durkheim puts it, "to their original state."[10]

Institutions. Education, religion, and the economy represent the main institutions of societies in Durkheim's view—the first two his principal and enduring concerns. Institutions provide the guiding norms and laws for a society, and they differ by virtue of the different tasks, or functions, that they provide. Education is central because it furnishes the earliest basis for the instruction of children in the ways and norms of a particular society. If societies fail, in the sense that there are high rates of deviance, such as crimes, that failure in part can be traced to the failure of educational institutions. Teaching must be firm and strict in such institutions, and it must cover the basic norms of the particular society.[11]

Religious institutions are equally central to Durkheim's view of the social world. Religion, in his view, seems to furnish the basic glue and integrity to the nature of a particular social order—whether it be a particular nation-state, as in France, or a more general form, as in the case of the modern or primitive social orders. Religious institutions provide the core laws, or values, for a society. Durkheim introduces certain important distinctions to help clarify the nature of religion and its centrality to a society. The most critical and famous is that between the *sacred* and the *profane*.[12] The sacred refers to that special, or holy, quality that particular objects or practices hold, and which are so identified by religious institutions. They include special holidays, but also special figures and material objects, such as the cross for Christians or the shank of lamb for Jews on Passover. The profane stands entirely apart from the sacred: It deals with everyday mundane activities and practices, such as the manner in which work is done.

In his last great work, *The Elementary Forms of the Religious Life,* Durkheim traced the centrality and importance of religion as an institution, but also as the kind of core institution for societies.[13] Religion provides the core values for any given society, and thus furnishes the elements that can hold a society together. Not only does Durkheim seek a sociological answer to questions raised by Immanuel Kant in his analysis, but he provides his view of the underlying critical institution in understanding how any society, or nation, works. In this respect, his emphasis on religion stands in considerable contrast to that of Marx on the economy.

Culture, Symbols, and Rituals. Norms and laws are critical to the working of societies. Sometimes they can be taught explicitly, as in the case of education and schools. But often they are taught in more subtle ways.

Durkheim insists that there are common symbols around which the members of societies unite, and which are important to sustaining societies over long periods of time. Such symbols might include the more trivial, as in the case of flags or national songs, as well as the more central, such the admiration and respect given to special figures, such as the founding figures of societies. In the case of a particular regime or nation, the symbols might be a flag or some special personage, like Washington in the United States. They invoke images, which, due to the constant repetition of lessons about them, serve to remind members that they all belong to the same nation.

Ritual is vital in invoking and reminding people of these symbols. "(R)ites," Durkheim observes, "are means by which the social group reaffirms itself periodically."[14] In effect, rituals are the regular and periodic occasions in which the people gather together to celebrate themselves, as a nation or society. Voting can be considered such a ritual, in the sense that it reminds people of the freedoms they enjoy under democracy. Durkheim's most penetrating example concerns the case of rituals observed in more primitive groups, such as those that celebrate the origins and life of their gods:

> men would be unable to live without gods, but, on the other hand, the gods would die if their cult were not rendered. . . . The real reason for the existence of the cults, even of those which are the most materialistic in appearance, is not be sought in the acts which they prescribe, but in the internal and moral regeneration which these acts aid in bringing about. The things which the worshipper really gives his gods are not the foods he places upon the altars, nor the blood which he lets flow from his veins: it is his thought.[15]

By gathering periodically and regularly to celebrate harvests, or the birth of particular animals, such groups not only celebrate the obvious facts, but they also engage in a rebirth of themselves.

These wonderful insights have had profound influence among social anthropologists as well as sociologists. They are employed, for example, by the sociologist of religion Robert Bellah to speak about the "civil religion" of the United States, as we shall shortly learn.

The Division of Labor. The last critical element to Durkheim's view of the nature of societies lay in his conception of the division of labor. Whereas Marx and Weber had spoken of social classes, roughly the common position of people with regard to their work or place in the economy, Durkheim wrote of this thing he called the division of labor. He picked up this theme, in part, from Herbert Spencer, who had developed a thesis about the increasing complexity and differentiation as societies evolved over time.

The division of labor consists essentially of the different tasks and functions done in a society to maintain the material survival of its members. Among primitive tribes, they consist of the process of hunting and gathering by tribal members, whereas in more modern societies they consist of a variety of different ways—of what we would call specific jobs and occupations today. The division of labor, rather than setting people apart as in the case of Marx, actually serves the same integrative function for Durkheim as norms and laws: It furnishes the basis for cementing and solidifying the character of society. If each person has a particular position in the working of the social order, and all major tasks are fulfilled to keep the society an ongoing enterprise, then it can survive. Thus, by a kind of similar process as the "invisible hand," societies manage to sort and shuffle people into particular jobs and tasks that must be performed if they are to persist as societies. Moreover, as societies grow, by number and in complexity, there is also a growing division of labor. One of Durkheim's more profound, but also controversial, suggestions is that as the population density of a society, or group, increases, there will be an inevitable pressure for the division of labor to become more complex, thus sorting people into new and different positions. "(A)ll condensation of the social mass, especially if it is accompanied by an increase in population," he writes, "necessarily determines advances in the division of labor."[16]

States, Politics, and Societies

Durkheim's view of states and politics emerges completely from his view of societies. States, or governments, are simply another kind of social institution. Rather than ruling on behalf of some illegimate, or temporary, dominating class or group, states represent the whole of society, seeking to engender overall agreement and consensus. They embody, in a sense, the *volonte generale* of Rousseau. They represent the articulate norms and laws of the underlying social order, and thus to oppose them is to oppose the social order, or society itself. In this reckoning, power and authority are not exercised illegitimately nor on behalf of any class or other grouping; society is *the basis of authority*, and the state must come to represent its basic workings and operations.

Opposition, in Durkheim's view, is not the opposition of a group that represents the future of society, or some overall or higher good. Opposition is "deviance" from the general norms of society.[17] States thus are compelled to act with force to impose their will. To Durkheim, the state is essentially a police force, responsible for ensuring that the norms and rules of society are, in fact, obeyed. Moreover, there was never any question of its illegitimacy or illegality—its authority is rooted in the very nature of the fact that it represented the political form of society itself.

Nevertheless, Durkheim fully recognized that as societies modernized, the hold of the state, like that of society, lessens over the lives of individuals. Deviance, in the form of suicides and of homicides, increases with modernization precisely because the common bonds that hold individuals to societies lessen in their strength and power. Thus, in modern societies integrity is based less on the general and total power of the social bonds, as of the states, and more on the manufacture of new bases for integrity and integration. States, like other social institutions, must seek guidance in the new social order.

Though Durkheim never fully explains or articulates this vision of the modern polity, he provides his clearest exposition of how it might work, in principle, toward the end of *Suicide*. Noting that the division of labor in modern societies had become more complex, he argues that the division of labor, one of the core elements of society, could furnish the basis for linking the state effectively to modern society and the lives of individuals:

> The only way to resolve [the antimony between excessive force and excessive neglect by the State] is to set up a cluster of collective forces outside the State, though subject to its action, whose regulative influence can be exerted with greater variety. . . . To [such corporations] . . . falls the duty of presiding over companies of insurance, benevolent aid and pensions, the need of which are felt by so many good minds but which we rightly hesitate to place in the hands of the State, already so powerful and awkward; theirs it should likewise be to preside over the disputes constantly arising between the branches of the same occupation, to fix conditions . . . with which contracts must agree in order to be valid, in the name of the common interest to prevent the strong from unduly exploiting the weak, etc.[18]

The new, modern society, in other words, is to be found in the proliferation of occupations among workers, and it is there that the lives of individuals will unfold. Social groups close to this experience, then, will be closest to the experience of individuals as social change happens and marks their lives. States will work best that best provide a means for organizations representing such occupations to voice the concerns of workers.

What is so remarkable about this passage from Durkheim is that it fits so neatly with a view that was propounded only decades earlier by his fellow Frenchman, Alexis de Tocqueville. The heart and soul of society should be the form and workings of the organizations around which the lives of individuals are fashioned, and such organizations must be connected integrally to the workings of the state, the highest level of authority in society. What Durkheim truly failed to appreciate—though he probably understood at some level—is that the state could come to have its own strong purposes, and that such purposes often ran deliberately counter to the needs and interests of the vast majority of citizens.

ALEXIS DE TOCQUEVILLE ON CIVIL SOCIETY AND POLITICS

The Essential Tocqueville

Alexis de Tocqueville, born into the French aristocracy, has become justly famous as the author of arguably the most penetrating analysis ever of American democracy. Born in 1805, he died in 1859. In the space of fifty-four years he created at least two memorable works of history and comparative analysis. Most of his life was spent doing the work of a politician and writer; his writings, on democracy and on the French Revolution, gained him both fame and wealth. Although he and Durkheim share much in common—in their emphasis on the civil basis of the political order and the underlying continuities of societies—they also differ markedly. Indeed, to many Tocqueville is the more compelling thinker for he managed to weave both an historical and a sociological imagination together at one and the same time. In the course of so doing, he also provided some of the earliest and still the very best of comparative historical and social analysis.

Tocqueville's major writings cast light on two important historical events. One concerns the French Revolution of 1789 and the collapse of the *ancien regime*.[19] Why, he wondered, did the ancien regime collapse? In raising this question, he anticipated the analyses of revolution and change among many of his successors. He argued, in essence, that the old regime had collapsed because of the failure of the nobility itself and because of the changes engendered in French society over the course of the eighteenth century. It was not the simple acts of 1789 and shortly thereafter that led to the revolutionary overthrow, but a set of sources that had earlier ripened and matured in French society. When the regime collapsed, it had basically exhausted its resources. Moreover, it failed in the middle of a general movement across the world for a greater social and political equality, a movement highlighted in the nineteenth century by the United States. The violence and terror of 1789 came about because citizens believed they needed to make a clean and abrupt break with their feudal and inegalitarian past: To do away with all remnants of the old society meant to do away completely and violently with that society.

The other and related question for Tocqueville was this: Why and how did American society develop in the manner it had? How was it able to create a novel set of social and political institutions that were keynoted by their emphasis on equality and democracy, when all older societies—which should have had some edge—were unable to do so? (In fact, rather than having an edge, the older societies, like France, bore an historical albatross.) This question, which later became the basis for many other important and original historical works, including that of Louis Hartz, Tocqueville set about to answer in an extended and detailed comparative analysis.[20] His methods would become as central and innovative as his actual analysis. He managed to show that a scholar could think of nations as whole entities, and therefore could compare nations in terms of both the differences in their outcomes and in the courses of such differences. And he did so with a subtlety and power that remains exemplary to this very day.

Equality in America

Democracy in America, Tocqueville was convinced, represented a very special and unique accomplishment. Looking around him at the world of the nineteenth century, he could find no other society that included the notable political institutions of America. The main feature of American democracy was its emphasis on the equality of its citizens. In his introduction to Volume 1 of *Democracy in America* he wrote that in his visit to America "nothing struck me more forcibly than the general equality of condition among the people . . . it gives a peculiar direction to public opinion and a peculiar tenor to the laws; it impacts new maxims to the governing authorities and peculiar habits to the governed."[21] All people, he observed, were held to be equal before the law and deserving of equal respect and treatment by the law. The very nature of American republican institutions furnished the basis for this equality.

General political institutions provided the framework for political equality in America. All people—but, of course, at the time it meant all white men—were to be granted suffrage and the equal capacity to influence the outcomes of the political process. Suffrage Tocqueville regarded as one of the central elements to democracy in America. The other was that of the abolition of the law of primogeniture, and the inheritance of wealth and privilege from one generation to another. Such a system, which characterized European countries, fundamentally undercut the ability of people to pursue their own wishes and desires on an equal footing. Other features of the court system and law also upheld the condition of equality, requiring that all people be treated with respect and dignity in the legal system. The federal system of government provided the framework for institutional equality, among the states and between men. The Constitution secured the basic principles, including the right of assembly, among others, permitting people to join with one another easily and to share their opinions in an equal and unfettered manner.

The Conditions (Causes) for Equality

The key analytical problem for Tocqueville was to discover the conditions that promoted such equality. Why, among all nations, should the United States have managed to create this special and virtually unique situation? What was it about the American people, and the country of America, that permitted equality to be achieved?

In a fundamental sense, the basic answer to this question is simple: In all other societies people suffered under oppression, from the nobles or the growing wealth of the manufacturing class, but in America, citizens in effect were born free. "The social conditions of the Americans is eminently democratic; this was its character at the foundation of the colonies, and it is still more strongly marked at the present day," he would write.[22] A relatively new and unburdened set of peoples, most of whom came to America as immigrants and to escape oppression in Europe, reached this continent and were free. As Louis Hartz pointed out, the critical notion of Rousseau—that men are born free and everywhere they are in chains—was simply not true, in Tocqueville's view, in America. In America, they were in effect born free since they had escaped the chains of their former existence abroad. Hereditary authority and the transmission of wealth and property did not operate in nineteenth-century America as they did in nineteenth-century Europe. Hence men were able to pursue wealth and material satisfaction, unburdened by the debts and chains of a feudal past.

Freedom, then, is the *sine qua non* of democratic equality in America. But, by itself it is insufficient to secure such equality. After all, men could be free—but free for what? To what ends? In America, in Tocqueville's eyes, men were not only free, but they engaged in actions to continually secure and parade their freedom to one another. There are two critical sources and elements to this activity on the part of Americans. The first, and to this day the most prominent, is the continuing activity of men to develop, support, and engage in voluntary associations. People voluntarily act with one another to secure their freedom: They engage in causes with one another in new organizations that pursue political ends; such organizations are critical, in fact, to the success of the American revolutionaries. "In their political associations the Americans, of all conditions, minds and ages, daily acquire a general taste for association and grow accustomed to the use of it," Tocqueville observed.[23]

There grew up in America a strong social infrastructure of voluntary associations of all stripes—political groups, social groups, cooking clubs, organizations among women to support the Revolutionary effort. This massive structure of organizations and associations, in Tocqueville's eyes, ensured that democracy would continue because all such organizations treated people in them as equals and all such organizations became the vehicle for expressing to the authorities their opinions and concerns. People cherished this freedom to act and to express their opinons almost in the same measure as they did in the energy with which they pursued wealth and material well-being. As Tocqueville would write in *Democracy in America:* "The most natural privilege of man, next to the right of acting for himself, is that of combining his exertions with those of his fellow creatures and of acting in common with them. The right of association therefore appears to me almost as inalienable in its nature as the right of personal liberty."[24]

An equally critical element to ensuring democratic equality in America is what Tocqueville called a free press and the freedom of speech. Freedom of speech is the first principle on which American government had been established and founded. And in reality Tocqueville found it displayed in the many and various activities undertaken by newspapers in America. Here, unlike Europe, one could read and see the free opinions of Americans expressed, opinions that were shared among themselves and that were also available to be read and understood by their rulers. To Tocqueville the sheer number and variety of different publications underscored the importance of the principle of free speech and a free press enshrined in the First Amendment to the Constitution of the United States.

In the absence both of voluntary associations, which Americans seemed to join in record numbers, and of a free press, freedom would have been an empty and vacuous notion. More important, it was the simultaneous absence of such associations and a free and vigorous press in Europe, along with the absence of a set of norms that affirmed equality, that convinced Tocqueville that such a strong social infrastructure was an absolute necessity for democracy to take root. "My aim has been to show," he writes, "by the example of America, that laws, and especially customs, may allow a democratic people to remain free."[25]

Threats to Democracy in America

Just as America seemed to show a path that other countries of the world might follow on the way to democracy, it also displayed the major threats that might occur to such equality. Three such threats seemed critical to Tocqueville.

The first of these was the element of race. Though he wrote of widespread equality, and the underpinnings of equality in American institutions, Tocqueville was not so naive to believe equality existed everywhere. It did not. In fact, he found three races among Americans revealing deep inequalities in social conditions. The races were the Indians, or native Americans;

black Americans; and white Americans. It was among blacks that he found the most potent threat to widespread equalities. He noted that blacks lived under conditions of slavery and in far worse circumstances than other Americans. The conditions of servitude might diminish, as in the North, but there still appeared to be deep and irreconcilable differences between blacks and whites in America. "Whoever has inhabited the United States must have perceived that in those parts of the Union in which Negroes are no longer slaves they have in no wise drawn nearer to the whites. On the contrary, the prejudice of race appears to be stronger in the states that have abolished slavery than in those where it still exists."[26] Such a powerful and prescient observer was Tocqueville that his observations on race sound as though they were written yesterday! One century later, Gunnar Myrdal and his colleagues would revisit Tocqueville's emphasis on equality in their masterpiece on race and inequality in mid-twentieth-century America.[27]

In addition, while America did not show the deep social and particularly economic inequalities of Europe, Tocqueville noted that if inequality ever did reach American shores, industry and manufacturing would be the culprits. Manufacturing, he argued, created divisions among people in terms of their wealth. And as businesses expanded and developed they could promote a new kind of inequality. "(T)he friends of democracy," he wrote, "should keep their eyes anxiously fixed in this direction; for if ever a permanent inequality of conditions and aristocracy again penetrates into the world, it may be predicted that this is the gate by which they will enter."[28]

But the most dangerous threat to equality in America, in Tocqueville's eyes, was the threat posed by the widespread equality itself:

> In my opinion, the main evil of the present democratic institutions of the United States does not arise, as is often asserted in Europe, from their weakness, but from their irresistible strength. I am not so much alarmed at the exceptional liberty which reigns in that country as at the inadequate securities which one finds there against tyranny.[29]

If all men were regarded as equal, then no man was more equal. This meant that everyone's opinion and idea would count the same. Under these conditions, the policies and principles of the people would be implemented through majority rule—on any key question, the majority would govern. But what was to become of the opinions and ideas of the minority, Tocqueville wondered. He went on to speculate that the great danger of equality in the governance of a society was that of *the tyranny of the majority*. Since all were equal, only the greatest number could gain advantage, unlike in European countries where advantage came to those with inherited privileges of wealth and property. It was such tyranny that Americans would have to guard against, both in the development of their political institutions, and in the general manner of their social ways of doing things among themselves.

Concluding Observations

In sum, Tocqueville provided both a vision and a map for the future of America. It rested upon the principles of equality and freedom, and was grounded in the general character of American society and culture. His was a vision not of a society divided by classes nor of one in which the state would dominate, views held respectively by Marx and Weber. Instead his was a view of a society grounded in a specific and unique culture, supported and maintained by an array of associations and organizations through which Americans gave voice and expression to their equality. It was, in other words, a civil society through and through—civil in its nature and civil in its relations among its citizens. Though it could come to harm, through the divisions between the races and the looming danger of excessive business, it was a portrait at the time unique, very different in its consequences and causes from that in European nations.

THE NEO-CONSENSUALISTS

Talcott Parsons

Talcott Parsons is one of the greatest social theorists of the twentieth century—and also one of the least well understood. Much of Parsons' problem arises from a writing style that is, at best, often impenetrable. The prolixity of his prose is due in part, however, to the complexity of the ideas he sought to convey. Here I shall briefly highlight only the most central of those ideas, ones that also bear upon matters of civil society.

Parsons attempted to meld the key concepts of Durkheim and Weber, seeing them—and not Karl Marx—as the true progenitors of modern-day sociology. From Weber he adopted the emphasis on the role of ideas and culture in the creation of societies, while from Durkheim he assimilated an emphasis on the integrity of societies and the factors that contribute to such integrity.[30] Societies, to Parsons, represent ongoing enterprises—or social systems—that are able to reproduce and recreate themselves from one generation of people to another.[31] How they do so, and other elements of their survival, are key questions he tried to answer.

What holds societies intact, in Parsons' view, is the set of basic values and norms shared by and disseminated among their members. Such values and norms are the key elements to the constitution of societies, playing a role for societies that atoms—and quarks (or even now, strings)—play for modern physics. In the United States the equality of opportunity may be considered as such a value, and norms can be found in the form of such practices as affirmative action in educational institutions and the workplace, norms that act to translate values to real-world activities. The work of societies, in

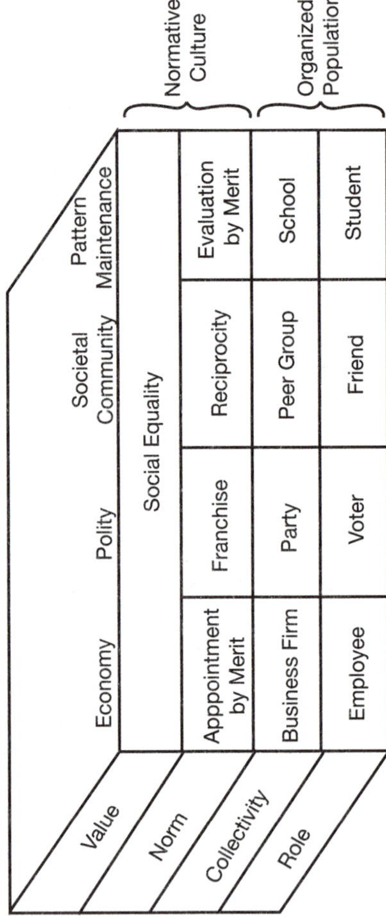

Figure 4-1 The Components of Social Structure

effect, is to ensure that such values and norms are transmitted to and acted upon by their members.

Parsons possessed a clear sense of what today we call *civil society,* but he named it the *societal community.*[32] It is, for him, that part of an ongoing society that is composed of the institutions of religion, education, and the family, and through which new members acquire the basic values and norms of society. The family plays a vital role in society for it transmits the basic norms of the society, such as the emphasis on equality. Religion plays an equally important role, especially in societies like the United States. Religion acts to teach and instruct people about the values that members must share, such as social and political tolerance. And education is especially important for it is through the school and classrooms that young people learn not simply—or even mainly—the basic elements of reading and writing, but rather the fundamental values of society. Here, of course, he follows the path pioneered by Emile Durkheim.

Parsons views the social world in terms of the shared and common elements on which it is grounded—the common beliefs, the norms and values, of people. Division and conflict are not present in his view of the world, nor is politics as we conventionally think of it. Politics is not the oppression of one class by another; nor is it the use of power by the state against both citizens and external enemies. Rather, power is "the capacity of a social system to mobilize resources to attain collective goals,"and politics concerns questions of how best to proceed in the mobilization of such resources.[33] The system is the key that unlocks all puzzles: Goals, purposes, and strategies are essentially those of the social system and the actors who play their bit parts on behalf of the system.[34] The game of politics, as Parsons pointed out in a famous critique of the work of C. Wright Mills, is not a zero-sum game in which the players are competing to control a fixed supply.[35] Instead, societies actually can create more and more of it. Yet, one might argue that had Parsons lived longer and taken greater recognition of the political divisions and poverty in America and the rest of the world, he might have been forced to change his tune on these matters.

Parsons continues to represent an important influence and voice in political sociology, if only because of his emphasis on the crucial significance of an underlying set of values in the workings of any nation or country, and because of his impact on such modern theorists as Jürgen Habermas. Where Durkheim had pointed to the importance of social solidarity, and Tocqueville to the value of equality in America, Parsons wrote of the world as a social system, an entity whose basic outlines he did much to clarify. His is a voice that remains important to the effort to uncover those points of unity, either in the form of symbols and celebrations in the polity, as in the writings of Robert Bellah, or in the work of more recent scholars such as sociologist Jeffrey Alexander.

Seymour Martin Lipset

One of the most interesting and provocative social scientists of the twentieth century—and the most widely cited—is Seymour Martin Lipset. He also is one of the principal founders of the field of political sociology. Lipset has been a prodigious and creative scholar, writing over twenty books and countless articles. It was Lipset who first gave shape to the intellectual agenda of political sociology in his justly famous work, *Political Man*.[36] There he identified Marx, Weber, and Tocqueville as the main intellectual founders of political sociology.

Like Tocqueville, Lipset's main intellectual passion has been to study America and, in particular, the nature of democracy in America. He has used this interest as a kind of intellectual probe also to explore the nature of other societies and their political systems. Thus, in a pioneering comparative analysis he examined the character of democratic governments in a number of societies, concluding that the main condition making for democracy is a strong middle class and a prosperous economy. He also focuses on America as a way of asking what became for him a lifelong query—why no socialism in America? To answer this question he undertook to explore the origins of agrarian socialism in Canada, basing his analysis on the emergence of the Cooperative Commonwealth Federation in Saskatchewan, Canada. He argued that the unusually high rate of political interest and participation in that province helped to lay the foundations for the Federation's appearance. Years later he would add to this analysis by suggesting, too, that the Canadian system of proportional representation, as compared to America's winner-take all system, greatly facilitated the rise of the socialist Federation in Canada.[37]

Though Lipset has been much influenced by the writings of Marx and Weber, it is the sensibility and passion of Tocqueville that seem to shine through his thought and writing most clearly. Consider the powerful and provocative analysis of the International Typographical Union in New York City, a work Lipset wrote in collaboration with James Coleman and Martin Trow.[38] Taking this single case, they ask why the ITU was able to sustain a democratic form of governance and administration whereas most other trades unions were unable to? His answer comes virtually straight from the pages of Tocqueville. Most other unions discouraged the active participation of their members in union activities, whereas, because of the high level of education and skill of the printers in the ITU, such participation became a way of life. "The printers' strong identification with (their) craft," the authors note, " . . . meant that they were more likely to be involved in the affairs of their organization than workers in other occupations. . . . [Moreover], their occupational community [further[stimulated the desire of the printers to participate in their union."[39] Democracy, so unique to this union, became grounded on a deep sense of commitment and widespread participation among the union members.

Lipset's analysis in *Union Democracy* represents an important illustration of the way that the civil institutions of a society—or in this instance, an organization—provide the means and foundations for politics, democratic politics in particular. To Lipset, as to Tocqueville before him, such institutions assume the form of the voluntary organizations and the informal networks that exist among people, as well as the customs and values on which they are grounded and that they serve to express. Activity in such social groupings provides both a means for understanding the nature of the larger social group and a way of communicating and securing a sense of trust among the others with whom one has contact.

Lipset's vision of democracy—a vision at one point illustrated with the claim of Joseph Schumpeter that democracy is "the free competition between elites for the right to govern"—is a vision that he continues to pursue and works hard to understand. Much of his writing makes sense only when understood as his passion and quest to understand the underpinnings of democratic governments. The central elements he has found—a high degree of education; an advanced economy; a broad and deep middle-class—represent the elements that he believes are necessary to sustain democratic governments.[40] Together these elements constitute one view of the way that civil society anchors democratic governments.

Moreover, his is a view that sees working democratic governments like that in the United States as good, in and of themselves, and that does not consider them either as pursuing the ends of power or as ruling on behalf of a small and illegitimate class of capitalists. Democratic government works effectively to process the different and varied opinions of people in society. It is a perspective that, while recognizing the important changes and shifts which have taken place, is deeply indebted to the imagery and questions raised first by Alexis de Tocqueville. And it is also a perspective that has gone to great pains to temper the influence of Marx's ideas on modern sociology.[41]

Lipset's empirical expertise and knowledge has proven to be exceptional. His work on the International Typographical Union helped to show how useful single case studies could be to the sociological study of the world of politics. Much of his writing has been about sample surveys and employs the perspective of the modern behavioral sciences, with their emphasis on questionnaire construction, surveys, and the opinions of the public. Though he has crafted exceptional historical work, to some degree modern sociology, and other social sciences, have moved beyond him in their emphasis on the institutional and historical underpinnings of modern societies.

Robert Bellah

Robert Bellah has been more often associated with the sociological study of religion than of politics. But as a scholar who works in the traditions of Emile Durkheim and Alexis de Tocqueville, and as a student of Talcott Parsons, what he has to say about sociology also has important bearing on one's view of politics. Indeed, Bellah's perspective on the world is a distinctive way of talking about the bearing of civil society, or the civil order, on the character of politics.

Civil Religion. One of Bellah's main contributions to sociology over the past several decades is his thesis about the nature of *civil religion*.[42] Adopting an idea from Durkheim, Bellah has argued that politics in America has become what he calls a civil religion. Durkheim originally suggested the germ for this argument in discussions like the following:

> There can be no society that does not feel the need of upholding and reaffirming at regular intervals the collective sentiments and the collective ideas which make its unity and its personality. . . . What essential difference is there between an assembly of Christians celebrating the principal dates of the life of Christ, or of Jews remembering the exodus from Egypt, or the promulgation of the decalogue, and *a reunion of citizens commemorating the promulgation of a new moral or legal system or some great event in the national life*? [my italics].[43]

Bellah argues that one may think of politics, not as politics in the conventional sense, but as a kind of way of life, or religion, for American citizens.

The roots of American civil religion, Bellah observes, can be found in some of the major statements and interpretations of our leading political figures. One illustration he uses is the Presidential Inauguration of John F. Kennedy in 1961. He notes that Kennedy used the word "God" three times in his speech. But the American Constitution calls for a separation of the state and church. How exactly, then, could one interpret Kennedy's invocation of the term in his national address? Bellah insists that "the separation of church and state has not denied the political realm a religious dimension. . . . [There are] certain common elements of religious orientation that the great majority of Americans share [and] . . . these have played a crucial role in the development of American institutions and still provide a religious dimension for the whole fabric of American life, including the political sphere."[44]

American civil religion is represented both by the symbols and by the rituals in which Americans engage to celebrate the nation and the elements they hold in common. Moreover, there are national crises that serve as tests of the state of nationhood and that offer the opportunity for restoring the sense of common fellowship among Americans. One such crisis was represented by the Civil War, when the North and South divided on the issue of slavery. It became both a moment of moral division and when the War was over, a moment that provided an opportunity for healing. In many respects, such healing has happened. And yet, the nation must continue to live through the trauma and make efforts to heal its moral wounds. Racism is a kind of modern-day crisis around which Americans are joined, and through which they make efforts to heal and to make themselves a common people. Its continuing presence also provides a continuing sense of crisis and the continuing possibility that the nation will never be whole.[45] It is such elements as these, in the history and sense of nationhood, in which Bellah finds his sense of civil religion to be revealed.

Habits of the Heart. To date Bellah's most famous work is one written jointly with several colleagues. Bellah wrote *Habits of the Heart*, along with fellow sociologists Richard Madsen, Stephen Tipton, and Ann Swidler, and philosopher William Sullivan. It not only is an original and important study of America, but it also became a bestseller, one of the few works ever by academic sociologists to achieve such recognition.[46]

The authors endeavor to probe and to understand the nature of American culture. They do so by assembling a series of interviews with a group of middle-class white Americans, the "middling group of Americans," who, they believe, are so representative of American customs and ways. They are after what Tocqueville termed *habits of the heart:*

> I am very much convinced that political societies are created not by their laws but by the feelings, beliefs, ideas, the habits of heart and mind of the men who compose those societies, by that which nature and education have made them, have prepared them to be.[47]

Theirs is a study, then, not of behavior or even of political events and institutions, but of the deep cultural traditions of American society. It is these traditions, they argue, that can explain both the strengths of America circa 1990, and of its weaknesses as well. The tone of their work is deliberately moralistic: Culture is not simply a set of habits and patterns, but it is a set of moral expectations for how people are to lead their lives.

The main pattern Bellah and his colleagues uncover is that of *individualism*. There are different varieties—the variety most often encountered in the activities of Americans, that takes the form of self-interested behavior and individual initiative, is what they call *utilitarian* and *expressive individualism*. Two other forms, the *biblical* and *civic republican* traditions, have receded from contemporary experience, but the authors believe these represent the most positive forms of individualism. The American tradition of individualism, which is responsible for the energy and activity of many in the business world, also has its impact over other spheres of life. Bellah and his colleagues portray various personal exemplars of individualism, some of whom reveal in very clear and graphic ways the value they attach to great personal success and ambition, and, in the lingua franca of the day, "being their own person."

These deep cultural foundations of American life, the same to which Tocqueville pointed more than a century earlier, have consequences for public life and politics. Americans, Bellah and his colleagues show, have a preference for individual pursuits, and a reluctance to engage in broad civic activities. The strength of the American tradition is to foster the individual pursuit of excellence, but the weakness is to diminish the sense of charity and compassion Americans might have for others. In a section in which they consider the activity of Americans in broad civic and public associations, they contrast the view of politics found in local government and the view advocated by a citizens' group:

> Two images of American life confronted each other: the efficient organizational society of private achievement and consumption versus the civic vision of work as a calling and contribution to the community, binding individuals together in a common life. . . . This (latter) view of politics depends upon a notion of community and citizenship importantly different from the utilitarian individualist view. It seeks to persuade us that the individual self finds its fulfillment in relationships with others in a society organized through public dialogue.[48]

The consequence, then, of such a strong belief in individualism is that Americans tend to think of civic ventures only in terms of personal gain and achievement, rather than in terms of promoting a stronger sense of community among themselves while acting to help others.

While Bellah and his coauthors decry the limits that individualism imposes on American public life today, they are careful to argue that the older, more subdued traditions, which emphasize a greater trust and commonality even among individuals, might always be resurrected. Such traditions exist as a kind of silent language, always available but mute in the face of utilitarian individualism's success. Moreover, though they do not link individualism much to signs of public inactivity, it also is clear that the authors believe such things as diminishing turnout for elections and the growing indifference of Americans to associational activity represent the "nihilism" to which individualism, when carried to an extreme, can lead.

James S. Coleman and Robert Putnam

Over the course of the past decade, there has been an explosion of interest in the bearing of civil society on the nature of a nation's politics and political institutions. Much of this work has been stimulated by theoretical formulations that owe their origins to the writings of two scholars—one a sociologist, the other a political scientist. I group them together here because the work has really grown in tandem, even though they never worked in direct collaboration with one another. But both were equally inspired by a kind of vision of civil society, and civic virtue, a vision whose roots may be traced back to both Durkheim and Tocqueville.

The beginnings of the perspective are to be found in the writing of James C. Coleman, a most brilliant sociologist. Shortly before his death, Coleman completed a massive work, *The Foundations of Social Theory*.[49] In it, he proposed a general social theory of action that was intended to rival the works of the great masters of sociology, like Marx and Weber. Though it remains to be seen whether the work will have that sort of lasting influence, there is one critical idea that has proven quite fruitful and provocative to recent scholars. Coleman proposed that individuals possess something he called *social capital*, drawing his inspiration for the term from the economist Glenn Loury. Social capital refers to the social resources that individuals possess and on which they can draw in making critical decisions and taking critical action. Loury had intended the concept to refer to the family and its network of relations in explaining the economic accomplishments of individuals.[50] Coleman intends the concept more broadly, to refer not only to the social relations of people, but also to the sense of underlying trust and confidence that people have in one another.

Coleman illustrates the idea of social capital with various references. He refers, for example, to the idea of the "rotating credit association," an association made famous by an article by Clifford Geertz.[51] The rotating credit association is a form of cooperative economic venture among people from Southeast Asian societies. By joining together, in a common venture, people pool their meager resources, and then can rotate in drawing on the general fund of credit created by the larger pool. It provides a successful answer to a situation in which no single member has enough funds to begin an economic enterprise, but in which a collection of such individuals can furnish on a regular basis such funds to their fellow members. Once a member draws on the funds, he is required to pay them back from the earnings of his venture. And the process continues. It is not only evident in Southeast Asian societies, where Geertz viewed it, but it also has been used to explain the economic success of Korean entrepreneurs in Los Angeles, especially by comparison with the economic failures of their African-American counterparts.[52]

Coleman believes that there are many such examples of social trust and cooperation evident in the larger world. They are to be found in extended families and in small groups. They also may be discovered in urban areas, and in the differences between them. Thus, for instance, Coleman notes that a mother who moved to Jerusalem felt more comfortable in allowing her children to play unattended there than in Detroit, precisely because she felt a greater sense of trust in the residents living in Jerusalem. In sum, Coleman argues that social capital consists of the networks and relations among individuals, and that it is also evident in the deeper sense of trust and comfort people feel in some cultures and locales than in others. Moreover, it provides an important resource on which they can draw in making individual decisions, a resource that is different from, and may even underlie, economic capital itself.

Coleman died before he was able to trace out and explore the various possibilities of his rich concept of social capital. Fortunately for him—and for us—it was an idea that prompted later pathbreaking research by the political scientist Robert Putnam, who acknowledges his deep debt to Coleman as well as to the sociologist Mark Granovetter.[53] Putnam, along with his colleagues Robert Leonardi and Raffaella Nanetti, was able to study the formation of new regional governments in Italy from the moment of their birth in the early 1970s.[54] The Italian government had decided to embark on a major effort to break out of the inertia of its national programs and to create new governments that could cover policy-arenas and also work more closely with local citizens. It was an historic venture for Italy, and one that Putnam and his colleagues were asked to evaluate. In the end, their assessment covered a period of a quarter of a century, during which a major evolution took place in the regional governments.

Putnam and his colleagues studied the regional governments by doing periodic surveys with the local officials as well as local citizens. They examined, among other things, the citizens' reactions to and sense of satisfaction with the work done by the local governments. In addition, Putnam and his colleagues also measured the effectiveness and performance of the regional governments. They quantified such performance along twelve different dimensions of the workings of the regional government, including the following: reform legislation; day care centers; housing and urban development; legislative innovation; cabinet stability; bureaucratic responsiveness; and budget promptness. Each of the twelve dimensions was put into quantitative form, and each covered somewhat different time periods over the course of the entire lifespan of the regional governments. The investigators finally created an overall index of institutional performance; as it turned out, each of the measures was related to one another, though the degree of such a relationship was not always strong.

The three social scientists then proceeded to put their data together. They looked for and discovered variations in the institutional performance of each of the twelve regional governments; they also uncovered important variations in the satisfaction of citizens with the effectiveness of each government's performance. As it turned out, citizens were more satisfied with those regional governments that performed better, thus satisfying both the Italian authorities and the investigators. Then the research became more interesting.

Putnam, who assumed responsibility for the main lines of the argument, embarked on a theoretical excursion as an advocate of the kind of view put forth by Alexis de Tocqueville. He assumed that something like civic traditions, or habits of the heart, were present among people, and that they could account for democracy in general, and for the link between the effectiveness of government and the satisfaction of citizens. He put his claims to the test. He showed, for instance, that variations in the institutional effectiveness of the regional governments could not be explained by variations in the level of their local wealth. This constituted both a test, and a disproof, of the hypothesis linking wealth and democracy provided by Seymour Martin Lipset. Next he turned to see whether the civic trust and traditions of a region were at all linked to institutional effectiveness, creating an index comprised of measures of voting turnout, and associational involvement by local citizens, among other things. An examination of the correspondence between his measure of the civic community and institutional performance provided overwhelming confirmation of his argument: where the local civic community was strong, there, too, institutional performance was the most effective by the regional governments. Indeed, the correlation was on the order of +.90, surprisingly strong evidence of correspondence in the social sciences.[55]

Not content to let his case rest simply on this evidence, Putnam considers alternative explanations, finding all of them wanting. He also expands on the argument about the civic community, an argument he links directly to the work of Tocqueville on American democracy. He finds that the civic community is something that can be linked to the Italian past, in particular, that stronger such communities grew in the Italian north as early as the Middle Ages, whereas the south was weaker in such traditions. The difference between the north and south of Italy is also parallel to the difference between those regions where the regional governments were ineffective and effective, respectively. To ground his case firmly, he then expands on the theory of the civic community, noting the importance of social networks and social trust, drawing explicitly on the work of Coleman and Granovetter.

Putnam's work has won him much praise and several awards, and it is the strongest evidence yet of the continuing importance of civic traditions, and of civil society, for the grounding and development of democratic politics. Moreover, as we shall discover in Chapter 9, he has extended the thesis of social capital and democracy even further, landing it on the shores of modern America.

CONCLUSION

Over the past few years, civil society has emerged among sociologists, and to a lesser degree, among political scientists, as the place to turn for interesting explanations of everything from democracy to revolution. There has been a virtual explosion of interest in the form and nature of civil society, much of it springing from works like Robert Putnam's *Making Democracy Work.* Though not all observers agree with Putnam—and many are now searching more carefully for evidence on such things as voluntary associations and social networks—most agree that Putnam has reinvigorated this long-neglected paradigm.

The interest in Putnam and civil society represents a return to the kinds of arguments and explanations offered a century ago by Emile Durkheim and, especially, Alexis de Tocqueville. The appeal of these arguments is quite simple. People are now searching for ways both to understand and to create, if not restore, democracies in the world. Neither Karl Marx, with his emphasis on social classes and the illusion of state power, nor Max Weber, with his concern about the actions of aggressive states, offer nearly as much hope for those wishing to establish and create new democracies. Moreover, many analysts find in the notion of civil society a way for understanding how the collapse of older regimes, like that of Poland, came about. Timothy Garton Ash, one of the earliest commentators on the collapse of communism in Eastern Europe, used the notion of civil society to portray the efforts of the movement Solidarity to rise up against the communist regime and to succeed. Ash argued that the success of Solidarity lay precisely in the fact that it had helped to create new associations in civil society, able to replace those of communism once it was overthrown.[56] It is likely that as long as our world remains in some turmoil, with the collapse of old regimes and efforts to create new ones, there will also continue to be a strong interest in understanding how the institutions of civil society work.

NOTES

1. Emile Durkheim, *The Rules of Sociological Method*, 8th edition, translated by Sarah A. Solovay and John H. Mueller and edited by George E.G. Catlin (New York: The Free Press of Glencoe, 1938; 1950), 2–3.
2. Ralf Dahrendorf, *Class and Class Conflict in Industrial Society* (Stanford, California: Stanford University Press, 1959).
3. On the origins of the distinction, see *Hegel's Philosophy of Right*, translated with note by T.M. Knox (London: Oxford University Press, 1952;1967), especially subsections 2 and 3 on civil society and the state, respectively.
4. Durkheim, *Rules of the Sociological Method*, lvi.
5. Emile Durkheim, *Suicide: A Study in Sociology*, translated by John A. Spaulding and George Simpson; edited with an introduction by George Simpson (Glencoe, Illinois: The Free Press, 1951).
6. Immanuel Kant, *The Critique of Pure Reason*, translated by Norman Kemp Smith (New York: St. Martin's Press, 1929; 1965).

7. Emile Durkheim, *The Elementary Forms of the Religious Life,* translated by Joseph Ward Swain (New York: Collier Books, 1961).
8. Emile Durkheim, *The Division of Labor in Society*, translated by George Simpson (New York: Free Press, 1964), 408–9.
9. Emile Durkheim, *Moral Education: A Study in the Theory and Application of the Sociology of Education,* translated by Everett K. Wilson and Herman Schnurer (New York: The Free Press of Glencoe, 1961).
10. Durkheim, *The Division of Labor in Society.*
11. Ibid.
12. *Elementary Forms of the Religious Life*, Book I.
13. Ibid.
14. Ibid., 432.
15. Ibid., 388.
16. *The Division of Labor in Society*, 268.
17. See, for example, *Suicide.*
18. Ibid., 380.
19. Alexis de Tocqueville, *The Old Regime and the Revolution,* edited and with an introduction and critical appraisal by Francois Furet and Francoise Melonio; translated by Alan S. Kahan (Chicago: University of Chicago Press, 1998).
20. Louis Hartz, *The Liberal Tradition in America: An Interpretation of American Political Thought Since the Revolution* (New York: Harcourt Brace Jovanovich, Inc., 1955).
21. Alexis de Tocqueville, *Democracy in America*, the Henry Reeve text with notes and bibliographies by Phillips Bradley (New York: Vintage Books), Volume I, 4.
22. Ibid., 48.
23. Tocqueville, *Democracy in America*, II, 127.
24. Op. cit., *Democracy in America*, I, 203.
25. Ibid., 342.
26. Op. cit., *Democracy in America*, II, 373.
27. Gunnar Myrdal, with the assistance of Richard Sterner and Arnold Rose, *An American Dilemma: the Negro Problem and Modern Democracy* (New York: Harper, 1944).
28. Tocqueville, *Democracy in America*, II, 171.
29. Op. cit., *Democracy in America*, I, 270–71..
30. Talcott Parsons, *The Structure of Social Action,* Volumes I and II (New York: The Free Press, 1937; 1968).
31. Talcott Parsons, *The Social System* (Glencoe, Illinois: The Free Press, 1951).
32. Talcott Parsons, *The System of Modern Societies* (Englewood Cliffs, New Jersey: Prentice-Hall, 1971).
33. Talcott Parsons, *Politics and Social Structure* (New York: The Free Press, 1969), 206.
34. Parsons, *The Social System.*

35. Parsons, "The Distribution of Power in American Society," in Parsons, *Politics and Social Structure*, 185–203.
36. Seymour Martin Lipset, *Political Man: The Social Bases of Politics* (Garden City, New York: Doubleday & Company, 1959).
37. Seymour Martin Lipset, *Agrarian Socialism*, updated edition (Garden City, New York: Doubleday, 1968).
38. Seymour Martin Lipset, Martin A. Trow, and James S. Coleman, *Union Democracy: The Internal Politics of the International Typographical Union* (Garden City, NY: Doubleday Anchor, 1962).
39. Ibid., p. 442.
40. Seymour Martin Lipset, "Some Social Requisites of Democracy," *American Political Science Review*, vol. 53 (March 1959), 69–105.
41. *Class, Status and Power*, Seymour Martin Lipset and Reinhard Bendix, eds. (New York: Free Press, 1966).
42. Robert N. Bellah, *Beyond Belief: Essays on Religion in a Post-Traditional World* (New York: Harper and Row, 1970).
43. Emile Durkheim, *Elementary Forms of the Religious Life*, 475.
44. Bellah, op. cit., 171.
45. See Robert Bellah, *The Broken Covenant: American Civil Religion in a Time of Trial* (New York: Seabury Press, 1975).
46. Robert N. Bellah, Richard Madsen, William M. Sullivan, Ann Swidler, and Steven M. Tipton, *Habits of the Heart: Individualism and Commitment in American Life*, Updated Edition with a new Introduction (Berkeley: University of California Press, 1996).
47. Letter from Tocqueville to Corcelle, September 1853; as quoted in Tocqueville, *The Old Regime and the French Revolution*, Volume One, op. cit., 10.
48. *Habits of the Heart*, 218.
49. James S. Coleman, *Foundations of Social Theory* (Cambridge, Massachusetts: The Belknap Press of Harvard University Press, 1990).
50. Glenn Loury, "Why Should We Care About Group Inequality?" *Social Philosophy and Policy*, 1987, 5, 249–271.
51. Clifford Geertz, "The Rotating Credit Association: A 'Middle Rung' in Development," *Economic Development and Cultural Change*, 1962, 10, 240–263.
52. Ivan Light, *Ethnic Enterprise in America: Business and Welfare Among Chinese, Japanese and Blacks* (Berkeley: University of California Press, 1972).
53. Mark Granovetter, "Economic Action and Social Structure: The Problem of Embeddedness," *American Sociological Review*, Volume 91 (November 1985), 481–510.
54. Robert D. Putnam, with Robert Leonardi and Raffaella Y. Nanetti, *Making Democracy Work: Civic Traditions in Modern Italy* (Princeton: Princeton University Press, 1993).
55. Ibid., p. 98.
56. Timothy Garton Ash, *The Uses of Adversity: Essays on the Fate of Central Europe* (New York: Random House, 1989).

Chapter 5

Basic Forms of Political Rule

Democratic, Totalitarian, and Authoritarian Regimes in the Modern World

> If there were a people of gods, it would govern itself democratically. Such a perfect government is not suited to men.
>
> Jean Jacques Rousseau, *The Social Contract*

> So a prince need not have all the . . . good qualities, but it is most essential that he appear to have them. Indeed, I should go so far as to say that having them and always practising them is harmful, while seeming to have them is useful. It is good to appear clement, trustworthy, humane, religious and honest, and also to be so, but always with the mind so disposed that, when the occasion arises not to be so, you can become the opposite. It must be understood that a prince and particularly a new prince cannot practice all the virtues for which men are accounted good, for the necessity of preserving the state often compels him to take actions which are opposed to loyalty, charity, humanity, and religion. Hence he must have a spirit ready to adapt itself as the varying winds of fortune command him. As I have said, so far as he is able a prince should stick to the path of good, but, if the necessity arises, he should know how to follow evil.
>
> Niccolò Machiavelli, *The Prince*

Our current thinking about the nature of politics has been shaped as much by the writings of ancient Greek philosophy as by those of any other civilization or time. We are indebted to the Greeks, particularly Plato and Aristotle, for helping us to conceive the setting of politics and of the rules that regulate it—in their words, the polis and the laws. Politics today is still thought to be how those people who are the members of a given community or society act, and should act, as members of its body politic. Politics continues to provoke the questions first raised and probed by the ancient Greeks: the questions of the rights of people to become involved in the body politic; of the willingness of those who occupy center stage—the aristocrats, the oligarchs, or whoever—to permit the great majority of people to enter into the deliberations that go on in the body politic.

This chapter considers some of the basic features of the political arena in modern societies as well as some of the variations that exist from one arena to another. Among other things, the discussion deals with the character of modern democratic societies—societies that are focused on throughout this book. It is most appropriate that the discussion depart from ancient roots, and thus it begins with a review of the classical Greek conception of the polis.

BASIC TYPES OF POLITICAL RULE: THE CLASSICAL GREEK CONCEPTIONS

Aristotle's conception of the Greek body politic, the *polis*, rested on two features: the qualities of its residents and the nature of its rules.[1] First, the polis was made up only of the body of citizens in a city-state; citizens were those who were governed and who could exercise the privilege of governance. Lower classes, including mechanics, artisans, and the large number of slaves, were not included among the people who qualified as citizens and hence as members of the polis. Second, the rules of the polis consisted of the laws and traditions of the Greek city-state; the laws were for Aristotle the most sovereign feature of the city-state. The governance of the citizens of the polis meant the "rightly constituted laws . . . and personal rule, whether it be exercised by a single person or a body of persons, should be sovereign only in those matters on which law is unable, owing to the difficulty of framing general rules for all contingencies, to make an exact pronouncement."[2]

There were, Aristotle further thought, two broad sets of political arenas: those in which men achieved all the prime moral values—wisdom, goodness, beauty, justice—and those in which men lived in more debased, if not more "real" circumstances.[3] Within each of these two sets were three subsets of polis: The moral set contained kingship, aristocracy, and polity; the other comprised tyranny, oligarchy, and democracy. Each of the three also possessed its counterpart in the other set. Thus, kingship had tyranny as its counterpart; aristocracy had oligarchy as its counterpart; and polity possessed democracy as its counterpart. The chief element that the three pairs held in common was the number of rulers in the polis; in kingship and tyranny there was only a single ruler, in aristocracy and oligarchy there existed several rulers, and in polity and democracy the large majority of citizens were their own rulers. There were other differences among the several forms, but Aristotle reserved most of his attention for democracy, oligarchy, and polity.

Oligarchy was thought to represent the perversion of the aristocratic form of rule. Aristotle believed that under the rule of oligarchy those individuals who held property, a minority of the population, limited the exercise of governance to themselves and ruled in ways that would advance their interests exclusively. Democracy represented the perversion of rule in polity—a polis in which the large majority of people had become sovereign, but in so doing violated the rights of the minority, the property holders. Each of the two forms violated the sense of justice that should prevail in the ideal community. Instead of adhering to the principle of distributive justice—the contribution of an individual to a society's well-being is rewarded in an amount commensurate to his contribution—democracy and oligarchy rewarded citizens on the basis of special qualities having nothing to do with their contributions to the vitality of the community. Hence, a democracy held all citizens to be equal although not all of them contributed equally to the well-being of the polis; an oligarchy insisted that all citizens are unequal although such inequality existed only by virtue of their disproportionate property holdings, not by the degree of their contribution to the well-being of the polis.[4]

In contrast to Plato, Aristotle maintained that in principle a democracy could possess certain desirable traits. For one thing, he believed the people as a whole possessed a better combination of qualities of judgment and good sense than any small number of individuals. "Each of the [people]," he wrote, "may not be of good . . . quality; but when they all come together it is possible that they may surpass—collectively and as a body, although not individually—the quality of the few best."[5] He further claimed that the governance of the polis by the people, or by their elected magistrates, could be justified on the grounds that the people represent the best judges of their own interests.

Polity and tyranny appeared to him as the best and the worst of political arenas. Although at first polity seemed to be only the virtuous counterpart of democracy, on further analysis it appeared as a mixed form of government, incorporating features of democracy and oligarchy. Citing the examples of Sparta, Aristotle claimed that polity ought to be construed by some observers as an oligarchy, by others as a democracy. He remarked:

> There are many who would describe [Sparta] as a democracy, on the ground that its organization has a number of democratic features. In the first place, and so far as concerns the bringing up of the young, the children of the rich have the same fare as the children of the poor, and they are educated on a standard

> which the children of the poor can also attain. . . . No difference is made between the rich and the poor: the food at the common mess is the same for all, and the dress of the rich is such as any of the poor could also provide for themselves. . . . A second ground for describing Sparta as a democracy is the right of the people to elect to one of the two great institutions, the Senate, and to be eligible themselves for the other, the Ephorate. On the other hand there are some who describe the Spartan constitution as an oligarchy, on the ground that it has many oligarchical factors. For example, the magistrates are all appointed by vote, and none by log; again, the power of inflicting the penalty of death or banishment rests in the hands of a few persons; and there are many other similar features. *A properly mixed "polity" should look as if it contained both democratic and oligarchic elements—and as if it contained neither* [my italics].[6]

Moreover, polity, if properly planned, corrected for the extremes of democracy, the rule by the many, and of oligarchy, rule by the few, by basing its form of rule upon the majority, the middle class. Asserting his preference for moderation in all things, Aristotle argued that polity, by being based upon a large middle class, assisted in eliminating the conflicts and tensions evident in democracies and in oligarchies. Yet, he noted, the establishment of polities was unlikely, for in most Greek city-states the middle class was very small, and disputes inevitably arose between the very rich and the very poor. Tyranny, in contrast to polity, represented the very worst sort of government. It was a base type of rule because it benefited the smallest possible number of citizens in a polis. Also, it represented a form of government in which the rule of the person replaced the rule of law; lawlessness for Aristotle was the most perverse form of governance.

To complete this brief portrait of the Greek view of politics, it is important that we remind ourselves that in actual practice the constitutional orders of ancient Greece comprised many different features, including magistrates, councils, and sometimes, assemblies of the entire body politic. Still, the differences between democracy and oligarchy pervaded the entire polis. Leonard Whibley, a close student of the Aristotelian conceptions of the polis and of the actual practices of the ancient Greek constitutional orders, summarily observed some of these differences between the two types of polis:

> In the fully developed democracy the people wanted to exercise their powers directly, they were jealous of all institutions in the state other than the assembly, and both council and magistrates were rendered in every way subordinate agents of the popular power. The duties of government were divided amongst a great number of magistrates whose authority was restricted as far as possible: the lot secured that ordinary men would be chosen (so that it was impossible to leave much to their discretion): their tenure was short, reelection was usually forbidden, offices were intended to rotate and all who exercised the smallest authority did so with a full responsibility to the governing body. In the oligarchies almost every one of these conditions is reversed. The functions of government were not so thoroughly divided, the magistrates had larger inde-

> pendent powers, they were appointed by and from a small privileged body, the same men might be reelected.[7]

In sum, the basic principles that Aristotle revealed through his analysis of the nature of democracies—in particular, the size of the ruling group, their social foundations in property, and the interests on behalf of which their leaders ruled—were in practice found to be operating down to the very smallest details in the Greek city-states

How useful are these conceptions to the analysis of contemporary political orders? Can we transport them across 2,500 years of time and use them to illuminate the features of current political realities? They are useful in isolating some of the basic outlines of the political order and some of the fundamental differences that exist among such orders. But there are at least two reasons why they cannot be transplanted unchanged from Aristotle and the Greek world to the contemporary world. First, the Aristotelian conceptions are useful primarily for the study of social groups no larger than the common city-states of ancient Greece—communities typically numbering in the tens of thousands. Many twentieth-century nations number in the tens, if not hundreds, of millions of people; simply by virtue of the difference in magnitude of population there is less than a perfect fit between the Aristotelian notions and contemporary circumstances.[8] Second, the revolution in industry and technology that in the eighteenth and nineteenth centuries helped to lay the economic foundations for the modern world brought about a number of changes of great political consequence—changes in our conception of citizenship, changes in our sense of the legitimate boundaries between public concerns and private interests, and transformations in the technical means that rulers may employ in cultivating the obedience of those whom they rule. One reflection of this feature of the modern world is that both Marx and Weber wrote of bourgeois or capitalist democracies, not simply democracies, suggesting that to them this form represented something unique. Thus, it is unwise to apply the Aristotelian conceptions to social and economic circumstances that are so very different from those of 2,500 years ago. The classical Greek conceptions, therefore, are broad guidelines on the nature of the significant features of current political orders.

TYPES OF POLITICAL RULE IN THE MODERN WORLD

In recent history there have been two almost opposite forms of political rule. First, there is *modern democracy*, a form that retains the ancient name because it shares certain features with the Greek polis of the same description—for instance, an emphasis upon widespread and voluntary citizen involvement in public life. Second, there is a new form, one that has elements of the ancient tyranny to which Aristotle referred but that also has a number of unique features; this is *totalitarianism*, represented in its purest respects in the former Soviet Union and in Germany under the rule of Adolf Hitler. Today its closest empirical counterpart is that of the People's Republic of China, though China is becoming something of a hybrid regime. A third form, which lies somewhere between democracy and totalitarianism, is that of *authoritarianism*. We shall discuss all three, with most of our emphasis on democratic and totalitarian regimes.

Democracy

There are two different sets of ideas about modern democracy. Scholars sometimes refer to the differences as that between substantive democracy, or how democracy really is intended to work, and formal democracy, or that which characterizes many of the so-called democratic nations in the world today. Here I shall refer to the two types as the *moral vision of democracy*, and the *empirical view* of it. The first, similar to that of the ancient Greeks, envisions the shape of democratic rule in utopian terms and thus seeks after the very best and the most just form of political rule under which citizens may live. In somewhat different fashion, this view of a democratic society was shaped by political philosophers such as Jean Jacques Rousseau, John Locke, Montesquieu, and John Stuart Mill in the eighteenth and nineteenth centuries, and was assisted by the writings of John Dewey and Robert MacIver, among others, early in the twentieth century.[9]

The Moral Vision. At heart, the moral vision of a democratic society claims that individuals are the best judges of their own interests. Eschewing a society sustained by a small number of rulers, a group of oligarchs in other words, this vision insists that individuals can exercise the faculties of sound judgment and wisdom required to maintain the well-being of the body politic. The authors of these ideas, moreover, believe that the political capacities of individuals, their skills as well as their actual comprehension of the mechanics of politics, are capable of improvement through self-governance. Even those individuals without sound judgment on politics benefit from engagement in the institutions and processes of the political arena. These premises suggest to some of the authors of the moral view that all persons should be permitted an equal opportunity to participate in politics, and to secure protection from political institutions. "The very fact of natural and psychological inequity," Dewey wrote, "is all the more reason for establishment by law of equality of opportunity, since otherwise the former becomes a means of oppression of the less gifted."[10]

The moral vision of a democratic society also insists that the involvement of individuals in the process of self-governance is a desirable goal in and of itself. Writing of the American experiment in democracy begun at the end of the eighteenth century, Hannah Arendt observed that the fundamental assumption underlying popular political participation "was that no one could be called happy without his share in public happiness, that no one could be called free without his experience in public freedom, and that no one could be called either happy or free without participating, and having a share, in public power."[11]

Contemporary theorists continue to mull over and modify the moral vision of democracy as articulated by such theorists as Dewey and Arendt. In a widely read work, political scientist Benjamin Barber argues on behalf of a vision of strong democracy as compared to the weaker, liberal—or thin—version.[12] Barber insists that democratic nations such as the United States or Great Britain do not represent true democracies. Instead, he believes true democracy

> in the participatory mode resolves conflict in the absence of an independent ground through a participatory process of ongoing, proximate self-legislation and the creation of a political community capable of transforming dependent private individuals into free citizens and partial and private interests into public goods.[13]

Strong democracy demands that citizens be active in the political process, and that they engage with one another in dealing with and resolving disputes among themselves. It also means that there are opportunities and facilities through which individuals, even in large-scale societies like the United States, are able to proceed with their engagement. "Strong democracy requires unmediated self-government by an engaged citizenry," Barber writes, "(and) institutions that will involve individuals at both the neighborhood and the national level in common talk, common decision-making and political judgment, and common action."[14] Like Arendt and Dewey before him, Barber was unsatisfied with modern arrangements, such as representative government, believing that individuals engaged with one another can create for themselves the best form of democratic action.

More recently, the political philosopher, Joshua Cohen, has argued on behalf of what he calls *deliberative democracy*.[15] To Cohen the essential feature of democratic governance is that there exists a forum through which individuals can engage in continuous deliberation over issues of common concern to them. *Deliberation* is the central concept. It requires continuity on the part of the participants as well as their trust in one another's capacity to engage and discuss issues with one another. It demands a complete faith and trust in the process of deliberation as a principle, and requires that no other grounds be chosen to arrive at a common choice among participants. In essence, it goes back to the very earliest meanings of democracy, yet it appends to them modern concerns—owing, in particular, to theorists like Jürgen Habermas—with the importance of public settings and debate and negotiation over the issues of common concern to participants.[16] Finally, as

Cohen notes, it is a pluralist configuration of actors rather than people of uniform faith or constitution. "The members (of the association)," he writes, "have diverse preferences, convictions, and ideals concerning the conduct of their own lives. While sharing a commitment to the deliberative resolution of problems of collective choice, they also have divergent aims."[17]

These latest versions and reworkings of the moral vision of democracy reflect much of the contemporary debate over the root meaning of democracy, especially in light of the collapse of the older totalitarian regimes of Eastern Europe. Many theorists struggle to define the essence of democracy, an essence that could comfortably fit such circumstances as large global economy and the development of postindustrial societies. Obviously, they also find unsatisfying the notion that nations like the Unites States, which call themselves democracies, actually reach anywhere near the ideal, or moral vision. And, in any case, they are a far cry from the empirical view of democracy today.

The Empirical View. There is a second body of thought that considers the nature of modern democratic societies; it seeks the creation of a theory of democracy inductively, based upon the study of current political realities. It is this stream of scholarship that furnishes many of the ideas and facts for the discussion in this book; this theory, for instance, in one way or another incorporates views described in the chapters on power in the United States, power in communities, and citizen participation in politics. The general set of notions embodied in this empirical view of democracy are found in some of the writings of Bernard Berelson, Robert A. Dahl, Giovanni Sartori, and Joseph Schumpeter, among many others.[18]

At its root the empirical conception of democracy shifts attention from the qualities of individual citizens and their fundamental rights of self-government to the rulers and the public competition that has brought them into office. In particular, this conception lays claim to the premise that modern democracy consists of institutions that furnish contenders for public office; typically, if not invariably, these institutions are political parties. The empirical theory holds, moreover, that there usually exist rival claimants for the opportunity to occupy the highest public offices. It incorporates the notion of citizen into its purview by asserting that citizens have the right to select among the rival sets of leaders those whom they believe best represent their interests. A now classic quotation from Joseph Schumpeter succinctly serves to portray these features of the empirical theory be asserting that the democratic method is "that institutional arrangement for arriving at political decisions in which individuals acquire the power to decide by means of a competitive struggle for the people's vote."[19]

Having transferred the emphasis from citizens to leaders in democratic societies, the empirical theory further reduces the necessary role of citizens in their own self-governance. It asserts that in order for a society to lay claim to the label "democratic," its leaders merely need to be responsive to the wishes of the majority of citizens. This is accomplished in two ways: first, through the medium of elections—if the candidates for public office fail to respond to the wishes of the majority of citizens, the candidates would fail to be elected—and second, through the development of policies in office that are supposed to anticipate the wishes of the citizens. In other words, it is not necessary for citizens to engage actively in the process of politics. In fact, the widespread active and continuous engagement of the citizenry in the body politic constitutes for some empirical theorists a greater danger than benefit to a democracy—a claim that echoes Alexis de Tocqueville's fear of the "tyranny of the majority" (see Chapter 4). Berelson, for example, makes the following observation:

> How would a mass democracy work if all the people were deeply involved in politics? Lack of interest by some people is not without some benefits, too. True, the highly interested voters vote more, and know more about the campaign, and read and listen more, and participate more; however, they are also less open to persuasion and less likely to change [sic]. Extreme interest goes with extreme fanaticism that could destroy democratic processes if generalized throughout the community . . . [whereas low] interest provides maneuvering room for political shifts necessary for a complex society in a period of rapid change.[20]

Thus, the empirical conception virtually transforms the root meaning of democracy—whether defined in Aristotelian terms as rule by many citizens or in those of the modern political philosophers. Democracy is no longer a body politic in which the engagement of citizens exists as its *sine qua non*, but one in which active involvement may be unnecessary, even undesirable.

Since these two perspectives, the moral vision and the empirical theory, exist as countervailing views of the nature of modern democratic societies, one must carefully scrutinize and compare them to search for similarities as well as advantages and disadvantages of each. The moral vision is founded upon both ancient and modern ideals, and represents a set of prescriptive statements about the conditions necessary for the working of a democratic society. The empirical theory, on the other hand, is grounded in a set of facts uncovered in societies conventionally thought to be democratic, and constitutes a set of descriptive statements about the actual conditions of governments. One obvious danger in the facile adoption of the moral vision is that one might fail to understand the actual workings of a democracy by not attending to their realities. The dangers of an easy acceptance of the empirical theory might prove more harmful, however. First, the empirical view too readily accepts the conventional definitions of societies as "democratic"; this definition is sometimes more myth than reality. After a review of many facts, it remains possible to draw the conclusion that the United States more nearly resembles an oligarchy than a democracy (see Chapter 6). Second, adoption of the empirical theory can lead to an ideological justification of existing political forms. Berelson's previous cited observations, for instance, are couched within a broader analysis that implies not only that democracy actually performs in a certain manner but that it also *should* perform in this fashion. Last, by abandoning a commitment to the utopian ideal of widespread citizen participation in the body politic, the empirical view dismisses, perhaps unwittingly, a rich heritage of political thought and tradition; more important, it relinquishes a position it could serve in the modern world of revealing how modern democratic societies could be refashioned in ways to approximate more closely the ancient ideal of a democratic society.

Regardless of this dispute—a dispute likely to remain unresolved—I want to provide a few of the more salient empirical details of modern democratic societies. These introduce the nature of these societies as well as provide a benchmark for a comparison with totalitarian orders.

Constitutional and Procedural Foundations. Democratic societies invariably are based upon a tradition of law with an emphasis upon broad civil rights for the citizens, including, among others, the right of dissent. There is a separation of functions among the various branches of government, producing three separate organs, an executive, a legislative, and a judicial branch; the actual functions of each of these varies from one democratic society to another. The process of governance is carried out through a system of representatives; the institution in which the representatives serve is variously called the parliament or the congress. Suffrage is widespread, and elections occur frequently. The occupants of the executive branch are either elected directly, as in the presidential democracy of the United States, or indirectly, as in the parliamentary democracy in Great Britain.[21]

In the twentieth century these constitutional and procedural foundations have been supplemented through the continued or new growth of a large bureaucratic apparatus. The scope of the operations of this bureaucracy, initially designed to aid and to protect the constitutional rights of the citizenry, have begun to encroach seriously upon these rights in places such as the United States.

Ideological Foundations. Modern democracies are founded upon beliefs in equality of individual citizens, in widespread public liberties, and in the desirability of citizen involvement in politics.

Social Foundations. Fundamental to the social foundations of modern democratic societies is a widespread plurality of groups and diversity of interests. A large number of voluntary organizations have been developed for citizen membership and involvement, and these serve as an infrastructure or a buffer zone between the lives of individual citizens and the political control exercised by the rulers. Chief among these many groups are political parties and factions within a single party that serve, among other things, as means for organizing and expressing citizen concerns and for attaining the constitutional right to exercise power.

Economic Foundations. Modern democratic societies, Great Britain and the United States in particular, developed concomitantly with the growth of capitalist institutions. Thus, their fate is inextricably linked to the fate of these institutions. General conditions of affluence seem to have been most favorable to the growth of democratic governments, as in the United States, and the governments themselves have acted in important respects to further the conditions of affluence. However, even in settings of pervasive poverty, as in India, modified forms of democracy exist or have existed. In the twentieth century especially, the institutions of the state have increasingly assumed widespread welfare responsibilities for the citizenry; the extent of such responsibilities varies from extensive, as in Sweden, to only moderate, as in the United States.

This description of the principal features of modern democratic societies should provide at least a general impression of them; details of their composition are etched more sharply in later chapters. In addition, this capsule portrait helps to distinguish between democratic and nondemocratic societies in the modern world.[22]

Totalitarianism

The idea of totalitarianism, or totalitarian dictatorship, is meant to convey the absolute domination of a nation and its people by a single political party as well as by those who control the party.[23] Totalitarian rule seeks to obliterate the social ties and groups typical of democratic societies, for instance the ties of the nuclear family, and to substitute for them new forms of social ties that are intended to absorb the individual completely as a member of the society. Between the party and its leaders, no groups or individuals are permitted to intervene and to replace the party as the single object of the individual's loyalty and commitment. The concept has been used primarily to describe two different historical regimes in the twentieth century, those of the former Soviet Union, especially under the rule of Joseph Stalin, and Nazi Germany. The combination of these two historical forms under a single rubric overshadows certain differences between them, in particular the distinction between the nature of communism and of Nazism. For many purposes this does not seem to create too much distortion, though some observers regard the dissimilarities between the two as more substantial than their common features.[24]

Carl J. Friedrich and Zbigniew K. Brzezinski, two scholars who have contributed greatly to our understanding of totalitarian societies, claim that such societies can be singled out for six distinctive qualities: (1) an elaborate ideology that covers every phase of an individual's life; (2) a single political party that typically is led by one individual, the "dictator"; (3) a widespread system of terror, channeled both through state and party institutions and directed alike against external and internal enemies of the regime; (4) a virtually complete control of the apparatus of mass communication that is unique because of its technological sophistication and complexity; (5) a monopoly over the weaponry and men associated with the armed forces; and (6) the direction of the entire economy, or at least its most significant sectors, by the state bureaucracy.[25] Alone, however, these six characteristics of totalitarian societies do not sufficiently convey the true nature of such regimes. Thus, as a counterpart of the capsule analysis of modern democratic societies, the features of totalitarian ones are briefly elaborated. Nazi Germany is discussed in particular, but many of the same features describe equally as well the general characteristics of the former Soviet Union.

Constitutional and Procedural Foundations. One of the principal features of Germany under the reign of Adolf Hitler and the National Socialist Party was the absence of constitutional and legal foundations; the only procedural foundations were those established through the auspices of the party. To all outward appearances, however, Nazi Germany seemed to constitute an extension of the government inaugurated as the Weimar Republic in 1918. Actually the National Socialist Party committed a legal revolution, overturning the Weimar's Constitution by employing that constitution's own provisions. Among the means used to achieve this end were a series of decrees and enabling acts passed in 1933 and 1934 that placed all power in the hands of Hitler as Chancellor and, later, President of Germany. In addition, the regime represented a virtual morass of offices and rules; Hitler fashioned a regime in which the National Socialist Party and the state bureaucracy seemed to share equal power—though the party and Hitler ultimately were dominant—and in which for each office in the state bureaucracy there existed a parallel and competing one in the National Socialist Party. From Hitler's point of view, of course, the result of this morass was to create rule through *divide et impera;* the competition among occupants of parallel offices secured the effectiveness of his own leadership. Apart from Hitler, only key members of his immediate coterie—Martin Bormann, Joseph Goebbels, and Heinrich Himmler, mainly—were able to exercise reasonably free and unrestrained rule; yet even they were not entirely free, for they remained in positions of unquestioning obedience to the commands of Hitler. During the early years of the Third Reich, there was also a facade of apparently democratic procedures that were consistent with the provisions of the Weimar Constitution. Thus, for example, there were several nationwide elections, but despite the large turnout of voters and the overwhelming support for the National Socialist Party, these elections were thoroughly manipulated by Hitler and his staff through their exclusive command of the radio and most newspapers, and their ability to assemble at a moment's notice large rallies of supporters.

An important part of the Nazi regime in Germany were the organs of the party and the state that were designed to combat the internal enemies; these agencies included the Gestapo, or secret police, and the S.S. troops under the authority of Heinrich Himmler. Both agencies were employed as means for combating dissent and for eliminating the enemies of the state, particularly Jews. The S.S. troops, in particular, assumed responsibility for the administration of death camps.

Ideological Foundations. One of the most visible and unique features of Hitler's totalitarian dictatorship was its ideology, an assortment of myths that were transplanted, in toto, from the declarations Hitler had earlier set out in his autobiography, *Mein Kampf*. Hitler and the National Socialists dispensed a doctrine of racial and national dogma that established the myth of the Aryan race as world saviors and made Jews appear as the scum of the earth; moreover, they sought and gained widespread popular acceptance of this doctrine. After 1938 these principles became transformed into actual practices of the Nazi regime, first through random terror committed against Jews inside Germany—as, for example, during Kristallnacht—and later through the terror organized under the auspices of the concentration camps and the wartime hostilities undertaken against many nations.

Social Foundations. In their effort to secure total commitment and obedience from the people, totalitarian regimes literally seek to declassify citizens. Upon their accession to positions of leadership in the German government, for example, the National Socialist Party leaders, through their practices of terror, tried to eliminate the many diverse social groups that existed during the Weimar Republic. Trade unions, for one, were eliminated and replaced by the Labor Front, which simply became an organized means for the National Socialist Party to manipulate the interests and lives of the workers. Except in a few instances, independent news media were either destroyed or taken over by the party. The churches remained more or less institutionally intact, but priests became the object of intense and unremitting attacks by members of the Nazi regime. In place of older organizations, new ones arose under the management of the National Socialist Party; thus, for instance, Nazi youth groups designed to socialize young Germans in the new, official system of thought were developed in large numbers. Symbolic of this gigantic program to design German society anew were the mass rallies that took place in the early years of the Third Reich; in those that occurred in Nuremberg, for example, thousands of people were arrayed across the floor on the arena—attentive, obedient, and absolutely mesmerized by Hitler.

Economic Foundations. Many analysts characterize the totalitarian economy as a command economy, noting such particulars about its structure as the regular plans for its expansion—five-year programs in the Soviet Union, four-year plans in Nazi Germany—the regimentation of the labor force, the special organization of the industrial plants, and the centralized form of planning concerning the budget and industrial output. These characteristics, like others, matured more fully in the former Soviet Union than they did in Nazi Germany; moreover, it is difficult to know precisely how the German economy might have performed under extended peacetime circumstances, since Germany went to war in 1939, only six years after the inception of Nazi rule. During its brief existence, however, the German economy actually comprised two different sectors: (1) the command sector that was controlled through the National Socialist Party and state administrations; (2) the large private sector that comprised many cartels in manufacturing and other forms of industry.[26]

This brief description naturally cannot do full justice to the range and depth of the features of different totalitarian societies; hence, I urge you to consult other materials on Nazi Germany as well as to consult discussions in later chapters of this book concerning such nations as the former Soviet Union. Nonetheless, the overview here helps to introduce two of the most prominent features of totalitarian regimes—the elimination of all autonomous institutions of the civil society, thus leaving the distinction between the public and private realms absolutely meaningless, and the genuine dominance of the party, its leaders and ideology, over all other institutions of the society. This last point, in particular, seems to render Marxist interpretations of Nazi Germany fundamentally incorrect; Hitler's dictatorship effectively supplanted all of the conventional features and processes of a capitalist economy with an administration less driven by economic doctrines than by national and racial dogma. These latter doctrines represented the motive force behind the establishment and short-lived reign of the Third Reich.

There is one nation today that most closely fits the defining features of totalitarian regimes, that of the People's Republic of China. China appears to fit most of the features associated with the concept, for example, a complete and total control of the country by the Communist Party, including all major institutions, ranging from the educational to the religious. However, China is today engaged in a massive experiment designed to discover whether a country tightly controlled by its leadership from the top can also become open to the introduction of major economic reforms from below. In the past decade there have been major reforms in the economy, resulting in the introduction of many foreign companies. In addition, the government has engaged in an effort to produce massive investment in its Special Economic Zones, a range of regions on the Southeastern border of the country that includes Hong Kong. Whether, and how, these economic transformations can influence the control of the Party remains to be seen. So far, however, the Party seems to have effectively walked the tightrope between its economic reform measures, which have loosened its control over industries and even over regions, and the demand, mainly from abroad, for more democracy and freedom for its citizens.

Authoritarianism

One of the problems that now confronts analysts of political rule is how to depict regimes that are neither totalitarian, in the classic sense of the Soviet Union or Nazi Germany, nor democratic, in the sense of the United States or Great Britain. There are many such forms of political rule today, and many seem to resemble nothing so much as the rule of absolute dictators. Examples easily come to mind. Consider the case of Mommar Khadaffi in Libya. He rules his country with an iron fist, controls and is backed by a loyal military, and has the admiration of most of his countrymen. Then there is the more notorious case of Saddam Hussein in Iraq. He obviously does not preside over a democratic society, is in firm control of the military, and also appears to have secured, somehow, the loyalty of his fellow citizens. Both rulers exercise their power as virtual dictators, but their regimes also lack some critical features of totalitarian rule, such as the reign of continuous terror against their enemies and the absence of a single political party in which authority and power actually are lodged. And there are countless other examples—governments that are clearly not totalitarian but lack the features of democratic regimes such as regular elections and widespread civil liberties.

Analysts have puzzled over these different forms of rule for years and have tried to capture their most essential features, especially as compared to democratic and totalitarian regimes. Years ago, the sociologist Edward Shils wrote of different kinds of oligarchies, drawing on the classic Greek distinction.[27] He suggested that in many of the developing nations of the world there was a tendency for the leadership to rule in a very authoritative fashion, in part because such nations, if they were to advance economically, almost required absolute political control by their leaders. Identifying such forms of rule as oligarchies, Shils distinguished among different types. They included tutelary democracies, in which there is both a concentration of power among the leaders and representative parliaments, and traditional oligarchies, characteristic of many African nations, in which leadership is run through tribal councils and there are very few of the elements of either advanced democratic countries or totalitarian ones.

Shils' distinctions draw attention to two special features of many of the regimes in the developing countries of the world: (1) the tendency for leaders to govern in an almost dictatorial fashion; and (2) the effort by these same leaders to promote the economic development of their countries. It is precisely these two features that have prompted today's scholars to conceive of a third form of political rule, one they believe lies somewhere between that of democratic and totalitarian regimes. It is called *authoritarianism*, and in the original words of the inventor of the concept, Juan Linz, it refers to

> . . . limited, not responsible, political pluralism—without elaborate and guiding ideology (but with distinctive mentalities); without intensive nor extensive political mobilization (except at some points in their development); and in which the leader (or occasionally a small group) exercises power within formally ill-defined limits but actually quite predictable ones.[28]

Linz developed the concept especially to apply to the regime of General Francisco Franco in Spain, for he believed that the regime was certainly not democratic, but that it also did not exhibit many of the excesses of the totalitarian governments of Hitler or Stalin.

Since Linz offered his original definition, the concept of authoritarianism has become further refined. Analysts point out, for example, that there are authoritarian regimes that are deeply populist: they cultivate the sentiments of and are much admired by the mass of citizens. An example would be that of Juan Peron in Argentina. Perhaps even the regime of Saddam Hussein today would qualify for such a description. In a recent study of the links between capitalism and the development of different kinds of political regimes, Dietrich Rueschemeyer, Evelyne Stephens, and John Stephens refine the notion of authoritarianism. They take it to mean, in general, those regimes that lack regular, free and fair elections of representatives with universal and equal suffrage, and a state apparatus which is responsible to an elected parliament.[29]

Over the past two decades, the most widely used conception of an authoritarian regime has been that of Guillermo O'Donnell. He developed a concept he called a *bureaucratic authoritarian* regime.[30] He meant by the term the following elements: (1) the exercise of political rule by a small group of leaders, often backed by the military; (2) the reliance of the political rulers also on a large group of technical personnel (technocrats), who exercise much of the day-to-day control over the operations of the society; (3) an effort to promote the economic growth of the society, in part as a response to a period of economic stagnation; (4) the extensive repression of the various classes in the society, especially the rising and expanding middle class. O'Donnell invented the term to depict a situation he had witnessed both in Argentina and in Brazil during the 1960s and 1970s—countries that had experienced rapid economic growth but in which the political leadership, rather than promoting and developing the institutions of civil society, sought to repress them.

The notion of bureaucratic-authoritarianism, while useful to depicting the often unstable governments in a number of advanced Latin American countries, also has been applied to nations outside of Latin America. Some have perceived somewhat similar regimes in the great economic advances made by the nations of Taiwan, South Korea, Singapore, and Hong Kong, the "four little dragons."[31] Like Brazil and Argentina, these places had experienced considerable economic success, but they did so at the expense of the civil liberties and exercise of freedom by their citizens. In fact, while there was great improvement in the economic fortunes of these countries as a whole, there was also considerable economic inequality, the lower classes and poor citizens suffering immense hardship while the wealthy accumulated much of the gains.[32]

Regardless of which precise term one uses, it is plainly evident that a number of the governments in today's nations are run by leaders who seek to exercise a very tight control both over the direction of governmental policy and the expression of free opinions by citizens. In many cases, such control is justified by leaders who claim they want to advance the fortunes of their country and insist that the only way to do so is to have absolute power, free from the interference of meddling parliaments or citizens. What remains to be seen is whether such regimes can endure over a long period of time. Like the charisma of authority, the success of authoritarian regimes pretty much depends on the success of their individual leaders and their allies. Once Franco died, for example, Spain became a more open and resilient political system. And, since the late 1980s, the exercise of authority in South Korea has also become more democratic.

The other, and equally pressing, issue is whether such regimes might make a transition to more democratic forms of rule, as in Spain or South Korea, or whether they will swing in the opposite direction, becoming more totalitarian. This is the difficult question facing many of the regimes in Eastern Europe and the former Soviet Union. What may decide the outcome in the end is the health and success of their economies, always a decisive factor. If the Eastern European countries can achieve growth and prosperity, this could reduce the tendency to revert to the totalitarian governments of the past half century or more, thus promoting more open and democratic governments. And yet, as the cases of Argentina and Brazil both illustrate, such success may in fact require an ever tighter control on both the citizenry and the economy from the top, a kind of control that is only a short step from the long arm of totalitarianism.

CONCLUSION

In the coming decades, there will be one issue that will face many of the world's nations—the issue of whether they will make a transition from authoritarian regimes either to democratic or to totalitarian ones. Authoritarian regimes, it seems clear, are both intermediate forms and transitional ones. They tend not to be stable over the long run. Even within the span of a single regime, as in the case of Argentina, authoritarianism can become transformed into a ruthless purge and search for the regime's enemies. The most glaring and horrendous example of such a regime in recent memory is that of Pol Pot in Cambodia in the 1970s, the scourge which became known as "the killing fields."

As we have pointed out, there are many pitfalls and quandaries that face the developing nations of the world. Most regimes want to make the great economic leap forward, but it almost is impossible to do so unless there is some considerable concentration of power among the leadership of the country. But once such power becomes concentrated, there can be a tendency for power to wish to perpetuate itself in office; power does not necessarily always corrupt but it is nevertheless a very seductive force for many officials. The problems become even more difficult as the global economy expands. Firms wish to deploy their capital funds in ways that will be most profitable, and many will search to invest them in the developing markets of the world. But if the regimes in those markets are unstable, then the very volatility of the market itself can further destabilize the regimes.

Francis Fukayama, in his famous thesis about the "end of history," suggested that with the collapse of communism, capitalism was on the way to achieving its hegemony as the reigning economic system of the world. Fukayama may have been premature. It is one thing for communism to collapse, quite another for it to be replaced by a stable democratic system. Indeed, it is likely that the pressures for the developing economies to swing back to some form of authoritative regime—whether authoritarian or totalitarian—will be very great in coming years. The recent chaos in Russia, as well as in other Eastern European nations, provides evidence of such pressures. And similar pressures are likely to be found in Southeast Asia as well as in many Latin American nations.

NOTES

1. Aristotle, *The Politics of Aristotle,* translated by Ernest Barker (London: Oxford University Press, 1975), III, IV, and V.
2. Aristotle, *Politics,* 127.
3. The reader must remember that Aristotle, like other Greek philosophers, did not make a distinction between idealized visions constructed for the purposes of realizing a certain moral aim and idealized visions constructed to achieve certain analytical goals. In other words, Aristotle drew a distinction only between the ideal and the real, whereas today we distinguish between the ideal in moral terms, the ideal in analytical terms—for instance, Weber's notion of the Protestant ethic and Marx's notion of capitalism—and the real. Thus, when Aristotle wrote of the ideal set of constitutional orders, he wrote of a moral vision; when he described the debased set, he spoke both of an unjust and a

more realistic portrait of their character. This may explain why Aristotle spent so much more of his effort in *Politics* writing of the nonideal polities; he simply meant to concede that they represented those forms more likely to achieve realization in ancient Greece.

4. Aristotle, *Politics,* II, Chapter 9.
5. Ibid., 123.
6. Ibid., 178.
7. Leonard Whibley, *Greek Oligarchies: Their Character and Organization* (New York: G.P. Putnam's Sons, 1896), 144.
8. For interesting observations on the matter of size and the character of the body politic, see Robert A. Dahl and Edward R. Tufte, *Size and Democracy* (Stanford: Stanford University Press, 1973).
9. For writings that illustrate these themes, see Jean Jacques Rousseau, "The Social Contract," in *The Essential Rousseau,* translated by Lowell Bair (New York: New American Library, 1974), 1-124, and John Stuart Mill, "On Liberty" and "Representative Government," in *Utilitarianism, Liberty, and Representative Government* (New York: E.P. Dutton and Co., 1951), 81–229, 231–532.
10. John Dewey, "Democracy as a Way of Life," in *Frontiers of Democratic Theory,* ed. Henry Kariel (New York: Random House, Inc., 1970), 15.
11. Hannah Arendt, "On Public Happiness," in *The Frontiers of Democratic Theory,* ed. Kariel, 5. This very short condensation of the utopian vision, in addition to having been based upon the writings of Rousseau and Mill, was aided in its formulation by several important secondary analyses of these matters. In particular, the reader is urged to examine the following excellent studies: Graeme Duncan and Steven Lukes, "The New Democracy," *Political Studies,* II (1963), 156–77; Lane Davis, "The Cost of Realism: Contemporary Restatements of Democracy," *Western Political Quarterly,* 17 (1964), 37–46; Kariel, *The Frontiers of Democratic Theory;* Carole Pateman, *Participation and Democratic Theory* (Cambridge: Cambridge University Press, 1970), Chapter 2 especially; and Dennis F. Thompson, *The Democratic Citizen* (Cambridge: Cambridge University Press, 1970).
12. Benjamin R. Barber, *Strong Democracy: Participatory Politics for a New Age* (Berkeley: University of California Press, 1984).
13. Ibid., 151.
14. Ibid., 261.
15. Joshua Cohen, "Deliberation and Democratic Legitimacy," in *Deliberative Democracy: Essays on Reason and Politics,* eds. James Bohman and William Rehg (Cambridge, Mass.: the MIT Press, 1997). See also the various other illuminating essays in this original and thoughtful work.
16. See, for example, Jürgen Habermas, *Between Facts and Norms: Contributions to a Discourse Theory of Law and Democracy,* translated by W. Rehg (Cambridge, Mass.: the MIT Press, 1996).
17. Cohen, op. cit., 72.
18. Bernard Berelson, "Democratic Practice and Democratic Theory," in *Voting,* ed. Bernard Berelson, Paul Lazarsfeld, and William McPhee (Chicago: University

of Chicago Press, 1954), 305–23; Robert A. Dahl, *Who Governs? Democracy and Power in an American City* (New Haven, Conn.: Yale University Press, 1971); Robert A. Dahl, *Polyarchy: Participation and Opposition* (New Haven, Conn.: Yale University Press, 1971), Chapter 1; Giovanni Sartori, *Democratic Theory* (New York: Frederick A. Praeger, 1965); and Joseph Schumpeter, *Capitalism, Socialism and Democracy,* 3rd ed. (New York: Harper & Row Publishers, 1962), 21.

19. Schumpeter, *Capitalism, Socialism, and Democracy,* 3rd ed., 269.
20. Berelson et al., 318–19.
21. There has been a good deal of recent discussion among scholars of the comparative strengths and weaknesses of parliamentary and presidential democracies. Much of the discussion was stimulated by an article by Juan Linz in which he argues that parliamentary democracies have decided advantages over presidential ones. Among other things, he observes, presidential democracies can result in a stalemate of power if the president and the congress are from different political parties; parliamentary democracies can more easily resolve differences because the leader of the victorious party also becomes the prime minister, and head of government. See, Juan J. Linz and Arturo Valenzuela, eds., *The Failure of Presidential Democracy* (Baltimore, Maryland: Johns Hopkins University Press, 1994).
22. This portrait of democratic societies is based upon a large number and wide variety of materials—too many, in fact, to cite here easily. Some of the broader treatments include: Robert A. Dahl, ed., *Political Oppositions in Western Democracies* (New Haven, Connecticut: Yale University Press, 1966); Robert A. Dahl, *Polyarchy: Participation and Opposition;* Leon D. Epstein, *Political Parties in Western Democracies* (New York: Frederick A. Praeger, Publishers, 1967), Chapters 1–4; and Edward Shils, *Political Development in New States* (The Hague: Mouton, 1962).
23. For somewhat different definitions of this concept, compare the following works: Hannah Arendt, *The Origins of Totalitarianism* (Cleveland, Ohio: World Publishing Co., 1958); Benjamin R. Barber, "Conceptual Foundations of Totalitarianism," in *Totalitarianism in Perspective: Three Views,* ed. Carl J. Friedrich, Michael Curtis, and Benjamin R. Barber (New York: Praeger Publishers, 1969), 3–39; and Carl J. Friedrich and Zbigniew K. Brzezinski, *Totalitarian Dictatorship and Autocracy,* 2nd ed. rev., by Carl J. Friedrich (Cambridge, Mass.: Harvard University Press, 1965), Chapter 1 especially.
24. For one observer who found the difference to be highly significant, see Barrington Moore, Jr., *Social Origins of Dictatorship and Democracy: Lord and Peasant in the Making of the Modern World* (Boston: Beacon Press, 1975), Chapters 7–9 especially.
25. Friedrich and Brzezinski, *Totalitarian Dictatorship and Autocracy,* Chapter 2.
26. This portrait of totalitarian regimes, with special attention to the Third Reich, is based upon the following sources: Hannah Arendt, *The Origins of Totalitarianism,* Part 3 especially; Lucy S. Dawidowicz, *The War Against the Jews: 1933–1945* (New York: Holt, Rinehart and Winston, 1975), Part 1; Joachim C. Fest, *Hitler,* trans. Richard and Clara Winston (New York: Avon Books, 1971), Parts 5–8 especially; Carl J. Friedrich and Zbigniew K. Brzezinski, *Totalitarian*

Dictatorship and Autocracy; Adolf Hitler, *Mein Kampf,* translated by Ralph Manheim (Boston: Houghton Mifflin Company, 1971), Vol. 1, Chapter 11 especially; Helmut Krausnick et al., *Anatomy of the SS State,* translated by Richard Barry et al. (Collins: London, 1968), especially Chapters 2–3; Franz Neumann, *Behemoth* (New York: Oxford University Press, 1952); and Albert Speer, *Inside the Third Reich,* translated by Richard and Clara Winston (New York: Avon Books, 1971), Parts 2–3 especially.

27. Edward Shils, *Political Development in New States.*
28. Juan J. Linz, "An Authoritarian Regime: Spain," in *Cleavages, Ideologies and Party Systems: Contributions to Comparative Political Sociology,* ed. Erik Allardt and Yrjo Littunen (Helsinki: the Academic Bookstore, 1964), 297.
29. Dietrich Rueschemeyer, Evelyne Huber Stephens, and John D. Stephens, *Capitalist Development and Democracy* (Chicago: University of Chicago Press, 1992), 43–44.
30. Guillermo O'Donnell, *Modernization and Bureaucratic-Authoritarianism: Studies in South American Politics* (Berkeley: Institute of International Studies, University of California, 1973; 1979). Also see his more recent excellent collection of essays, *Counterpoints: Selected Essays on Authoritarianism and Democratization* (Notre Dame, Indiana: University of Notre Dame Press, 1999).
31. Ezra F. Vogel, *The Four Little Dragons: The Spread of Industrialization in East Asia* (Cambridge, Massachusetts: Harvard University Press, 1991). Hong Kong was part of the British Commonwealth until 1999, when Britain transferred its authority over Hong Kong to the People's Republic of China.
32. Frederic C. Deyo, *Beneath the Miracle: Labor Subordination in the New Asian Industrialism* (Berkeley: University of California Press, 1989).

Chapter 6

Power and Equality in Modern America

The business of America is business.
Calvin Coolidge

Writing in the nineteenth century, Karl Marx offered us the first view of how power might operate in a large and growing industrial society. He insisted that capitalism was the foundation of the growth and development of modern societies, and that the arm of the state under capitalism served mainly to promote the interests of capitalists, that is, of business and industry. The capitalists had become a ruling class; they not only controlled the operations of the economy, but they also controlled those of the state. Thus, they, or their agents, made policies and decisions that in the long run would benefit their interests and secure their dominance over the rest of society.

Marx's view had an elegance and a ring of truth to it, so much so that even today, a century and one-half later, many still believe this is the way the world of power and politics operates. But not everyone does. And what we, as students of politics, must do is to consider the evidence about power with great care and decide whether the view of Marx or someone else might be correct. The object of political sociology, here as elsewhere, must be to develop empirically grounded theory and then to subject it to careful and thorough empirical scrutiny.

In this chapter I will review the evidence we have today about the nature and operations of power in America. Twenty years ago, when I wrote the first edition of this book, this chapter looked very different from the one you are about to read. At a minimum, the research and hard work of political sociologists in this most difficult of intellectual terrain has come far and made some clear advances. The chapter will consider these themes: (1) the nature of the government, or state as I shall call it, and some of the important variations among states; (2) the nature of the modern economy, particularly the modern corporation, and its power; and (3) issues of economic inequality and political equality in contemporary America.

At the end, I hope you will ask yourself: Is there an answer to the question of who holds and exercises power in America? I believe there is one, but it is a bit complicated, like all such matters. I hope to show you that while America clearly possesses a democratic state, of the form we discussed at length in the last chapter, such a state operates in ways that run counter to our general sense of what democracy is all about.

PROLOGUE

At the risk of complicating a fluent narrative, I will make a brief detour at the start to provide you with a short history of the debates and issues that have surrounded the study of power in America. My rendition will show you where the field has come as well as how it has arrived here. Moreover, this tale also is essential to understanding how political sociologists approach the study of power in America today—in particular, what issues remain alive for them and what issues no longer are relevant. Some of their concerns, you will see, draw freely on the writings and ideas of Karl Marx, Max Weber, and Alexis de Tocqueville.

For as long as Americans have thought and written about power, there have been debates about what it looks like and how it operates. Many scholars–and members of the lay public, too—preferred to take American democracy at its word. They emphasized the underlying values of American democracy, and how the processes and debates of politics actually favored the workings of democratic government. Democracy was rooted, it was thought, in the very nature of a system of checks-and-balances, the design of government that was created by the framers of the Constitution. Three different branches of government exist—an executive, a legislative, and a judicial–and each pursues a separate task of governance—to make policy, to debate policy, and to make judgments about the implementation of policy.

Still there always have been dissenters from the dominant view of American democracy. There have been those who do not take the system at its word, who believe there are forces that operate behind the scenes, as it were. Some dissenters, for instance, have drawn explicitly, or implicitly, on the writings of Karl Marx. One such dissenter was the famous economic historian, Charles Beard, who believed that the economic foundations of American society actually held the key to the operations of government. Beard pursued this thesis in a number of ways, including a famous book in which he insisted that the Constitution of the United States was a flawed and biased document precisely because most of the framers of the Constitution were themselves wealthy plantation owners and businessmen.[1] How, then, he asked, could they possibly create a government that would be impartial to their interests?

The debates over the nature of American democracy continued beyond Beard, but the dominant view always remained more or less intact. Democratic politics was to be taken at its face value. It was a matter of give-and-take, negotiations, the workings of the different branches of government, each pursuing its own task, until, in the end, the process resulted in policies and actions that favored the interests of the majority of Americans.

At roughly mid-twentieth century, the intensity of the debate heated up. Fresh from a victory over Germany, Japan, and Italy in World War II, Americans returned home from the war and began to work hard at moving themselves ahead. Work was on their minds, but politics was, too. Although America and its allies had won the war, there were important new political alliances and divisions that had been created. The most important division was created by the rise of the Soviet Union and Communist China to new roles as players in world politics. "An iron curtain," had been dropped across part of the world, in Winston Churchill's famous words delivered in 1946, one that would not only divide nations, but also Americans one against another. In America, at the end of the 1940s, a new movement began under the name of McCarthyism, a movement led by Congressman Joseph McCarthy of Wisconsin that was intended to root out Communists and other fellow-travelers in the United States. The movement would divide Americans against one another and result in the tragic and premature end to the careers of many highly successful people. The effect was not only to destroy the careers of many Americans, but also to act to stifle dissent in the United States.

It did anything but stifle dissent. Among social scientists, two different views came to prevail about the nature of American democracy. One, authored by the political scientist Robert Dahl, insisted that the nature of American democracy was such that every dominant group played a role in the game of politics, and that the rules of the game permitted and sustained an equal participation of their roles. Dahl's view, which came to be known as the pluralist view of American politics, articulated the dominant, mainstream interpretation of politics for Americans. It was a view that was elegantly expressed and that, owing to the research by Dahl and his research assistants, was supported by evidence showing, among other things, that on different political issues, different parties came to the table to play, no one party being more dominant than another.[2]

At about the same time, another, and very different, perspective was offered on the nature of American politics. Though various forms of Marxist analyses of American democracy had been around ever since Beard, and even before, the new view represented a radical departure from the past. This new view was advanced by C. Wright Mills, a young sociologist from Texas who would die prematurely at the age of 46 in 1961. Mills argued, in effect, that American democracy was something of a sham.[3] Politics did not allow everyone an equal opportunity to participate. Some people possessed and exercised much more power than others; they, in effect, were the ones who made decisions that controlled and directed the lives of other Americans. And there was little Americans could do about such matters, in large part because of the origins and positions of those in power. There were three critical axes to this new coalition of power, which Mills called "the power elite": big business, or corporations; the leading military officials, especially members of the Joint Chiefs of Staff of the military; and the members of the executive branch of government. Americans could only choose one part of this "power elite," the figure who sat in the White House. They certainly could not determine the people who ran the corporations, nor could they select the high-ranking members of the military.

Mills's view was to become popular among younger Americans, especially those just off to college. Just as Dahl's view possessed a *prima facie* element of truth, so too did that of Mills. The President of the United States, after all, was a great military hero, Dwight D. Eisenhower, who led the American troops during World War II. Many of the men who served in his Cabinet had been members of leading business firms and corporations prior to their service in government. Moreover, it also appeared true, as Mills argued, that power had moved from Main Street to Wall Street and to 1600 Pennsylvania Avenue—and, in particular, that it was the federal government, both under the New Deal administration of Franklin Delano Roosevelt and then under Eisenhower, that was making the key decisions over the lives of Americans. For many Americans, these were important issues, yet for the great majority, such issues did not matter as they worked hard to support young families and to furnish their new homes in the suburbs.

To sociologists, the debate raged on between the proponents of the Dahl, or pluralist, view of American politics, and the proponents of the Mills, or elitist, view. Each camp was able to assemble an arsenal of evidence to support its own view. Over the course of the late 1950s and early 1960s, the Dahl camp was able to assemble evidence that showed how different groups came to play prominent roles in urban politics. Using research studies from work in New Haven, New York, Chicago, and other cities, the pluralists gradually accumulated a great deal of evidence to support their perspective.[4] The adherents of the Mills view also accumulated evidence, plus a great deal of new enthusiasm for the work by some younger sociologists, who, locked in their own debate with government about the War in Vietnam, came to believe deeply and firmly in the truth of Mills's view.

By the early 1970s, the debate had become something of a stalemate, each side claiming a kind of intellectual victory. But then the grounds of the debate began to shift, and new angles were taken on the matter of power in America. A version of the Mills's thesis began to circulate that insisted that America was run not merely by a power elite, but by a ruling class. Advanced by the sociologist, Ralph Miliband, (see Chapter 2), it argued that those people who held high political office in America represented, in effect, agents of the ruling class, or capitalists. Therefore, it could be expected that their views and decisions over policy would ultimately advantage business in America—as clearly they seemed to do based upon the various government policies made over the course of the 1950s, 1960s, and 1970s. Another neo-Marxist view at the time was that of the economists Paul Baran and Paul Sweezy.[5] They argued that America had reached a new phase in its development, that of "monopoly capitalism." Among other things, this meant that the structure of the country was designed to favor the interests of the dominant corporate monopolies, and to do so by engaging in wars abroad to promote and extend the economic power of these corporations.

One other view also emerged, representing yet a different twist on the nature of politics. It was the view of the French sociologist, Nicos Poulantzas (see Chapter 2). He insisted that the structures of the state actually had, in effect, taken on a life of their own, thus becoming "relatively autonomous" from control by members of the ruling class, or capitalists. The state advanced the interests of the capitalists, or businessmen and women, in America in a way that did not require the continuous, or even periodic, oversight by the capitalists themselves. In other words, it no longer mattered who held office on Pennsylvania Avenue, because it was the office, not the occupant, that mattered. What gave Poulantzas's argument a special appeal to sociologists was that his view accorded with the deepest dictates of the discipline—that it was the institution and the office, *not the individual occupant*, that mattered in the long-run operations of all institutions, whether they be political, business, or otherwise.

We thus arrive at today's platform from which to view power in America. The debate between the pluralists and the elitists is effectively moribund. Although there are elements of the pluralist view that still have a ring of truth to them, as, for example, that there are different players in politics in America, there is very little evidence today to support the main tenets of this view. Granted that the broad legal and historic outlines of the American state remain democratic, almost all political sociologists seem to agree that some players are simply much more powerful in the game of politics than other players, though they disagree on the precise reasons for their power. Many agree that the federal government is a key player in the structure of American power, if only because of the resources it controls and can manipulate. In addition, major corporations remain key players in American politics, again because of the resources they control. In general, there also has been a shift away from identifying individuals as the loci of the exercise of power to viewing organizations and broad institutions as the loci of such power. This shift is in keeping with the growing emphasis among sociologists on the significance of the concepts of social networks and institutions.

Three specific views today dominate the writings of students of power in America. The first is what we might call the *dominant*, or *ruling, class* view, a variant on the original conception of Karl Marx.[6] It claims that the critical decisions in America are more or less made and dominated by an upper class of people, who serve on the boards of major corporations, intermarry with one another, go to school with one another, and the like. The second is what has been called an *institutional elite* model, so coined by the sociologist G. William Domhoff. It argues that it is the people who occupy the positions of great authority in major institutions in America that control the dominant decisions of the society, and that such institutions include both those in the federal government and in major corporations. The third is the *state-centered* view of American politics. It originated with the important work of sociologist Theda Skocpol (see Chapter 3). It argues that the state is actually the main locus of power, and that the individuals who occupy the major positions in the state, such as the President and his advisors, act in decisive and deliberate fashion to further the interests of the state, not those of capitalists *per se*.[7] In matters of power, in the game of politics within America and in dealings with other nations, it is the decisions of those who are in the government that really matter, according to Skocpol, not those of the members of the upper class. Such decisions, Skocpol appears to suggest, spring not from the class or other background interests of those in government, but from the immediate organizational dictates and broad policies of the state itself.

Our discussion in this chapter about matters of power in America today will be guided by the general focus provided by these three views and by the evidence, much of it quite sophisticated, assembled by their proponents. As to which of the views is most correct, that is another matter. But let us first review the evidence on the main lines of the arguments that follow, and then return at various points in the chapter to reassess the key questions of power, and of democracy, in modern America.

THE POWER OF THE AMERICAN STATE

The American state, as compared to other states, is defined as a weak system.[8] By this analysts mean that American government lacks the same degree of centralization of authority and decision making so characteristic of European democracies. In England, for example, the authority of the government is concentrated in the hands of the national government at Westminster. The national government makes decisions over the most important matters of taxation and revenues, schooling, and public buildings, where local governments have a limited authority to spend and disburse funds on such matters as local public housing. In France, too, the authority is concentrated in the hands of the national government, and provincial governments exercise only limited authority over issues of concern to the public. The centralization of authority in the governments of these nations, and in those of other European countries as well, have roots in the far distant past, dating back to the seventeenth century.

The American state, by comparison, has from its founding and in the terms of the Constitution been one in which the authority to make policy is divided and dispersed among different agencies and branches. There is, first, the system of checks-and-balances, produced by the three different branches of government. In addition, and equally important, power also is dispersed among different levels of government—the federal government in Washington, the state governments of the fifty states, and the local governments of the many municipalities. Such a system of federated government has resulted in a kind of dilution of central power, purposefully limiting throughout much its history the ability of the federal government to exercise authority over the lives of American citizens. On matters of school funding, for example, both state and local authorities make the critical decisions. On issues of public spending for parks and for police and fire departments, it also is the local and state authorities that have the final say. This dispersal of authority is written into the very nature of the American Constitution, and thus sets limits on what the federal government can and cannot do.

Yet while the rules and regulations produce considerable dispersion of authority among different agencies and across different levels of government, over time there has been a *de facto* growth of authority in the hands of the federal government. Local governments began as the real centers of authority in America, creating a kind of system that can best be described as a *bottom-up* rather than a *top-down* democracy. The achievements and accomplishments that were made by government, especially in nineteenth-century America, often were the achievements of local or state governments. Critical decisions were made about such matters as schools, or railroads, or other modes of transportation, and such decisions frequently were made, and had the force of binding authority, by local and state officials. But as the nineteenth century unfolded, the character and locus of power began to shift, from the local levels to the state and thence to the federal level of government.

The political scientist, Stephen Skowronek, in a masterful work, characterizes this period in the development of the American state not as one of weakness, but as one in which the "courts and parties" exercised great control.[9] Such a state, he finds, had its beginnings in the nineteenth century when both the judiciary and the political parties were the dominant players in the lawmaking and decisions taken by the federal government. For example, even after the Pendleton Act of 1883, which would make merit the primary qualification for the holding of a civil service appointment, political parties continued to play a central role in helping to determine who the potential occupants for such offices would be. The courts likewise exercised a great influence over the manner of federal policymaking, not merely helping to interpret the law but also acting as active arbiters in establishing the substantive nature of law itself. The American state, in Skowroneck's view, ultimately came to represent a special historical/cultural mix of tendencies built into the Constitution and of the needs for an expanding society to provide governmental decisions over a broad range of issues and a wide expanse of territory. It was not a weak state, so much in his view, as a state whose hands were tied by the penetration of the forces on behalf of courts and parties into its innermost workings. Moreover, as America was buffeted by the winds of industrialization, winds that would demand a centralization of authority, the state changed, but in ways that continued to reveal the deep imprint left on it by the power both of the courts and of the two dominant political parties.

The most dramatic period in the centralization and concentration of authority in the hands of the federal government (what Skowronek refers to as the "national state") took place during the course of the Roosevelt Administration from 1933 to 1945. Stimulated largely by the economic devastation of the Great Depression and, then, by entrance into World War II, the Roosevelt Administration was able to develop a degree of authority unmatched by any other Presidential Administration. Here I will review a few general details about Roosevelt and the power of the Executive branch of government in America. I shall also consider several other key agencies of the federal government—the military, the CIA, and the FBI. This review will cover some of the key episodes in the growth of power in the federal government and will introduce us to a central, if not the central, aspect of the federal government—the state as a war-maker.

The American State as a War-Making State

The Executive Branch. Franklin Delano Roosevelt was a figure of enormous charisma and equally unbounded ambition. He and his administration managed during his tenure in office to initiate a number of federal programs that eventually served to reshape the links between the federal government, the world of business, and the broader public. Under his administration, for example, there came into existence the Social Security program in 1935, the Tennessee Valley Authority in 1933, and a host of general welfare programs designed to extricate the United States from the depths of the Great Depression. Under Roosevelt, too, owing both to the circumstances of the Depression as well as to the Second World War, the Congress seemed to become less and less an equal partner in the operations of the federal government. Roosevelt's influence, because of his special gifts of communication, extended well beyond the confines of 1600 Pennsylvania Avenue. Thus, during the 1930s he managed to fashion a structure of partisan loyalties and identities in the United States that would not disappear for at least another thirty years.

Yet, Roosevelt was only the first of several presidents to have succeeded in expanding the power and influence of the presidency, though he surely was one of the most skillful. Owing in part to the more aggressive role the United States sought in world affairs during as well as after World War II, the incumbents of the presidency came increasingly to make decisions that had worldwide, not to say historic, significance. Harry Truman made the decision to drop the atomic bombs both on Hiroshima and Nagasaki, acts that set into motion an entirely new understanding of the meaning of war and human violence. John Foster Dulles, Dwight Eisenhower's Secretary of State, made decisions that reshaped the nature of the balance of power in the Middle East, and with it the relations between the United States and the Soviet Union as well

During the presidential administrations of Kennedy, Johnson, and Nixon, observers agree, the power of the presidency truly came into its own. During this period, which began with the Kennedy administration in 1960, the United States government sought to extend its influence abroad, creating new alliances in Asia, Africa, as well as with the Latin American nations. In 1960, for example, the Organization of American States was created under the initiative of the Kennedy administration. Ostensibly designed to furnish American aid to the Latin American countries and to solidify the American alliance in the north and south, many observers saw the OAS in truth merely as a device to extend and to protect American political and economic interests in Latin America.[10] The Peace Corps, too, was an innovation of the Kennedy administration, apparently created to furnish aid to citizens of other countries with no strings attached; yet, once more, from another angle observers saw it as simply a means of extending the hegemony of American political power abroad. In addition, there was the famous abortive Bay of Pigs invasion of 1962, taken under the initiative of the Kennedy administration. Carried out with the cooperation of the Central Intelligence Agency (CIA), it marked still another attempt by the American president and his counselors to extend American influence beyond the shores of the United States.

The event that decisively contributed to the growth in the power and influence of the president and his counselors, to the development, in the words of Arthur Schlesinger, Jr., of an "Imperial Presidency," was the Vietnam War.[11] To all outward appearances, the United States government should have had little, if any, interest in Vietnam. Here, after all, was a country in the midst of an internal conflict, a war that had only a decade earlier led to the humiliating defeat of France. It was a country thousands of miles from the shores of the United States; yet, for some reason only later to be clarified, the president and his counselors believed it necessary to introduce American troops into the struggle. Hence, in 1963, the United States commenced to increase aid to the tottering Diem regime in South Vietnam. With the assassination of President Kennedy, and after winning election on a platform in which he condemned his opponent for his trigger-happy intentions in Vietnam, Lyndon Johnson presided over a major escalation of the United States' effort. He did so, moreover, through actions, such as the Gulf of Tonkin incident in 1965, that seemed to be strategically designed to force the United States into ever greater participation, and he did so, most significantly, without the free and ready advice and consent of the American Congress.

Why should the United States have become involved in such a war? And why did the president and his advisors, particularly the members of the National Security Council under the leadership of Walt Rostow and McGeorge Bundy, seek to assert American influence in this far-flung region of the world? Those who have studied documents that bear the imprint of these officials argue that American advisors believed the national interest was at stake, in fact, that the Communist nations posed a major threat to American democracy. Hence, they reasoned, it was important for the United States to put up an aggressive front, in the words of Richard Barnet, to display a "macho and aggressive style," as a means of protecting the national interests of the United States. If Vietnam fell, it was assumed in terms of the so-called domino theory, so too would other nations in the region fall, leading eventually to the dominance of the Communists in that part of the world and thereby shifting the balance of power between the Communist and non-Communist countries.[12] Such an event, the Kennedy and the Johnson administrations both believed, must be avoided, and thus they engaged in almost reckless use, and sacrifice, of American troops and weaponry.

The end of the Vietnam War in 1975, coupled with the resignation of President Nixon following the Watergate fiasco, helped restore Congress to a more powerful role in the workings of the federal government by diminishing the power of the presidency. Nevertheless, the administration of President Ronald Reagan might be credited, in part, for helping to bring about the demise of the Soviet Union and its Communist allies throughout Eastern Europe. Though Reagan was a decidedly uncomplicated man, he was a powerful opponent of the Soviet Union, insisting that the Communist menace must be wiped out. In his administration, the United States government continued to put pressure on the Soviet Union. Although there were a number of internal problems and issues that helped to bring about the collapse of Communism, many observers believe that the policies of the Reagan presidency assisted as well.

The end of Soviet-style Communism has created a vast new and uncertain terrain for world politics and economics. The power of the American presidency today is far less than during the Roosevelt years. Apart from the NATO action against Kosovo, the United States was not involved in a major war effort during the administration of Bill Clinton. Moreover, both Clinton's enemies and his own missteps limited the power that he might have exercised in office. Indeed, the failure of his effort to create a major national health plan, one that would have been a revolutionary effort to promote welfare for many millions of Americans, might well be regarded, in retrospect, as the decisive turning point in his administration. In addition, the election in 1994 of a Republican Congress spelled further doom for the Clinton presidency and for the ability of Clinton to take decisive new steps in reshaping America.

The Military, the Central Intelligence Agency (CIA), and the Federal Bureau of Investigation (FBI). C. Wright Mills insisted that much of the authority wielded by the federal government lay in the role of the military and its capacity to control resources. Mills argued that the military principals of the government had come to assume an enormous impact on the making of public policy after the end of World War II. In fact, individuals with experience in the American military have come to occupy high positions in the government over the course of the past five decades. A favorite example for Mills was Dwight Eisenhower, who moved from being the Commander of Allied Forces in Europe to become President for two terms, beginning in 1952. Other military figures who have been important in the shaping of American foreign and domestic policies in the years since the close of World War II include General Maxwell Taylor, who during the Vietnam War furnished key advice to the Kennedy and Johnson administrations.

Although the power of the military to influence American policy has declined in recent decades, even during the 1980s military figures exercised power in the federal government. Consider the case of General Alexander Haig. Haig first rose to prominence as chairman of the Joint Chiefs of Staff of the armed forces, later became a personal and controversial counselor to Richard Nixon, and, it was said, played a large role in the final days of Nixon's presidency.[13] In the administration of Ronald Reagan, Haig achieved the penultimate position, perhaps, for a military figure, apart from the presidency itself, serving as secretary of state. His influence undoubtedly was part of the reason for the Reagan administration's highly aggressive stance on foreign policy, not to say the recommended increases for spending on defense. Moreover, Haig entered the 1988 presidential campaign, vying for the highest office himself. Other prominent military officers continue to play a role in the policymaking of the federal government, including General Colin Powell, who served as the Commander of the Joint Chiefs of Staff during the administration of George Bush.

Over this same period of time, spending on the defense budget also revealed the extent to which the United States relied on the military, and defense, for its policies and directions. In 1970, for example, while the United States was still in the midst of the War in Vietnam, the federal budget targeted $78.7 billion for defense, fully 40 percent of the entire federal budget at the time.[14] In 1980, a figure of $130.4 billion was directed to the Department of Defense, about one-quarter of the national budget. By 1999, the portion of the federal budget devoted to military expenditures had risen somewhat, to 32 percent, still quite a bit lower than it was during the 1970s.

Besides the military, there have been other agencies of the federal government that, since the end of World War II, have exercised considerable influence over American foreign and domestic policies. The two most significant have been the CIA and FBI. The CIA came into being as a result of the National Security Act of 1947, the same act that created the Department of Defense and established the National Security Council.[15] Originally it had been the intention of its creators that the CIA remain under the control of the National Security Council, and that it operate explicitly to gather intelligence overseas. But after its establishment, and particularly under the leadership of Allen Dulles, brother of Eisenhower's secretary of state, the role of the CIA expanded considerably. It began to initiate various clandestine activities abroad, among them efforts to overthrow governments perceived to be unsympathetic to American national interests. Ever since the enlargement of its role under the tutelage of Dulles, the CIA has acted in important ways to shape and to direct American foreign policy.

There appear, in fact, to have been countless instances of foreign conflicts and episodes in which the CIA somehow has been involved, including of course the major fiasco, the Bay of Pigs, in which the CIA virtually sponsored an effort to oust Fidel Castro and his regime. There also was the famous U-2 spy plane incident of 1960, when Francis Gary Powers was shot down while flying over Russia. Later it was discovered that his mission was under the supervision of the CIA. The CIA also participated in the overthrow in 1954 of the Guatemalan regime, another government claimed to be unfriendly to American interests, and it is reported to have assisted in undermining the Marxist government of Premier Salvador Allende in Chile in 1973. The Reagan presidency was itself implicated in scandal involving the CIA. As the Iran-Contra hearings during the summer of 1987 revealed, there were deep machinations and plots involving administration officials, from William Casey in the CIA to Oliver North, on the staff of the National Security Council, perhaps even to Vice-President George Bush—although he disclaimed any active involvement. The plans involved a complicated exchange of people and goods, with American captives in Lebanon freed, and aid shipped surreptitiously and illegally to support the antigovernment Contra effort in Nicaragua. At the center of this plot, it now appears, were the CIA and its former director, William Casey. To the chagrin of many people, officials and public alike, the CIA has not overstepped the tacit limits of national sovereignty on foreign soil exclusively. In the early 1970s, for instance, it was learned that the CIA had for a time provided financial support to certain members of the National Student Association in return for their help in collecting information on alleged radical students. Elsewhere, on campuses and in research laboratories throughout the United States, it has been reported, the CIA has also provided financial support to people who were willing to inform on the activities of their colleagues and friends.

All such acts, and many other foreign engagements abroad, have been done in complete secrecy, conceived and produced by an inner council within the CIA, known as the Special Group. Moreover, the budget of the CIA, although artfully disguised from the curious eyes of wary congressmen, is reported to rival in size that of its Russian counterpart, the KGB. In short, as David Wise and Thomas Ross tersely claim in their important analysis, the CIA has during the years of its existence operated almost as an "invisible government" in the United States.

With the death of J. Edgar Hoover in 1970, the influence of the FBI declined in importance, aided in no small part by investigations of its activities by the Congress. Yet, during the reign of Hoover the FBI represented a very powerful agency of the federal government; Presidents, themselves, even occasionally seemed to reverse the Constitutional relationship between the president and his subordinates, showing enormous respect and deference toward Hoover. Over the years the FBI has limited its own intelligence work to American soil, but it has ranged far and wide in the pursuit of information on alleged dissidents. During the late 1940s and into the 1950s, the FBI played a major part in collecting information on so-called Communist agents or sympathizers in the United States, helping to feed American political paranoia in that decade.[16] Where the FBI began to overstep itself, in terms simply of gathering intelligence, was in the fabrication of information that could be used to discredit otherwise important and respected Americans.[17] For instance, it has been reported that the FBI fabricated stories about alleged sexual liaisons of the Reverend Martin Luther King, Jr., during the mid-1960s in an attempt to diminish his influence as a spokesman for the civil rights of African Americans. And, in even more controversial operations, in 1980 the FBI undertook the ABSCAM effort, an intelligence operation in which an FBI agent who posed as an Arab oil magnate tried to bribe various congressmen. Defense attorneys for several of the congressmen indicted for accepting such bribes have tried to show that the FBI did not merely "gather" information, as is its mandate from the government, but tried to create it instead.

The American State as a Welfare State

The power of the Executive Branch of government to make critical decisions about war, coupled with the authority of the military, the CIA, and the FBI, all represent one side of the operations of the state—the *war-making*, or social control side, of state policy. But there is another, equally important side to the exercise of power by the federal government, what we can call the *welfare* side of state policy. It was during the course of the Roosevelt administration that major measures were made to promote the well-being of American citizens, including the Social Security Act of 1935. It is this side of the state that has come to be seen increasingly as a crucial feature of the state—that side whose actions actually can promote the well-being of its citizens.

The welfare state, in general terms, came into being during the course of the twentieth century.[18] Various nations of Western Europe introduced a number of policies and measures designed to improve the well-being of their residents. Such measures included provisions for the cost of general health care, pensions for the elderly, aid to orphans and widows, and other such benefits. Some nations became exemplary for the broad array of benefits they furnished for their citizens. The Scandinavian countries, especially Sweden and Norway, stand out among all Western nations for the level of benefits they provided.

As compared to other nations, however, the United States has provided far less for its citizens, creating "safety nets" which are less secure and comprehensive. Although the United States has provided pensions, through the Social Security Act, such benefits are not nearly as comprehensive as those of other countries. In addition, though the United States provided funds to cover the costs for young children of single parent families, those funds, too, were fairly meager. The economist Gosta Esping-Andersen speaks about three different kinds of welfare systems. There are those of the Scandinavian countries, which he refers to as social democratic welfare systems: These furnish the most comprehensive benefits to the largest number of citizens. Then there are the welfare systems of countries, like Germany, which he refers to as corporativist welfare systems. They provide benefits for workingmen's compensation and unemployment, but their provisions are tied to a worker's previous earnings and are not nearly as generous as those of the Scandinavian countries. Finally, there are what Esping-Andersen refers to as the "residualist" welfare states. Such nations provide benefits, but these benefits are limited and cover only specific areas of welfare. The United States is an example of this more limited kind of welfare state.

Since the mid-1970s, there have been general changes in the nature of the welfare state. Most nations were forced to reconsider the amounts of money they provided in benefits to their citizens primarily because of a financial crunch they experienced after the worldwide oil crisis of 1973–74. When the welfare state first came into being it was argued, by such key figures as William Beveridge in Great Britain that the state could afford to be generous in the monies it provided citizens so long as unemployment remained low. With low rates of unemployment, there would be plenty of cash reserves, secured by taxes from the employed citizens, to provide benefits for the small number of people who were unemployed and for other

TABLE 6–1 Public Social Security and Health Expenditures as a Percentage of Gross Domestic Product in Selected Countries, 1980–1990

OECD Countries[1]	1980	1990
Canada[2]	17.3	18.8
Denmark	26.0	27.8
France	23.9	26.5
Germany	25.4	23.5
Netherlands	27.2	28.8
Norway	21.4	28.7
Sweden	32.4	33.1
United Kingdom	21.3	22.3
United States	14.1	14.6
Other Countries[3]	**1975**	**1986**
Czechoslovakia	17.2	21.5
Hungary	14.9	16.2
Ukraine	13.8	17.3
USSR	13.6	15.5
Australia	10.3	9.2
New Zealand	14.5	17.9
Japan	8.9	12.2
Argentina	6.8	6.1
Brazil	5.2	5.0
Chile	11.0	13.1
Costa Rica	5.1	7.3

[1]These figures are based on OECD definitions which are not comparable with the ILO's.
[2]Data for Canada refer to 1982 and 1990
[3]ILO-based data. For the ex-communist nations, spending is calculated in terms of net material product.

Sources: OECD, *Employment Outlook,* Paris, 1994, Table 4.7; ILO, *The Cost of Social Security,* Geneva, 1991. Reprinted by permission of Sage Publications Ltd. from Gosta Esping-Andersen, *Welfare States in Transition: National Adaptations in Global Economies* (London: Sage Publishers, 1996), p. 11.

items, such as pensions for the elderly and health care aid. But by the early 1970s, unemployment rates had increased worldwide, and pressures began to build to find ways to solve the problem.

For a number of nations, especially European ones, the solution was to be found not in increasing employment, but in reducing the amounts of expenditures on welfare items.[19] Prime Minister Margaret Thatcher of England led the way, arguing the radical position that the state should no longer provide welfare in the amounts it had. She insisted that the welfare programs, created after World War II in England, were a bad idea, and that people had to become more responsible for their own lives. The Thatcher Revolution, as it was called, resulted in a change of attitude, and eventually a change of policy, in Great Britain, signaling a change that would happen in other nations as well. In Great Britain, for example, public housing, which had been a guarantee for poor families for several decades, changed course, and the Council houses were put up for sale and rent. This was only one of the measures instituted in changing the course of the welfare state.

Other nations today have not made so many dramatic reductions in their welfare policies, but all countries have been compelled to reconsider the nature of their benefits. In the absence of full employment, it becomes difficult to provide government funding for the array of measures and benefits previously guaranteed to all citizens. Even in the generous welfare states of Scandinavia, for example, important rethinking has been done about the nature of the benefits to be provided.[20] In the United States, which has lacked the generous benefits of the Scandinavian countries, the reduction in the size of the safety net happened not simply through a cutback of benefits but also because of an unparalleled degree of economic expansion over the course of the 1990s. In fact, from 1991 through 1999, economic growth continued high in the country, and the rates of unemployment saw levels they had not seen in more than thirty years. The effect was to provide the foundations for a sea change in the limited American welfare state, creating new workfare programs that provided jobs for many people, often single mothers, previously on the welfare rolls. As of late 1999, the revolution in the nature of welfare in America seemed to be doing better than even the most vigorous critics had believed, with thousands of Americans now working rather than subsisting on welfare benefits such as monies for families with young children. But the jury remains out on whether the economic boom really helped the most impoverished families in America.

Sociological Perspectives on the Power of the State Today

Much of the controversy among political sociologists in recent years has been over the nature of the state, not as a war-making but as a welfare-providing state. While all observers agree that the American welfare state operates in a less generous fashion than other welfare states, there remain questions about the reasons for its different character. Theda Skocpol, for example, has argued that American welfare policy is the result of "polity-initiated decisions," a number of which took place before the actual policies developed and implemented by the Roosevelt Administration (see Chapter 3).[21] She insists that the United States was on a course to create strong welfare measures, such as pensions for widows and Civil War veterans, but that such decisions came to nothing because of the political efforts directed against them early in the twentieth century. For her, the source and origins of the American welfare state, however limited it might be, lay in the efforts of political associations and state managers to develop coherent policies. Central to her argument is that such policies were being fashioned well before the years of the Great Depression and the consequent material misery suffered by many Americans. Hence, she concludes, it was state officials, and a broader body of political figures, who were responsible in the end for the welfare measures adopted during the 1930s. The timing of the development and adoption of the measures is critical for her argument.

G. William Domhoff counters her view by insisting that the origins, and limits, of welfare policy in America can be traced directly to the actions, not of the state and its managers, but rather to business groups and the corporate community.[22] Domhoff argues, for example, that the Social Security Act of 1935 was a product not of the Roosevelt administration, per se, but rather of self-interested business figures in the administration and business organizations in the United States. He writes about old-age pensions that

> the experts who wrote it were direct employees of one of the most powerful upper-class families of the day, the Rockefellers; . . . several top executives supported the plan; . . . the level of benefits was tied to salary level, thus preserving the values established in the labor market; there were no government contributions from general taxes, an exclusion that business leaders insisted on; (and) there were both employer and employee contributions to old-age pensions, which business leaders insisted on.[23]

A variant of this view is that of sociologist Jill Quadagno, who insists that it was class-related issues that produced limits to the welfare policies of the United States government. Quadagno argues that "the struggle for old age pensions (in the United States) was part of a broader process of class struggle, shaped first within the marketplace and later within the electoral-representative political system."[24]

This is one of those important debates that is difficult to decide on the basis of the available evidence. Mainly that happens because each view uses somewhat different evidence to furnish support for its argument. Domhoff emphasizes the immediate business backgrounds of state officials who helped to draw up the old-age pension plan as part of the Social Security Act, whereas Skocpol emphasizes the policies and ideas about pensions developed well before the Roosevelt administration took office. Skocpol also argues that the limited character of the American welfare state springs, not from the power of business, but from the political contests early in the twentieth century. These were contests that were won by the political parties and organizations that opposed, for a variety of reasons, such benefits as workingmen's pensions.

In this debate, I have my own preference—that of the state-centered view. There are good reasons for the state-centered view. One important one is quite simple and basic. People who occupy the major offices of the government are bound, by the nature of their office, to promote the interests of the government, or state. Their tenure, indeed their success, rests on their ability to promote these interests. Granted many such officials come from the business community, as in the case of the very effective former Secretary of the Treasury, Robert Rubin, a former Wall Street banker. Such officials are compelled to take a view of the state as a player in world politics and the world economy. They act, in effect, to further the interests of the state. If they did not, they, and their associates, would quickly be out of office.

Yet I also would argue that the power of the American state and its officials is indeed constrained, limited by its own history and structure, and by contending powers in America. The institution of the American state does not exercise nearly the power of the state under the People's Republic of China, or that of the various authoritarian regimes throughout the world. Business provides a far greater presence in America than in many other nations. Nevertheless, while the business community can limit what the state can do, it cannot initiate and pursue new policies and actions. Those remain the prerogatives of the state.

Moreover, the power of the state compared to that of business can vary from one time period to another. Clearly during the 1930s the American state exercised great power over the nation; it was responsible in large part for bringing the country out of the depths of the Great Depression. During the economic prosperity of the 1990s, however, the business community grew more than ever forceful and prominent in American politics—far more so than during the years of the Cold War, when state officials were forced to exercise much greater authority. Just how important the business community has been, and may become, is the issue taken up in the next section.

THE POWER OF BUSINESS AND CORPORATIONS

When Alexis de Tocqueville wrote of the nature of equality in America, he identified three major features of the society that could pose threats to such equality (see also Chapter 4). One, of course, was the element of race. Though white Americans, especially males, enjoyed unparalleled freedom, especially as compared to their counterparts in Europe, African Americans and Native Americans alike suffered at the hands of the whites. Another possible threat was that of the *tyranny of the majority*, a threat that lay in the fact that in a society where everyone was deemed equal, decisions would rest with the majority opinion, which by definition carried the most weight. But the major threat, in Tocqueville's eyes, lurked in the form of business. Business and great industry posed a potential threat to equality because, like social class in Europe, they held the potential to undermine democracy through the unequal distribution of material wealth. Tocqueville may have been a great believer in democracy, but he also was a practical enough thinker to realize that there were no real barriers to preventing wealth from exercising its influence over politics.

Many observers have come to realize that great wealth can influence, and has influenced, the course of politics in America. The historian David Potter, for instance, acknowledged that one of the features that enabled the American political system to run as well as it has, and to survive many obstacles over the course of two hundred years, has been its history of affluence and wealth.[25] America has had more than its share of natural resources on which to draw, including an abundance of land and territory, and it has been able to make its way, relying as much on domestic markets as on its success in invading markets abroad. Even today, at the beginning of the twenty-first century, America stands out for its prosperity, able to withstand the difficulties of a global economy even as other nations struggle abroad.

But prosperity and wealth are not equally divided among Americans. Nor have they been. By the early part of the twentieth century, it had become clear that large business organizations would furnish the direction to the American economy and that they would do so based upon their ability to accumulate and invest financial resources. The pioneering work to identify that trend was the singular book by Adolf Berle, Jr., and Gardiner Means, entitled *The Modern Corporation and Private Property*.[26] Berle and Means took note of a startling fact—that much of the business conducted in the American marketplace was done at the time by very large firms. In fact, they observed that a comparatively small number of such firms actually controlled a disproportionate amount of the assets in each of several fields. For instance, in 1929, shortly before the crash on Wall Street that resulted in the Great Depression, 130 of 573 companies that did business on the New York Stock Exchange could be classified as corporations. Furthermore, these 130 companies controlled fully 80 percent of the assets in the market. It appears from research done by sociologist William Roy that the tendency for corporations to become the real players in the American economy had begun decades before, as a number of corporations began to accumulate large amounts of resources and to overshadow the wealth of other businesses.[27] Today virtually all sociologists take for granted that the dominant players in the modern economy are not people, but rather large corporations, and among them those corporations that control the greatest amount of assets.

The lopsided distribution of resources, which Berle and Means uncovered in the 1920s, continues to be a prominent part of the American economy. In the early 1980s, for example, there were about 260,000 manufacturing firms in the United States. Only a handful of them, 657, actually controlled 80 percent of the assets of all manufacturing firms. Likewise, there were about 15,000 commercial banks at the time, of which 478 held 63 percent of the assets of all banks. Moreover, the concentration of resources has grown over the decades: in 1950, the 200 largest manufacturing firms held 48 percent of the assets of all such firms, but by the early 1980s, the 200 largest firms held 61 percent of the assets of all firms.[28] In the prosperous 1990s, the trends continued in the same direction. Although the economy boomed and jobs were abundant, large corporations continued to control most of the assets and resources.

Able to control such resources, it is the large corporations, everyone agrees, that can exercise the most clout in the American market. But even if they do exercise a control over assets and wealth, it is the nature of the market, so the argument goes, that such corporations are in competition with one another. Berle and Means, after having uncovered the vast wealth of a few large corporations, went on to make another startling argument—that control of corporations had moved out of the hands of a few rich families like the DuPonts and the Rockefellers into the hands of managers and shareholders. It was the managers of the corporations, Berle and Means claimed, who actually controlled the destiny of corporate wealth in America.

But is it so? Are managers, working more or less in competition and in isolation from one another, the ones who control the destiny of the large firms? It is on this and related questions that sociologists have reached some of their most important discoveries in recent years.

The Corporate Community

The largest corporations in America today not only control a vast amount of wealth and resources, but they also are part of what G. William Domhoff calls a "corporate community."[29] This community has taken form because of the social networks that bind one large corporation to another large corporation. Sometimes such networks happen as a result of friendships, or even schools and clubs held in common among the members of the larger corporations. But most often the networks occur at the highest decision-making level of the corporation—the board of directors. Various studies by sociologists over the past two decades document these networks, or what are called, "interlocking directorates."[30]

In the most recent version of his writings on power and authority in America, Domhoff studied the corporate interlocks among the top 1,029 corporations in America, based upon the level of their assets. Among these wealthy corporations, which included General Motors, Coca-Cola and Kmart, Domhoff found a surprisingly large number of overlapping memberships among individuals. For example, people who sat on the board of the Chase Manhattan Bank held forty-eight similar positions among the top corporations. Altogether, about 20 percent of the top firms had extensive ties with other firms by virtue of the interlocking memberships on their boards of directors.[31]

Even within the corporate community, some players may be more significant to the activities of the market than other players. There is an old argument, which can be traced back to the writings of Rudolf Hilferding, that says as modern capitalism grows and develops, financial capital will be more important than other kinds (see Chapter 10).[32] Hilferding argued that financial capital helps to open new markets abroad for domestic firms, and that even in domestic markets it plays a key role in helping the development of new firms. Domhoff's study reveals that a number of banks were among the most connected of corporations, including the Chase Manhattan, Bank of America, and the Wells Fargo Bank.

Sociologist Richard Ratcliff was among the first sociologists to document Hilferding's general thesis in a series of important studies of firms in the St. Louis area. Ratcliff found, for example, that while many local manufacturing firms began to decline during the 1970s and 1980s, local financial firms continued to flourish, largely because of the investments they were able to make in new markets and developments outside of St. Louis. He notes that the

> evidence thus suggests that Saint Louis, despite its image as a declining older industrial metropolis, was actually producing a net capital surplus that was deposited in the major banks and then exported for investment elsewhere, presumably to the Sunbelt and other high growth areas.[33]

Sociologists Michael Schwartz and Beth Mintz have also uncovered similar evidence of the key role of financial institutions among American corporations. They find that banks and savings and loan associations appear to stand at the center of corporate interlocks among corporations, though their power is limited by market forces and by the autonomy of various industries. Yet, they conclude, that the "portrait that emerges is that of a loosely structured system which follows the dictates of the market but under the leadership of the money market commercial banks."[34]

The Corporate Inner Circle

The argument about the significance of the corporate community in America and its actions received its most sophisticated and sustained attention by the sociologist Michael Useem. In research among corporations and their leaders in the United States and Great Britain, Useem uncovered evidence of several forms of a corporate community. He relied on interviews with members of the boards of directors, done in 1979 and 1980, and on data about the largest corporations.[35]

Useem's main discovery was of an *inner circle* among the members of the boards of directors, a kind of core group or central elite. The inner circle members were those who were at the center of the social and business networks. They also possessed a decidedly different view of the business and political world than their contemporaries. Thinking not of their own particular corporate or business interests, they sought to view the "bigger picture" of the world, taking what Useem refers to as a *classwide* scan of the world. This meant that they thought in broader and more general terms about politics than other directors. Moreover, Useem adds that the developing of the inner circle is a growing moment in the development of modern capitalism. At the end of the nineteenth century, families like the Rockefellers were in control of firms. Then came the managerial revolution, identified by Berle and Means, and managerial capitalism. At the close of the twentieth century, Useem sees an emergent form of *institutional capitalism*, a form in which business institutions have become dominant, and the members of their boards of directors the leading force on behalf of a unified, classwide view of the world.

Multinational Corporations and the Growth of the Global Economy

In the early 1960s, long before there was talk of a global economy, there was talk of something else—the multinational corporation whose power extended beyond the boundaries of nation-states.

These firms, variously called transnational, multinational, or even global corporations, and exemplified especially by firms like Exxon, General Motors Corporation (GM), International Telephone and Telegraph (IT&T), and International Business Machines Corporation (IBM), introduced an even more novel phenomenon, but one entirely consistent with the forecast by Berle and Means. Operating in more than one nation, they not only rivaled the economic resources of some nation-states, but it seems they could operate free of any meaningful sanctions or penalties of the nation-states themselves. Richard Barnet and Ronald Müller, coauthors of the definitive treatment of these organizations, thus quote the president of the IBM World Trade Corporation who declared that

> For business purposes the boundaries that separate one nation from another are no more real than the equator. They are merely convenient demarcations of ethnic, linguistic, and cultural entities. They do not define business requirements or consumer trends. Once management understands and accepts this world economy, its view of the marketplace—and its planning—necessarily expand.

The same gentleman concludes by remarking that the "world outside the home country is no longer viewed as a series of disconnected customers and prospects for its products, but as an extension of a single market."[36]

With the collapse of the Soviet Union, and the opening of new democracies like South Africa, the large multinational corporations now exercise considerable influence throughout the world. Such corporations include IBM, McDonalds, and a wide variety of firms that now seek to make profits in worldwide markets. Such firms act as the spearheads of capitalism and penetrate new markets easily. Many such corporations, moreover, are financial ones that invest in the new markets abroad. In fact, it is their investments, or the withdrawal of them, that may have helped to account for the financial collapse of a number of the Asian economies over the past decade.[37]

Does America Possess a Ruling Class—or Even a Dominant Class?

Recall Marx's image of the ruling class. It is a class of capitalists who exercise power not only over markets, but also over the running of the state. The state rules on its behalf. The state makes policies that further the interests of the capitalists. Such policies would include capital gains taxes that are only minimal, providing only a small dent in the earnings of people of great wealth. They would also include policies that exercise only limited control over the business dealings of corporations.

But there are all sorts of questions that arise in trying to determine the existence of a ruling class that, in effect, runs the machinery of state. How does the ruling class operate? It certainly does not operate as it would in the early days of the "robber barons," when the wealthy moguls of America seemed to control the fate of its citizens. If the corporate community lies at its center, how does the community make its influence felt? Moreover, if there is a ruling class at work, why do large corporate chieftains, like Microsoft boss Bill Gates, get called to Washington to defend the practices of his company against the charge of monopoly? These are the kinds of questions that must be asked, and for which the evidence must be uncovered, to satisfy ourselves whether or not America is run by a ruling class.

Several methods of inquiry have been developed to try to learn whether such a ruling class exists. One method for discovery, on which G. William Domhoff relies, is to find evidence of some kind of social networks that link the corporate chieftains to the rulers of state.[38] Presumably if there are such networks, of the same kind found at the highest levels of the largest corporations, this provides prima facie evidence of a community of interest, even if it does not tell us how the influence flows—whether from the corporate leaders to the leaders of state, or in the other direction. The best work along these lines has been furnished by sociologist Gwen Moore.[39] Moore and her associates conducted a survey of the leaders of some different institutional sectors, including the federal government, in 1971–1972. The results showed evidence of communication among a number of leaders in each sector, along with the presence of over thirty social cliques, consisting of 227 men and women, all of whom possessed relationships with one another, as well as crucial links to other cliques. This inner group, drawn largely from the members of Congress, political appointments, and business circles, not only possessed common social ties to one another, Moore found, but in some cases certain of its members belonged to the same social clubs, thereby adding a further contribution to a common sense of purpose.

Another method is to inquire whether the corporate community also acts in concert on matters of state and politics. This is the method that sociologist Mark Mizruchi pursued in his very fine analysis of the structure of corporate power in America.[40] Examining several top corporations, Mizruchi made a series of inquiries about the nature of the corporate interlocks and the unity on political matters among the corporations. He found clear evidence that the largest corporations not only possessed important interlocks but that they also acted in common to make sizeable contributions to political campaigns, to provide testimony on business issues to Congress, and to exercise a kind of unified voice in politics. His research, he notes, tends to support the view of Michael Useem about the existence of an inner circle among America's corporations, one that acts in concert in politics.

There is additional evidence, of a more indirect and circumstantial nature, that suggests that the corporate community can exercise great power over the actions of the state. Political action committees, for example, have been the subject of study by sociologists.[41] This research reveals that such committees are very careful in the funds they disburse to candidates, and also that such funds can make a large impact over the course of a campaign. In fact, the financial contributions that the corporate community makes to the political campaigns of different candidates can make a major difference in who runs and who wins—a difference that seems to be increasing rather than diminishing in its effect.

Such is the piecemeal and diverse evidence to suggest that via social networks and such key elements as campaign contributions the corporate community can make its great influence felt in the design of American politics. But does it act as a cohesive and coherent ruling class? The evidence at this point is just circumstantial but suggestive. From his research on the directors of the top business organizations in the United States and Great Britain, here is the way Useem sums it up:

> The rise of institutional capitalism in the U.S. and U.K. contributed to the rise of more conservative political climates in the early 1980s. Though the new corporate political activity was not decisive, its significance should not be underestimated. A central objective of the business political mobilization on both sides of the Atlantic was to restore company profits to levels of an earlier decade. . . . The electoral success and political thrust of the Thatcher and Reagan governments were in no small part products of this business venture into politics . . . the rise of the new conservative forces that were among the pillars of the Republican and Conservative governments was a product of the formation on both sides of the Atlantic of informal and formal organizational networks linking together most large corporations.[42]

In other words, business represented a substantial force in shaping government policy even in the 1980s.

My own view of the matter can be summed up like this: Big business does play a role in American politics, but such a role is not as the captain of the ship of state. A more apt image is this: Think of the large corporate interests as the winds that blow the sails on the ship of state. State officials, themselves, steer the ship across the seas, but the corporate community can affect the course that is sailed. Ultimately, however, it is the skill of the sailors, i.e., state officials, and the durability of the ship, i.e., the state, not the winds, that determine where the ship of state will head and where it will land.

EQUALITY AND INEQUALITY IN MODERN AMERICA

Any assessment of the nature and structure of power in modern America must come to grips with the prevailing inequalities among individuals in the society. Wealth is not distributed equally, as we have seen in the case of corporate power, nor has it ever been. And in the past decade or so, during a period of record high employment rates during peacetime, the differences between the wealthy families and the poorest families have been increasing rather than diminishing.

Economic Inequality

In a society in which capitalism is the dominant force in the economy, economic inequalities are likely to arise. In the early years of modern industrial capitalism in America, the inequalities were sharp and deep. Certain families, founders of great corporations like Standard Oil or the plutocrats like Andrew Carnegie and J. Pierpont Morgan, held a tremendous amount of wealth. This wealth gave them an ability to exercise influence, both over the economy and the polity, which was not available to the average American. Most Americans held jobs as members of the working class, many employed in factories or firms engaged in various forms of manual labor.

But as America developed it appeared that the distribution of wealth had evened out. More and more families were now able to move up the ladder of wealth and to join the ranks, if not of the upper classes, surely of the middle classes. By the middle part of the twentieth century, many observers were hailing America not simply as the land of opportunity, but as a land where the middle class had become dominant, thereby making political democracy a reality.[43] The kind of imagery which Alexis de Tocqueville had imagined—of America as a land of equality and freedom for all—seemed to have become a reality just after the close of World War II. Many Americans now were able to move to the suburbs and secure their dream homes.

Granted that not all were able to do so. African Americans, in particular, still suffered from inequality in America, even after slavery had ended.[44] But if the fortunes of African Americans could be uplifted, it appeared that even in the midst of some inequality the fortunes of the great majority of Americans were prospering, giving rise to the image of America as an "affluent society."[45]

The corporate wealth of the 1990s should silence those who parade America as a land of equality. For just as corporate wealth has become concentrated in the hands of fewer and fewer large corporations, so, too, there are dangerous signs of a growing economic inequality in America—between the very rich and the very poor.[46] Since the 1970s, America has become home to a large "underclass," in the words of William Julius Wilson, a noted sociologist.[47] The underclass is made up largely of African Americans who live in the inner cities of the major metropolitan areas of the United States. These are people, often unmarried women with young children, who over a period of several decades became part of a large group of people dependent on the state for their resources. Many simply did not have the skills to work, but most, particularly the men, were unemployed because jobs had left the American city. There developed a growing class of the unemployed, left inside the American city with little access, either because of education or residence, to the new fortunes that had grown up on the fringe areas, in the edge cities of the American metropolis (see also Chapter 7).

The early indications are that, with high rates of employment, many of the members of the underclass are now securing jobs, able to support their families in ways they were not able to do before. Special programs in the states of Wisconsin and Pennsylvania reveal that with intensive help and aid, many of the underclass who previously lived off the state now have joined the workforce and are able to bring home salary checks. But many of their jobs tend to be temporary. While work has provided such people with a new sense of self-esteem, the tenure of their employment still remains in question.

In addition, even while the underclass has gained, there is a growing concentration of wealth at the very top of American society—a disparity that is growing between the wealth of the richest Americans and that of the poorest. A 1999 report, done by the Center on Budget and Policy Priorities, a nonprofit organization in Washington, D.C., finds that the "gap between rich and poor has grown into an economic chasm so wide that this year the richest 2.7 million Americans, the top 1 percent, will have as many after-tax dollars to spend as the bottom 100 million."[48] Even more significantly, just as the American welfare state has been less generous than that of other welfare states in the twentieth century, so, too, the economic inequality in America is more pronounced today than that of other Western nations. Edward N. Wolff, an economics professor at New York University, notes that the United

States is "the most unequal industrialized country, in terms of income and wealth, and we're growing more unequal faster than the other industrialized nations."[49]

America thus is not a society of economic equals, where wealth is evenly distributed. And as the inequality increases, what will happen to the society as a whole? Will a growing number of Americans become disenchanted with the society? Or will they simply be content to live with the economic disparities? It was such inequalities, you will recall, that Marx believed would spell the end of modern capitalism. But they have not, and one of the reasons they have not is because of the other key feature of American society. This is the opportunity to be able to exercise a kind of freedom and voice in politics that, however imperfect, is a far cry from the oppression of people under other regimes, particularly totalitarian ones.

Political Equality

One of the crucial facts about the nature of Western democracies over the course of the twentieth century is this: Citizenship, the very essence of democratic rights, has been extended to an ever-growing number of people and groups. One of the most famous arguments along these lines is that of T.H. Marshall.[50] His argument has been seen as the underlying rationale and groundwork for the development of the welfare state in the twentieth century. He proposed that there were three sets of rights: civil rights, or the rights of individuals under the law; economic rights, or the rights of individuals to labor and to work; and social rights, or the rights of individuals to be entitled as citizens to support and benefits provided by the state. He further claimed that these rights gradually became granted by the state over the course of three centuries, culminating in the provision of social rights during the course of the twentieth century.

Although there are those who take issue with some of his claims, Marshall's key insight is that as Western democracies have developed, citizenship rights have been expanded and extended, both in terms of what individuals can expect as citizens, and in terms of the broad array of groups that are covered under the terms of citizenship. A similar argument has been made by the sociologist Michael Schudson. Countering the view of many sociologists, Schudson argues that America has become increasingly a rights-based nation, one in which rights have been extended over time to more and more groups of people.[51] It is this rights-based society that, from my point of view, provides the foundations that limit the impact of economic inequalities on the lives of average Americans. Sharp economic differences are critical to the lives of people, but if people also believe they have the freedom to move ahead, the inequalities will never appear so sharp nor sting so much.

The meaning of citizenship in the United States has almost from the very first been defined in terms of equality. The Declaration of Independence proclaimed that all men are created equal, and that they are by nature free to pursue ends of their own choice. Decades later, Alexis de Tocqueville declared that Americans seemed to feel themselves the social equal of one another, and this has come about, he further suggested, because America avoided the obstacles inherited from a feudal past. That very same theme was articulated a century later by the great Swedish economist Gunnar Myrdal. He claimed that the central foundations of American society had been erected on the fundamental notion that all people were created equal. Yet he went on to observe that while true in principle, in fact there was considerable inequality in the United States, particularly between the races.[52]

Myrdal in some sense turned out to be the more accurate observer. Even while Tocqueville was claiming evidence for the presence of considerable social and political equality in the United States, large numbers of people did not share in it. In the mid-nineteenth century slavery still remained widespread, and only men could exercise the principal right of citizenship, that of suffrage. Not until the twentieth century did the idea of equality come to be extended to the great majority of people, and it happened because they were claimed to be citizens, thereby entitled to exercise certain basic Constitutional rights.

Citizenship in the twentieth century has become expanded in the first instance through the extension of certain fundamental rights to ever larger and more varied types of people. The passage in 1920, for example, of the Nineteenth Amendment to the Constitution meant the guarantee that women now could exercise the right to vote and thus join their male counterparts after being so deprived for almost 150 years. In 1948, the armed forces became integrated by a presidential order, putting African Americans and white combat troops on an equal social footing for the first time in American history. Yet, it seems, the major breakthrough so far as the extension of citizenship rights was concerned, took place with the Supreme Court decision in the case of *Brown v. Topeka* in 1954, the famous ruling on school desegregation. Under the guiding hand of Earl Warren, the Court decided that no African American should be denied the right to an education the equivalent of that of whites, and it thus declared that public schools should become desegregated "with all deliberate speed."

The decision of the Court proved historic in more than one sense, for by overturning the earlier ruling in the case of *Plessy v. Ferguson*, the case in which the Court decided in 1896 that Plessy, an African American man, was not entitled to travel in the same public accommodations as whites, it proclaimed that African Americans were entitled to equal treatment before the law *simply* and *primarily* because they were citizens of the United States. That legal interpretation, together with subsequent Congressional decisions in the Civil Rights Acts of 1964 and 1965, served to shore up the extension of citizenship to African Americans. At the same time, the implications of those actions were that no citizens could be deprived of equal and fair treatment in education, politics, or even in such public domains as housing and public accommodations on the basis of their race, color, or creed. By implication, then, other non-Anglo groups, such as Hispanic Americans and Native Americans, fell under the rule of these new laws and the new interpretation of the Constitution; thus, like African Americans, they too came to benefit from the extension of citizenship to all groups that previously lay beyond the pale.

Soon, the movements inspired by these historic legal and Congressional decisions worked to the advantage of the largest minority group in America—women. Working hard and long hours, many women together with their male supporters managed to get an Equal Rights Amendment passed by the Congress. This further ensured that the rights of citizenship would be extended to women much along the same lines they had been expanded for religious and racial minorities; that, in particular, women, too, could not be subject to any type of occupational discrimination based simply upon their sex. Yet, the battle for full and complete citizenship for women is likely to be the longest and most difficult; this became clear when the necessary number of state legislatures failed to ratify the Equal Rights Amendment, and thus it did not become law. On balance, however, a greater variety of people, including women, in late twentieth-century America can enjoy the benefits of citizenship and the implementation of the Constitutional provisions for equal treatment and opportunity than in times past.

The extension of citizenship in the twentieth century took another, one must say, greatly more profound, turn. For until the 1954 Supreme Court decision, citizenship only included the most minimal kinds of rights. In the case of women, for example, it only meant the right to vote; even in the case of African Americans, until the 1954 Court ruling, citizenship only covered, in a limited fashion, suffrage. The greater significance of the 1954 decision was that citizenship now came to take on a new meaning—people regarded as citizens of the United States were now to be further guaranteed, as part of their Constitutional heritage, a right to receive the same education as one another. The philosophy of "separate but equal" claimed legitimate in 1896 now was deemed to be invalid; true citizenship meant the full and complete implementation of the notion of equality, taking in the widest possible spectrum of the social domain. In light of this reinterpretation and fundamental extension of the meaning of citizenship, it only could be a matter of time before citizenship actually took on a more substantial form. It is in this regard, then, that the Congressional acts of the 1960s served simply to secure the 1954 Supreme Court ruling. Moreover, this very same period, the 1950s and 1960s, witnessed additional elaboration upon the basic redefinition of the meaning of citizenship. Thus, with the passage of the various welfare measures in the 1960s, the Johnson administration was not merely creating a dependent population, as some social critics have claimed.[53] In fact, the administration was saying, in effect, that citizenship in the United States now furnished a person not merely the chance to live, to work, and to be educated—by themselves extraordinary extension of rights—but it also guaranteed a certain minimum standard of living to those people, who, for whatever reasons, were unable to secure one for themselves.

The effort to extend the rights of citizens to larger and larger segments of the American community continues apace. Over the course of the next three decades new policies were effected that were intended to secure and protect the rights of citizens. Such measures included the American Disabilities Act of 1991, which extended protection to people who were disabled; new policies to protect women against sexual harassment in the workplace; and several other new policies. A very minimal interpretation of citizenship at the beginning of the twentieth century has, by the end of it, turned out to be an extraordinarily broad one.

But all is not rosy for the rights of citizenship in America. Two portentous signs on the horizon are those efforts designed to counter the extension of the liberal ethos in America. One is the new controversy that has been raised about the matter of affirmative action. In the 1970s new guidelines came down from the federal government, designed to protect the rights of groups that were historic minorities in America. In particular, they were guidelines designed to enable African Americans to secure opportunity in arenas which were denied them in the past, especially in terms of entrance to forms of higher education. Many colleges and universities adopted such guidelines and proceeded to admit African American applicants when the qualifications of such applicants were roughly comparable to those of white applicants. Litigation was brought against such affirmative action guidelines that challenged the principle—in particular, the famous challenge offered in the case of Allan Bakke in 1978. Bakke had been denied admission to the Medical School of the University of California at Davis, even though his credentials were as good as those of a number of minority applicants who were admitted ahead of him. In their ruling on this case, the Supreme Court argued that the Davis Medical School could not, in effect, discriminate against Bakke by admitting minority applicants less well qualified than him, and therefore ruled that he had to be admitted. Nevertheless, the case did not establish a clear rejection of the general affirmative action guidelines; later federal laws even managed to sustain the intent of affirmative action policies.

By the mid-1990s there were serious challenges to affirmative action, however. A federal court ruled, for example, that the University of Texas could no longer provide special consideration of African Americans and Hispanics in the admission to Law School. The effect initially was quite dramatic, resulting in many fewer applications and admissions. In California, an action by the Board of Regents also had the same chilling effect: applications and admissions from minority candidates were down. The controversy continues, however, and there is no end in sight. Affirmative action was a set of policies designed to extend the rights of citizens in ways previously denied them. Challenges to affirmative action are seen as challenges to the whole extension of citizenship. Moreover, the recent efforts in California to limit the benefits available to recent immigrants, particularly undocumented immigrants, further reveal the challenge that now exists in the United States in a century that has become known as the century of citizenship—through the welfare state and other such measures.

America, like many other Western countries, now finds itself at a critical kind of turning point. Immigration, for example, will continue, and probably increase as various barriers to immigration come down. Since 1965 and the initiation of the new immigration law in the United States, millions of immigrants have come to this country. Their very presence here poses some fundamental challenges and issues for the coming century. Will citizenship rights be rolled back, and will they become limited to only certain groups of immigrants? How will America as a whole deal with the vast new groups of immigrants? What will happen in the process to the situation of African Americans, the largest minority group now, but by the year 2050 only the second largest, next to the Hispanic population?

The presence of the new immigrants, coupled with the continuing economic troubles of African Americans, will once again test the fundamental tenet of American democracy, that of the breadth and depth of equality. Will equality be limited, as it was during de Tocqueville's time, only to certain groups? Or will it be extended to greater and greater numbers of people? This is *the* American dilemma, and it is one that cannot be avoided.

CONCLUDING OBSERVATIONS

America has been seen as both the land of economic opportunity and as the site of great corporate giants, organizational plutocrats of the twentieth century. It is a place where citizens are free to exercise their rights to vote, to engage in free speech, and to assemble for peaceful purposes, but it also is a country in which the modern state can exercise great, even decisive, power over the course of world events.

Different sociological observers treat different features of American society and history as though they were the only features. Neo-Marxists, and even those who are not, such as G. William Domhoff, believe there is a dominant class, a group of corporate powers that more or less runs the country. Theda Skocpol, and her followers, maintain in contrast that the modern American state is the essential locus of power and that agency that drives the country forward, particularly during times of great national crisis. Alexis de

Tocqueville, and those who have adopted his point of view, including Gunnar Myrdal, point to the essence of America in the emphasis on equality, and equality of opportunity for all people. Such opportunity, even if imperfectly granted, clearly has expanded over the course of the twentieth century.

Each view can find some support and comfort for itself in the actual empirical evidence we have at hand. And perhaps that is the main point. As a large and massive international force at the beginning of the twenty-first century, America is complex. Its laws insist on equality and guard against infringements on the rights of others, but many of the forces that drive it are forces of considerable resources that aim to gain for themselves and not for the larger public. Capitalist democracy, even in a nation known as the best in an imperfect world, is not a simple matter.

NOTES

1. Charles A. Beard, *An Economic Interpretation of the Constitution of the United States* (New York: Free Press, 1935; 1965).
2. Robert A. Dahl, *Who Governs? Democracy and Power in an American City* (New Haven, Connecticut: Yale University Press, 1961).
3. C. Wright Mills, *The Power Elite* (New York: Oxford University Press, 1959).
4. Edward Banfield, *Political Influence* (New York: Free Press, 1961); Wallace S. Sayre and Herbert Kaufman, *Governing New York City* (New York: Russell Sage Foundation, 1961).
5. Paul Baran and Paul Sweezy, *Monopoly Capitalism: An Essay on the American Economic and Social Order* (New York: Monthly Review Press, 1968).
6. G. William Domhoff, in the latest edition of his book, *Who Rules America?*, insists on a distinction between the ruling class and the dominant class (his version) about power in America. The chief difference, as I understand it, is that his view insists on a looser coordination among the components of the class view. That is, there is not a close and intimate correspondence between the interests and dominance of the class and the actions by political leaders. But the difference, as I understand it, is only one of degree; his argument, for all intents and purposes, is closely similar to the argument advanced by Marx in the last century.
7. See, for example, Peter Evans, Dietrich Rueschemeyer, and Theda Skocpol, eds., *Bringing the State Back In* (Cambridge, Massachusetts: Cambridge University Press, 1985).
8. Bertrand Badie and Pierre Birnbaum, *The Sociology of the State* (Chicago: University of Chicago Press, 1983).
9. Stephen Skowronek, *Building A New American State: The Expansion of National Administrative Capacities 1877–1920* (Cambridge, UK: Cambridge University Press, 1982).
10. See Julio Cotler and Richard R. Fagen, eds., *Latin America and the United States: The Changing Political Realities* (Stanford: Stanford University Press, 1974).

11. Arthur M. Schlesinger, Jr., *The Imperial Presidency* (New York: Popular Library, 1974).
12. Richard J. Barnett, *Roots of War* (Baltimore, Maryland: Penguin Books, 1972).
13. Bob Woodward and Carl Bernstein, *The Final Days* (New York: Simon and Schuster, 1976).
14. *Statistical Abstract of the United States*, 1980, Tables 432 and 436.
15. David Wise and Thomas B. Ross, *The Invisible Government* (New York: Random House, 1974); Bob Woodward, *Veil: The Secret Wars of the CIA, 1981–87* (New York: Simon and Schuster, 1987); Scott D. Breckinridge, *CIA and the Cold War* (Westport, Connecticut: Praeger Publishers, 1993).
16. See, for example, Gary T. Marx, "Thoughts on a Neglected Category of Social Movement Participants: The Agent Provocateur and the Informant," *American Journal of Sociology*, 80 (September 1974), 402-421; James Rule, Douglas McAdam, Linda Stearns, and David Uglow, *The Politics of Privacy* (New York: New American Library, 1980).
17. Gary Marx, "The Agent Provocateur and the Informant"; also see more generally, Gary T. Marx, *Undercover: Police Surveillance in America* (Berkeley, California: University of California Press, 1988).
18. For some recent discussion, see: Rodney Lowe, *The Welfare State in Britain Since 1945* (London: Macmillan, 1993); John Brown, *The British Welfare State: A Critical History* (Oxford: Basil Blackwell, 1995); Gosta Esping-Andersen, ed., *Welfare States in Transition: National Adaptations in Global Economies* (London: Sage Publishers, 1996).
19. Gosta Esping-Andersen, "After the Golden Age? Welfare State Dilemmas in a Global Economy," in Esping-Andersen, ibid., pp. 1–31.
20. John P. Stephens, "The Scandinavian Welfare States: Achievements, Crisis and Prospects," in Esping-Andersen, ibid., pp. 32–65.
21. Theda Skocpol, *Protecting Soldiers and Mothers: The Political Origins of Social Policy in the United States* (Cambridge, Massachusetts: The Belknap Press of Harvard University Press, 1992).
22. G. William Domhoff, *Who Rules America? Power and Politics in the Year 2000*, Third Edition (Mountain View, California: Mayfield Publishing Company, 1998).
23. Ibid., p. 272.
24. Jill Quadagno, *The Transformation of Old Age Security: Class and Politics in the American Welfare State* (Chicago: University of Chicago Press, 1988), p. 189.
25. David M. Potter, *People of Plenty: Economic Abundance and the American Character* (Chicago: University of Chicago Press, 1954).
26. Adolph A. Berle and Gardiner C. Means, *The Modern Corporation and Private Property*, revised edition (New York: Harcourt Brace Jovanovich, 1968).
27. William Roy, *Socializing Capital: The Rise of the Large Industrial Corporation in America* (Princeton, NJ: Princeton University Press, 1997).
28. *Statistical Abstract of the United States*, 1986, Tables 821 and 893.
29. Domhoff, *Who Rules America?*, Chapter 2.

30. On important early work, see: Michael Patrick Allen, "The Structure of Interorganizational Elite Co-optation: Interlocking Corporate Directorates," *American Sociological Review*, 39 (June 1974), 393–406; Michael Patrick Allen, "Management Control in the Large Corporation: Comment on Zeitlin," *American Journal of Sociology*, 81 (January 1976), 885–94; Maurice Zeitlin, "Corporate Ownership and Control: The Large Corporation and the Capitalist Class," *American Journal of Sociology*, 79 (March 1974), 1073–1119; and Maurice Zeitlin, "On Class Theory of the Large Corporation: Response to Allen," *American Journal of Sociology*, 81 (January 1976), 894–903. On somewhat later work see: Michael Schwartz, ed., *The Structure of Power in America: The Corporate Elite As a Ruling Class* (New York: Holmes and Meier, 1987), Part I; and Mark S. Mizruchi and Michael Schwartz, eds., *Intercorporate Relations: The Structural Analysis of Business* (Cambridge, Massachusetts: Cambridge University Press, 1987).

    For the most recent and careful assessment of network interlocks in the corporate sphere, see Mark S. Mizruchi, "What Do Interlocks Do? An Analysis, Critique and Assessment of Research on Interlocking Directorates," *Annual Review of Sociology* (1996), Volume 22, pp. 271–98.
31. Domhoff, *Who Rules America?*, pp. 36 ff.
32. Rudolf Hilferding, *Das Finanzkapital* (Vienna: I. Brand, 1910).
33. Richard Ratcliff, "The Inner Circle and Bank Lending Policy," in Schwartz, ed., *The Structure of Power in America*, pp. 154–162, at p. 161.
34. Beth Mintz and Michael Schwartz, "Corporate Interlocks, Financial Hegemony, and Intercorporate Coordination," in Schwartz, ibid., pp. 34–47, at p. 46.
35. Michael Useem, *The Inner Circle: Large Corporations and the Rise of Business Political Activity in the U.S. and U.K.* (New York: Oxford University Press, 1984).
36. Richard J. Barnet and Ronald E. Muller, *Global Reach and the Power of the Multinational Corporations* (New York: Simon & Schuster, 1974), pp. 14–15.
37. James Bearden, "Financial Hegemony, Social Capital and Bank Boards of Directors," in Schwartz, ed., *The Structure of Power in America*, pp. 48–59.
38. G. William Domhoff, *Who Rules America?*, Chapter 2.
39. Gwen Moore, "The Structure of a National Elite Network," *American Sociological Review*, 44 (October 1979), 673–92.
40. Mark S. Mizruchi, *The Structure of Corporate Political Action: Interfirm Relations and Their Consequences* (Cambridge, Massachusetts: Harvard University Press, 1992).
41. Dan Clawson, Alan Neustadtl, and Denise Scott, *Money Talks: Corporate PACs and Political Influence* (New York: Basic Books, 1992).
42. Michael Useem, *The Inner Circle*, op.cit., p. 192.
43. Essentially this is the interpretation taken by Seymour Martin Lipset. See Seymour Martin Lipset, "Some Social Requisites of Democracy," *American Political Science Review*, Vol. 53 (March 1959), 69–105.
44. See, for example, Gunnar Myrdal, *An American Dilemma: The Negro in A White Nation*, Volumes I and II (New York: McGraw-Hill, 1944; 1962).
45. John Kenneth Galbraith, *The Affluent Society* (Boston: Houghton Mifflin, 1958).

46. Edward N. Wolff, *Top Heavy: A Study of the Increasing Inequality of Wealth in America* (New York: Twentieth Century Fund Press, 1995).
47. William Julius Wilson, *The Truly Disadvantaged: The Inner City, the Underclass, and Public Policy* (Chicago: University of Chicago Press, 1987).
48. David Cay Johnston, "Gap Between Rich and Poor Found Substantially Wider," *The New York Times*, Sunday, September 5, 1999, p. 14Y.
49. As quoted in *The New York Times*, Monday, April 17, 1995, pages A1; C4. For other recent data on the inequality of wealth in the United States and other nations, see: Denny Braun, *The Rich Get Richer: The Rise of Income Inequality in the U.S. and the World* (Chicago: Nelson Hall, 1997), and the United Nations Human Development Report, 1999.
50. T.H. Marshall, "Citizenship and Social Class," in T.H. Marshall and Tom Bottomore, *Citizenship and Social Class* (London: Pluto Press, 1950; 1992).
51. Michael Schudson, *The Good Citizen: A History of American Civic Life* (New York: The Free Press, 1998).
52. Gunnar Myrdal, *An American Dilemma*, Volume 1, Chapter 1.
53. Frances Fox Piven and Richard A. Cloward, *Regulating the Poor* (New York: Pantheon, 1971).

Chapter 7

Power and Politics in the Modern Metropolis

> All politics is local.
>
> Tip O'Neill, former Democratic Speaker,
> United States House of Representatives

Today, as the world becomes an increasingly smaller place, aided in large part by the new information technology, it would seem that many older institutions and structures might lose their influence over our lives. Nation-states, for instance, no longer seem to be such a powerful force. New alliances have formed, erasing old divisions and creating the basis for new, more broad-ranging policies in the future. Consider the case of Western Europe. Here are nations that are several centuries old, with long-lasting divisions and conflicts with one another, about to embark on a great economic and political experiment—the European Union. Or, consider the case of cities. Once, in the fifteenth and sixteenth centuries, cities wielded great power over the world. Recall the city-states of Venice and Florence. These were medieval empires, with their own navies and armies, acting like the nation-states of today. And yet they have disappeared, replaced by nations, and now transnational alliances.

One must ask: Are cities still an important force over our lives? And in what ways? Those are the two central questions that will drive this chapter. I will argue that cities represent a significant part of our lives, and that how they wield power—and we wield power as citizens living in them—remain significant features of the contemporary world. In some countries, particularly the United States, cities retain a great deal of their power, largely because of the federated structure of American government and the evidence of local autonomy in the rule of municipalities over many of their own affairs. In other countries, like Great Britain, the power of the locality is more limited. The national government controls much of the funding for local communities, and the exercise of politics and power, while quaintly seated in local councils, is really fought out in the House of Commons. But things can always change. In just the past decade, for example, the People's Republic of China has witnessed a major shift of control in cities. Special economic zones (SEZs) have been created in which the role of local leaders and businessmen plays a larger part than ever before. In cities like Shanghai, the role of local officials has become ever more important, a startling change from the pre-1978 period under the rule of Mao Tse Tung.

This chapter will consider the following prominent themes: (1) the varying and competing theoretical perspectives on cities and politics; (2) the nature of the city in American history, and how historical changes are reflected in the nature of its politics; and (3) the changing fortunes of cities as the effects of a global economy become ever more present in the destinies and lives of citizens living in cities, particularly in the largest cities of the world.

THEORETICAL PERSPECTIVES ON CITIES AND POLITICS

Beginning in the 1950s, various battles were waged among social scientists competing to understand and interpret the nature of politics in American cities.[1] The first, and most major, skirmish occurred between scholars who called themselves *pluralists*, on the one hand, and those who referred to themselves as *elitists*, on the other. The issue boiled down to the question of how much power the citizens of local communities in America had—very little, or a lot. The pluralists maintained that citizens possessed considerable opportunity to exercise power over their lives, whereas the elitists thought that the politics of cities were controlled by fairly small handfuls of officials and business figures.

Fortunately, some time has passed and the residue of that debate has been more or less swept away. But new debates and issues now dominate the urban scene—and new perspectives as well. Here I shall consider several of the more important perspectives on cities and how they and their politics work. I begin with the old standard, the pluralist view. Though it suffered some serious blows as a result of work in the 1960s, with the growing importance of work on civil societies and politics it is likely that the pluralist view will be revived. Besides, it remains an important, if nevertheless flawed, way to think of the politics of American cities.

Political Pluralism in the City: Civil Society and the Dispersal of Power

Though pluralism has a long and rich history in American political thought, it was only with the writings and theory of the political scientist Robert A. Dahl that pluralism shifted from a rough paradigm to a full-fledged theory of urban politics.[2] Dahl's argument was cast very broadly, and though he spoke of an urban polity, he really intended his general view to be applicable more broadly to the making of modern democracies. His is a view that grows out of the general notion that the institutions of a society, or place, are very significant to the politics of that society.

Dahl's view is based on an analysis and interpretation of politics in the city of New Haven, Connecticut, in the early 1960s. He begins by insisting that life in New Haven, like that of the rest of America, can best be seen in terms of dominant institutional sectors—the economic, the political, the arts, and the religious institutions. Within each of these major institutional sectors, special organizations and groups produce for and demand the special talents of members of the general public. Next, Dahl claims that the ongoing character of each of the institutional sectors and, of course, the organizations within them operates through the accumulation and investment of basic resources. Moreover, the operations of each sphere tend to require specialized forms of resources; the economic sphere deals in the accumulation and investment of material wealth, the sphere of high society in the accumulation and investment of prestige, and the political sphere in the accumulation and investment of political power. Here, of course, he follows Max Weber in specifying, in effect, the crucial differences among class, status, and parties (see Chapter 3).

In addition, he argues that most people do not care much about politics. There are those who are active and concerned in a regular fashion about politics, including mainly political officials but also some citizens, but most citizens are subject to inertia and do not care what happens in the political world. Nevertheless, the world still operates well in Dahl's pluralist universe, primarily because the leaders always seek *to anticipate* the wishes and desires of the citizens—that, of course, is the essence of the democratic electoral process—and because all citizens, leaders and lay citizens alike, share the same common values and goals. Finally, Dahl actually put his theory to a test and, with the aid of several key research assistants, closely examined the process of decision making over the period of a year. Dahl more or less confirmed his expectations: Power was dispersed widely among the public. On different issues, such as schools and parties, alternative groups came into play; and the most powerful, or influential, figure in the city was the Mayor, Richard Lee.

A number of important studies in the 1960s generally confirmed and supported Dahl's pluralist portrait of the city, including important work by

Wallace Sayre and Herbert Kaufman on New York City.[3] Indeed, for a time the pluralist view was the most widely accepted view of the way politics operates in the cities and communities of America. Even today, there is much to recommend the notion that different groups can exercise their will over the nature of urban politics, depending on the particular kinds of issues up for discussion. But there also are important reservations about the pluralist view. These come from camps based more centrally on a neo-Marxist, or political economy, rendering of the city.

The City as a Growth Machine: The Political Economy of the City

In the early 1970s, the pluralist view of the urban polity came under heavy fire. In part, there was criticism that the pluralists did not possess an objective view of politics, but rather a view that had become entrenched as the American ideology.[4] In part, the criticism came from the other school of urban sociology, the elitists, who believed that the pluralists failed to understand how much power the rich and wealthy exercised in many American communities. But the main criticism of the pluralist view was leveled by the sociologist who, as it happened, provided a new interpretation of the urban arena—sociologist Harvey Molotch.

The pluralists had argued that essentially all policies and all groups were equal in the urban polity. Everyone had a voice; every group could exercise power, but political officials seemed to exercise more of it. Molotch, trained at the University of Chicago, argued that the pluralist view was mistaken. Not all issues count the same; not all voices are equal. In fact, the main emphasis of cities and other communities, Molotch insisted, is that of growth. Growth is the driving force of the city; all other issues and principles are subordinate to it.[5]

The city, Molotch writes, is like a growth machine. It churns out policies that favor and promote its growth. This is, in effect, its *raison d'être:*

> the political and economic essence of virtually any given locality in the present American context, is *growth.* . . . [The] desire for growth provides the key operative motivation toward consensus for members of politically mobilized local elites. [This] growth imperative is the most important constraint upon available options for local initiative in social and economic reform. . . . [Thus] the very essence of a locality is its operation as a growth machine.[6]

The very nature of the American city is to expand and to grow. Real estate brokers and entrepreneurs are growth's main proponents. They play a large role, transforming the land and space of the city into commodities. But other actors in the city also profit from growth. Political officials, Molotch argues, stand to gain from growth because the greater the number of residents and territory over which they rule, the greater their power. Eventually a kind of unholy alliance emerges in the city—of real estate entrepreneurs, bankers, political officials, even the media brokers—all of whom generally favor and sponsor growth because they benefit from it.

In a sequel to his article, Molotch and John Logan expand on the theory of the urban arena.[7] Drawing from some important other work, such as that of the geographer David Harvey, they argue that cities, like other forms of property under capitalism, are subject to two kinds of valuation.[8] One is valuation based on the market, otherwise known as *exchange value;* the other is valuation based upon the use to which residents put their property, otherwise known as *use-value.* The distinction is one first introduced by Karl Marx to explain the nature and emergence of *commodities* under modern capitalism. Logan and Molotch go on to argue that urban land and space, themselves, become subject to an eventful history of *commodification.*

The political struggles and tensions of cities are waged over how, and whether, land and space will become commodities. They write: "[the] legal creation and regulation of places have been primarily under the domination of those searching, albeit sometimes in the face of use-value counter-demands, for exchange value gains."[9] Citizens have their own preferences for land, particularly for their own land, and land in their neighborhoods. As Logan and Molotch observe, there are several different use values evident among property owners and their neighbors. They include "the daily round," that residents make about their neighborhood, the sense of identity connected to a place, and the presence of social support networks.[10] When the purposes of real estate brokers and entrepreneurs come into conflict with those of local residents, essentially over the nature of the values for land and space, then major political battles break out, often visible in the contentious politics of city hall.

In my own research on a Sunbelt city, I found that there can be deep, cultural differences between those who view the land of these areas in terms of the profit they can gain from them, and those who view the land for its main value for them. In Austin, Texas, and other cities across the Sunbelt, the main use value lay in terms of the broader environmental meaning that the land held for main people. In particular, I discovered that

> On the one hand, there are those people who today define the land purely and simply in terms of modern-day capitalism, that is, as a commodity. To them, the land in and around Austin has meaning only insofar as it can be sold, and it can bring them a profit, perhaps of considerable proportions. . . . On the other hand, there exists another group of people, who possess an entirely different conception of the land. To them, humans and nature possess a special kind of relationship, one of balance, a harmony that must not be based by the senseless abuse of land. To this group of people, the land is to be preserved as much as possible in its natural, primitive state, and equally as much to be used for the enjoyment of the broad public rather than simply the large-scale developer, or even the private landowner.[11]

Indeed, the sense that nature possesses a value in and of itself has come to characterize many of the more rural areas subject to development and growth now in America, a part of the broader effort to implant environmentalism as a new and important American value.

Other research also has emphasized the role of real estate entrepreneurs and developers in the urban arena. Sociologists Joe Feagin and Mark Gottdiener argue that real estate entrepreneurs play a major role in shaping the city, and that their power acts, often invisibly, to determine the choices that cities make.[12] Other urban scholars, like Susan Fainstein, make similar points.[13]

The growth machine view of the city, and of urban politics, has become immensely popular over the past twenty years, certainly the most widely cited interpretation of urban politics. While many voices often can be and are heard, it is clear that in early twenty-first century America, urban growth continues to be a central issue, and those who advocate it frequently represent an unholy alliance of actors on its behalf.

City Limits

The pluralists and the proponents of the growth machine theory alike work on the assumption that cities make a difference, not only to the lives of their residents, but also to the character of American politics. But other astute observers of the American political scene take a radically different view of the matter.

In 1981, the political scientist Paul Peterson made a major departure from past work on the American city.[14] Peterson argued that cities no longer mattered very much to American politics, a view that echoed an earlier argument by the sociologist C. Wright Mills.[15] He insisted that, in fact, cities make little difference to power in general. "[Cities] cannot make war or peace; they cannot issue passports or forbid outsiders from entering their territory; they cannot issue currency; and they cannot control imports or erect tariff walls."[16] Cities, in brief, experience limits to the exercise of their influence and power.

To elaborate his view Peterson sets about in a very careful and precise demonstration of the limits of cities. One of his most powerful points is to demonstrate that while many citizens in the late 1970s were in desperate need for resources, cities that were best able to meet the needs of such citizens were, in general, the wealthier and more affluent cities. In effect, cities with many impoverished citizens failed to meet their needs because they did not possess the resources. There was only one political agency in America at the time that could meet the needs of the poorest citizens of cities— the federal government. In effect, Peterson's argument bore witness to the centrality of the federal government in late twentieth century America, yet another way in which his argument resembled that of Mills.

Peterson's most important contribution is to suggest that there are three major policy domains for cities. They are: *allocational*; *redistributive*; and *developmental*. Allocational policies cover the regular and daily workings of local government, in other words, the "housekeeping" policies. Policies that deal with the cost of the fire department or police department, the running of the government accounting office, or the need for new political structures, all are examples of allocational decisions. In effect, they make little real difference to citizens' lives; they simply keep the operations of government running. Redistributive policies cover most of the concerns we think important to the lives of the needy and frail of local citizens—the effort to provide monies, welfare assistance, and other forms of aid to local residents. But, as Peterson showed, the poorest cities are the least able to handle such costs for their citizens. And thus it was left to the federal government to help such citizens through various kind of federal relief and welfare measures.

Finally, there are developmental policies—tax inducements to lure business, the establishment of industrial parks, the effort to create a strong new tourism base in cities. They are the only policies, Peterson believes, that cities can control. They are the policies that cities use to compete with one another in order to attract new business firms and citizens to their locales. And they are the policies that truly make the difference between booming cities and cities that fare less well. In other words, just as Molotch and Logan argue that the central purpose of American cities is to promote their growth and expansion, so Peterson makes the same argument but from a very different vantage point. Cities cannot make war, but they can compete with one another by offering better packages to residents looking for a new and better place to live.

Since its publication, Peterson's argument has been one of the most influential in the study and examination of urban politics. It is as widely cited as that of Molotch and Logan, but for entirely different reasons. Moreover, because it has come to be viewed as a radical and abrupt break from the pluralist view of American political scientists, it has also prompted a strong debate from those social scientists who continue to insist that cities are important, and that cities still matter on a whole range of issues to their residents. And that group includes those scholars who advocate the last important theory of urban politics today, regime theory.

Regime Theory: History and Local Governance

The fourth theory that attracts some proponents of the continuing importance of urban politics today has become known as *regime theory*. Its origins are due to the work and writings of two political scientists, Stephen Elkin and Clarence Stone.[17]

The argument of regime theory takes up, in a sense, where that of Robert Dahl and the pluralists left off. Dahl and the pluralists emphasized the wide dispersal and distribution of power in cities, noting that the capacity to make decisions in local politics varied to some extent with the particular issue at hand. To the pluralists there are, in effect, multiple, or plural, bases of power. But the problem with this view, as shown by later analysts, is that not all groups are equal in their capacity to make decisions. Some, in particular the business community, hold far more sway, being able to effect their decisions much more easily than other groups.

Stone counters this criticism by arguing that even if cities become dominated by a coalition of business interests, this does not necessarily mean they will simply become committed to measures designed to enhance growth and the profits of business. He suggests, to the contrary, that urban politics is not a zero-sum game, in which the presence of power on the part of the business community means its absence for other groups. Rather, the city must be viewed as a "world in chaos." The formal institutional arrangements have little impact on what happens in the city. In fact, the way cities are run is through a set of informal arrangements of cooperation that take place over time: in other words, an urban regime.

Stone argues that many cities can be seen as possessing such regimes, and even though the business elite appears to dominate the structure of power, actual decisions take place through a process of negotiations, selective incentives, and the seizing of "small opportunities." Nothing can be taken for granted or as predictable under regimes, even those dominated by the business community. Where Peterson's formal, rational choice model, based upon economic reasoning, suggests an opposition between, let us say, redistributive and developmental policies, Stone's more careful examination of the process reveals far greater complexity—and a trade-off between an effort to be efficient and an effort to be just, or equitable in urban politics. Consider this illustration he furnishes of politics in Atlanta:

> In 1946, the central element in the governing coalition was a downtown business elite organized for and committed to an active program of redevelopment that would transform the character of the business district and, in the process, displace a largely black population to the south and east of the district. At the same time, with the end of the white primary that same year, a middle-class black population, long excluded from power, mobilized its electoral strength to begin an assault on a firmly entrenched Jim Crow system. Knowing only those facts, one might well have predicted in 1946 that these two groups would be political antagonists. They were not. Both committed to an agenda of change, they worked out an accommodation and became the city's governing coalition [over the next several decades].[18]

Stone's point is quite simple. The nature of urban politics in America is such that formal arrangements and positions mean very little, and that the actual process involves a series of compromises, all of which are designed to create productive decisions for the city. Various groups draw on the resources available to them, for instance, power or numbers of people, and then come together in cooperative ventures.

The main difference between regime theory and those of the growth machine and Peterson is this: all three agree on the importance of business figures and on issues of growth and development for cities. But whereas the growth machine views the power of business alliances as pernicious, Peterson sees it as natural to the city, and Stone believes that the actual processes of urban politics lead to compromise and negotiation between business leaders and other key groups. Business may appear to be dominant, but it works for cooperative arrangements with its political neighbors out of a sense they are "all in this together."

Concluding Observations

It always is difficult, especially for beginning students, to understand and appreciate competing views of how cities work. In the social sciences, in general, old theories do not disappear to be replaced by newer ones; instead there is a kind of recycling of old theories. Primarily that happens because no theory ever seems able to convey the richness of the empirical reality with which we deal. Reductionist theories seem to miss the boat altogether; abstract theories fail to make historical sense much of the time. Yet we do move ahead, however slowly. The Molotch-Logan theory—and later, Peterson—recognize one central fact of modern American cities: the unparalleled significance of growth. Not all policies make a difference today—growth is the watchword, the *sine qua non* of the American city. Good cities are those that grow; bad cities are those that do not. And we harbor the notion that collections of citizens can make a difference to such policies.

But theories may rise and fall with the ebb tides of history. Growth has not always been the dominating factor of American cities—and the growth machine has not always looked the same. We shall get a better sense of the significance of historical change to the politics of cities as we delve, however briefly, into the history of American cities.

THE METROPOLIS IN AMERICAN HISTORY

Social scientists, because of the nature of their discipline, often have a blind spot for history. New theories get invented and seem to represent the final answer to understanding such things as urban politics. But they remain influential only so long as the historical circumstances to which they point also remain in place. In fact, when the broad sweep of urban history is understood, then and only then do we understand why some theories are right—because they are applicable only to certain points in history and time. In this regard, then, the social sciences are very different from the natural and physical sciences. To better understand American cities, and the theories we use to describe them, I shall turn now to a discussion of some of their historical ebb and flow.

The Rise and Fall of the Industrial Metropolis

In American history there have been different forms and kinds of cities. In the eighteenth century there was the *mercantilist city*. This was a city in which commerce and local business played a prominent role. The economic philosophy of the day was mercantilism, a philosophy that emphasized the limited role of government, and the central significance of commerce to the fortunes of the city. It was a city of limited size, and even more limited growth. Local government did matter to the fortunes of local residents. It was a city that the historian, Sam Bass Warner, Jr., would characterize as a "walking city."[19] Distances meant nothing to travel. The city, especially the central part, was small. Residents could walk and visit one another often. They came to be neighborly, and to know one another intimately. It was the kind of city that the nineteenth-century sociologist, Ferdinand Toennies, and the twentieth-century urbanist, Louis Wirth, would characterize for its qualities of *gemeinschaft*, or community: small, friendly, commercial, sociable.[20] Early Boston and early Philadelphia represent examples of such a city.

By the middle part of the nineteenth century, however, the nature of many American cities began to change. They changed under the weight of the industrial revolution, the great revolution that brought about such fundamental transformation to the way business and commerce were done in America, and the American city in particular. Over the course of the next century, the American city would become, in effect, an industrial city. And the nature and fortunes of industry would leave their mark deeply etched on the character of this city.[21]

We can trace the growth and development of the industrial city in terms of a series of stages. Four stages are evident. They are: (1) a *pre-industrial stage* that represents the early origins of many such cities; (2) an *early industrial stage* in which the city becomes radically transformed; (3) a *mature industrial stage*, in which the rapid growth declines, and the nature of the city also becomes altered; and (4) a *stage of incipient decline*, when industry begins to depart the city, looking for more profits elsewhere, and when the city—and local citizens—begin to face substantial crises. Each stage has become associated with a different form and type of politics and governance. In fact, because the stages also are associated with differences in the form of internal politics, they may also help to explain why there can be differences among cities at the same point in time.[22]

The Reign of Local Notables and the Engagement of Ordinary Citizens. The first stage of the industrial city was for many the stage of their origins. It was a time when certain fairly small groups of men dominated the life of the city. In particular, those people who specialized in the purchase and sale of land for the city exercised dominance over its business and political life. They were men who were among the founders of the city. They were the city's earliest businessmen, and often the most successful. In part because of their importance to the commerce of the city, their fellow citizens often selected them to become the first public officials of the city. Thus, in the city of Milwaukee, Wisconsin, for instance, Byron Kilbourn and Solomon Juneau, among the city's founders, were also among the city's earliest mayors. The same pattern—founders and early mayors—characterized other cities at a similar period in their development.[23] Moreover, because the nature of government was primitive and undeveloped—essentially there was no local government—many local citizens became engaged in the activities of the time, giving a sense of a genuine commitment to and involvement in the local community. It was at this stage for many American cities in the 1830s and 1840s, incidentally, that Alexis de Tocqueville would come to America, observing what for him was a defining characteristic, the extensive and active participation by Americans in its many forms of associations and politics.[24]

The Industrial Revolution and Rise of the Capitalist Class. Almost overnight the character of the preindustrial, or commercial, city changed. In many older American cities, this took place in the 1860s and 1870s.[25] There was a great industrial boom, brought about by such inventions as the steam engine and other apparatus that made work go more easily. Manual labor was replaced by the labor of machines. One invention after another piled up, resulting in a whole range of new implements, from farm equipment to new forms of leather and leather manufacture. New industry meant a new slew of jobs and job opportunities as well. This was a time when many immigrants came to America from abroad because of the new opportunities they found here. Within the city itself, the nature of politics changed as well. The early entrepreneurs, who had specialized in the sale and purchase of land, now were overtaken by the new businessmen, who were making fortunes hand over fist. Industry, in general, came to drive the overall expansion of the city, replacing the earlier forms of commerce.[26]

This stage also witnessed the rise of a new capitalist class in the city, in general, those whose wealth came from profits and fortunes in the industrial sector. Though much remains to be learned about the precise nature of this class, in cities like Milwaukee there is clear evidence that the power at this time was not only lodged in the hands of individuals of great wealth, but such individuals came to form, along with others, a tight-knit class.[27] At the same time, there emerged in many American cities a class of laborers who themselves came to form groups in opposition to the capitalist class. Moreover, their organization often took the form of unions, or radical politics, which provided a wedge and division from the capitalists.

Government in this phase remained small and comparatively primitive, showing only tentative signs of the kind of expansion and dominance that came to highlight business and industry. If there were, in contemporary terms, a growth machine, it was not government at all, but industry—hard, heavy industry that brought in many, many workers from abroad and drove the expansion of the city forward.[28]

The Mature Industrial City: Emergent Government and Political Division. By the turn of the century, many of America's new industrial cities had changed dramatically from only two or three decades earlier. They were substantially larger cities, many having grown by the hundreds of thousands. The city of Chicago, for instance, grew from a city of 109,260 in 1860, to a city of 1,698,575 in 1900. But more than the growth of the local population was involved. There also came to be a new configuration of forces and structures that characterized and drove the fortunes of the city. In Milwaukee, Wisconsin, for example, local government had risen to prominence by the end of the century. New departments came into being, including the police and fire departments. Professional staffs ran them; they had hired numbers of new employees.[29] Compensation was now offered for the services of individuals, whereas earlier volunteer citizens had maintained such forces. The overall structure of local government had increased immeasurably by 1900, if not rivaling the value of local industry, at least approximating its worth.

The effect of the growth of government and the consolidation of local business was to transform government from being merely a kind of handmaiden to the work of business to becoming a rival for power in the city. Again, Milwaukee provides an illustration of how this happened.[30] In Milwaukee, local businessmen had long been strong supporters of local government. In fact, there was something of an alliance between the two groups: Business supported the work of government, and government supported the work of business. But as the powers of government grew, in terms of new departments, a professionalization of the staff, the very value of local political structures, a division also grew between local government and local business. Government demanded more resources for the needs of local citizens. Businessmen began to resist. In Milwaukee, the division was fueled because the Social Democrats had come to assume such strong power in the city.

This was a period for many cities when the institution of government had grown so much in its authority over the life of local citizens that some figures came to office and were corrupted by the power they experienced. It was, in a sense, the historical heyday both of local government and of local mayors, who could use the power of local government. For most of the older American industrial cities this stage took place in the early 1900s, when the power of local government provided a platform for ambitious officials to exercise and wield their dominance over the urban arena.[31]

Decline of the Industrial City: the Loss of Industry, Local Clout, and the Rise of Ethnic/Racial Conflicts. By the 1930s, many local governments would attain the pinnacle of their powers. Local mayors were critical to the success of local cities. This was as true of cities like Philadelphia as it was of cities like Boston or Chicago. The great financial collapse, caused by the Depression, soon changed the fortunes of cities and their local officials.[32] Many cities were again transformed, but now from bustling business local empires to places that could no longer meet the needs of their citizens. As businesses failed, more was asked of government, especially local government. Early welfare measures were begun, such as local relief efforts to provide food and clothing. But the main responsibility became shifted to the federal government. Only in a few places, like Milwaukee, did the local officials manage to work so effectively that they actually had surplus monies in their coffers by the end of the fiscal year. Most cities were virtually bankrupt.[33]

The decline of the American industrial city that had begun in the 1930s would diminish briefly during the period of World War II but accelerate once again in the 1960s and 1970s. This time truly was a time when the industrial city came to experience substantial decline and misfortune. Several events happened that would change the city once more. Many businesses began to depart the central city, leaving either for places in the South and Southwest or for abroad. They were lured to their new surroundings by one simple fact: bigger profits. In the South, they could expect to find few, if any, taxes; abroad, wage labor was far cheaper than in the United States. The net effect, however, was to leave many of the industrial cities in deep financial trouble.[34] Lacking the monies they secured from local businesses, by way of local taxes and by way of the wealth spent in the city, local governments now were left bereft of funds and resources.[35]

The American industrial city was thus left looking like a shell of its former self. In cities like Cleveland, Pittsburgh, and Detroit, the city was in great physical disrepair. Old manufacturing plants stood as the relics of a rich and flourishing past. Parts of Detroit, at the time, resembled nothing so much as a kind of urban concentration camp, old buildings having been boarded up, ringed by barbed wire fences to prevent people from getting in—or perhaps getting out. The loss of business and the inability of local governments to survive successfully especially hurt certain populations. Older residents were hurt, those in their 50s and 60s who were fired by the departing businesses. Many such employees not only were left without a job, but also without pensions to cover their old age. Ethnic minority populations, like that of African Americans, were left to become an underclass in the American city, particularly hard hit by the loss of industries.[36]

What is especially tragic is the way that the declines of the industrial city helped to fuel the tensions between different racial and ethnic groups. African Americans and Hispanics were hit particularly hard by the decline.[37] African American populations expanded in certain cities just as the jobs they sought left. Many such populations also became prey to the machinations of local businesses and industries. Certain areas of cities in which African Americans lived became areas in which local banks and savings and loans refused to provide money for the purchase of homes.[38] The suburbs, which began to grow after World War II, also made the situation doubly difficult because many such places, if they did not actively discourage minority residents, certainly did not welcome them with open arms.

This last stage of the American industrial city, that of decline, is a stage that many cities are just now leaving. It is a stage when both local industry and local government have been shown to be vulnerable. It is a stage when the federal government came to assume a great deal of the responsibility for helping the needs of the elderly and the African American underclass, but which, in recent memory, the responsibility has devolved back to state governments.

Concluding Observations. In sum, then, the American industrial city became transformed over time, as did its politics. Moreover, because it did change, the applicability of theories describing it also would change. Theories that emphasized the rule of elite figures, or notables, would be especially applicable to its earliest stage, while theories that emphasized its limits came to be most relevant only to its latest historical stage, from the 1960s to 1990s. Moreover, the growth machine theory, which speaks to the importance of land and real estate in the nature of the city, describes cities early in their origins but says little about the emergent institutions within them. In fact, the growth machine theory, with its emphasis on growth at all costs, is really a theory not of industrial cities but of postindustrial cities, as we shall soon see.

The Contentious Politics of the American Metropolis: Central Cities, Suburbs, and Edge Cities

One of the principal features of the American city, and larger metropolis, that emerged at roughly the same time as the industrial city itself, was a deepening division between the central part of the city and the suburbs.[39] Kenneth Jackson traces the history of American suburbs in considerable detail, noting that many of them began in the nineteenth century, an effort on the part of Americans to capture their bucolic past.[40] Many of the more wealthy residents of the city were able to move to its outer fringes, especially as facilities for transportation became available. Soon this began to leave the city looking somewhat like its growing class divisions—the poorer, laboring class living in the central parts, near work, while the richer residents were able to take advantage of the outer fringes, either for recreational housing or for year-round living.[41]

As time went by, the effect became very pronounced. By the early part of the twentieth century, many suburbs were incorporating themselves separately from the central cities.[42] Part of the effort was fueled by the growing class differences in their residents, but part was simply facilitated by the ability of small American municipalities to incorporate them. Thus began the deep, and continuing, division between the central cities and the suburbs of the American metropolis. The split was made more or less real, and legal, by key court decisions, such as that in the case of St. Louis in 1875. This decision said that localities were creatures of the state, and that the state had jurisdiction over such localities. It also gave permission to small local areas, like villages and burgeoning suburbs, to split off from the central cities. Cities like St. Louis, for example, soon became ringed by sets of small villages and suburbs, a fringe area that would eventually become a refuge for the city's wealthier residents.[43]

In some metropolitan areas, like Milwaukee, the spatial division became accentuated by the effort of local industrial suburbs to remain strictly autonomous of the city. West Allis, for instance, a suburban area that housed the Allis-Chalmers Manufacturing firm, refused to become incorporated as part of Milwaukee, largely because it wished to control its own resources. In Cleveland, new housing developments were built in suburban areas, and for their own reasons they too sought and secured legal and political independence from the city of Cleveland. When cities sought to annex or to consolidate with such suburban regimes, suburbs generally successfully fought off such attempts, supported by both the courts and rural-dominated state legislatures.[44]

As many older industrial cities entered the declining phase of their development in the 1960s and 1970s, the central city-suburban split came back to haunt them. What had begun as an effort by suburbanites to protect their wealthy lifestyle, now became the device that would further deepen the economic woes of many central cities. The highways and expressways built after World War II had accelerated the move to the suburbs. And by the early 1960s, suburban areas accounted for a growing percentage of the American metropolitan population. The suburbs not only had robbed the central cities of residents, but of their wealthier residents. And because local taxes were secured from local residents, the gap in the financial resources of the central cities and the suburbs widened considerably. Cities like New York and Cleveland went into default in large part because they no longer housed the residents able to provide the tax monies for their budgets.[45]

Such facts, historical and cultural in nature, provide the framework for understanding both the politics and the varied successes and failures of American cities over the past couple of decades. Recent research by David Rusk, former mayor of Albuquerque, New Mexico, suggests that those metropolises that have been able to expand and to incorporate their suburban regions generally have done better surviving the industrial decline than those that have not.[46] Such expandable, or elastic, cities are ones that somehow managed to escape the deep splits, and financial hardships of many other industrial cities. In addition, Minnesota state legislator Myron Orfield, has demonstrated that the blight and problems of inner cities have begun to move into the first ring of suburban areas of certain metropolises, like Minneapolis. Building on these discoveries, Orfield has argued that metropolitan areas must make an effort to create metropolitan solutions for themselves, thereby overcoming the historic divisions between cities and suburbs. Orfield, among others, has become the proponent of "regionalism," a movement that urges more cooperative programs between the cities and suburbs of the American metropolis.[47] It is likely that this movement, and this program, will in the near future become a more visible feature of the politics of American cities.

A corollary to the growth of the regionalism movement on behalf of American cities is the recent emergence of *edge cities*.[48] Such cities are found on the fringe areas of the American metropolis, their growth often stimulated by the interstate highway system. Generally speaking, they consist of a cluster of businesses and malls, along with nearby housing developments. Such edge cities have flourished in recent years, springing up almost everywhere in America. Like the earlier suburbs, they are separate and autonomous from the central cities of the metropolis, governed, in the words of Joel Garreau, by small "shadow governments" that exercise considerable control and regulation over the lives of their firms and residents. Moreover, they are also the sites where many of the new jobs are now occurring in American cities, and thus they only make worse the problems that the underclass faces in the inner city as they try to find new job opportunities for themselves.[49]

As edge cities increase, and as suburbs—rather than the central city—come to house more and more of America's residents, the fulcrum of American urban politics also has begun to shift. In the past, the suburbs represented the heart of the Republican strength of the American city, but recent signs suggest that the Republican Party can no longer take the suburbs for granted. Nevertheless, the social composition and political inclinations of the suburbs are vastly different from their counterparts in the inner cities, thus accentuating the longstanding divisions. How politicians will deal with these differences will, along with regionalism, represent some of the key political issues of the near future for the American city.

The Post-World War II City: Sunbelt Cities and Metropolitan Fragmentation

Just as the interstate highway system accelerated the movement of Americans to the suburbs, so it aided the development of cities beyond the pale of industrial America. Virtually all of the industrial cities developed in the

Northeast and Midwest, in places like Boston, New York, Pittsburgh, and Detroit. But as the decline of these cities took place, many industries and firms began to relocate where they would not face taxes—in places like Atlanta, Dallas, and Phoenix. Spurred also by the growth of the defense industry during World War II, a tremendous urban boom happened in the so-called Sunbelt, its first signs evident in the 1960s.[50]

Sunbelt, or postindustrial cities, seem to be very different in their form and politics from the older industrial cities, although their pattern of underlying development seems much the same.[51] Most have avoided the deep political divisions evident between the central cities and the suburbs. Some have managed to avoid them simply because they learned from the experience of these older cities; others have managed because they are in states in which home rule exists, and in which many localities exercise more control over their own affairs than in the older industrial Midwest or Northeast. Sunbelt cities as a result have grown massive, both in terms of the number of their residents and in terms of their spatial dimensions. Cities like Phoenix or Tucson, Arizona, have exploded in size over the past several decades, far outdistancing older places like Pittsburgh and Milwaukee. Many have become the refuge for older residents, migrating from the North to the Sunbelt. And, of course, one effect of their expansion has been to shift the political weight of America somewhat from the North to the South.

Because of the rapidity of their growth, and because they are seen as lying on the frontier edges of America, such cities have become the central locale for the "growth machine" furor and politics. It is these cities, which have mushroomed so quickly, that the divisions are not over class issues, in the older sense, or between Republicans and Democrats, as between the progrowth and antigrowth forces.[52] States like Florida or Georgia are states where these issues are fought out in urban areas, and where the growth machine theory is to be seen in full and complete detail.

Some such Sunbelt cities also provide evidence of virtually no governmental controls over the site and place of urban expansion. Sprawl, which has become the fashionable epithet for those who oppose such expansion today, is evident in many such metropolitan areas, including Dallas, Atlanta, and Tucson, among others. Houston, Texas, is the site of almost massive sprawl. Houston has virtually no zoning controls over its growth. Because of this, real estate developers have been able to exercise freely their dominance over Houston. Sociologist Joe Feagin refers to Houston as a "free enterprise city," a place where the business community exercises its power almost at will.[53] Real estate developers have been able to create various residential tracts almost free of any kind of zoning regulations. Moreover, Feagin suggests the absence of such controls has created decided disadvantages, including greater pollution of the atmosphere and uneven growth in the metropolis.

Many other Sunbelt cities have taken on a similar character. The earliest such example is that of Los Angeles, described by the urban historian

Robert Fogelson as "the fragmented metropolis."[54] Los Angeles, unlike the cities of the north, did not possess a large industrial empire to drive its growth and expansion. As a result, it came to lack the spatial character of many Northern cities: There was no industrial core downtown to act as a magnet for the new immigrants to the city. Instead, the city became the site of countless new housing developments, each searching for its new area on the fringe for a kind of "suburban dream." Key developers played a role in this process, among them Henry Huntington, Jr. Moreover, such businessmen exercised considerable power in the city, partly because municipal authority was relatively weak, and they were able to fuel the drive outward from the center of the city. New industries located not in the center but on the outskirts and the fringes. Finally, the failure to develop a comprehensive and effective municipal system of railways, brought about by the limited railways developed to expedite travel to individual housing developments, spurred the growth of the highway system and the attraction of the automobile. Los Angeles came to be the epitome of the new Sunbelt city—deconcentrated, laced with an extensive system of overlapping highways, and housing countless numbers of local governments and municipal bodies.

Can American Cities Make a Real Difference in the Lives of Their Residents?

Ever since Paul Peterson made his famous argument about "city limits," students of cities have come to believe that cities are, indeed, limited in what they can do to enhance the lives of their residents. But Peterson ignored important earlier research by Amos Hawley that had shown ways in which cities varied in their policies and showed that some could, indeed, make a difference.

The Concentration of Power and Urban Policy-Making. Hawley had proposed the following hypothesis: "the greater the concentration of power in a community, the great the probability of success in any collective action affecting the welfare of the whole."[55] Hawley tested the hypothesis by developing operational indices of his two principal variables, the concentration of power in communities and the success in collective actions affecting the welfare of the whole. His measures of each variable were ingenious. The concentration of power was measured as the ratio of the number of managers, proprietors, and officials in the labor force of a community to the number of people in the entire employed labor force, or as

$$\frac{\text{Number of managers, officials and proprietors}}{\text{Number of people in the employed labor force}}$$

According to Hawley, as the ratio—formally known as the MPO ratio—became smaller, the concentration of power in a community became higher, and conversely, as it became greater, the concentration of power in a community grew weaker. His reasoning was that a smaller ratio meant there were fewer managerial functions in a community relative to the labor force; therefore as a group, the managers, officials, and proprietors would likely be more cohesive and would certainly possess more unilateral power to get things done. His measures of policy outputs were whether communities had become involved and later executed urban renewal programs; Hawley assumed that such programs acted to promote the welfare of the community as a whole.

Thus, the specific hypothesis Hawley tested, which derived from his more abstract proposition linking power and policy outputs, was that in communities where the MPO ratio was smaller, there should be a greater likelihood of execution of urban renewal programs. Since a number of other factors naturally could affect involvement in urban renewal programs, Hawley had to control systematically for them; having done so, however, he still found a clear relationship between the MPO ratio and execution of urban renewal programs that conformed to his hypothesis.

Civic Capital and the Reconstruction of Industrial Cities. One of the features that characterized the recent period of decline of older industrial American cities is that some cities emerged from this period more quickly and more successfully than others. They managed to make decisions that helped them escape the ravages of decline, including the recruitment of new industry; some even made decisions that provided clear benefits for the large majority of their residents. In particular, cities like Minneapolis-St. Paul were successful in escaping the deep decline characteristic of Detroit, while Pittsburgh did much better than Milwaukee in remaking itself from a city known worldwide for its steel industry to a city that began to be known for its educational institutions and its high-technology industries.

Why, then, did some older industrial cities escape decline more quickly? Orum and Gramlich argue that there is a feature common to all cities, something they call *civic capital*.[56] They further suggest that civic capital consists of four basic components: a *vision*, or general plan and direction for the city, one that provides a map for the future of the city; a *strong commitment* to the city, or place, shared generally by the majority of residents, and especially by the leading figures and class; *alliances* between the leading political and economic figures of the city that helped to furnish a concentration of power at the top; and, finally, and most significantly, *bridges* that link the alliances of the city to its citizens, through such intermediary factors as neighborhood organizations, local voluntary associations, even trade unions. Together these four elements constitute the civic capital of a city. And cities appear to vary in their civic capital, which, in turn, makes a difference to their capacity to make decisions that will benefit the majority of their residents.

Consider the recent stories of three separate cities, all three of which experienced the growth of industry early in the twentieth century. The Twin Cities (Minneapolis–St. Paul) of Minnesota are cities that have managed to make critical decisions to move themselves forward. The most important was the creation of the Metropolitan Council in 1967. The Council was designed to make decisions that would aid the residents of the entire metropolitan region, not simply the central cities. It has helped to provide a means for making policies about regional resource sharing on matters such as water and sewage-treatment. It also provides the current framework for helping to attack more fundamental issues, such as local crime and problems in the local schools. The city of Pittsburgh is equally notable for some of its advances. Though hit hard by the decline of the 1960s and 1970s, and suffering the loss of many thousands of residents, Pittsburgh has bounced back much more quickly than some other cities. It has managed to create a first-rate set of universities, including Carnegie-Mellon University, and recently has been able to attract new industries. It also has managed to remake its downtown area, the Triangle, creating a beautiful park and area for residents to enjoy. In contrast to both the Twin Cities and to Pittsburgh, the city of Milwaukee has lagged far behind in its effort to move beyond industrialization. Until recently, Milwaukee has been unable to attract much in the way of new industry; what industry has come to the region has settled on its fringes. It had great difficulty making a decision about the future of its local baseball club, the Milwaukee Brewers. And it remains a city that is very segregated, in which racism has been labeled by the local newspaper as a major problem in the 1990s.

Three very different cities, three very different stories of success in climbing beyond industry. Orum and Gramlich argue that the differences can be explained by differences in the amount of civic capital available to the cities. The Twin Cities entity, which stands above both Pittsburgh and Milwaukee in making successful decisions on behalf of its residents, seems to have the most. It possesses a strong vision, nurtured by many community leaders; it possesses a strong commitment to place on the part of its residents, also fostered by such things as immense local philanthropy by its leading businessmen and businesswomen; it has a history of strong alliances between the leading political and business figures, evident in the work they did in the early 1950s to sponsor urban renewal downtown; and there is evidence of bridges that link the alliances to local citizens' groups. Pittsburgh has almost as much civic capital as the Twin Cities: in fact, it is very noteworthy for the alliances and the vision developed in the 1940s for its future by its key political and business leaders, such as H.J. Heinz and David Lawrence. What it may lack are the solid bridges, linking the alliances of the city to its citizens groups. Milwaukee, one should not be surprised to learn, is the weakest in terms of its civic capital. In fact, based upon my own research, it appears that the only element that has been evident in Milwaukee, at least until recently, is that of alliances. On the matter of commitment to place, vision, and bridges, the city of Milwaukee has been notably lacking.

In brief, a comparison among the three cities suggests that where there is more civic capital, then cities will be better able to make decisions that benefit the majority of their citizens. This conclusion awaits further research, but is highly suggestive.

CITIES AND THE NEW GLOBAL ECONOMY

One of the great transformations of our age is the development of the new global economy. Aided by the creation of vast new information technology, people and firms are now more closely connected and intertwined with one another than ever before. The effects are felt everywhere, including in metropolitan areas and among their residents. How these effects will play out in the future remains unknown, but there has been interesting speculation in the past few years, to which we now shall turn.[57]

Global Cities

The sociologist/urban planner Saskia Sassen has advanced the most arresting argument about global forces.[58] She argues that three cities, in particular, have become global cities. They are Tokyo, London, and New York. What has happened in these cities, she suggests, is that the economy has moved beyond the dominance of heavy industries to the dominance of new sectors. They are the sectors of finance, real estate, and information technology. Within these sectors there has been a considerable increase of employment and also the generation of great wealth. In New York City, certain real estate magnates like Donald Trump have risen to the top of the wealth hierarchy, while the financial sector on Wall Street has made immense profits and fortunes over the past decade. Information technology firms also make a difference, and there has been a rapid increase and growth of such businesses—not only in New York, of course, though it has come to be one home to these new firms.

In this postindustrial phase of the world economy, other important tendencies also have become evident. Sassen argues that there has been a tendency for an increasing inequality of wealth based upon the nature of these new businesses and the nature of the metropolises themselves. In effect, there has been a growing sector of the very rich and a growing sector of the very poor. The rich hold the professional and managerial positions in the new industries, while the poor are located at the bottom rung of the occupational ladder, holding the poorly paid positions in the service industries. Moreover, as these positions have opened up they also have become available to the many new immigrants who have come into these major metropolises, thereby providing them employment, though only at minimal wages. Sassen suggests that these tendencies can eventually have a real impact on the politics of the cities, heightening poverty, for example, and with it the need to make clear policies to aid the new urban poor.[59]

Moreover, Sassen argues that the new global cities have become a world unto themselves. Their economic and political players have become attuned to the actions of one another rather than to the actions within their own countries. Financial managers in London, for instance, are more apt to be attentive to the actions of financial managers in Tokyo or New York than to their fellow financial figures elsewhere in their home country. In effect, new business empires are being established that transcend national boundaries and divisions. The argument is an extension of an earlier argument by Richard Barnett and Ronald Muller on the emergence and development of multinational corporations (see Chapter 6). Sassen has extended the argument to examine the nature of these three metropolises and the important consequences, such as the polarization of income and wealth.

Sassen's view of these three modern areas also relegates other cities, in America as well as Japan and England, to lower rungs on the hierarchy of dominance. Ecologists have for a long time argued that cities exist in terms of a hierarchy of dominance, based on their flow of goods and traffic, and Sassen now suggests a new kind of dominance, based on the emergence of the global economy. But while elegant and attractive, much of Sassen's argument remains at this point speculation. Economists argue that the polarization of wealth we see may be due to other forces and factors. In addition, it remains to be seen whether the other large metropolitan areas will be propelled automatically into the new arena of global cities, or whether, in fact, they will continue to be shaped and modified by the culture and politics of their own countries.

Other Postindustrial Cities

One of the real questions raised by the analysis of Sassen, and by the changing nature of the world's economy, is the extent to which cities will become like one another, or if they will remain uniquely bound to the culture of their own nations. Some analysts have argued on behalf of a convergence thesis, claiming that cities around the world are becoming more and more similar. Such is the analysis of Michael A. Cohen who insists:

> while the causes of urban unemployment in the [Northern and Southern Hemispheres] are certainly different, their manifestations and consequences are similar, if not identical. Increasing numbers of low-income earners, working in the service sector, face rising prices for many needed urban services and the satisfaction of basic needs. Homelessness, youth unemployment, and growing social problems of the poor, including crime and drugs, are evident in both northern and southern cities.[60]

But the problem with such an analysis is that it completely ignores the history and culture of individual countries and their places, and by ignoring different causes of similar outcomes cannot provide coherent policies.

What is clear is that many of the older industrial cities around the world are taking political actions to improve themselves and their fortunes, which tend to be very similar. In a powerful and insightful analysis, Weiping Wu, a professor of urban studies and planning at Virginia Commonwealth University, finds both important similarities and critical differences in the postindustrial development of several cities in very different parts of the world: New York, Barcelona, and Santiago.[61] Drawing on the work of Sassen, she notes the major transformations in New York, especially the loss of manufacturing jobs and the growing income disparities between the very poor and the very rich. Such inequality, she observes, could ultimately prove to have serious political consequences. But she also observes the ways in which the city has managed to overcome such inequalities and measures it is taking to improve the lives of the poor.[62]

In the case of Barcelona, a city once built on an important manufacturing base, the city has been able to overcome its loss of industry and other decline because it stimulated "competitive economic development by establishing visions for the city, building public consensus, and encouraging public-private cooperation."[63] Moreover, the public officials in Barcelona took important steps to promote its fortunes, creating, among other things, municipal funds that would help the city recover from the loss of so many manufacturing positions. Santiago, by contrast, is an entirely different story. Like many other Latin American cities, it houses many impoverished residents who have been unemployed for years. It also has serious problems of pollution, great traffic congestion, and much physical decay. But the Chilean government shifted many resources to the city in the mid-1970s, and the city itself managed to attract much new industry. Thus, it too met its challenges and managed to overcome them in a way unlike many other older industrial cities in the world. In brief, Wu finds that while cities may differ in the world, and many may face the challenges of the loss of jobs and growing poverty, cities like New York, Barcelona, and Santiago are able to overcome these challenges by the special ways in which both the national and local governments develop modes of cooperation and, especially, by the shifting of more autonomy and resources to the cities themselves.

Regional and Urban Experiments of Major Developing Nations: China, South Korea, and Taiwan

One of the most important experiments of our current era is that which is taking place in the People's Republic of China. Since the end of the Cultural Revolution in 1978, and under the reforms of Deng Xiao Peng, the Chinese government has sought to wed two seemingly different forces—control by a dominant political party and its leaders with the introduction of new economic reforms. Some of the most imaginative steps, in fact, have been taken with regard to the development of China's urban areas, in particular cities like Shanghai. The Chinese government has granted to these new areas, indeed, entire regions, an autonomy they previously did not possess in the hope of stimulating and expanding the local economy and eventually the regional economies.

Several different developing nations have experimented with new regional economic zones. In China such zones have become known as Special Economic Zones, whereas in Taiwan and South Korea they are known as Free Economic Zones. The purpose of such zones is to stimulate both the local and the national economies by providing special kinds of incentives to foreign investors. Incentives include such things as lower rates of taxation on profits and fewer trade restrictions. In Taiwan such zones were first established in the mid-1960s, in Korea in 1970, and in China in 1979, just at the end of the Cultural Revolution. So far the results have confirmed the hopes of officials.[64] In each country these zones have stimulated considerable investment by foreign enterprises: Japan has invested heavily in Taiwan and South Korea, while Macao and Hong Kong were the major investors in Shenzhen in China until 1990. Each of the zones also has grown rapidly in terms of its population. China's experiment may be the most promising of all. Between 1979, when Shenzhen was begun, and 1990, the number of firms in the zone grew from 224 to 2,470. There was a great growth of the labor force, and the city has emerged as one of high-rises and become the most modern and attractive of China's cities. Moreover, the pace of investment in the city has not only contributed to the wealth of the local population, but appears to have generated wealth across the region—which was the original intention.

Such zones represent new kinds of economic experiments for developing nations of the world. The hope is that the economic development they engender will both provide direct benefits to the nation and serve as models of what other cities and businesses might achieve. In China the experiment is the most unusual for, although the city represents a kind of free economic zone intended to encourage foreign investment, the entire experiment is controlled and regulated from above by the Chinese State Council. Shenzhen thus represents in model form the effort of China to try to marry a socialist government with a free-market economy. Besides the innovations of the SEZs, the Chinese government has also permitted local metropolitan officials, like those in Shanghai, to exercise more authority over local decisions.[65] Such decisions concern both the political administration and the economic decisions for their areas. In Shanghai, there are also new zones such as that of Pudong, in which an effort is being made to foster both a new strength in foreign industry as well as in the financial sector.

The questions raised by the greater autonomy now permitted by the

Chinese government over localities is whether the economic payoff will be great enough to offset any disadvantages. In particular, if polarization of wealth and income should happen in the SEZs, or in Shanghai, what are the likely political consequences of such outcomes? And how much leeway will the government permit, especially if the resistance to it increases? These are intriguing and important questions, and they could pose serious threats to China's new experiment, a mix between a strong socialist government that seeks to encourage deep reforms and an open market economy that runs on principles of supply and demand.

CONCLUSION

Over the course of the past thirty years there have been tremendous changes in the world economy and in the nature and configuration of nation-states. Such changes have made themselves felt in several ways. In this chapter we have considered both the local configuration of metropolitan governments in America and some of the impact that the world situation has made upon the local American scene. We also have considered the nature of cities in the new global economy and some of the new forms, such as global cities, that have appeared.

The difference between city politics today and those only three decades ago are quite extraordinary. This chapter is vastly different from one I wrote in the late 1970s. How different will one be twenty years hence? It is not clear, but if the differences are anything like those of the past twenty years, local politics again will have undergone major transformations. In the end, however, one thing remains constant—the needs and welfare of people.

NOTES

1. For a good review of different perspectives at the time, see *Community Politics: A Behavioral Approach*, Charles A. Bonjean, Terry N. Clark, and Robert L. Lineberry, eds. (New York: Free Press, 1971).
2. Robert A. Dahl, *Who Governs? Democracy and Power in an American City* (New Haven, Connecticut: Yale University Press, 1961).
3. Wallace S. Sayre and Herbert Kaufman, *Governing New York City* (New York: The Russell Sage Foundation, 1960); Edward Banfield, *Political Influence* (New York: Free Press, 1961).
4. Theodore J. Lowi, *The End of Liberalism: the Second Republic of the United States* (New York: W.W. Norton, 1969; 1979).
5. Harvey Molotch, "The City as a Growth Machine," *American Journal of Sociology*, 82 (September 1976), 309–32.
6. Ibid., 310.

7. John Logan and Harvey Molotch, *Urban Fortunes: the Political Economy of Place* (Berkeley: University of California Press, 1987).
8. David Harvey, *Social Justice and the City* (Oxford: Basil Blackwell, 1973; 1988).
9. Logan and Molotch, *Urban Fortunes*, op. cit., 37.
10. Ibid., 103–110.
11. Anthony M. Orum, *Power, Money and the People: the Making of Modern Austin* (Austin, Texas: Texas Monthly Press, 1987), 309.
12. Mark Gottdiener and Joe R. Feagin, "The Paradigm Shift in Urban Sociology," *Urban Affairs Quarterly*, 24 (December 1988), 163–187.
13. Susan S. Fainstein, *The City Builders: Property, Politics, and Planning in London and New York* (Oxford: Basil Blackwell, 1994).
14. Paul E. Peterson, *City Limits* (Chicago: University of Chicago Press, 1981).
15. C. Wright Mills, *The Power Elite* (Oxford: Oxford University Press, 1959).
16. Peterson, op. cit., 4.
17. Stephen L. Elkin, *City and Regime in the American Republic* (Chicago: University of Chicago Press, 1987); Clarence N. Stone, *Regime Politics: Governing Atlanta, 1946–1988* (Lawrence, Kansas: University of Kansas Press, 1989).
18. Stone, ibid., 240.
19. Sam Bass Warner, Jr., *The Private City: Philadelphia in Three Periods of Its Growth* (Philadelphia: University of Pennsylvania Press, 1968).
20. Louis Wirth, "Urbanism as a Way of Life," *American Journal of Sociology*, 44 (July 1938), 1–24.
21. Raymond Mohl, Jr., *The Making of Urban America*, 2nd edition (Wilmington, Delaware: Scholarly Resources, 1997); *Urban America in Historical Perspective*, Raymond A. Mohl and Neil Betten, eds. (New York: Weybright and Talley, 1970); Dennis R. Judd and Todd Swanstrom, *Private Power and Public Policy* (New York: HarperCollins, 1994), Chapters 2–7; Bayrd Still, "Patterns of Mid-Nineteenth Century Urbanization in the Middle West," *Mississippi Valley Historical Review*, 28 (September 1941), 187–206; and Charles N. Glaab and A. Theodore Brown, *A History of Urban America* (New York: The Macmillan Company, 1967).
22. Much of the general framework in the discussion below is drawn from my own work, but it is generally supported by the historical literature as noted above. See Anthony M. Orum, *City-Building in America* (Boulder, Colorado: Westview Press, 1995).
23. Ibid., Chapter 3.
24. Also see Robert A. Dahl, *Who Governs?*
25. Mohl and Betten, op. cit., Part IV.
26. Dahl, op. cit.
27. Orum, *City-Building*, 91–95.
28. Ibid., Chapter 4; Mohl, op. cit.
29. Orum, *City-Building*, Chapter 5. Also see these important works on a similar theme: Eric Monkonnen, *America Becomes Urban: The Development of U.S. Cities*

and Towns, 1780–1980 (Berkeley: University of California Press, 1988); and Jon Teaford, *The Unheralded Triumph: City Government in America, 1870–1900* (Baltimore, Maryland: the Johns Hopkins University Press, 1984).

30. Orum, *City-Building*, Chapter 5.
31. Judd and Swanstrom, op. cit., Chapter 3.
32. Ibid., Chapters 5–7.
33. Orum, *City-Building*, Chapter 5; also Mohl, Jr., *The Making of Urban America.*
34. See, for example, Todd Swanstrom, *The Crisis of Growth Politics: Cleveland, Kucinich and the Challenge of Urban Populism* (Philadelphia: Temple University Press, 1985).
35. Peterson, *City Limits*, Chapter 10; Orum, *City-Building*, Chapters 6 and 7; Judd and Swanstrom, *Private Power and Public Policy*, Chapter 7.
36. William Julius Wilson, *The Truly Disadvantaged: Public Policy and the Making of an Underclass* (Chicago: University of Chicago Press, 1987).
37. Ibid.; and Orum, *City-Building*, Chapter 7.
38. Gregory D. Squires, *Capital and Communities in Black and White* (Albany, New York: State University of New York Press, 1994).
39. See, especially, Jon Teaford, *City and Suburb: the Political Fragmentation of Metropolitan America, 1850–1970* (Baltimore, Maryland: the Johns Hopkins University Press, 1979).
40. Kenneth Jackson, *Crabgrass Frontier: the Suburbanization of the United States* (New York: Oxford University Press, 1985).
41. Orum, *City-Building*, Chapter 4.
42. Teaford, *city and Suburb*, Chapter 2.
43. Teaford, op. cit., *infra.*
44. Ibid., Chapters 2 and 3.
45. Swanstrom, op. cit.; Peterson, op. cit.
46. David Rusk, *Cities Without Suburbs* (Baltimore, Maryland: the Johns Hopkins University Press, 1993).
47. Myron Orfield, *Metropolitics: A Regional Agenda for Community and Stability* (Washington, D.C.: the Brookings Institution, 1997).
48. Joel Garreau, *Edge City: Life on the New Frontier* (New York: Doubleday, 1991).
49. For a number of fine articles on these spatial changes, see *Interwoven Destinies: Cities and Nation*, Henry G. Cisneros, ed. (New York: W.W. Norton, 1993).
50. Carl Abbott, *the New Urban America: Growth and Politics in Sunbelt Cities* (Chapel Hill: University of North Carolina Press, 1987), and *Sunbelt Cities: Politics and Growth Since World War II*, Richard M. Bernard and Bradley M. Rice, eds. (Austin, Texas: University of Texas Press, 1983).
51. Orum, *City-Building.*
52. Mark Baldassare, *The Growth Dilemma* (Berkeley: University of California Press, 1981); *The Politics of San Antonio: Community, Progress and Power* (Lincoln, Nebraska: University of Nebraska Press, 1983); and Orum, *Power, Money and the People.*

53. Joe R. Feagin, *Free Enterprise City: Houston in Political and Economic Perspective* (New Brunswick, New Jersey: Rutgers University Press, 1988).
54. Robert M. Fogelson, *The Fragmented Metropolis: Los Angeles, 1850–1930* (Berkeley: University of California Press, 1967; 1993 reissued).
55. Amos Hawley, "Community Power and Urban Renewal Success," *American Journal of Sociology*, 68 (January 1963), 422–31.
56. Anthony M. Orum and James Gramlich, "Civic Capital and the Construction (and Reconstruction) of Cities," *Colloqui: Cornell Journal of Planning and Urban Issues*, XIV, 1999, 45–54.
57. H.V. Savitch, *Post-Industrial Cities: Politics and Planning in New York, Paris and London* (Princeton: Princeton University Press, 1988); *Preparing for the Urban Future: Global Pressures and Local Forces*, Michael A. Cohen, Blair A. Ruble, Joseph S. Tulchin, and Allison M. Garland, eds. (Washington, D.C.: Woodrow Wilson Center Press, 1996).
58. Saskia Sassen, *The Global City: New York, London, Tokyo* (Princeton: Princeton University Press, 1991); Saskia Sassen, *Cities in a World Economy* (Thousand Oaks, California: Pine Forge Press, 1994).
59. See also, *Dual City: Restructuring New York*, John H. Mollenkopf and Manuel Castells, eds. (New York: The Russell Sage Foundation, 1991).
60. Cohen, "The Hypothesis of Urban Convergence," in *Preparing for the Urban Future*, op. cit., 29.
61. Weiping Wu, "Economic Competition and Resource Mobilization," in *Preparing for the Urban Future*, ibid., 123–54.
62. Roger A. Waldinger, *Still the Promised City:African-Americans and New Immigrants in Postindustrial New York* (Cambridge, Massachusetts: Harvard University Press, 1996).
63. Wu, op. cit., 134.
64. Xiangming Chen, "The Changing Roles of Free Economic Zones in Development: A Comparative Analysis of Capitalist and Socialist Cases in East Asia," *Studies in Comparative International Development*, 29 (Fall 1994), 3–25.
65. Xiangming Chen, "Urban History as Contemporary City (Re)Building: Shenzhen's Rise and Shanghai's Renaissance in Post-Mao China." Paper presented to the 55th Annual Meeting of the Midwest Political Science Association, Chicago, April 10–12, 1997.

Chapter 8

Political Parties and Political Partisanship

> Among the numerous advantages promised by a well-constructed Union, none deserves to be more accurately developed than its tendency to break and control the violence of faction. . . . By faction, I understand a number of citizens, whether amounting to a majority or a minority of the whole, who are united and actuated by some common impulse of passion, or of interest, adverse to the rights of other citizens, or to the permanent and aggregate interests of the community. . . . The inference to which we are brought is that the causes of faction cannot be removed, and that relief is only to be sought in the means of controlling its effects. . . . A republic, by which I mean a government in which the scheme of representation takes place, . . . promises a cure for which we are seeking. . . . As each representative will be chosen by a greater number of citizens in the larger than in the smaller republic, it will be more difficult for unworthy candidates to practice with success in the vicious arts by which elections are too often carried; and the suffrages of the people, being more free, will be more likely to center in men who possess the most attractive merit and the most diffuse and established characters.
>
> James Madison, *The Federalist*

Like many of his fellow revolutionaries, James Madison hoped to protect the liberty and freedom of citizens in the newly founded United States of America against any danger. One of the most serious was that of factionalism. Factions, he believed, could attract disproportionate amounts of political power and eventually become the inevitable centers of political controversy. They thus could rob politics in a free society of the fluid and responsive fashion in which it should work. To guard against such threats, Madison and the other founding fathers designed a federal republic. In *The Federalist* Number 10, he provided a stirring and elegant defense of the architecture of this constitution that would prevent the formation of factions. But less than ten years after the ratification of the Constitution, political parties, a form of faction among the most despised by Madison, had appeared in America.

Had James Madison, a founding father of the United States and one of its most revered thinkers, merely been a poor judge on a minor aspect of the new republic? Or had it been, perhaps, merely a strange twist of historical fate that political parties arose? As it turns out, Madison was only one of many political observers who failed to foresee the appearance of political parties. The classical writers on democracy, as we saw in Chapter 5, never imagined a day when powerful bodies could arise to intervene between the political wishes of the mass public and its elected representatives. Nevertheless, at the beginning of the twenty-first century, political parties can be found everywhere. In industrialized nations there are parties, numbering anywhere from two to fifteen, and in the developing nations as well there are parties that often prove essential to the national aspirations and development of these countries.

Why have political parties come about? Do they serve special purposes that other organizations fail to provide? How have they managed to escape the efforts of politicians who wished to prevent their rise to power? These and other questions will serve as the main agenda for this chapter. In particular, my discussion will cover: (1) the nature and origins of modern political parties; (2) variations in the organizational structure both of modern and older political parties; (3) the politics internal to party organizations; and (4) the nature and development of parties, and political partisanship, mainly in contemporary American politics.

THE NATURE OF MODERN POLITICAL PARTIES

Modern political parties first arose in the nineteenth century. In the United States, their birthplace, parties surfaced just prior to the presidential election of 1800, but the complete trappings of the modern party—the strength of organization and the involvement of the public—did not fully appear until the 1820s and 1830s. In Great Britain, political clubs and cliques existed long before the advent of nineteenth-century politics, but only after the passage of the electoral reforms of 1832 and especially of 1867 did parties develop into something akin to contemporary institutions in the United States. Elsewhere in Europe, modern parties were somewhat slower in arising; in the

Scandinavian countries, for instance, they did not emerge until the turn of the twentieth century.[1]

As the parties in the United States and Britain evolved, they became transformed, eventually assuming many of the special features we now associate with the modern political party. William Nisbet Chambers, in his definitive analysis of the early American parties—the Federalists of Hamilton and Washington, the Republicans of Jefferson—identifies the several unique qualities of the modern parties through a comparison with their predecessors, the cliques and factions.[2] Chambers observes, first of all, that the modern political party involves an active leadership group committed to goals that advance the party rather than individual personalities. The club or clique, in contrast, is typically a temporary alliance of individuals. It is not identified by specific party labels, and members are more concerned with their own personal advancement than that of the group to which they belong. In addition, Chambers notes, the modern party has developed specific practices designed to further its own expansion and to allow it to work within the government. They include the practices of electioneering for campaigns, the techniques of nominating candidates for office, and the special arts of compromise required to maintain a hold over high political office. To clubs and cliques of politicians such practices appear quite foreign. The party, moreover, also encompasses a wide variety of interests and supporters, each of which attempts to shape the opinions of party leaders; in contrast, the club is only based on a narrow range of concerns. Coherent programs, or ideologies, flow from the structure and activities developed by the modern parties, partly as a means of further securing their continuity both in and out of government; while clubs or factions rarely, if ever, advance programs or statements of principle. Last, Chambers notes, modern political parties rely heavily upon the support of the public to remain in office and thus seek to solicit and mold opinion among the public, whereas factions or cliques, which are highly self-contained groups, manifest little concern, or need, for broad public support.

Such are the principal features of modern political parties. They should be seen as representing a kind of Weberian ideal-type, an abstraction created from a number of similar features of modern parties everywhere.[3] There is, however, considerable diversity among modern parties, as we shall see. First, however, let us look at some of the circumstances that gave birth to the modern parties.

THE BIRTH OF MODERN POLITICAL PARTIES

There are a number of reasonably good theories and accounts of the origins of modern political parties.[4] Some take a specifically historical tack, attempting to locate the origins of parties in the special circumstances and setting of a nation.[5] Others take a broad, comparative stance, identifying the origins of modern parties in features common to many nations.[6] Among these many accounts, perhaps the best is found in the work of Joseph LaPalombara and Myron Weiner; their account is notable for its emphasis on the broad preconditions and unique historical forces associated with the rise of parties.[7]

Several broad social and economic circumstances, LaPalombara and Weiner claim, seem to account for the emergence of modern political parties. Four are particularly crucial for the development of parties: secularization, voluntary associations, and communications together with transportation. First, secularization must take place in a society prior to the rise of modern parties; modern parties are founded on the fact that "individuals come to believe that through their actions they are capable of affecting the world in ways which are favorable to their interests and sentiments."[8] Second, the emergence of modern political parties is also likely to be preceded by an extensive network and variety of voluntary groups. Modern political parties reveal an intricate organizational machinery, and it appears that the development of this machinery is especially likely where people are accustomed to organizational participation and activity. Third, LaPalombara and Weiner suggest, the emergence of modern political parties also has been encouraged by an extensive network of communications and transportation. Some of the key features of the modern party, such as electioneering and extensive contacts between the parliamentary party and the hinterlands, simply could not have come about in the absence of a system of communication and transportation.

LaPalombara and Weiner fully realize that these conditions only assist in the emergence of modern political parties. Thus, they suggest several additional features that seem to represent the special historical precipitants for the formation of modern parties.[9] The features represent three "historical crises" that occur as societies attempt to achieve nationhood—a crisis in the legitimacy of the new social-political order, a crisis in the integration of the new order, and a crisis in participation by the masses in the new order. Each of these crises seems to provide the last shove toward the formation of the modern parties; or, from another perspective, modern parties seem to be the unique devices for resolving these crises.[10]

The first crisis, that of legitimacy, concerns the broad sense of viability that a new order's institutions and symbols have for its citizens and residents. The modern political parties help, so LaPalombara and Weiner suggest, to furnish this sense of viability. The second crisis, that of integration, involves the extent to which the territories and groups of a new order are divided by seemingly irreconcilable conflicts. Often, modern political parties seem to arise to provide a means for resolving these differences, for integrating the residents of a developing nation. The third crisis, that of participation, is the most crucial; most modern political parties seem to have emerged to cope especially with this particular crisis.

The account of LaPalombara and Weiner, at first glance, seems to fit many historical circumstances. In the United States, for instance, both the general preconditions and the historical crises were present about the time of the formation of the Federalist and Republican parties at the end of the eighteenth century. For one thing, just as Alexis de Tocqueville perceived, there had been a widespread network of associations in existence in the colonies long before the emergence of the two parties. The network of correspondence committees and patriotic organizations had been instrumental in the development of the Revolution. For another thing, a system of communications and transportation also existed prior to the development of the political parties, and this, too, later proved invaluable to the development of these organizations, especially that of the Republican Party. In particular, a crisis of legitimacy of the new order and another of participation by the people were also evident at the time of the formation of the first parties. These were resolved in part through the successful efforts of the Federalists and Republicans. In addition, a second crisis of participation that occurred in the 1820s shortly after the passage of laws to extend suffrage and disbanding of the Congressional caucus as a means of political nomination was almost immediately followed by the birth of the Democratic Party.[11]

Accounting for the origins of modern political parties remains a difficult but important intellectual task. LaPalombara and Weiner have given us some insight into the nature of the events and the circumstances associated with the rise of the modern party

VARIATIONS IN MODERN POLITICAL PARTIES: HIGHLIGHTS OF CURRENT AND FORMER PATTERNS

The notion of modern political parties I introduced at the outset of this chapter should serve as a guide to help us sort out and to better understand the real world. Like all such abstractions, however, it represents a composite of many common, yet subtly different, forms; it advances our understanding by showing us what apparently disparate groups hold in common, and yet retards an even deeper appreciation by downplaying important differences. This section considers some of these differences by looking at some of the contemporary and earlier variations.

Current Patterns

The most illuminating discussion of differences among current parties can be found in the analyses of Maurice Duverger in *Political Parties: Their Organization and Activity in the Modern State*. Duverger provides an exhaustive taxonomy of party structures; two criteria he uses to distinguish among parties—their constituent units and their form of membership—are of special interest.[12]

Constituent Units. According to Duverger, there are three principal forms of the constituent units of modern parties: the caucus, the cell, and the branch. By closely examining the structure and activities of these units, Duverger suggests, one is better able to understand the nature and relative effectiveness of the political parties that employ them.

The caucus, which, for example, is characteristic of the Democratic and Republican parties in parts of the United States, is fairly limited as an organization. The number of its full-time members is small, and it seeks only the most minimal expansion of its membership in the public. It rarely engages in efforts to generate much enthusiasm and support in the broader society because it wishes to remain a closed and, to a large extent, select organization. Moreover, it incorporates a wide expanse of geographical territory; American caucuses cover such large units as counties and municipalities. Consonant with its limited aims for expansion, the caucus operates only on an intermittent basis, becoming active just at election times.

At the lower levels of organization, caucus leaders are typically precinct captains and other agents whose responsibility is to see that the voters turn out for the party's candidates at election time. The precinct captains also have the responsibility of disseminating information and generating enthusiasm among party members for the nominating conventions, those few occasions when party adherents gather together for the purpose of electing people to run for office. The membership, however, rarely plays a part in the selection of candidates; the primary tasks of choosing candidates are left up to the major party figures.[13]

Duverger regards the caucus with no little disdain, especially as compared with the cell and the branch forms. He notes, for instance, that in European countries the caucus is on the decline and is generally being replaced by the cell or the branch. Duverger observes that the caucus remains a viable organization only in the United States, largely because it appears to be more compatible with special features of the United States' historical setting, particularly the strength of individualism and the absence of a sense of class-consciousness.[14] Among other things, he notes, that "caucuses are an archaic type of political party structure *[sic]*. . . . In their composition as well as in their structure [weak collective organization, predominance of individual considerations] they represent the influence of the upper and lower middle class. . . . The greater efficiency of recruiting techniques directly adapted to the masses [for example, the system of branches] has usually brought about the decline of the caucus."[15]

The branch, which is characteristic of most Socialist parties in Europe, is in most respects fundamentally different from the caucus as a form of party organization. In general, the branch represents a highly centralized form of organization in which the membership is tightly locked through an intricate division of labor and in which there is a clear emphasis on control from above. It incorporates a fairly large number of members, is ever after new ones, and attempts to establish for itself a broad base among the public. It generally seeks an open stance with regard to the broader society, hoping thereby to establish itself as a permanent and broad point of reference and to be able to mobilize people for a variety of purposes.

One of the striking features of the branch is that it exists for more than simply the election of candidates to high political office. This explains, for example, why the branch takes an expansionist approach among the public. This also accounts for the regularity and intensity of the branch's activities; the leaders of the branch attempt to keep in constant communication with their membership and to encourage informal ties among the members. The branches of the Socialist parties, for example, generally hold meetings twice a month at which they provide a broad form of political education in addition to the more routine forms of information pertaining to elections.

Comparing the branch and the caucus, it is evident that Duverger far prefers the former type of organization, partly because he believes that it enables all people to play a much more prominent role in the internal affairs of the party and, hence, that it is fundamentally more democratic: "There is no doubt the caucus is undemocratic . . . ; this small closed group, composed of semi co-opted, well-known figures, is obviously oligarchic in character. The branch, on the other hand, which is open to all, and in which the leaders are elected by the members (at least in theory), corresponds to the requirements of political democracy."[16]

The third, and last, principal form of constituent unit of modern parties is that of the cell, a form similar in most respects to the branch. Like the branch, for example, the cell is always seeking to expand its membership base among the public and actively searches for new members through regular meetings and extensive propaganda. The cell, an invention of the Communist parties of Europe, also possesses two features that make it an even more tightly knit and cohesive unit than the branch. First, the cell is based on the occupational locus of individuals rather that the residential one—it is found not in the commune or district as the branch is but instead in the factory of the office. Naturally this provides the cell with an unusually firm and vivid presence among its membership and thereby secures its psychological hold upon the loyalties of members. Second, the size of the cell is smaller than that of the branch; whereas the branch typically has more than one hundred members, the cell rarely achieves this size. Its comparatively smaller membership provides the cell with an additional basis for creating an intense solidarity and loyalty on the part of its members.

The cell, Duverger further suggests, represents a profound change in the conception of a political party. Whereas the caucus is organized principally for electoral victory and the branch for establishing a broad base of adherents among the public in addition to electoral victory, the cell is organized as a means of overthrowing the established governmental order. He observes, moreover, that "instead of a body intended for the winning of votes, for grouping the representatives, and for maintaining contact between them and their electors, the political party [under the cell] becomes an instrument of agitation, of propaganda, of discipline, and if necessary, of clandestine action, for which elections and parliamentary debates are only one of several means of action, and a secondary means at that. The importance of this change cannot be overemphasized. It marks a breach between the political regime and the organizations it has produced to ensure its working."[17]

Form of Membership. A second means to illuminate the differences among modern parties and thus to cast light on their relative advantages and disadvantages, Duverger claims, is through classification on the basis of form of membership. There are two broad types of parties based upon this criterion, the *cadre* party and the *mass* party. The cadre party, which most closely resembles the American political parties, is a limited enterprise that restricts membership to a very few people and attempts to attract important and familiar faces that provide the party with a blue-ribbon image. It is a party that is loosely knit in its organization and that rarely maintains a high level of control over its organizational bases in society. The cadre party, moreover, seeks only to prepare itself for the electoral battles. Therefore its leaders are principally interested in maintaining their contacts with candidates; in stirring up the public, members and nonmembers, just for electoral campaigns; and in winning the allegiance of voters, not of citizens *per se*. Duverger further asserts that the cadre party is generally on the decline—at least in Western countries—having been replaced in most areas at the end of the nineteenth century and beginning of the twentieth century by the *mass* party.

The mass party, which is a creation essentially of the broad modern extension of suffrage and most characteristic of the branch- and cell-based European Socialist and Communist parties, is interested in gaining converts to its cause as well as in generating votes at the polls. Thus it attempts to create widespread as well as intense support among members of the public. As it is primarily interested in attracting adherents, it creates a sophisticated machinery for the recruitment and enrollment of large numbers of dues-paying members. Moreover, it is necessary to differentiate clearly between degrees or levels of membership in the mass party. These are the categories: supporters, who simply pay dues and infrequently attend the meetings of the party; militants, who are the active members and the ones upon whom the success of the party chiefly depends; and the inner circle, or core group, which exercises complete control over every facet of the party's structure.

Although these and other taxonomic devices employed by Duverger have been criticized, they still remain highly illuminating and useful.[18] Duverger, for instance, draws attention to the fact that the cadre, caucus-based political parties, like those in the United States, tended to develop historically from within the legislature; in his view, this may explain why they have also retained an emphasis on limited membership of the public and an elitist quality. In contrast, the branch- or cell-based mass parties, like the Communist and Socialist parties in Europe, developed outside the legislature; this perhaps accounts for their greater responsiveness to the participation of the public and for their more frequent attempts to promote rand and file members to posts of leadership.

Candidate Campaign Organizations. In recent years, there have been some noticeable changes in the structure of political parties, particularly in the United States. The most important one has been the development of the candidate campaign organizations, especially of candidates for major political offices. These campaign organizations rely heavily upon the appeal of the candidate and are also responsible for creating large war chests of funds for the rigors of the campaign itself. They also become the means through which large amounts of money are funneled to the candidates, often well in advance of the actual election campaign. By the fall of 1999, for example, George W. Bush, Jr., Republican candidate for President in 2000, had already assembled more than $50 million for his race, even though the election was more than a year away. It was the largest amount of campaign money ever assembled by any Presidential candidate in American history.

The effect of these new candidate campaign organizations, which essentially are run independently of the party, has been to reduce the impact of the political party even more in the United States, and to promote a greater emphasis upon the strengths of the individual political candidate. But this has been a long-term tendency in the nature of American political parties, noted years ago by V.O. Key in his seminal analysis of American parties. In Europe, by contrast, the political party today continues to be a strong component of any political campaign, providing an important structural and ideological integrity to the character of political races and contests often lacking in the United States.

Electoral Laws. The history of politics and political organization provides one key to understanding the nature of parties in general and to the differences between parties in Europe and the United States. Another, perhaps the most crucial, key lies in the nature of electoral laws, themselves.[19]

The electoral system of most continental European nations has been based upon what is called the system of proportional representation, or some variation of it. This is a method that awards seats in the legislature on the basis of the proportion of votes gained by a candidate in the electoral contest. For example, if there are 100 seats up for election, those seats will be awarded to parties based upon the proportion of the vote they secure. If Party A secures 35 percent of the vote, then it will also secure 35 of the seats in the contest; likewise, if Party C secures 10 percent of the vote, it will also secure 10 seats. Through this method, which is the most common method of election throughout democratic countries, a variety of political parties can be represented in a nation's legislature.[20]

The method of election in the United States is much different. Here there is a winner-take-all, or plurality, system of election. Victors are determined on the basis of who secures the majority of votes in a single election, or a single district. The long-term effect has been to produce the two major party contestants in America, the Republicans and the Democrats. Other political parties, because they cannot secure any form of representation based upon their overall share of the electoral vote, get tossed aside.

There are several obvious and not-so-obvious consequences of the differences in the form of electoral laws. One is that the electoral system in the United States has made it almost impossible for third party candidates to secure any continuing form of representation in the legislature, either state or national. Over the course of American history, various third party candidates have run for office. They include Theodore Roosevelt, who won as the Progressive Candidate in 1912; Strom Thurmond, who ran for President as a rump Dixiecrat candidate in 1948; and most recently, Ross Perot, who ran for President under the banner of the Independent Party in 1992 and 1996. Perot did better as a third party candidate than any other figure in recent memory, securing almost 20 percent of the vote. The effect of his popularity was to give the Presidency to Bill Clinton on a mere plurality, not a majority, of the popular vote that was cast. Perot's candidacy took its toll—it cost him many millions of dollars from his own personal fortune for the campaign—and he failed to gain nearly the same popular vote in 1996. In 1998, Jesse "the body/mind" Ventura ran and won as the Independent Party candidate for Governor of Minnesota, the first such third party victory for gubernatorial office since Robert LaFollette ran and won on the Progressive Party ticket in Wisconsin.

Another important consequence of the different form of electoral laws in Europe and the United States is that the parties in Europe have been based more heavily on a strong ideological platform and appeal than in America. Proportional representation allows parties to run on the basis of particular ideological platforms and appeals as they seek to gain a share of the overall vote for themselves. In general, it favors the representation of minorities.[21] This method, for instance, was clearly helpful in the rise of the Green Party in Europe as the party sought to campaign based on its concern with important environmental issues. In general, proportional representation helps to encourage the development and success of even small parties. In comparison, the winner-take-all system in America has forced parties to appeal to the sympathies of the large group of middle-of-the-road voters, people who generally do not take strong ideological positions on any issue but are necessary to electoral victory. It is the vote of these citizens that will determine who wins a particular contest. The effect, observers note, has been to diminish the distinctive ideological character of both American parties as they seek to gain the vote of the great middling sector of the electorate.

Former Patterns: The Political Machine of Urban America

Party machines dominated the political life of many large American cities for a number of years.[22] The rise of the machine roughly corresponded to the waves of European immigrants in American cities; in New York City, large numbers of immigrants arrived in the 1840s and 1850s, and the political machine showed a parallel rise in strength. In most cities, the machine was run by the Democrats, but in a few cities, like Philadelphia, it was run by the Republicans. Control of the machine was typically in the hands of members of distinct ethnic groups. In Boston, for example, it was the Irish—most notably Boss Curley—who found their way into the positions of control over the machine; while in New York City, it was the Irish and later the Italians who controlled the party machine. As the case of New York City illustrated, it was not simply that the reins of power were held by distinct ethnic groups, but also that these reins were transferred over time from one ethnic group to another.[23]

What did the party machine look like? How did it wield power? The machine seemed to have both the structure and the internal discipline of an army and often worked as effectively. Typically at its top was a single leader, a boss, who exercised principal control over the operations and inner structure of the machine.[24] Slightly lower in the hierarchy were his associates, or lieutenants, whom he relied upon for information and for the successful implementation of his commands. The social ties between the boss and his lieutenants often began in childhood, as Mike Royko's insightful analysis of Richard Daley's Democratic machine in Chicago reveals; these were hardened through the years by common political battles and enemies.[25] Beneath this top echelon, there were further niches in the machine's structure, including those of various party functionaries.

The principal goals of the machine were electoral victories and, through such victories, the control of the privileges and reward of public office in the city. Insofar as the winning of political office was concerned, the strength of the machine lay far down in the recesses of the organization—in the vast networks that punctuated the many wards and precincts of cities. In each precinct, there was a captain, beneath him were lieutenants, and further beneath them were other functionaries; it was these officials who helped to keep the wheels of the machine greased and upon whose shoulders rested the fate of the machine's candidates at the polls. The men of the machine knew the members of their district, and when the time came to get them to the polls, these men had carefully laid the foundations for a large, and sometimes overwhelming, victory of the machine. The classic revelations of how the local members of the machine performed their tasks are found in the discourse on practical politics offered by George Washington Plunkitt. Plunkitt was a member of the Tammany Machine in New York City at the height of its power in the late nineteenth and early twentieth centuries. Consider just a few of his pearls of practical political wisdom:

> What tells in holdin' your grip on your district is to go right down among the poor families and help them in the different ways they need help. I've got a regular system for this. If there's a fire in Ninth, Tenth, or Eleventh Avenue, for example, any hour of the day or night, I'm usually there with some of my election district captains as soon as the fire engines. If a family is burned out I don't ask whether they are Republicans or Democrats, and I don't refer them to the Charity Organization Society, which would investigate their case in a month or two and decide they were worthy of help about the time they are dead from starvation. I just get quarters for them, buy clothes for them if their clothes were burned up, and put them up till they get things runnin' again. It's philanthropy, but its politics, too—mighty good politics. Who can tell how many votes one of these fires bring me? The poor are the most grateful people in the world, and let me tell you, they have more friends in their neighborhoods than the rich have in theirs.
>
> If there's a family in my district in want I know it before the charitable societies do, and me and my men are first on the ground. I have a special corps to look up such cases. The consequence is that the poor look up to George W. Plunkitt as a father, come to him in trouble—and don't forget him on election.
>
> Another thing, I can always get a job for a deservin' man. I make it a point to keep on the track of jobs, and it seldom happens that I don't have a few up my sleeve ready for use. I know every big employer in the district and in the whole city, for that matter, and they ain't in the habit of sayin' no to me when I ask them for a job.
>
> And the children—the little roses of the district. Do I forget them? Oh, no! They know me, every one of them, and they know that a sight of Uncle George and candy means the same thing. Some of them are the best kind of vote getters. I'll tell you a case. Last year a little Eleventh Avenue rosebud, whose father is a Republican, caught hold of his whiskers on election day and said she wouldn't let go till he's promised to vote for me. And she didn't.[26]

For a long time, the machines of political parties exercised a tight control over municipal governments and the political arena generally in many urban settings. They did so because they were able to provide the needy and dependent immigrants with material inducements not available elsewhere.[27] The machines provided jobs to recently arrived immigrants who could not otherwise secure positions. The machine provided general forms of welfare, including money and clothing, again to those people who could not otherwise secure the basic necessities of life. These, plus other benefits, served as inducements and enabled the machine to secure the compliance of voters on election day—a rather minor request after all was said and done.

POWER AND POLITICS WITHIN MODERN POLITICAL PARTIES

Though the modern political party is recognized for a number of distinctive and innovative features, the scope and vitality of its organization—the neatly defined hierarchies, the vast network of communications, and the overriding commitments of leaders to organizational goals and growth—rank as the characteristics of singular historic significance. Many writers have drawn special attention to them.[28] One of the most persuasive was Moise Ostrogorski, the first and possibly still the most brilliant analyst of modern parties.[29] Writing at the close of the nineteenth century, Ostrogorski took special note of the political organizations formed by the Jacksonian Democrats in the United States and of the Liberal Party's Birmingham Caucus in England. Painting his analysis with a good deal of cynicism and moral condemnation, Ostrogorski emphasized the ways in which the organizational strength of the Democrats in the United States and the Liberals in England enabled their leaders to manipulate the sentiments of the electorate. Ostrogorski feared, moreover, that the strength of these party organizations might grow so considerable that citizens could be deprived of their right to choose political representatives free from party interference, and that party leadership could dominate the public representatives in the legislature.[30]

Robert Michels's Iron Law of Oligarchy

The seminal analysis of the organizational features and internal processes of modern parties, however, remains that of Robert Michels, a German-born sociologist.[31] Michels's analysis principally concerns the German Social Democratic Party at the turn of the twentieth century but deals as well with trade unions and other parties both in Europe and in the United States. He considers why seemingly fluid democratic organizations like parties become transformed into highly ossified structures with members robbed of rights to participate in decisions and leaders granted inordinate power. His examination, known chiefly by its identification of an "iron law of oligarchy," is so important that it is worth dwelling on at some length.

To begin with, Michels asserts that the members of the working classes, and by implication those of the mass public, can only achieve privileges for themselves by combining their numbers into organizations. Adopting a position roughly equivalent to that of V. I. Lenin—though apparently unaware of Lenin's own analysis—Michels maintains that the "principle of organization is an absolutely essential condition for the political struggle of the masses."[32] Nevertheless, he claims, once a party organization has been formed by the masses, the reins of power inevitably fall into the hands of an oligarchy. Psychological factors contribute to the inability of the masses to retain control of the organization. These include their suggestibility to orators and propaganda in general and their willingness to submit to the commands of leaders.[33] Besides these there are also technical factors that produce organizational incompetence on the part of the masses. For instance, once the representatives of the membership of the organization have been elected, Michels avers, they achieve a level of expertise and a degree of control over the means of communication that individual members of the rank and file could not even hope to attain.

There are also qualities of the positions of leadership, however, that enhance the tendencies for oligarchies to emerge in party organizations. The attainment of expertise by the leaders falsely encourages them to believe that they are indispensable to the life of the party. The financial benefits that accompany office in the organization provide an incentive for leaders to retain their positions, particularly if their prior positions in the organization were as impoverished as those of other members of the rank and file. Michels writes:

> When the leaders are not persons of means and when they have no other source of income, they hold firmly to their positions for economic reasons, coming to regard the functions they exercise as theirs by inalienable right. Especially is this true of manual workers, who, since becoming leaders, have lost their aptitude for their former occupation. For them, the loss of their positions would be a financial disaster, and in most cases it would be altogether impossible for them to return to their old way of life.[34]

Ultimately those who serve as leaders become so enamored of the power and privileges of their positions that they seek to retain the positions indefinitely. Among other things, they try to co-opt future leaders from among the rand and file members and thus, to prevent members' free choice in the selection of their future leaders. They also create further positions within the leadership ranks, multiplying the benefits that can be obtained from holding office and simultaneously further insulating themselves from contact with and influence by the rank and file.

Michels is fully aware that leaders cannot dominate the membership of party organizations indefinitely, even by using such ploys as co-optation. To explain the change that occurs in the leadership of party organization, he adopts a form of explanation similar to that which Vilfredo Pareto used to explain the changes in the composition of the governing class in society.[35] Michels argues that there never is a clear break between the composition of the old leadership group and that of the new one. Instead of a *circulation des elites*, there is a *reunion des elites*, that is, an amalgam of elements from the old leadership group with elements drawn from the new one. Change in leadership through amalgamation is coupled with change through decentralization, Michels further observes, with smaller and smaller oligarchies emerging from the original large one. Nonetheless the acts of amalgamation and decentralization do not detract from the one essential fact of every party organization—oligarchy—or, the concentration of power at the top of the party organization and the resulting loss of power incurred by members of the rank and file.

Michels's thesis about the accumulation and concentration of power at the top of party organizations might as easily be called the "ironic law of oligarchy." It is nothing short of a major irony that socialist parties, such as the German Social Democratic Party, which preached the end of class rule and the equal dispersion of power and privilege among all people in society, displayed vast internal inequities in the distribution of power and wealth. The irony in the discovery further convinced Michels that he had uncovered an eternal verity about party organizations, in particular, and, perhaps even about mass organizations, in general.

Most contemporary scholars of parties and political organizations seem about as dogmatic and unreflective in their conviction of the truth of the iron law of oligarchy as Michels was steadfast yet thoughtful in his. But some have chosen to inquire further into the nature of the iron law, seeking either to discover whether it accurately describes current party organizations or to find out the conditions under which it might fail to come true. Maurice Duverger, for example, found evidence of oligarchical structures in many different political parties, especially the Communist parties in Europe that introduced systematic methods for recruiting and training new leaders.[36] He observes that even in presumably democratically administered parties, oligarchical leadership seems to surface: "In theory, the principle of election should prevent the formation of an oligarchy; in fact, it seems rather to favour it. The masses are naturally conservative; they become attached to their old leaders, they are suspicious of new faces."[37]

Renate Mayntz and Samuel Eldersveld find reasons for making revisions on Michels's iron law. Mayntz, in a study of a district unit of the Christian Democratic Union in West Berlin, uncovered some signs of oligarchy. She found, in particular, that new leaders often received their positions through the influence of older members of the leadership group, and the rank and file hardly exercised much power at all in the selection of new leaders.[38] Yet the leadership was not oligarchic in the sense portrayed by Michels; the leaders did not deliberately attempt to maintain themselves in office through the devices to which Michels pointed, for example, control of communications and monopoly of organizational skills. Instead, certain features of the party organization contributed to a high degree of autonomy on the part of the leadership. Such autonomy included: an election process that prevented the rank and file from exercising much choice over the selection of leaders; a strict hierarchy in the organization that prevented the rand and file from easily evaluating the performance of the leadership; and an absence of regular channels that would permit the rank and file members to participate in the formulation of party policies. Mayntz concludes that while this party organization, at least, may not strictly conform to the pattern and sources of oligarchy noted by Michels, it also is a far cry from the achievement of a democratic process in which leaders and followers freely interact and influence one another. Eldersveld, basing his ideas on his observations of local party organizations in Michigan, argues that the current political party is best conceived as a special kind of organization. It is one in which command does not clearly flow down from the top but rather is diffusely partitioned among several layers of the organization, resulting in a very loosely coordinated structure.[39] Furthermore, he claims, the cohesiveness of the elite groups at the top of the political party organizations is less real than apparent; instead of a single oligarchy, Eldersveld believes that there are several different suboligarchies that are only loosely coordinated and only infrequently in contact with one another.

Among the efforts to reexamine Michels's thesis, none ranks as more imaginative and thorough than the classic analysis of Seymour Martin Lipset, Martin Trow, and James Coleman.[40] Recognizing considerable truth in Michels's iron law, Lipset and his colleagues set out to discover the conditions under which oligarchies fail to arise in large organizations (see also Chapter 4). The site of their study was a trade union, not a political party, but the choice was propitious nonetheless since trade unions, like parties, are often as vulnerable (if not more so) to the growth of oligarchic leadership. Moreover, the particular union they examined, the International Typographical Union (ITU), represented the single trade union in the United States that had a long history of democratic politics. There were two political parties that regularly competed for union offices and that just as consistently alternated in the control of the offices. Inasmuch as all other unions were run by oligarchies, the specific question for Lipset, Trow, and Coleman became: Why does the ITU have democratic (competitive) rule instead of oligarchic control?

There were, as Lipset and his colleagues found, both historic and structural reasons for the presence of democracy, or absence of oligarchy, in the ITU. First, at the founding of the ITU, the printers revealed a strong identification and commitment to their craft; this loyalty became transformed into an interest and concern about their union. As a result, they were less apt to fall into the trap of membership passivity that Michels thought assisted the rise of oligarchies. Second, the ITU was somewhat notable among unions for the autonomy of the local branches; instead of having been created from the top down, it had been created as a federation of autonomous units. This fact played an important part in the subsequent politics of the union, facilitating as well as sustaining dissent against established practices and policies in the union. Third, among blue-collar workers, printing carries high prestige and also considerable financial rewards. These attributes perhaps serve to reinforce the printers' commitment to their craft, and they also create less of a disparity between the job of union leader and that of rand and file worker. Hence, the incentive for a leader to retain his office for its special perquisites was notably absent in the ITU. Fourth, as a result of their general concern and participation in the union, the printers as a group seemed to be especially skilled in the informal and formal ways of politics. Such skills on the part of the rank and file further encouraged engagement in union politics, even enabling some rand and file members to achieve high office in the union. These, too, are qualities that Michels did not find in the membership of the oligarchic parties and unions he observed.

In short, the study of the ITU is instructive for the lessons it may provide to political parties—and other organizations—wishing to avoid oligarchy. The following qualities are especially important to achieve democracy within parties: encourage commitment to the party, foster participation by the rank and file, create a climate receptive to dissent and innovation, and breed social and political skills in the rank and file.

The nature of the internal structure of political parties will remain an interesting matter of study as long as parties remain important institutions. Michels's analysis provides an important insight into the basic character of these organizations; its essential truth seems hard to disprove even now, almost three-quarters of a century after its initial declaration. Moreover, his insight raises intriguing and difficult questions about the relative advantages and disadvantages of parties that exhibit oligarchic tendencies over those that exhibit democratic ones. A true democrat may believe that any form of oligarchy is reprehensible and to be avoided at all costs. However, organizations that permit competition and dissent to arise among factions are often so debilitated by the internal conflicts they are incapable of attaining their goals in the larger society. Those, by comparison, that insist on unity within the ranks and manifest cohesive leadership, perhaps even oligarchy, frequently are the more successful in attaining the broader goals.[41] Which should one prefer—democracy within the ranks or victory outside the ranks? That is a question we all are left to ponder.

POLITICAL PARTISANSHIP: CONTEMPORARY PATTERNS AND TRENDS IN THE UNITED STATES

To what degree does partisanship actually pervade the consciousness of citizens? In particular, to what extent have people come to accept political parties as guides for their electoral behavior? And to what degree do they remain loyal to political parties? These are the sorts of questions I shall address in this section. I shall limit my analysis, for the sake of brevity, to the national level of politics, to presidential or congressional elections, as well as to related phenomena at this level.

The Breadth of Political Partisanship

Political partisanship can be studied in different ways. One is by looking at how people identify with political parties, if they do so at all. Party identification, researchers have found, is a very important dimension of how people think and act in politics.[42] Generally, people who adopt a particular party identification will vote for that party in national elections. But over the course of the past several decades there have been some significant changes in the nature and impact of party identification in the American electorate.

When the first studies of voting behavior and party identification were done in the 1950s, the patterns were quite clear. About one of every two voters identified themselves as Democrats, another three of every ten identified themselves as Republicans, and the remainder—twenty percent—claimed they were Independents, with no regular party identification.[43] Those who identified with the Democrats tended to vote Democratic in national elections, whereas those who identified with the Republicans tended to vote Republican. Independents, as you might expect, were a kind of free-floating electorate that would vary in their choice of candidates from one election to another.

This pattern of party identification and voting remained more or less descriptive of the American electorate for about fifteen years, until the late 1960s. Then the pattern began to crumble and important new shifts began to appear. In particular, there was a growing number of Independents to be found among the party identifiers, and a smaller number of people who identified themselves as Democratic partisans. The changes began to appear just after the election of Richard Nixon, a Republican president, in 1968. And, when he was re-elected in 1972, the shift to Independents became somewhat more marked.[44] What was evident is that the old New Deal Democratic coalition, created under the regime of Franklin Delano Roosevelt, had begun to come apart. The elections of Dwight Eisenhower, another Republican presidential candidate, in the 1950s, were the first signs of the demise of the Democratic coalition; Nixon's two victories cemented the change.

The Theory of Realignment. The appearance of more and more Independents among voters, coupled with the two elections of Republican Nixon, forced electoral observers to rethink the structure of the American electorate. For years, the Democrats had been the majority party in America, but now the Republicans were challenging their dominance. Did this change signal something more profound?

Among scholars seeking a deeper explanation of the changing partisan patterns, there was one theory that attracted much attention. It was the theory of "realignment" of the electorate proposed by the prominent political scientist, V.O. Key, Jr.[45] Key proposed that American electoral history had seen a series of almost different party systems, each with its own dominant party and with its own pattern of alignment of segments of the population supporting the majority and the minority parties. One important system had come into being in the Presidential contest of 1896. The Republican won this contest, which pitted the great Democratic orator William Jennings Bryan against the Republican William McKinley. Over the course of the next generation, the Republicans would remain as the dominant national Party, winning more often than not. But there was something even more important that Key discovered. The social alignments of the two parties remained more or less the same over the course of the period: The Democratic voter was apt to come from a rural agrarian background whereas the Republican voter tended to come from an affluent urban setting.

With the election of 1932, a new majority power and a new alignment of the electorate took effect. The Democrats became the majority party of the nation as they would win the office of the Presidency consistently from 1932 to 1968, losing only to Eisenhower in 1952 and 1956. Moreover, Roosevelt's victory in 1932 brought about a "critical realignment" in the electorate: The Democrats now became the party of the city, the Republicans the party of rural America. The Democratic voter tended to be a working-class ethnic American, whereas the Republican voter tended to be a white rural or small-town resident.

Key argued that such realignments in the American electorate were a product of generational shifts in the sympathies of voters and in the appeal of candidates. Once their loyalties were formed, voters tended to remain attached to a particular party over the course of their voting lifetime. As they aged, and as world events changed, something of a seismic shift began to occur that resulted in a new majority party and a new configuration of social groups behind both the majority and the minority parties.

Now if Key's theory were correct, it appeared that 1968 signaled the end, more or less, of the dominance of the Democratic Party. The Nixon victories, together with the growing number of Independent partisans, seemed to be the first real signs of the major partisan shift about to occur in America. But were they?

Partisan Realignment; or Dealignment? One of the great debates today among students of voting is whether America has actually witnessed a critical realignment of the form predicted by Key's theory, or whether something different has happened. In one sense there seems to have been something resembling a realignment. Out of the last eight Presidential elections, dating back to 1968, the Republicans have won the majority of the contests, five. In the previous ten Presidential elections they had won only two. Moreover, Clinton's victory in 1992 was won with just a plurality–43 percent of the vote—not a majority, owing to the large number of votes that went to Ross Perot.

But appearances can be deceiving, especially in this case. One of the main features of a period of critical realignment, according to Key's theory, is that there is a major shift in the sympathies of specific social and economic segments of the electorate. Thus, in 1932, the shift took place as urban voters began to flock to the Democrats, replacing rural America as the main force behind the Democrats. But no such shift seems to have taken place during the past couple of decades—and certainly not in 1968 as might have been expected. Instead, what observers find is a growing number of people who identify themselves as Independents, thus neither Democrats nor Republicans.

The growth in the proportion of Independents in the American electorate began in the late 1960s. Over the course of this early period, the proportion of the electorate that identified itself as Independents was on the order of about 12 to 15 percent.[46] Including Independents who leaned toward the Democrats and Independents who leaned toward the Republicans, it actually came to about one of every three voters at its peak. In 1952, when the New Deal coalition was still in place, only one of every four voters identified as an Independent. By the mid-1980s, the shift toward Independents had leveled off. And by 1996, the proportion of people who identified themselves as pure Independents had diminished to only 8 percent of the electorate.[47]

Some analysts, such as political scientist Everett Carll Ladd, Jr., argue that we are in the midst, not of a realignment but of a *dealignment* of the voters.[48] Voters have not shifted away from the Democrats to the Republicans on a regular basis so much as they are simply refusing to identify with either of the major parties on a consistent basis. In part, this new era may be a product of two different demographic trends among citizens. One is the growth in the education of the electorate, signaling that voters are bringing more of their knowledge to bear on their electoral choices. The other is that many of the new Independents are younger voters, hence they share few of the entrenched political loyalties of their parents.[49]

And yet not everyone agrees with this particular assessment. There is some evidence to suggest that some kind of partial realignment has taken place. Sociologists Clem Brooks and Jeff Manza argue that there is evidence that more professional workers, like lawyers and doctors, are now drawn to the Democratic Party than in the past.[50] They suggest that this disproportionate strength of the Democrats among the professions represents a sign of the actual realignment. Brooks and Manza, however, are the only social scientists thus far to detect such a trend.

Values and Partisanship

There is another way to think about the partisan views of the electorate. This is in terms of the values that people hold. Although there is a good deal of evidence to suggest that there seems only a limited degree of ideological thinking among voters, especially in America, there may be values held by voters that escape the usual net of partisan loyalties and identification. This is the line of analysis that has been pursued by political scientist Ronald Inglehart.[51]

Inglehart argues that over the course of the last three decades there has been a growing shift in the values held by citizens living in Western industrial democracies. We can think of the values held by people, he suggests, in terms of whether they reflect a concern with issues of safety and defense, or whether they reflect a concern with the environment and matters of equality. The first orientation is what he terms a *materialist* view of the world, whereas the second is a *post-materialist view.* He theorizes that since the later 1960s there has been a shift in the value orientations of citizens, from a materialist to a post-materialist view of the world. Those holding to a materialist view still remain in the majority, but the post-materialists are becoming a larger percentage of the population. The shift is associated with other structural changes in the economies of Western industrialized countries, including a shift away from primary manufacturing to high technology.[52]

Inglehart and his colleagues have done a number of studies to confirm and identify the various dimensions of the materialist and post-materialist view of the world. As Figure 8-1 reveals, for example, between 1970 and 1994 there was a noticeable increase in the proportion of people who held post-materialist orientations.

Among other important implications of this work is that the difference between the materialists and post-materialists influences their partisan attachments and preferences at the voting booth. Political scientist Russell Dalton, in a study of value-orientations among citizens in four nations, shows that the post-materialists clearly prefer more left-wing parties, while the materialist prefer more right-wing parties. In the early 1990s, for instance, 67 percent of the post-materialists preferred the Democrats compared to only 50 percent of those holding materialist values. In Great Britain the link between value orientations and party preferences was even more pronounced. Seventy percent of the post-materialists preferred the left-wing Labour Party, while 70 percent of the materialists preferred the right-wing Conservative Party.[53]

One can speculate that if the industrialized nations continue to move in the direction of great technological development and expansion, there is apt to be a corresponding increase in the proportion of citizens who hold to post-materialist values.

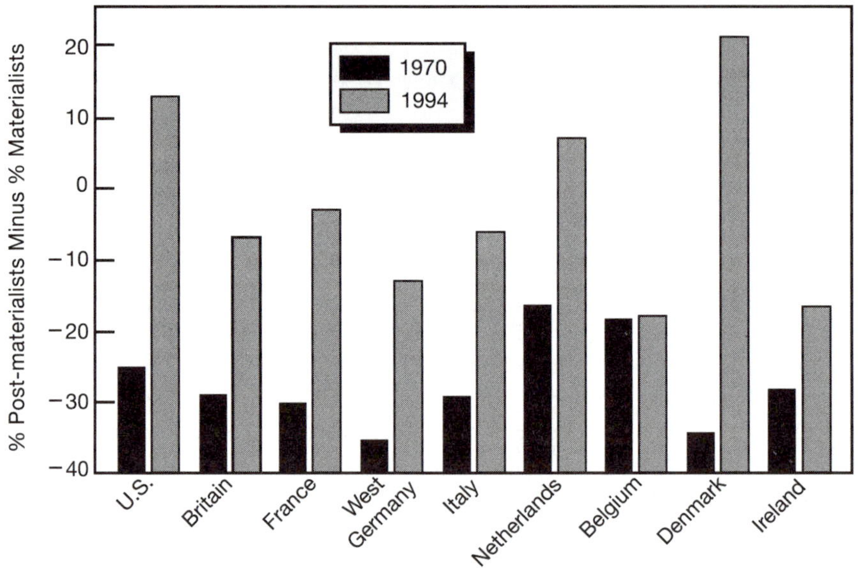

Figure 8-1 The Shift Toward Post-materialist Values Among the Publics of Nine Western Societies, 1970–1994

Source: European Community surveys, February 1970 and fall 1994; and (despite the legend above) U.S. National Election Surveys from 1972 and 1992. From Terry Nichols Clark and Michael Rempel, eds., *Citizen Politics in Post-Industrial Societies* (Boulder, Colo.: Westview Press, 1997), p. 65. Reprinted by permission of the publisher.

The Social Foundations of Partisanship

Social Class. The earliest studies of political parties, especially in the United States, revealed a very consistent set of findings.[54] Upper-class voters were apt to support the Republicans, while lower- and working-class voters tended to support the Democrats. The differences often were quite striking, among the major sources of variation to be found in the kinds of people who divided along party lines. The most important and interesting research on the matters is the classic work on stratification and partisanship by sociologist Robert Alford.[55]

In research conducted in the early 1960s, Alford compared the impact of social class, measured in occupational terms, on voting for left- or right-oriented parties in each of four countries, Australia, Canada, Great Britain, and the United States.[56] He found that class voting—by which he means the relative degree of support provided by manual and nonmanual workers for each party—was considerably lower in the United States than it is in either Great Britain or Australia. Even in Great Britain, class voting, which Alford expected to be strong, was comparatively weak. This pattern remained consistent from about 1940 to 1965.

National elections in recent years reveal, however, that the pattern of class differences in voting has become less marked. Working-class citizens no longer prefer the Democrats in large numbers, nor do upper-class citizens regularly prefer the Republicans. As noted previously, for example, sociologists Clem Brooks and Jeff Manza find a growing number of professional workers shifting to the Democratic Party in America over the period 1972 to 1992.[57] Other studies reveal a similar decline in class voting in America. Sociologist Norval Glenn, for instance, found that in non-Southern areas of the United States there has been a decline in the degree to which members of the different classes vote for the Republican presidential candidates. In 1936 there was a difference of almost 23 percent in the rate of support provided by blue-collar and white-collar workers for the candidacy of Alf Landon, whereas in 1968 there was a difference of only 11 percent between the classes in their support for the candidacy of Richard Nixon.[58] Political scientist Paul Abramson found somewhat similar results in an analysis of patterns of party voting during recent presidential contests. He observes, moreover, that the decline in the level of class voting can be attributed to a greater proportion of Democratic partisans among members of the post-World War II middle class as compared with the pre-World War II middle class.[59]

In the most recent Presidential elections, there continues to be a decline of class-linked voting in the United States. Abramson and his colleagues found that in the 1996 Presidential election, the supporters for Bill Clinton were more likely to come from the middle class rather than from members of the working and lower classes. And the traditional differences in class backgrounds of the Democrats and Republicans continued to weaken.[60]

What is even more interesting is that the differences in the social class backgrounds of left-wing parties, like the Democrats and the Labour Party in Great Britain, and right-wing parties, like the Republicans and the Conservative Party in Great Britain, are diminishing in other industrial democracies as well. This seems to be part of a general shift on the part of a number of political parties across nations to broaden their appeal to the middle classes, much like the Democrats have done in America in the 1990s.[61]

Social Networks. Some of the earliest studies of partisanship in the mass electorate, notably those by Berelson, Lazarsfeld, and their colleagues, reflect a central concern for the impact of primary group influences. Because of the early development of party preferences, it becomes somewhat difficult to assess the manner in which primary groups influence the voting behavior of adults; that is, it is uncertain whether primary groups mold opinions or whether they are self-selected by the individual. Nevertheless, two findings from this early research stand out as particularly interesting. First, Berelson, Lazarsfeld, and McPhee report that the greater the homogeneity in the opinions of the members of one's primary groups—family and friends—the greater the conviction of the individual for a particular political candidate. Specifically, if one's friends and family all intended to vote for or prefer the Republican candidates for president, then one would have a stronger conviction for that Republican candidate than he or she would if such persons were divided in their opinions. The second major finding of this early research emerges as a corollary to the first; people who are subject to conflicting opinions from the members of their primary groups are apt to behave reluctantly and uncertainly. For example, either they tend to put off making their decision about whom to support until the end of the campaign, or they fail to vote at all. Such a pattern became characterized as one of "cross-pressures" and, in various forms, became the basis for a considerable amount of later theoretical and empirical work.[62]

The importance of social networks and social context continues to be underscored by recent research. Political scientists Robert Huckfeldt and John Sprague find that people construct social networks that will tend to reinforce their own political preferences during electoral campaigns. Moreover, these same networks may work to supply people with a continuing flow of political information, some of which is incorrect and may be misperceived by its recipients. Huckfeldt and Sprague argue that, in general, such social contexts today play a very important part in the transmission and reception of political information.[63]

Partisanship and Rationality in the Electoral Process. Political theorists often claim that in order for a democratic society to survive in a healthy and suitable fashion, citizens must take an active interest in public affairs. They must be willing to guard against offenses by their elected officials, to hold those officials accountable for their policies, to make sure that the ship of state is being properly guided through both the calm and the rough waters of world events. Many citizens, however, have neither the time nor the interest to remain constantly vigilant. Therefore, elections are looked on by theorists of democratic politics as the one special occasion when the public can take an active interest and decide, individually and collectively, who will serve their interests and concerns best in public office. It is further assumed, by these accounts, that the public acts in a rational fashion to select their officials: People establish priorities for themselves, weigh what candidates say, and then, through the magical device of electoral procedures, come up with candidates who will serve their interests, or those of the majority, best.

Political parties, which are everywhere dominant in democratic societies, introduce a complicating but not an insurmountable obstacle in this reckoning about the rational method whereby the public chooses to express its will. All that is required to introduce the factor of parties into the decision-making procedure is the additional assumption that parties become the specific organizational devices whereby the public is offered a choice; parties, by this logic, have a responsibility to offer distinct choices to the electorate for their decision. At the same time, however, the electorate is expected to make its choices, not constrained by party labels, among the candidates of the parties. The policies of the parties, the special stands of the candidates, and the voter's own special priorities are expected to come together in a measured fashion and to result in a rational choice of elected officials.

This is only theory about rationality in the electoral process. What does experience show us? Prior to the 1960s in the United States, a large proportion of the electorate seemed unable to discern any of the apparent ideological differences between the major political parties and incapable of thinking about political choices and issues in any consistent conceptual fashion. That is, they seemed unaware of the issues or choices that confronted them and were in no sense prepared for exercising rationality in the electoral process. Given the sizable proportion of people who were loyal to one or the other major political party, it appeared that their motivations in elections stemmed from a *faith*, or a *loyalty*, to the party rather than from a decision based upon the issues and their own priorities.

Researchers at the University of Michigan developed a model of the decision-making process by individual voters that highlighted forces of party loyalty and concern with issues most forcefully. Angus Campbell and his colleagues hypothesized that choices among candidates at election time spring essentially from one of three forces: party loyalty or party identification, the attractiveness of a particular candidate, and issues of the campaign. If the rational model presupposed by democratic theories were an accurate one, issues should turn out to be the most powerful force, and candidate appeal and party loyalty should be considerably less powerful. What happens?

Table 8-1 reproduces estimates of the magnitude of these effects as judged from one of the Eisenhower-Stevenson presidential contexts in the 1950s.[64] Party identification refers to party loyalty; orientation to Eisenhower and Stevenson refers to the appeal of the candidates; and domestic and foreign issue partisanship refers to the impact of issues. Looking at the first row, that of the simple correlations, it is evident that party identification exerts the most powerful impact on the voter's choice, but that each of the issue components also has a very powerful effect. However, examining the coefficients in the second and third rows, which represent the effects of each variable—controlling for the influence of the other variables—the pattern of coefficients is markedly different. In fact, party loyalty exerts the most powerful influence on the individual voter's choice; it is far greater than that of issues or candidate appeals. Thus, loyalty, or party preference, rather than rational calculation, underlies the voter's choice.

These estimates of the effects of each of these forces on the individual

TABLE 8-1 Relation of Partisan Attitudes to Preference Among All Respondents Expressing a Preference for a Major Party Candidate (N = 1522)

	Party Identification	Orientation to Eisenhower	Orientation to Stevenson	Domestic Issue Partisanship	Foreign Issue Partisanship
Simple correlation with preference	0.59	0.35	0.23	0.48	0.38
Partial correlation with preference (all other attitudes held fixed)	0.42	0.16	0.12	0.23	0.20
Standard regression coefficients	0.40	0.13	0.09	0.20	0.16
Multiple correlation of five partisan attitudes with preference 0.68					

Source: Adapted from Angus Campbell and Donald Stokes, "Partisan Attitudes and Presidential Vote." Reprinted with the permission of The Free Press, a Division of Simon & Schuster, Inc. from *American Voting Behavior* edited by Eugene Burdick and Arthur J. Brodbeck, p. 356. Copyright © 1959 by The Free Press.

voter's choice, of course, come from the pre-1960 period, which, as we have observed already, is in many ways very different from the post-1960 era. In the post-1960 period there has been a marked decline in loyalty to each of the two major parties and, simultaneously, a marked jump in the mass electorate's consistency of conceptual thought about politics. Are these changes further reflected in the changing weights assigned to each of the three major forces that figure into the voter's choice? Are voters in some sense now more calculating and deliberative about their choices than several decades ago?

Regrettably there are no data comparable to Campbell's for the post-1960 period; thus, precise estimates are impossible. But there are some scattered clues that suggest there has been an increase in the extent to which issues figure into the choices of voters. Some of the increase apparently is due to short-term forces. Thus, in the 1964 Presidential election, which pitted Republican Barry Goldwater against Democrat Lyndon Johnson, two researchers found that issues, springing mainly from Goldwater's very conservative perspective, figured more prominently in voters' decisions than they had in the elections of the 1950s.[65] Similarly, Philip Converse and his colleagues found that the 1968 campaign of Independent George Wallace generated an unusual interest, and division, among the voters on such issues as civil rights, law and order, and Vietnam.[66]

However, some of the increase in the salience of issues can be attributed to the secular rise in the salience of issues, generally, for the American public. Political scientists Norman Nie and Kristi Andersen, for instance, discovered several indications of the increasing importance of issues for presidential voting and of the simultaneous decline of party loyalty. In 1956, the gamma association between attitudes toward various issues and the presidential vote was +.16; this association rose dramatically to +.58 in the 1964 election and remained at about the same level in the 1972 election. While the influence of issues was rising, that of party loyalty dropped from a high of +.89 in the 1956 election to +.70 in the 1972 election. From another perspective, the influence of party loyalty in the 1972 elections was only somewhat higher than that of issues, +.70 as compared to +54.[67]

The most recent evidence, from the Presidential election of 1996, suggests that issues continue to play an important part in the choices of voters. Those who voted for the Democrats and those who voted for the Republicans sensed a marked difference between the parties in the major issues of the campaign. And those differences played a part in whether voters chose Bill Clinton or Robert Dole. In his research, Russell Dalton found that the issue positions of voters, not only in the United States, but also in Great Britain, Germany, and France, made a large difference in their partisan preferences in the early 1990s.[68]

To sum up the evidence: Party loyalty continues to exert a strong influence on the choices of voters. But issues are coming to play an increasingly important role in such choices. Voters are depending less than before on the identifying label of a party and more on the stands that candidates take on important issues—about the economy, abortion, the environment. Why is this happening? Why the change from the 1950s to now—and why not only in the United States but also in several other Western countries?

At best, answers to these questions must be tentative; much of the hard and secure evidence is now lacking, but there seem to be three possible explanations. First, the general increase over the past several decades in the level of education among the public has produced voters who are more sophisticated about the nature of parties and politics. Voters are becoming educated to be more deliberative and rational in their choices of candidates to support. Although increases in the average level of education over the past two decades are fairly slight, they could be sufficient to account in part for the growing rationality of voters. The fact that the movement toward partisan independence occurs especially among the young who are receiving the greater educational training underscores the plausibility of this explanation. Second, the magnitude of domestic and foreign conflicts in the 1960s—the civil rights issues, the students issues, and the Vietnam War, among many others—left people with the impression that political parties are simply no longer capable of handling political conflicts, a task almost exclusively their domain. The argument is also partly supported by evidence that shows a marked cynicism on the part of the public toward the effectiveness of the federal government. Such cynicism, coupled with the diminishing loyalty of voters to parties, are an unquestionable part of a broader pattern of voter disenchantment with many political institutions. The third explanation assumes that political parties are an important part of social life and that the ties of people to parties are the result of the parties' deliberate efforts to cultivate their loyalties. Thus, the declining loyalties of people to the parties is the result of diminishing strength in the party organizations and their failure to exact the commitments of people for more than electoral contests. Parties in the United States, as Duverger remarked, have been noted historically for their limited interest in the loyalties of citizens; moreover, their strength has been on the decline since the close of the nineteenth century. Both circumstances may finally have caught up with parties and produced a reduction in the overall proportion of loyal partisans.

Any or possibly all of these explanations may help to account for the new patterns we have observed. In any event, the main conclusion is best put by Dalton: "(M)ore citizens now have the political resources to follow the complexities of politics; they have the potential to act as the independent issue voters described in the classic democratic theory but seldom seen in practice."[69]

THE PAST AND FUTURE OF MODERN POLITICAL PARTIES: THE CASE OF THE UNITED STATES

The halcyon days of the political parties in the United States were those in the last quarter of the nineteenth century. The party organizations performed with an efficiency, a discipline, and an intensity since unmatched; as Richard Jensen notes, political campaigns at this time were carried out with the vigor and precision of military campaigns.[70] The feelings engendered among the voters were also more intense than in recent years; Ostrogorski provides a most vivid description of the party feelings at the time:

> The name of the party is its own justification, in the eyes of millions of electors. They say, with a well-known politician, an ex-Senator of New York, "I am a Democrat" (or "I am a Republican," as the case may be), just as a believer says, to explain and justify his faith, "I am a Christian!" The reader knows how, and through what political sentiment all the world over, has been intensified in the United States and raised to the level of dogma—the dogma of "regularity," which makes the party creed consist in voting the "straight party ticket," whatever it may be. The sins against the religion of the party are sins against the ticket.[71]

Turnout among voters for presidential, state, and local elections was considerably higher than it has been recently. It reached an average near 80 percent, while in the past several presidential elections it has declined steadily, from a figure of 63 percent in 1960 to one of slightly over 50 percent in the 1996 presidential election.[72] The competition between political parties for elective office was also usually considerably keener than at present. In short, the party organizations were usually vigorous at the end of the nineteenth century in the United States and were considerably stronger than at present. Inasmuch as the change appears to represent a more or less continuous decline that has been interrupted only occasionally, it is appropriate to inquire into the conditions that have led to the gradual atrophy of parties in the United States.

There appear to be a number of sources. Perhaps the most significant is the Progressive movement that developed in the 1890s and was largely organized and advanced by white middle-class Protestant Americans who saw party organizations and their adherents as threats to their own values and lifestyles. The tensions between the Progressives and their opponents grew out of a clash of many different interests and beliefs: the genteel and impersonal outlook of the indigenous Americans against the rough and personal orientations of the ethnics; the Protestantism of the indigenous Americans against the Catholicism of the ethnics; the wealth of the middle-class Americans against the poverty of the ethnics; and so on.[73] The specific results of the Progressive movement, though designed ostensibly to promote greater participation in politics by the public, were really intended to deprive the ethnic groups of control of the party organizations that were their one hold on and source of satisfaction in American life. As the reformers intended, the ethnics ultimately lost control of the party organizations, but this loss resulted in serious and permanently crippling blows to the vitality of the party organizations.

Several products of the Progressive movement undercut the party organizations; the most prominent one was the establishment of direct primary elections. Direct primary elections took the nomination of candidates away from parties and their leaders and gave it to the public. Having lost their right to nominate candidates, parties lost their ability to establish and to enforce a firm party line among their candidates. Fights eventually came to prevail more between the personal factions within political parties than between the parties themselves. The actual candidacy of people for office came to rest less on their loyalty to the party beliefs and hierarchy than on their capacity to generate funds for the political contests. In short, the direct primary stripped the political parties of an important function of identifying and nominating candidates for office; thus, it assisted in the decline of the party organizations in the United States. (One could justify the party's loss as the public's gain, but apparently the public does not see it that way for it turns out for primary elections in even smaller numbers than for regular elections.)

Two other circumstances that made their first appearance at the end of the nineteenth century also contributed to a decline in the vitality of party organizations. One was the loss of patronage that was one of the mainstays of the political party. The Pendleton Act passed in 1883 opened civil service positions to competition on the basis of merit; initially, it covered only 10 percent of the civil service positions in government, but it now covers 90 percent of them. The loss of patronage meant that the parties could no longer provide the attractive inducements that secured a large and loyal staff of workers; the absence of other attractive substitutes was another crippling blow to party organizations. The other circumstance was the introduction in the early twentieth century of a new style of campaigning—advertising. Partly a consequence of the diminishing strength of the party organization and partly a cause for its diminishing even further, advertising as a mode of campaigning was adopted by candidates as an easy and efficient way to communicate with the voters. The earlier style of campaigning, the militarist in the words of Richard Jensen, relied heavily on precinct workers and various other party staff members to draw out the vote for candidates. Advertising relies upon the media to appeal to voters. In recent years, advertising has become even more heavily relied upon at the expense of party workers; television now makes the house-to-house rounds among voters. The effect of this new mode of campaigning, of course, is to rob the party of yet another of its principal functions and to further contribute to the demise of the organization.

One last important historical fact working against party organizations has been a trend I noted previously about the United States—that is, the gradual concentration of financial resources in the federal government and the use of these resources to provide welfare monies to the impoverished and disabled. The party organizations in urban areas relied upon their provision of funds as a means of securing services in precincts of poor immigrants—for a little cash, one could easily drum up a few more voters in a ward. During the Roosevelt administrations, the federal government began to provide these funds in the form of unemployment compensation and countless other programs, and party organizations lost their exclusive appeal. The poor could now turn to the federal government for money, and the parties had nowhere else to turn for staff replacements.

So what will become of party organizations in the future? Are they necessary and important to the survival of American democracy? Or are they, in fact, organizations whose importance has run its course, and which may now be scattered among the various ashes of political history? What is clear is that such organizations are vastly different than their nineteenth century—indeed, even mid-twentieth century—counterparts. They no longer wield the power for their bosses in urban areas, nor do their leaders exercise the kind of power they once held. They work well to provide a medium through which voters can express preferences, but obviously far from perfectly. The rise to prominence of the Independent Party in the 1990s suggests that third parties still provide a choice to voters, even in some specific local circumstances, but it is unlikely that the Independent Party will ever become a dominant force.

Instead Americans seem to live with parties, but when they do political work it is mainly through other forums—through local groups, civic organizations, and similar instruments. Whether America can survive with the limited involvement of the public in the activities of parties, and even of voluntary associations, is a question that, as we have seen earlier, has prompted a good deal of recent speculation by such figures as Robert Putnam, among many others. So long as the economy is booming in America, it is likely that such questions will be postponed. But what will happen if the economy turns sour? How will people express their voice and their dissatisfaction? If they have become unaccustomed to working and talking in the forum of public affairs, how will they know how to re-engage in such activities?

Such problems as these will remain on the agenda for political sociologists and political scientists to explore in the near future. The great irony is that America is held up as a model of an effective democracy for many of the emerging nation-states just at a time when a number of social scientists are voicing their concerns over the diminishing level of civic commitment and interest on the part of American citizens. Is it possible that democratic nations can reach the point where they continue to work effectively, even in the absence of a vigorous party system?

NOTES

1. A number of good general treatments of the history of parties in different countries can be found in Sigmund Neumann, *Modern Political Parties: Approaches to Comparative Politics* (Chicago: University of Chicago Press, 1956).
2. William Nisbet Chambers, *Political Parties in a New Nation: The American Experience 1776–1809* (New York: Oxford University Press, 1963), Chapters 1 and 2, especially pp. 45–49.
3. Max Weber, *The Methodology of the Social Sciences.* Translated and edited by Edward A. Shils and Henry A. Finch. With a Foreword by Edward A. Shils. (New York: The Free Press, 1949), 80.
4. See, for instance, Hans Daalder, "Parties, Elites, and Political Development in Western Europe," in *Mass Politics in Industrial Societies: A Reader in Comparative Politics*, ed. Giuseppe Di Palma (Chicago: Markham Publishing Company, 1972), pp. 4–36; and Maurice Duverger, *Political Parties: Their Organization and Activity in the Modern State,* revised edition, translated by Barbara and Robert North (New York: John Wiley & Sons, Inc., 1959).
5. Along these lines, for example, see Neumann, *Modern Political Parties.*
6. One of the most common explanations of this form is that which traces the rise of parties in both the United States and Western Europe to the extension of suffrage in the nineteenth century. See, for instance, Leon D. Epstein, *Political Parties in Western Democracies* (New York: Frederick A. Praeger, 1967), pp. 19–26.
7. Joseph LaPalombara and Myron Weiner, eds. *Political Parties and Political Development* (Princeton, New Jersey: Princeton University Press, 1966), Chapter 1.
8. Ibid., p. 21.

9. Actually, LaPalombara and Weiner consider these two sets of conditions as alternative explanations for the origins of parties; I have taken license and combined them here into a somewhat more comprehensive scheme.
10. The logical ordering of conditions prior to the emergence of the modern parties is a sticky issue that LaPalombara and Weiner never identify. It is evident that the three general sets of preconditions act as necessary circumstances for the rise of parties, but the logical status of the crises is not so clear. For our purposes, they are assigned the status of sufficient but not necessary conditions.
11. These events can be found in any standard treatment of American party history as, for example, Herbert Agar's *The Price of Union* (Boston: Houghton Mifflin Company, 1950). The illuminating analysis of Chambers, *Political Parties in a New Nation*, is particularly helpful in understanding this period.
12. Duverger, *Political Parties*, revised edition.
13. Epstein, *Political Parties in Western Democracies*, Chapter 8.
14. Duverger, *Political Parties*, pp. 22–23. Duverger, of course, is not the only observer of United States' history to point to the salience of these features for its institutions.
15. Duverger, *Political Parties*, pp. 20–21.
16. Ibid., p. 26.
17. Ibid., pp. 35–36.
18. For criticism, see, for example, Aaron Wildavshy, "A Methodological Critique of Duverger's *Political Parties*," *Journal of Politics*, 21 (May 1959), 303–18; and Epstein, *Political Parties in Western Democracies*, Chapters 2 and 4.
19. For two excellent works on electoral laws and their impact on party politics see: Douglas W. Rae, *The Political Consequences of Electoral Laws* (New Haven and London: Yale University Press, 1967), and Arend Lijphart, *Electoral Systems and Party Systems: A Study of Twenty-Seven Democracies 1945–1990* (Oxford, UK: Oxford University Press, 1998).
20. Actually the method of representation is more complicated than this simple explanation suggests. There are different methods for determining the actual proportion of a party's representatives to be awarded seats. The Hare system most closely approximates the form given in my explanation; other methods determine the outcomes in a slightly different manner. See Lijphart, ibid., Appendix A.
21. Ibid., Chapter 7.
22. The seminal work on the party machines in the United States during their early rise to power remains, M. Ostrogorski, *Democracy and the Organization of Political Parties*, vol. II, translated by Frederick Clarke (New York: Macmillan & Co., Ltd., 1902).
23. For an interesting analysis of this phenomenon, see Robert Dahl, *Who Governs*? (New Haven: Yale University Press, 1961), Chapter 4.
24. The following analysis is based principally on Mike Royko. *Boss: Richard J. Daley of Chicago* (New York: New American Library, 1971).
25. Ibid., Chapter 2 especially.

26. William L. Riordon, *Plunkitt of Tammany Hall: A Series of Plain Talks on Very Practical Politics* (New York: E. P. Dutton and Co., Inc., 1963), pp. 27–28.
27. For the analysis in this paragraph, see Fred I. Greenstein, "The Changing Pattern of Urban Politics," *Annals of the American Academy of Political and Social Science*, 353 (May 1964), 1–13. Also see Fred I. Greenstein, *The American Party System and the American People*, 2nd ed. (Englewood Cliffs, New Jersey: Prentice-Hall, Inc., 1970), Chapter 4. For the relationship between power and inducements, see the discussion of the notion of power at the beginning of Chapter 6 in this book. An insightful analysis and updating of the nature of political machines is to be found in Thomas M. Guterbock, *Machine Politics in Transition: Party and Community in Chicago* (Chicago,: University of Chicago Press, 1980).
28. See, for example, Duverger, *Political Parties*; and Philip Selznick, *The Organizational Weapon: The Study of Bolshevik Strategies and Tactics* (Glencoe, Illinois: The Free Press, 1960).
29. M. Ostrogorski, *Democracy and the Organization of Political Parties*, I and II.
30. On the first point, Ostrogorski's fear may have been well founded, even though he exaggerated them; on the second point, his fear turns out to have been less sound, as later scholarship on British parties reveals. See R. T. McKenzie, *British Political Parties: The Distribution of Power Within the Conservative and Labour Parties*, 2nd ed. (New York: Frederick A. Praeger, Publishers, 1964), pp. 642–49.
31. Robert Michels, *Political Parties: A Sociological Study of the Oligarchical Tendencies of Modern Democracy* (New York: Collier Books, 1962).
32. Ibid., p. 61.
33. Somewhat prophetically, given the rise of Hitler and the Nazi regime only decades later, Michels believed that the need for submission to a leader's will was possibly peculiar to the German people and the residue of a long tradition and of the recent leadership of Bismarck.
34. Michels, *Political Parties*, p. 207.
35. Vilfredo Pareto, *The Mind and Society* (London: Jonathan Cape, 1935) III, pp. 1427–31.
36. Duverger, *Political Parties*, pp. 116–68.
37. Ibid., p. 135.
38. Renate Mayntz, "Oligarchic Problems in a German Party District," in *Political Decision Makers*, ed. Dwaine Marvick (Glencoe, Illinois: The Free Press, 1961), pp. 138–92.
39. Samuel J. Eldersveld, *Political Parties: A Behavioral Analysis* (Chicago: Rand McNally & Company, 1964), pp. 1–13.
40. Seymour Martin Lipset, Martin Trow, and James Coleman, *Union Democracy: The Internal Politics of the International Typographical Union* (Garden City, New York: Anchor Books, 1962)
41. For relevant evidence on this matter, see William A. Gamson, *The Strategy of Social Protest*, 2nd edition, (Belmont, California: Wadsworth Press, 1990).
42. Angus Campbell et al., *The American Voter* (New York: John Wiley & Sons, Inc. 1960), and, more recently, Paul R. Abramson, John H. Aldrich, and David W.

Rohde, *Change and Continuity in the 1996 Elections* (Washington, D.C.: CQ Press, 1998).

43. Campbell et al., ibid.
44. See, for instance, Norval D. Glenn, "Sources of the Shift to Political Independence: Some Evidence from A Cohort Analysis," *Social Science Quarterly*, 53 (December 1972), 494–519.
45. V.O. Key, Jr., "A Theory of Critical Elections," *Journal of Politics*, 17 (February 1955):
46. Abramson et al., op. cit., Chapter 8.
47. Ibid., p. 167.
48. See, for example, Everett Carll Ladd, Jr., "The Shifting Party Coalitions—From the 1930s to the 1970s," in Seymour Martin Lipset, ed., *Party Coalitions in the 1980s* (San Francisco: Institute for Contemporary Studies, 1981), 127–49.
49. Paul R. Abramson, "Generational Change in American Electoral Behavior," *American Political Science Review*, 68 (March 1974), 93–105.
50. Clem Brooks and Jeff Manza, "The Social and Ideological Bases of Middle-Class Political Realignment in the United States, 1972–1992," *American Sociological Review*, 62 (April 1997), 191–208.
51. See, for example, Ronald Inglehart, *Culture Shift in Advanced Industrial Society* (Princeton: Princeton University Press, 1990).
52. Ronald Inglehart, "The Trend Toward Postmaterialist Values Continues," in Terry Nichols Clark and Michael Rempel, editors, *Citizen Politics in Post-Industrial Societies* (Boulder, Colorado: Westview Press, 1997), 57–66.
53. Russell J. Dalton, *Citizen Politics: Public Opinion and Political Parties in Advanced Industrial Democracies* (Chatham, New Jersey: Chatham House Publishers, 1996), 189.
54. Paul F. Lazarsfeld, Bernard Berelson, and Hazel Gaudet, *The People's Choice* (New York: Duell, Sloan and Pearce, 1944); also Campbell et al., op.cit.
55. Robert Alford, *Party and Society* (Chicago: Rand McNally, 1963).
56. Alford, *Party and Society*, and Alford, "Class Voting in the Anglo-American Democracies, in *Mass Politics in Industrial Societies*, Di Palma, pp. 166–99.
57. Brooks and Manza, op. cit.
58. Norval Glenn, "Class and Party Support in the United States: Recent and Emerging Trends, " *Public Opinion Quarterly*, 37 (Spring 1973), 1–20.
59. Paul R. Abramson, "Generational Change in American Electoral Behavior," *American Political Science Review*, 68 (March 1974), 93–105.
60. Abramson et al., op. cit., Chapter 5.
61. Dalton, op. cit., 175.
62. Careful examination of the results in *Voting* reveals that the authors believed cross-pressures characterized situations of conflicting social statuses, among many others; hence, their research in a way can be directly connected to the large amount of work on the effects of status inconsistency. Moreover, their research also figured quite prominently in the development of cognitive dissonance theory by psychologist Leon Festinger.

63. Robert Huckfeldt and John Sprague, "Networks in Context: The Social Flow of Political Information," *American Political Science Review*, Volume 81 (December 1987), 1197–1216.
64. Angus Campbell and Donald Stokes, "Partisan Attitudes and the Presidential Vote," *in American Voting Behavior*, eds. Eugene Burdick and Arthur J. Brodbeck (Glencoe, Illinois: The Free Press of Glencoe, 1959) pp. 353–71.
65. John Osgood Field and Ronald E. Anderson, "Ideology in the Public's Conceptualization of the 1964 Election," *Political Parties and Political Behavior*, Crotty et al., pp. 400–19.
66. Philip E. Converse et al., "Continuity and Change in American Politics: Parties and Issues in the 1968 Election," in *Political Parties and Political Behavior*, Crotty et al., pp. 356–99.
67. Nie with Anderson, "Mass Belief Systems Revisited."
68. Dalton, ibid., Chapter 10.
69. Ibid., 235; see also Abramson et al., op. cit. Chapter 11.
70. Richard Jensen, "American Election Campaigns: A Theoretical and Historical Typology," in Walter Dean Burnham, *Critical Elections and the Mainsprings of American Politics* (New York: W.W. Norton and Company, Inc., 1970), 72.
71. Ostrogorski, ibid., 353–54.
72. William Nisbet Chambers, "Party Development and the American Mainstream," in William Nisbet Chambers and Walter Dean Burnham, eds., *The American Party System* (New York: Oxford University Press, 1967), 14.
73. Richard Hofstadter, *The Age of Reform* (New York: Vintage Books, 1960), Chapter 6.

Chapter 9

Citizen Participation in Politics

Conventional and Contentious Forms

> And so, we have become convinced that the fundamental error committed by the "new tendency" in Russian Social-Democracy lies in its subservience to spontaneity, and its failure to understand that the spontaneity of the masses demands a mass of consciousness from the Social-Democrats. The more spontaneously the masses rise, the more widespread the movement becomes, so much the more rapidly grows the demand for greater consciousness in the theoretical, political and organisational work of Social-Democracy.
>
> V.I. Lenin, *What Is To Be Done?*

Political parties, as we saw in the last chapter, represent an important but only one of many media through which the public can express themselves in the political arena. There are countless other ways as well. People can circulate and sign petitions; stage mass rallies; engage in mass marches; even contact local political officials. In recent years, more and more citizens appear to be choosing these new forums to voice their views, whether about local neighborhood concerns, about issues of peace, or even simply to show their support of groups like the disabled. In this chapter, I will review what we now know about citizen participation, broadly speaking. For the purposes of providing a comprehensive portrayal of these matters I will draw a distinction between *conventional*, or routine, politics, like parties, and *contentious* politics, like more marginal and radical social movements, such as the Peace movement or the Pro-Life protestors in America.

These matters of how to participate and how to express our views about politics are of vital concern to us as citizens. No wonder then that so many students of political sociology have made the study and research about contentious politics, or what is otherwise known as the field of social movements, one of the most popular subfields of sociology.

CONVENTIONAL POLITICS

Consider the nature of citizen participation in *conventional politics* first. I use the term to refer to *the regular, or routine, institutional forms that political action assumes in society*. Typically political sociologists mean, in particular, such things as political parties and interest groups, such as the National Organization for Women (NOW) or the National Rifle Association in the United States. Such groups represent the vehicles that are available for participation by people, and that act, in a general sense, to express people's ideas and beliefs to the officials of government. In democracies like the United States or Canada, there is usually an array of such organizations, and a set of rights and laws of the society protect their presence.

Types and Levels of Participation

Political scientists Sidney Verba and Norman Nie completed the definitive study of participation in conventional politics more than three decades ago. That study helped to establish the basic benchmarks both for the nature of activities in which people participate and for their overall levels of participation.[1]

The study was undertaken in 1967 among a sample of American residents. Verba and Nie asked their respondents about their engagement in each of several different kinds of political activities. Table 9-1 presents the twelve different forms of participation they uncovered and the percentages of respondents who claimed to have engaged in each of the different forms. The forms represent a hierarchy of involvement in politics almost identical to another broad study of political participation by political scientist Lester Milbrath.[2] Seventy two percent of the respondents report regular voting in Presidential elections; only 8 percent claim membership in a political club or organization.

Using the results obtained from their questions about forms of participation, Verba and Nie developed a compact theoretical model of the clusters of activities they expected to find. The model was based on the amount of initiative required for the act of participation as well as on the scope of the act's outcome. For example, they expected to find that voting, an act of little initiative, would emerge as one mode of political participation independent of broader campaign activity by citizens. They then performed a statistical

TABLE 9-1 Percentage Engaging in Twelve Different Acts of Political Participation

Type of Political Participation	Percentage
1. Report regularly voting in presidential elections[a]	72
2. Report always voting in local elections	47
3. Active in at least one organization involved in community problems[b]	32
4. Have worked with others in trying to solve some community problems	30
5. Have attempted to persuade others to vote as they were	28
6. Have ever actively worked for a party or candidates during an election	26
7. Have ever contacted a local government official about some issue or problem	20
8. Have attended at least one political meeting or rally in last three years	19
9. Have ever contacted a state or national government official about some issue or problem	18
10. Have ever formed a group or organization to attempt to solve some local community problem	14
11. Have ever given money to a party or candidate during an election campaign	13
12. Presently a member of a political club or organization	8
Number of Cases: weighted 3,095 unweighted 2,549	

[a]Composite variable created from reports of voting in 1960 and 1964 Presidential elections. Percentage is equal to those who report they have voted in both elections.

[b]This variable is a composite index in which the proportion presented above is equal to the proportion of those in the sample who are active in at least one voluntary association that, they report, takes an active role in attempting to solve community problems. The procedure utilized was as follows: Each respondent was asked whether he was a member of fifteen types of voluntary associations. For each affirmative answer he was then asked whether he regularly attended meetings or otherwise took a leadership role in the organization. If yes, he was considered an active member. If he was an active member and if he reported that the organization regularly attempted to solve community problems, he was considered to have performed this type of political act. Membership in expressly *political* clubs or organizations was excluded from this index.

Source: Adapted from Sidney Verba and Norman Nie, *Participation in America: Political Democracy and Social Equality* (New York: Harper and Row, 1972), p. 131.

operation known as factor analysis. This means, in simplest terms, identifying the various kinds of political acts that tend to be performed by the same people. Verba and Nie uncovered six different forms or modes of such participation.

Here are the forms they found: *the totally inactive,* or those who perform no political acts whatsoever (22 percent); *voting specialists,* or those who just engage in voting in elections (21 percent); *parochial participants,* or those who report contacts with state or local leaders on personal problems only (4 percent); *communalists,* or those who engage in action only on local problems (20 percent); *campaigners,* or those who report engaging only in campaign activities, such as working for a candidate (15 percent); and, finally, *complete activists,* or those who engage in all the forms of political activity (11 percent).

In the years since Verba and Nie did their pathbreaking work, other research has uncovered roughly similar forms and percentages of activity in conventional politics. But there are some important nuances and variations that have been uncovered. For example, the voting turnout rate in the United States has been consistently lower than in other industrialized nations of the world. Moreover, over the past several decades the turnout for elections in the United States has dropped dramatically as compared to other countries (see Chapter 8). In nations such as France, Germany and Great Britain, the voting turnout over the past three decades has remained more or less stable, with fluctuations here and there. In the United States, by contrast, there has been a dramatic drop-off. Various reasons have been offered for the decline in the United States, as compared to other nations, including the greater activity and ideological polarization of European political parties.[3] Finally, recent research on patterns of participation in the United States reveals that Americans show very high rates of participation in voluntary associations and other social groups, especially as compared to the residents of other nations. What is particularly impressive is the activity of many Americans in religious organizations, an activity that seems to make up for somewhat more limited activity in strictly political organizations and groups.[4]

Social Cleavages and Conventional Political Participation

Besides the differences in the types of politics in which people routinely engage, there are also some important variations by virtue of the social groups to which people belong. The most important such variations are due to the significant social cleavages of our time: social class, race and gender.

Social Class. Since the first empirical work ever done about social differences and political participation, one discovery emerges time and again: citizens of higher social class standing, however measured, participate more extensively and deeply in the regular institutional politics of their societies.[5] So powerful is the influence of social class, or socioeconomic status, on routine political participation that Verba and Nie created a basic model of participation specifically organized about differences between people of different class rankings. Figure 9-1 provides one set of data from their study that reveal the pattern of SES differences in the general scale of political participation. There is a considerable increase in the rates of participation between the lower end of the socioeconomic scale and the higher end of it: The group at the very lowest point on the scale shows an average rate of 46 points below the mean for the entire sample, while the group at the very highest end of the scale shows an average rate of 66 points above the mean for the entire sample.

Scholars have offered different explanations for the link between social class and routine political participation. One argument is that people of

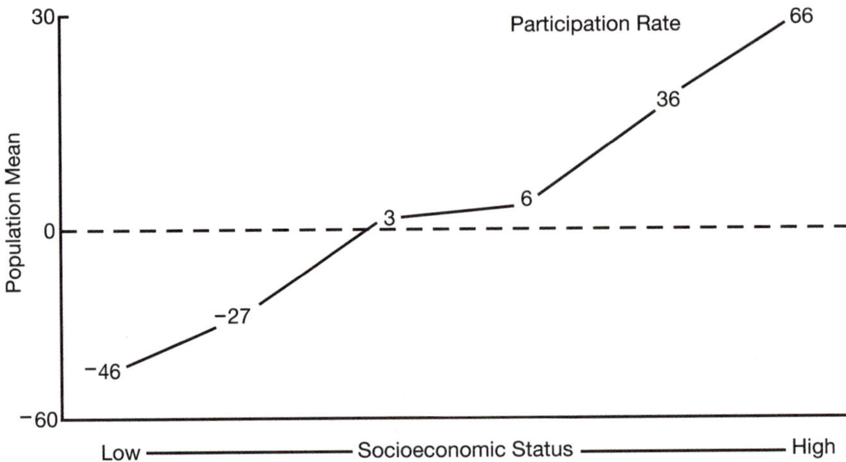

Figure 9-1 Socioeconomic Status and the Overall Participation Scale
Adapted from Sidney Verba and Norman Nie, *Participation in America* (New York: Harper and Row, 1972.

higher class standing have a greater stake in the political system, hence they are more likely to support it through regular forms of political activity. By contrast, citizens of lower class ranking, it is argued, generally are more likely to feel cut off from the activities of society, and thus are less inclined to take the time to participate in politics—however much it might benefit them.[6]

The connection of social class to participation in routine politics has prompted some recent speculation by political analysts. The central component of social class that seems so clearly connected to political participation is that of a person's level of education: The higher the level of education, the greater the participation in routine politics.[7] In part, this has been explained by the greater level of general interest and sophistication by those who are well educated. But now some social scientists wonder if this explanation is complete.

Over the past several decades, while the average level of education has increased in the United States, the actual level of participation, particularly in elections, has declined. How can this happen, if, in fact, people seem to have become more sophisticated? Should they not, as a group, also have become more aware and involved in politics? Political scientist Russell Dalton argues that this puzzle can be explained only if we understand participation in a larger historical and social context. There are broad macroscopic forces, he suggests, that can alter the seemingly natural connection of some social identities, like class, and routine political participation. Those forces in recent years, he argues, include the changing character of political institutions and their diminishing hold over people.[8] Hence, he urges that social scientists be aware both of the broad shift of historical circumstances, which can alter the general map of participation in politics, and the specific links that connect certain social cleavages to participation.

Gender and Race. There are both gender and racial, or ethnic, differences among people in the level of their interest and participation in routine politics. Generally speaking, men have been more active in routine forms of political activity, such as voting, than women, a difference that can be found once again in the very earliest studies of routine political participation. Likewise, among the American public, African Americans typically have shown lower rates of political activity than their Anglo-American counterparts.[9]

Observers argue that both the gender and the racial differences are partly the result of differences in the general sense of political effectiveness on the part of people.[10] Thus, women and blacks generally have not been as well represented among public officials as either men or whites; it is claimed, therefore, that both women and blacks would have less reason to want to participate in politics.

In the discussion of racial differences there is one other important point to keep always in mind. The difference in the level of political activity between African Americans and Anglo-Americans is also partly to be explained by the difference in the class standing of both groups. That is, African Americans, on the whole, are of lower class standing than their white counterparts and, thus, part of the black-white difference can be explained by overall differences in the class ranking of the two racial groups. Indeed, when one examines the racial differences in participation among members of the same social class, the racial difference becomes muted to some extent. African Americans and white Americans of the middle class, in particular, participate at roughly the same extent; only among members of the lower class are African Americans much less apt to participate in routine political activities.[11]

Major Alternative Interpretations of Conventional Political Participation. Most interpretations of the links between social cleavages and routine political participation rely on a kind of natural interest argument. Scholars will argue, as I have noted, that certain groups have a greater stake in the system or more personal resources such as education, and therefore, such groups will be more likely to become involved in routine political activity like voting or signing petitions.[12] This is what we might call the *society-centered* view of participation: People participate in politics owing to special social characteristics or resources they possess. Those who have more of such resources, whether they be members of the higher social classes or men, are likely to become more heavily engaged in politics than those people who have fewer such resources, such as members of the lower classes or women.

This general line of argument assumes, however, that political parties and associations are simply the passive recipients of their membership. In fact, as we know, they are not. Parties work hard to get people to vote; political associations, such as the National Organization for Women, often are aggressive in their efforts to generate new members. Acknowledging this obvious fact, political scientists Steven Rosenstone and John Mark Hansen offer an alternative explanation for differences in rates of participation.[13] We may think of it as the *polity-centered* view of participation.

Rosenstone and Hansen argue that differences among people in their levels of activity in routine politics can be traced to the effectiveness, or failure, of parties and other political groups to mobilize adherents. Drawing on a rich tradition in sociology they argue, for instance, that the decline in voting turnout in America is due to the failure of the political parties to mobilize voters effectively. They use this same reasoning to argue that the social class difference in the levels of routine political activity can be traced to the effort of parties, and other political groups, to mobilize the very wealthiest members of the polity. The assumption here is that parties and associations hope, among other things, to draw on the financial resources of the richest sectors of the public and thereby to provide funds for their efforts.

In the end, the differences between the upper and lower classes, men and women, blacks and whites, probably can be traced to a combination both of resources and of the differential efforts by organizations to recruit members.[14] The great merit of the polity-centered view, as I see it, is that it offers a perspective that is more realistic and grounded in shifting historical currents in various societies. It provides an accounting of differences in rates of participation that draws attention not merely to the social characteristics of people, but also to the larger setting of political rules, laws, and actions. Hence, for example, the difference in the rate of participation between blacks and whites historically has been much lower in settings in which there are organizations that deliberately seek to mobilize black voters, such as northern cities. These and other important empirical patterns of participation are simply another reminder of the importance of political organizations, as agents of mobilization, in the construction of routine politics.

Civil Society, Social Capital, and Conventional Political Participation

One of the liveliest debates about routine politics in recent years concerns the matter of *civil society*, or its equivalent in a sense, that of *social capital*. Democracies, in principle, appear to rely heavily on a strong civil society, especially in the form of intermediate organizations and associations which are available for citizens to support and through which their views can be expressed to public officials. This general argument, as we argued in Chapter 4, stems from the writings of Alexis de Tocqueville, and is also to be found imbedded in the writings of Emile Durkheim.[15]

In the early 1990s, the importance of civil society to sustaining democratic governments was revived by the writings of the political scientist Robert Putnam. Putnam argued that organizations and associations are critical to sustaining the work of modern democracies. Among other things, they help to promote a strong sense of civility and trust among citizens; or, as he put it, drawing on the work of James Coleman, they furnish the critical social capital necessary to making democratic institutions work. He offered this argument, first, in *Making Democracy Work,* a book written with two colleagues on the building of social and political institutions in modern Italy.[16]

But most attention was drawn to an article that he published two years later on the historic pattern of social and political affiliations in America.[17] He argued that American democracy is in danger because of the declining social capital among its citizens. His interpretation was based, among other things, on the results of sample surveys that show that while more people are bowling than ever before, more are bowling alone, not in bowling leagues. Moreover, he found other evidence of a decline in participation in organizations. This included declines in church attendance, participation in fraternal organizations, and in other public forms of association. His argument was also based on the results of surveys that show that more people are now engaging in leisure time activities on their own, rather than with other people. People are still doing things, but they tend to do them by themselves.

Putnam's article, entitled "Bowling Alone," became one of those social science arguments that touch a very responsive chord among citizens, but also draw the critical scrutiny and ire of many social scientists. Putnam became something of a household name almost overnight, moving out of the relative obscurity of his faculty position at Harvard University. He even rated a short feature in *People,* a magazine that is usually reserved for the fun and foibles of popular movie stars and other celebrities. Many public commentators claimed that his general thesis was right: Civility and social trust in America were on the decline, and this could help explain perhaps such anomalies as the increasing level of education among Americans, coupled with the sharp decline in voting turnout.

But many social scientists find fault with the details of Putnam's argument. Among them is Everett Carll Ladd, Jr., a respected political scientist and longtime analyst of polling and survey data. Ladd questioned whether the social capital of modern America actually had declined. Examining the results of survey data collected over a long period of time, Ladd claimed there was little evidence of a decline of social capital. In fact, he found that the level of volunteerism in the United States continues to be strong and that " the 'nation of joiners and volunteers, and givers' idea isn't myth; the foundation built from past experience is pretty strong."[18]

Political sociologist Theda Skocpol argues that Putnam's findings are also subject to a different interpretation. "The only thing that has changed recently," she writes, "[is that] members of a burgeoning upper-middle stratum of highly educated and munificently paid managers and professionals may have pulled out of locally rooted civic associations. At one time participation and leadership in the American Legion or the PTA were steppingstones for professionals, business people, and privileged homemakers. But now their counterparts do better if they work long hours and network with each other through extra-local professional or trade associations, while dealing with politics by sending checks to lobbying groups headquartered in Washington, D.C."[19]

At this point, the jury remains out on Putnam's thesis. Much remains to be learned about the historic trends in the participation of Americans in their various social and political associations, a key part of the argument. A number of studies are now underway to determine these trends more precisely. Other observers are making new inquiries into the nature of civil society in America, and trying to determine how the elements of civil society figure into the promotion of democratic institutions in this country. But the issue is one that ranges well beyond American boundaries. As a number of nations attempt to construct their own democratic institutions, the work on social capital, civil society, and democracy remains very pertinent to their efforts. If voluntary associations and the other trappings of civil society are, indeed, as crucial to democracy as Tocqueville once argued, then it is precisely those institutions that new nations will seek to construct, even revive, as they go about constructing the formal apparatus of modern democracies.

CONTENTIOUS POLITICS: POLITICS BY OTHER MEANS

Riots, rallies, and mobs. These are the forms through which unconventional politics often occur. Our image of them may be of the hundreds of citizens who gathered at the gates of Paris in the late eighteenth century, threatening to do away with the nobles. Or, it may be of the marchers who assembled in Washington, D.C. in August, 1963, to hear Martin Luther King, Jr., give his stirring speech, "I Have A Dream." Or, perhaps, even of the men and women on the streets of Los Angeles in 1993, just after the verdict that freed the police officers in the trial of Rodney King, a black man who, as videotapes later showed, was pummeled by officers as he lay defenseless on the ground.

In fact, however, it is very difficult to forge a precise conceptual distinction between conventional and unconventional politics, or what many observers today call *contentious politics*.[20] Often there are many features that both forms of politics share in common. Both are well administered, based upon organizations and associations available to people. They both often involve regularly scheduled activities, whether showing up to get a petition signed or assembling outside an abortion clinic every Saturday. And they often involve some of the most respected and well-educated members of a community.

The main difference between conventional and contentious politics, I would argue, is that *both treat themselves, and are treated by the established authorities and institutions of a society, in radically different ways.* In general, contentious political forms are defined by the established authorities as lying outside the normal institutional boundaries of a society.[21] Indeed, contentious political forms emerge in a society because their founders and organizers believe the regular institutional channels for political expression have become closed to them. Contentious politics often also represent a major challenge to the established regime and its officials, pursuing their agenda through unconventional tactics, such as street demonstrations and violent acts committed against the authorities.[22] Such challenges lie beyond the traditional left-right difference. In fact, such challenges can come both from the liberal left, as for example, those people who, on the issue of abortion, support Pro-Choice forces, and from the conservative right, as for example, those groups that support the Pro-Life groups.

Contentious politics are contentious so long as they remain outside the normal institutional apparatus in a society for voicing political ideas. Once they become "captured" by the regular institutions—that is, they become institutionalized, or legitimate—they may turn into something else, like a normal interest group so often found in modern societies.[23]

In the past twenty years, there has been a veritable avalanche of publications about contentious politics. In this section I shall review both the classic and the most recent statements. The field is, as we would say in contemporary parlance, a "work in progress." Therefore I shall try to convey the basic and underlying themes that guide the bulk of this work.

Contentious Forms

Contentious forms of politics can include a wide array of different concrete activities and actions: peaceful rallies, marches, lynches, even disorderly crowds. Some scholars focus their attention on the specific concrete forms of the nature of contentious groups themselves, seeking to uncover the nature of their dynamics.

Crowds, Mobs, and Other Public Assemblies. The earliest writings on the nature of contentious assemblies were those of several conservative, one might even say reactionary, political analysts.[24] Gustav Le Bon was the first such analyst to devote his attention to them. Envisioning crowds of the sort that assembled in Paris in the 1790s, he argued that such public gatherings of people were essentially assemblies of madmen, who in concert acted entirely irrationally. Rational action, he seemed to suggest, would dictate that people would argue over their differences in some kind of reasoned and orderly situation; if people took to the streets to air their complaints, this clearly was evidence of their lack of reason.[25] A somewhat similar line of argument was taken many decades later by the union member and popular writer Eric Hoffer.[26] Hoffer argued that groups of people who assembled in contentious forms, like crowds or other assemblies, consisted not of reasonable men and women, but rather of people who were alienated and estranged from their societies. They were, in his terms, *true believers*, totally dedicated to a cause. Having in mind the many assemblies of Communists in America in the 1930s and 1940s as well as the Nazis in Germany, Hoffer sought to discredit them by claiming their members were isolates and loners, not normal people.

The best of modern social science research on the nature of public gatherings completely undermines the view that participants in contentious politics are mad. Clark McPhail and his colleagues at the University of Illinois, Champaign-Urbana, have studied the nature of public gatherings like crowds and marches for several decades.[27] They find that such assemblies of people behave in very disciplined and orderly fashion, not in the manner Le Bon or Hoffer suggest. For instance, they discover that people generally assemble in clusters of friends and apparent associates in crowds. They term such activities as *milling behavior*, a kind of activity that occurs when there is a lull in the activity of the event. They also find that people march and walk in a very orderly fashion in most crowds, and that they do not engage in a kind of loose and random activity as alleged by Le Bon.[28] Altogether, then, large public gatherings, which represent the heart and soul of much of contentious politics, appear to be far more orderly and disciplined than the conservative reactionary analysts like Le Bon pictured them.

Changing Historical Forms of Contention. One of the most significant discoveries of Charles Tilly, a leading student of contentious politics, is that the form of contention can vary from one historical epoch to another (see also Chapter 3). In his early work, Tilly speculated that such forms represented a "repertoire of contention"(including such things as strikes, marches, and mobs), and that such repertoires were chosen by different groups of contenders in different historical periods.[29] In his extensive explorations of contentious politics in Great Britain and France, Tilly's major discovery is that over time there has been an important change in the form of contentious politics practiced by dissident citizens. Prior to 1850, contention tended to take the form of local and parochial demonstrations, including the seize of grant, or village battles. As time passed, however, contentious gatherings became national and autonomous, involving strategic strikes, rallies, and electoral campaigns.[30]

Historical Cycles of Contention. Contention is, as Tilly's research reminds us, an historically imbedded process, linked to the activities of specific actors and groups in specific times and places. The work of Sidney Tarrow and others takes this line of thinking a step further, showing us how forms of contention appear to arise in historical cycles.

Based upon research in Italy and other European countries, Tarrow argues that there are cycles of contention over time.[31] Some periods are relatively quiescent. Other periods, however, crackle with contention. Suddenly there arise a whole host of different social movements and organizations that challenge the ongoing order. Tarrow suggests that part of the way to understand the nature of contentious politics is to understand that some periods simply see a rich flowering of groups, and that such groups are stimulated by the energy and social resources of one another.

In the case of France, for instance, his research demonstrates that in the period in and around 1848, the period of great mobilization across Europe, the number of contentious events began slowly and then peaked at several points in time.[32] Such events included various mobs and other public assemblies of people. As the number of events peaked, of course, the challenge to the governmental authorities itself increased, laying the basis for more intense conflict between the established regimes and the challenging groups.

There are several periods in the twentieth century when such cycles arose in the United States. One such cycle took place about the time of the

Figure 9-2 1848 Events by Month, March 1847–August 1849

Source: Sarah Soule and Sidney Tarrow, "Acting Collectively, 1947–1949: How the Repertoire of Collective Action Changed and Where It Happened," paper presented to the annual conference of Social Science History Association, New Orleans, Louisiana, 1991. From Sidney Tarrow, *Power in Movement: Social Movements and Contentious Politics,* 2nd ed. (Cambridge, England: Cambridge University Press, 1998), p. 152. Reprinted with the permission of Cambridge University Press.

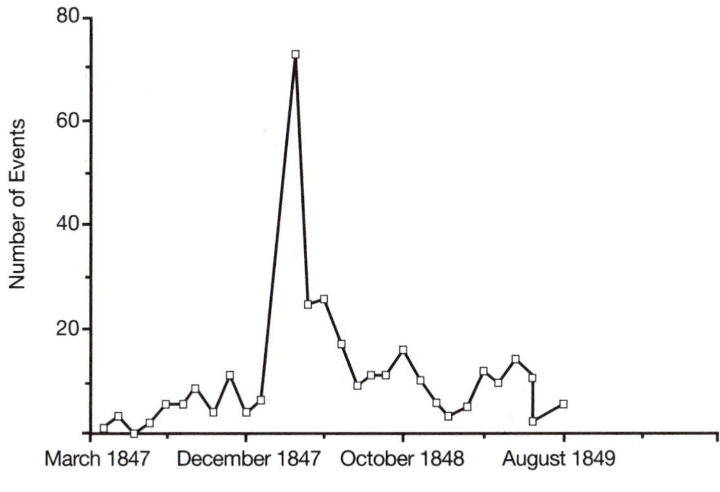

Great Depression in 1933. Displaced from regular employment and fearful of their future, many citizens took to the streets. Workers went on strike against various companies across America. Young students became involved in such groups as the Young Communist League and the Trotskyites. The peak of the movement in America probably occurred in the mid-1930s, and it began to recede as the Depression came to an end and mobilization for wars abroad began to occur early in the 1940s.

Another such period took place in the 1950s and 1960s. Again, this was a time that had begun as a period of relative political quiescence. The 1950s were known as a period of "social conformity" in America, marked by the publication of such signal works as William H. Whyte's *The Organization Man*.[33] Whyte maintained that work had become heavily bureaucratized, leading to a standard kind of white-collar employee, attired in a standard uniform of gray suit and numbing black tie and behaving in a socially conventional manner. The single dominating presence in the early to mid-1950s was the political mobilization of the young conservatives in America, headed by such groups as the Young Republicans and the Young Americans for Freedom. The other marked presence was that of the fiery campaign of Senator Joseph McCarthy to rid America of "Communists," a campaign that destroyed the careers of many talented people, including several Hollywood actors and directors. Both the conservative presence and the McCarthy campaign fashioned an atmosphere of political fear in America. As the 1950s unfolded, however, more and more liberal groups began to form. New issues dominated American politics, primarily the effort to secure greater freedom and civil rights for black Americans. By the early 1960s, America was virtually awash with many new organizations and countless contentious events, ranging from wade-ins to sit-ins to major marches on Washington, D.C.

In Tarrow's terms, then, the mid-1960s represented another peak period in the cycle of contention in America. Among the many new groups that formed were: the Student Non-Violent Coordinating Committee, which orchestrated the activities by black students throughout the South; the Southern Christian Leadership Conference, headed by Martin Luther King, Jr.; the Students for a Democratic Society, which became the pivotal center for student protests against the war in Vietnam; and the National Organization for Women. All these groups, and a number of smaller, less heralded (often more radical) ones arose in this period of great national crisis and contention. But, as in the case of the events of the 1930s, by the early 1970s both the number of events and the number of new organizations also began to decline.[34]

The notion of cycles of contention has become a popular one among modern students of contentious politics. Among other things, observers wonder what promotes not only the emergence but especially the decline of events and organizations. In the case of the black civil rights movement, a major part of contentious America during the 1960s and 1970s, observers have argued that the decline was brought about by the direct repression by the Nixon Administration, coupled with an economy in decline.[35]

Social Revolutions. Some forms of contentious politics are more important than others. Indeed, the earliest studies of contention and challenge to public authorities spent most of their time examining the nature of *revolutions,* and the difference between such contentious forms and other types of contentious action.[36]

Most scholars today, especially those who follow in the footsteps of figures like Tilly, Tarrow, and Doug McAdam, the leading advocates of what has become known as the "political process" approach to the study of contention (see page 226ff), prefer to think about challenges to political authorities as an extended process of political struggle, one that involves various groups and different key points of historic action. But others spend much time thinking mainly about revolutions. Theda Skocpol, as we noted in Chapter 4, has furnished the singular study of major social revolutions over the past several centuries.[37] Skocpol identifies a social revolution as a fundamental social and political transformation of a nation. Her argument is that such revolutions are produced by the failure of state regimes, often brought about by wars with other nations, coupled with the presence of major internal opponents and competitors to those state regimes.

A number of other scholars have followed Skocpol's line of analysis. One of her students, Jack Goldstone, has argued that social revolutions happen not simply when states fail, but that states fail, among other reasons, because of population growth. Goldstone claims that population growth, especially rapid growth, forces governments to tax their citizens more heavily in order to cope with the new needs and demands of the larger population. Such new taxation measures then can become an immediate cause for revolution, as were the new tax measures that helped to prompt the outbreak of hostilities in the American colonies in 1776.[38] More recently, Goldstone has collaborated with sociologist Bert Useem to argue that even prison riots may be thought of as a kind of "mini-social revolution."[39] Examining several instances of prison riots, Goldstone and Useem argue that there are many features of prison riots that can be explained by the same kinds of dynamics as state-centered social revolutions. Such parallels include administrative crises and a widespread sense of grievance and injustice among the prisoners, both factors that can be observed prior to great social revolutions.

Ultimately all the challengers to the authority of a given political regime, or state, hope to displace those authorities—or at least to challenge them so completely as to leave their mark on the political structure of the state. But very few such challengers have ever succeeded. In our own time, as we enter the twenty-first century, we are about to see whether new and stable political transformations will occur in nations like Russia and South Africa. Their history will eventually provide new ways for understanding both how revolutions begin and how—or even whether—they take a lasting and durable form.

Identity vs. Instrumental Movements. One of the major debates that marks the study of contentious politics has to do with the matter of recent forms of social movements. In the 1980s, Alberto Melucci, a European student of contemporary movements (virtually all others until that time had been American), argued that many new forms of social movements were different from earlier ones.[40] In particular, Melucci claimed that various "new social movements" were about the business of making different kinds of demands and pursuing different goals from older ones. He insisted that such demands often had more to do with the nature of the participants and their lives than with the accomplishment of specific political ends. New movements, he further argued, were often more intent on providing a home and refuge for their participants, and a basis for their identity—hence the name, *identity politics*—than they were in making inroads and changes in the current political regime.[41] Such new social movements, in his accounting, thus offered a very different picture from the older social revolutions of which scholars like Goldstone and Skocpol write—movements that seemed intent simply on displacing old regimes and creating new ones.

Today there are a number of newer social movements, especially in Europe, many more than there were just two or three decades ago. Such movements pursue various kinds of aims, including radical feminist groups, environmental organizations, peace movements, and new forms of ethnic nationalism. Even in the United States, some newer groups, including organizations on behalf of women and ethnic minorities, have emerged and offer a somewhat different view of the world than many of their predecessors. Such groups provide a way for asserting and sustaining issues of *collective identity* for their participants. They offer a variety of activities and often are intent more on reviving and sustaining cultural forms, include various parades and art forms, than in challenging governments and public officials. Moreover, the nature of their battles and public displays have less to do with achieving some specific political end than in making a point about whom the group represents and the importance of the collective identity of their members, whether they be blacks, Hispanics, or women.[42]

Melucci suggests that these new social movements not only possess different goals, but that their very essence differs from earlier groups of radicals. He also insists that, arising in an age dominated by information technology, they represent a new way for identifying and communicating with their potential membership and the larger public. Symbolic and cultural issues have become of central importance to the livelihood of these groups, far more than material or political gains. And because of this, certain social forces like the mass media also have assumed a more general importance to the creation and maintenance of social movements than they previously had.

Melucci observes of recent actions by young people, for instance, that the "poverty of the instrumental outcomes of action conceals a metabolic richness of stimuli, relations and exchanges. Mobilizing against racism, heroin, or the mafia in Italy, or merely for peace may not directly affect the phenomena themselves, but it promotes the creation of a solidarity network essential for the restructuring of individual and collective experience of youth."[43]

Yet other analysts of social movements take strong exception to this general line of argument. Craig Calhoun writes that "the new social movements idea is . . . problematic and obscures the greater significance of identity politics. . . . Without much theoretical rationale, it groups together what seem to the researchers relatively 'attractive' movements, vaguely on the left, but leaves out such other contemporary movements as the new religious right and fundamentalism, the resistance of white ethnic communities against people of color, various versions of nationalism and so forth."[44] And Nelson Pichardo argues that there is nothing essentially "new" about the new social movements. He maintains that in most respects the new social movements simply do not differ from the older ones. The main contribution of the emphasis Melucci puts on the new social movements, Pichardo writes, is to focus much greater attention on the role of culture and identity—both of which are non-instrumental matters—in the study of social movements.[45]

While much of the criticism seems justified, there remain some central benefits to be gained from the kinds of questions Melucci and others have raised about the new social movements. What will be especially intriguing to learn in the future is whether and how such movements have taken advantage of the new information technology, both as a source of their concerns and as a means of providing a different face to what they do.

The Origins of Contention

Over the past three decades or so, most of the attention of students of contentious politics has been devoted to the development of theoretical models that could help us understand how and why such forms arise. It is one matter to identify and describe the forms. But it is another matter to explain their origins, particularly the various conditions that give rise to them.

Some of the earlier writings about contentious politics devoted a considerable amount of attention to why such forms deviated from the routine politics of the day—from parties, interest groups, and other forms of association. Sociologists Ralph Turner and Lewis Killian, for example, devoted a good deal of time to trying to explain "collective behavior," or mobs and crowds in their terms, that was different from the usual forms, such as people at work.[46] They argued that events such as crowds and public lynches created their own rules and norms as they evolved, sparked at first by specific events, such as the shooting of a citizen. Norms emerged to guide and direct the behavior of people, they argued, thus suggesting that while crowds and mobs may have been different, they also had an imbedded set of rules though they were totally unruly forms of gatherings, as Le Bon had argued.

At roughly the same time, Neil Smelser, a Berkeley sociologist, offered a powerful and sophisticated treatment of contentious forms, like crowds and mobs, lynchings, and even social movements.[47] Smelser argued that forms of contention arose when people's access to their means of political expression became blocked, and when, at the same time, they came to feel both aggrieved and frustrated. Instead of seeking a normal path to resolve their concerns, such as contacting a Congresswoman or discussing them with others, people created different forms of collective behavior when they short-circuited the normal and regular institutional channels for resolving problems. Such short-circuiting took place against a backdrop of other important facilitating conditions, such as an institutional structure that permitted contention to arise, and the failure of the political authorities to act decisively and quickly to bring potential contention to a halt, Smelser argued.

Both the Turner-Killian and the Smelser accounts influenced many later analysts of forms of contention. Yet, the most recent research has moved well beyond these writings to suggest a much greater depth and focus on a key number of conditions and circumstances that promote various kinds of dissent. I will describe four specific models below: (1) *political process*; (2) *cultural forces*; (3) *social networks and other mobilizing structures*; and (4) *grievance/breakdown*. The first three today represent the most dominant and popular forms to explain the outbreak and dispersal of contentious politics.

Political Process. The political process view of the origins of contention began with the writings of Tilly (see Chapter 3).[48] In recent years it has been further developed and refined in the writings of Tilly, as well as Doug McAdam and Sidney Tarrow.[49]

The political process model of contention maintains that such politics must be seen as part of the ongoing range of political activities in a specific society. Though contentious politics begin as an effort to challenge the ongoing political regime, they happen because of specific conditions that characterize both the normal political regime and the broader social/economic context in which it operates. Contentious forms occur throughout history, so the argument goes, and it is the task of the analyst to trace the different historical conditions and settings in which they occur. In this sense, the intricacies and challenges of history are a very critical piece of the puzzle of explanation, occupying a far more prominent role than in the earlier explanations of writers like Neil Smelser.

The main element to which political process analysts direct attention is that of the political structure in which contentious politics arises. Features of this structure can either promote or impede the origins of contention. They do so, in the words of analysts, by providing certain *political opportunities* for contention to take effect. The inspiration for this concept comes from work done in the early 1970s by the political scientist Peter Eisinger. Examining the outbreak of race riots in different cities, Eisinger suggested that the probability of such riots depended heavily on the *structure of political opportunities* provided by the local urban setting. In particular, he wrote, "such factors as the nature of the chief executive, the mode of aldermanic election, the distribution of social skills and status, and the degree of social disintegration, taken individually or collectively, serve in various ways to obstruct or facilitate citizen activity in pursuit of political goals."[50]

Over the years scholars have discovered that the specific form and content of these opportunities vary widely. In the case of the 1917 Russian Revolution, for example, it was pressures on the rulers of state, brought about by failures in war, that ultimately provided a key opportunity for the Bolsheviks to rise and to topple the regime of the Tsars.[51] Yet, in the recent case of Poland, it was the simultaneous emergence of the Solidarity movement, coupled with the growing failure of economic performance of the Communist regime, that led to the collapse of Communist Poland and the rise of the new Polish state.[52]

McAdam, in his analysis of the emergence of the civil rights movement in America on behalf of African Americans, has argued that a structure of opportunities arose in the 1940s and 1950s that helped to encourage the emergence and to fuel the drive of African American civil rights organizations.[53] In part, that structure was promoted by critical changes begun at the level of the federal government. The presidential administration of Harry Truman (1945–1952) championed the cause of black civil rights in the late 1940s, ushered in by the required integration of the American armed forces. Other similar decisions followed on the heels of that decision, prompted in part by a growing influence of liberal forces in the United States government. The Supreme Court, under the leadership of Earl Warren, made a decisive step in 1954, ordering the desegregation of all public facilities in America, including restaurants, bus stations, and schools. The changes in the federal administration's view of civil rights provided an opening for other efforts, including new challenges such as that sparked by Rosa Parks in Birmingham, Alabama, when she refused to take one of the seats usually assigned for African Americans at the back of a public bus. Gradually more and more openings occurred in the longstanding hold of segregation over America, openings that permitted more and more African Americans to mobilize themselves against longstanding forms of segregation.

In the case of the African American civil rights movement, then, the opportunity structure was furnished by changes that took place in the nature of the government's policy regarding African Americans. Some of these changes took place because of the weakened power of some groups in America and the increased power of other groups. McAdam argues that as the Southern plantation economy began to recede, among other things it began to diminish the strength of the old Southern planters both over their own regional economy and within the ranks of the federal government.[54] At the same time, new social forces arose, those which championed a more liberal view of race and equality in America. The Warren Court was critical to this effort; and it was a Court that included not only Warren but also several other key figures that would help to promote a shift in the nature of the state's policy on matters of racial segregation. In addition, there were smaller efforts that gradually built up to the shift in the federal government. Among them were the work of the National Association for the Advancement of Colored People (NAACP) to challenge segregation on various fronts in the United States. Foremost in this effort was the work of Thurgood Marshall, a young African American lawyer who would eventually become the first African American appointed to the Supreme Court.

As this important example shows, the political process model requires a detailed yet broad attention to the shifting fortunes of different social groups and how such shifting fortunes eventually influence the nature of state policy. Other writings, influenced by the political process model, have focused on similar sets of events and how they open up opportunities for new groups to challenge and to contend with the authorities.[55] But, as Tarrow notes in his most recent work, much work remains to be done to specify the exact manner whereby the structure of political opportunities operate. Opportunity structures at this time, he notes, seem to represent a confluence of activities by different parties across several dimensions: (1) increasing access to participation in the political system; (2) shifting political alignments; (3) divided political elites, or authorities; (4) influential allies; and (5) repression or facilitation by the authorities.[56]

Cultural Forces. One of the most popular ways today for explaining the origins of different forms of contention and challenge against ongoing regimes is to seek such explanations in the broader cultural environment of movements. There is still a great deal of disagreement over how to put culture in a conceptual form useful to the analysis of contention, but important headway has been made in the past fifteen years or so by several analysts.[57]

The original writings about social and political movements attempted to capture the cultural, or belief, component by using the concept of *ideology.* But there were problems with this concept, the chief one being that it had come to mean many different things to different scholars. Karl Marx, for example, wrote of the ideology of modern capitalism, by which he meant the general systems of values and beliefs that pervaded capitalism and that sustained its hegemony over a long period of time (see Chapter 2). But other analysts used the concept of ideology to refer to the specific set of beliefs and ideals proposed by different social movements. Thus, the body of beliefs identified as "socialism" was viewed by some scholars as a specific kind of ideology that spoke to the nature and design of the economy and government under a regime that ruled on behalf of the working class. By the early 1970s, analysts had become so disgusted with the whole notion of ideology that they often turned to noncultural and nonideological explanations of contention.[58]

Frame Analysis. In the mid-1980s, sociologist David Snow and several of his students proposed a new scheme for thinking about the links between the broader cultural environment of social movements and the emergence of movements themselves.[59] Drawing on work originally proposed by the sociologist Erving Goffman, Snow and his associates argued that the origins of contention can be found partly in the ability of movements, and their proponents, to cultivate broad and wide-ranging appeals to the public. Movement organizations do so by furnishing *frames* through which they link their own concerns to those of a potential membership base in the public. As Snow and his colleagues defined them, frames represent general schemes that allow people to interpret and make sense of the world around them.

Frames thus are the scripts that movements used to define themselves. They provide the means through which the movement is identified as well as a way of identifying those groups and people who lie outside the movement. At their most complete, frames also provide a way of making full sense of the world—of drawing a distinction, among other things, between the insiders and the outsiders.

Consider, for example, the case of the recent heated debates between those who believe in the scientific origins of mankind, drawing on the theory of Charles Darwin, and those who believe that mankind is the product of some larger force, a Creator, or God.[60] This debate is as much a matter of political contention as it is one over some larger truth. There are two kinds of frames at war here: a scientific frame about the origins of humankind and a religious frame. Those who take the latter point of view, the *creationists,* have been very successful in forcing school systems to consider whether or not to offer texts on biology that mention the concept of human evolution. In the words of Snow and his colleagues, the creationists have manufactured a fully developed frame about the world. This frame claims that the manifold species and varieties of life on Earth were designed by a Creator, and that there is no evidence, or even theory, that would link the origins of man to the existence of primates. The frame of the creationists, which has proven to be popular especially among religious fundamentalists, is rooted in a specific religious vision of the world, and it draws upon a variety of texts and interpretations, including that of the Bible.

Snow and his colleagues have expanded and extended the concept of frame in various ways. In their original article, they write about what they term *frame alignment,* meaning the manner in which contentious movements seek to align their frames on the world with those frames of the larger public. Thus, to continue our example, the political successes of the creationist frame about the origins of mankind can be explained in large part by its ability to link the nature and variety of forms of life in the world to a fundamentalist belief in God. The frame, about the manifold forms of life, manages to resonate with those people who, themselves, are firm believers in God.[61]

The concepts of frame and frame alignment, along with related concepts, such as that of *frame amplification,* have proven to be enormously popular among contemporary students of contentious politics. There is a vast number of articles today, on a variety of different kinds of movements and other forms of contentious politics, that use these concepts to talk about the origins and unfolding of protest. But, at the same time, there is a certain degree of ambiguity about these notions. In their recent work on comparative social movements, for instance, McAdam, McCarthy, and Zald observe that "little systematic work on framing processes (or the cultural dimensions of social movements) has yet been produced."[62] Even Snow and his colleagues realize that more work needs to be done to make the concept of frame clearer.[63]

Information and Technology. There is a second way in which cultural forces can figure into explaining the origins of forms of contention. This is the nature of information, in general, and the new information technology created in the past decade or so.

Both Manuel Castells and Alberto Melucci point to the great importance of the new information technology in the creation of modern forms of contention and protest. Castells argues that the new information age represents a new form of society, replacing in a sense the older, industrial forms of capitalism.[64] Information has come to replace other forms and media of communication. In addition, the technology that people use to communicate with one another has changed the relationships among them, and with those changes, it has altered the nature of power and power relations.[65] Castells sees both the new information technology and the rise of "identity movements" among women and ethnics as symptomatic of the new age of protest. Similarly, Alberto Melluci also believes that information represents a new wrinkle to the modern world, and that it will alter the forms of politics and protest among people. In addition, he believes that in this new age, issues of meaning and its construction have become ever more important to the development and unfolding of social movements.

Those sociologists like Castells and Melucci, I would argue, may be on to something very important. In the late 1990s, the Internet emerged as an important way for different contentious groups, particularly hate groups, to advertise their message and to attract great attention to themselves. One sociologist has identified more than five hundred different hate groups with websites on the Internet.[66] Moreover, there is mounting evidence that links 1999 shootings—by Benjamin Smith in Illinois, who shot and killed an African American as well as an Asian, and Benjamin Furrow in California, who shot young students at a Jewish day school and killed an Asian immigrant postal worker—to hate groups that advertise on the Internet. More and more such terrorist kinds of activities are apt to emerge in coming years, as groups become more accessible on the Internet and as individuals succeed in connecting themselves to such groups.

Social Networks and Mobilizing Structures.[67] Writings about contentious politics earlier in this century often portrayed contentious participants as very different from the usual participant in politics. Such a stereotype probably can be traced in part to the nineteenth-century writings of LeBon.[68] The political activist in left-wing, or even right-wing, contentious movements was seen as someone who did not fit into the normal routines of society. Often such a figure was seen as estranged or cut off from the world. At its most extreme, this "true believer" was an individual so cut off that he, or she, was something of a social isolate, bereft of companions and family, a loner.

While this portrayal sometimes appears accurate—as in the recent cases both of Benjamin Smith and Benjamin Furrow—most often the typical participant is very different from this, quite the opposite of a loner. If anything, people who become active in social movements are drawn to them, in part, through a social circuitry of personal connections and ties to the movement itself. Anything but a social isolate, the participant actually is someone who is socially tied and connected to the form of contention. Taken more broadly, and abstractly, then, social networks and social clusters of people—friends, family, or simply acquaintances—have become a critical piece of puzzle in the effort to explain both why contentious politics starts up and why contentious forms become successful in recruiting participants.

Building on earlier work, David Snow and his colleagues argue that social networks become a means through which people are recruited for individual events as well as for participation in contentious movement organizations.[69] They argue that social networks provide a link between the larger public and the movement organization. And movements succeed to the extent that they are able to activate and draw upon such networks to recruit participants. This basic insight, so sociological in character, has furnished the inspiration for a number of other writings about the importance of networks and clusters of contacts to movements. The sociologist Roger Gould, in research in France, for instance, shows that neighborhood social networks, in addition to formal organizational ties, operated in complex and different ways to mobilize people to support the Paris Commune of 1871.[70]

Networks have been shown to be important to the development of a variety of different forms of contentious politics in recent times. Jo Freeman, in some of the best and earliest research on the rise of feminism in the 1960s, discovered that social networks were vital to the origins of the 1960s feminist revival in the United States.[71] Similarly, in his research on the origins of the civil rights movement, McAdam notes the importance of indigenous social networks to the development and mobilization of various contentious African American groups.[72]

More than networks, there are also important indigenous organizations among groups of potential challengers that serve as key elements to mobilize them.[73] In his prize-winning writing on the origins of the civil rights movement, Aldon Morris has shown that various kinds of networks and organizations proved absolutely essential to the mobilization of participation on behalf of the civil rights effort.[74] Most important in this regard, he finds, was the black church. It was in the African American church that many figures first began to articulate their concern about the injustices suffered by African Americans. African American ministers proved important to this effort, in part, because they held a special and important place in the African American community, as well as having a regular acquaintance with many African Americans. But there were other important organizations and groups as well, including the famous Highlander Folk School in Tennessee that actually served as a training ground for a number of important civil rights personages, including Rosa Parks. It is not so unusual, then, that Martin Luther King, Jr., would emerge as a key leader of the civil rights movement, for he personified the indigenous leadership in the African American community.

Bert Klandermans, a prolific writer about the social psychology of social movements, has done some of the most important recent theoretical work along these lines. He argues that movements depend for their strength and success upon *mobilizing structures*. Such structures include a diverse array of organizations and loosely coupled networks of informal groups, both of which seem to encourage the emergence of contentious movements.[75]

Grievance/Breakdown Theory. Somewhat at odds with most of the recent writing and thinking about contentious politics is the fourth model. This proclaims that the origins of movements are to be sought in conditions of personal grievance and social breakdown in the larger society. When he first offered his view of contentious politics, Charles Tilly made it a point to claim that the level of grievance is always the same in societies. What matters to the development of contention is not grievance, he insisted, but issues of power and the mobilization of resources among the challengers, or contenders.[76] At the time he made this original argument, there were many social scientists, myself included, who believed that grievances lay at the very heart of contention. Among them were the political scientist Ted Robert

Gurr, who argued that contention and protest in general were based upon the social psychology of people. When grievances were high, then people were more apt to engage in contention.[77] But Tilly believed this view to be totally wrong. And the latest generation of scholars of social and political protest generally have followed Tilly's lead.

Yet not everyone believes that it is political opportunities and resources in the larger society that explain the origins of protest events. In particular, sociologist Bert Useem argues strongly that personal grievance and societal breakdown conditions still are important to the explanation of different forms of protest and contention. In a recent article on the subject, Useem observes that such factors help to supplement the understanding of the emergence of social movements and other forms of contention. They are particularly useful in explaining episodes of great rupture and breakdown in the social fabric much like those that took place in the United States during the Great Depression, he insists. He also argues that is not useful for the other schools of social movement analysis to condemn breakdown theories as though they were morally corrupt and just supported the societal status quo.[78]

The Institutionalization of Contention

One of the classic concerns about contentious politics is what happens to the contentious organization, or other assemblies, over the course of their political lifetimes. The concern was raised first in the writings of Roberto Michels. As we showed in Chapter 8, Michels argued that even the most radical organization, such as the nineteenth-century German Social Democrats, could eventually turn into a conservative one, leading Michels to propose his famous "iron law of oligarchy." More recently, there is clear evidence that some groups that begin as contentious challengers to the reigning authorities eventually do become part of the regular assembly of politics. The most famous recent case is that of the environmental group, the Greens, in Germany, which began in the early 1980s as a form of radical dissent, but in recent elections actually has won important seats in the German *Bundestag*.

Other sociologists have taken up this same concern. Writing in the 1960s, Mayer Zald and Roberta Ash argued that a process of goal displacement is likely to occur among social movements as they develop over time. To improve upon the imperfections in both the Weber and the Michels formulations, Zald and Ash developed a series of propositions that would describe the ebb and flow of change in movement organizations.[79] Going a step beyond the earlier analyses, they observe that the elements of potential change in movement organizations can be identified as goal transformations, shifts to organizational maintenance, and increases in the concentration of power. To account for these potential forms of change, they stress, one must look at the nature of the movement organization, in particular whether the organization demands only minimal commitment (inclusive) or intense commitment (exclusive) from its members, and at its position within the larger society.

Among a series of propositions they develop several are worth noting. They observe that a transformation in the goals of a social movement organization is likely to happen because of its competition with other organizations within the same movement. For instance, they note, in the African American civil rights movement in the 1960s, organizations like the NAACP and the Urban League were compelled to become more ideologically radical simply to retain their hold on material resources that were beginning to shift to the more radical groups like the Student Non-Violent Coordinating Committee. They also contend that a movement that has lost its original dynamic quality and becomes a part of the status quo is most apt to follow the sort of sequence outlined by Michels. This happens because the viability of the movement no longer lies in the acquisition of major new gains from the established social and political institutions but rather in the protection of old gains. For no segment is this pattern more important than for that of the leadership. In one of their more insightful assertions, Zald and Ash remark that movement organizations whose ideology strongly recommends distrust of societal and political authorities are very likely to produce factions and splits among their members. The stance of distrust of authority almost inevitably shifts from a focus on authority outside the movement to that within it, leading to opposition groups which challenge the original leadership of the movement. Both the SDS and SNCC eventually experienced the development of factions, and later decay, precisely because of the pattern Zald and Ash formulate.

Soon after completing this analysis, Zald broadened his concern into what became a revolutionary break with past approaches and a vital stepping stone to the new contemporary approaches to the study of social movements. Along with sociologist John McCarthy, he argued that social movements are best construed as part of the panoply of organizations in modern society.[80] Thus, instead of speaking of movements as though they were an unorganized mass of people (what they term the "hearts and minds"approach), Zald and McCarthy urged that we think of them as part of a modern array of organizations, many of which are funded and become part of the regular institutions of modern society. They termed this novel view *resource mobilization* because it emphasized how groups of people mobilize resources to challenge the political authorities. The perspective helped to feed the current interest in social networks, mobilizing structures, and other institutional features of modern societies.[81] Perhaps its main contribution was to force observers of contentious politics to focus more attention on "social movement organizations," rather than simply movements of people.

In their recent writing David Meyer and Sidney Tarrow help to advance this general theme about the institutionalization of contentious politics.[82] They are interested, in particular, in the actual transformation of societies over time as they experience cycles that alternate between periods of protest and dissent. It appears, in fact, that contention grows, stimulates other forms of contention, and then even develops almost like other organizational forms. Tarrow suggests that there may be underlying processes of contagion and diffusion among contentious organizations, even those in different societies, which help to explain this pattern.[83]

In addition, Meyer and Tarrow wonder whether over a period of time, as the number of contentious actions and organizations flourish, there is a tendency for the reigning authorities to attempt to institutionalize contention. Such an occurrence would represent a form of *co-optation,* a process in which the authorities defuse the energy of contention simply by making contentious organizations a part of the routine array of political organizations. There is some preliminary evidence that contention has grown in popularity among the broad citizen publics of Western democracies. Thus, in his research on four industrial democracies, Russell Dalton finds that over time there is both a greater frequency of contentious activities, like signing petitions, as well as a greater acceptance of such activities.[84] Moreover, there also is evidence that in the United States as well as in the emerging democracies of Eastern Europe protest and contentious political forms, such as rallies, marches and dissenting electoral challengers, have become a part of the routine and regular display of politics. Thus, contention has been gradually moved out of the arena of marginal and radical expression, and made into a more orderly and regular part of the rules of the political game.[85]

Contentious Politics and Political Victories

Although, as Alberto Melucci rightly suggests, many forms of contention are apt to involve other than political goals, such goals, in fact, are the primary concern for many movements. From the African American civil rights to the feminist movements, from the pro-abortion to the anti-abortion movements, forms of contention have sought to achieve victory—not simply by changing the identities of their participants, but by altering the world around them.

How successful have contentious politics been? And under what conditions have they been most successful? As any student of contentious politics will tell you today, we have very few answers to this most vital of questions. Partly that is because it is simply very difficult to determine a clear, causal link between the means used—in this case, contention—and the outcomes achieved, which are often changed policies by the established authorities.[86] Partly it is simply that students of contentious politics have devoted much less effort to doing research on the question of outcomes. Paul Burstein and his associates note, for example, that "we know little about how movements get their demands on the formal political agenda or, most critically, about the ultimate impact of movement activities on people's lives."[87] Much of what we do now know, or, at least say, about the effectiveness of contentious politics, comes from a creative and pioneering effort piece of research by William Gamson, done almost one-quarter of a century ago.[88]

Gamson sets out to identify movements that are successful and those that are failures and then to locate the characteristics of movements and their social surroundings that are associated with success and failure. His analysis is based upon a representative sample of fifty-three social movement organizations in America, or what he refers to as "challenging groups," since the organizations represent innovative attempts to secure benefits from members of the status quo. Among groups represented in the sample are those as diverse as the American Association of University Professors, the Bull Moose Party (Progressive Party under Theodore Roosevelt, 1912–1916), and the Communist Labor Party. The time frame from which Gamson drew his sample is the period from 1800 to 1945, during which there were about 500 to 600 groups that could be classified as challenging ones.

Gamson defines success and failure with two separate indices. One is an index of *acceptance*; if a challenging group is invited to negotiate or consult, granted formal recognition, or actually incorporated as part of the organization of its antagonist, then it has received acceptance by its antagonist and qualifies as successful. The other is an index of *new advantages*; if the goals of a challenging group are somehow met, then the challenging group has received new advantages. How does one determine whether the goals have been met? As illustrations, Gamson suggests that "new advantages for the American Birth Control League . . . meant a change in practice by Americans—increased usage of contraceptive techniques. New advantages for the North Carolina Manumission Society are measured by their success in persuading individual plantation owners to grant freedom to their slaves."[89] In some cases, groups are identified as having more than one goal, and so they stand to gain more than one kind of new advantage. Of the fifty-three groups in his study, approximately the same proportion—38 percent—achieved success on both indices as achieved success on neither—42 percent. Six of the groups were not accepted in any way by their antagonists but did gain new advantages, while five achieved acceptance but no new advantages.

There are two kinds of results that prove to be the most illuminating from this study. First, Gamson finds that violence and other forms of constraints such as boycotts or strikes bring success to challenging groups. Separating the challenging groups into those that use violence, those subject to it, and those that fall into neither group, for instance, he finds that the greater proportion of the groups that use violence achieve both acceptance and new advantages. While there is a difference in the rates of acceptance, the difference is not statistically significant. "Virtue, of course, has its own, intrinsic rewards," Gamson concludes. "And a lucky thing it does too, since its instrumental value appears to be dubious."[90]

Gamson also discovers that, in general, challenging groups that are better equipped as organizations also achieve the higher rates of success, thus confirming with hard evidence the kind of intuitive understandings possessed by such successful revolutionaries as Lenin. For one thing, the challenging groups that are bureaucratic, that is, possess a written charter or constitution, have a formal list of members, and have at least three levels of authority, are far more likely to achieve acceptance and new advantages than their nonbureaucratic counterparts. For another, groups in which power is centralized, that is, there is only one center of power, are also the more likely to achieve success, though the achievement is more likely to occur in the case of new advantages than in that of acceptance. Both circumstances, moreover, operate independently so, for instance, 75 percent of those groups both bureaucratic and centralized achieve new advantages compared to only 15 percent of those groups neither bureaucratic nor centralized.

But there is strong disagreement with Gamson's overall discoveries and his general point of view.[91] Another major work, published by Frances Fox Piven and Richard Cloward, argues that the more disruptive contentious activities are, the more likely they will succeed in wringing concessions from authorities.[92] Piven and Cloward examined several different groups of challengers. They argue that the massive protests and strikes of the 1930s were victorious in producing important achievements, especially the creation of new industrial unions. "Industrial unionization," they write, "was not a management strategy, but a workers' victory."[93] Piven and Cloward also believe that the massive resistance by African Americans in the South had important benefits, including eliminating terror as a form of social control to be used against them, and helping to usher in important political gains in voting and the like in the 1960s.

Among students of contentious politics today, the debate continues—will disruption achieve more for the dissidents than, let us say, a strong internal organization? Disruption can produce changes, particularly if the contentious forces are dealing with authorities who are in a weak position. But it is also true that disruption can call into being greater repression and control of the dissidents, thus forcing the organization to halt its activities, even to go underground. Researchers are just now inquiring into the greater details of this matter, trying to determine when it will be repression against disruption, and when the contentious forces are most apt to succeed.[94]

CONCLUSIONS

The study of citizen participation, especially in contentious political forms like social movements, has moved well beyond the century-old characterizations of Gustav Le Bon, stereotypical claims that somehow dissidents were loners and irrational actors. Modern scholars and students have managed to create a new array of concepts and to make exceedingly important discoveries about how contentious politics now works. Moreover, they also have helped to refashion the study of conventional political participation by forcing scholars to attend carefully both to the difference between protest and routine politics, and to the explanations for participation, in general.[95]

Yet much remains to be done to extend this work so that it can also help to make a real difference in the impact of such politics. Years ago, the sociologists Robert Alford and Roger Friedland argued that political participation did not make all that much difference for the exercise of power in societies. Working largely from a neo-Marxist frame of reference, they insisted that the political participation of the lower and working classes in the United States brings them no power, while the power of the middle and upper classes is often maintained without participation.[96] To document their claim, they showed that regardless of the levels of interest and participation in politics by the lower classes, they achieved no greater benefits, particularly in material terms, from the American political and economic systems; they received no more substantial advantages in tax breaks, welfare assistance, and so on. Thus, Alford and Friedland maintain that political participation provides no guarantee that the material benefits of society will be more equitably distributed.

Alford and Friedland's argument, along with the limited knowledge we now have about the ability of contentious politics to wrest concessions and change from political regimes, provides a real challenge to the study of citizen participation in the future. In the end such work, like all work in the social sciences, must help to provide a better and more improved condition for all citizens. If the study of contentious politics provides nothing more than improved ways of understanding the world, is it really all that significant?

NOTES

1. Sidney Verba and Norman Nie, *Participation in America: Political Democracy and Social Equality* (New York: Harper & Row Publishers, 1972).
2. Lester W. Milbrath and M.I. Goel, *Political Participation: How and Why People Get Involved in Politics* (Chicago: Rand McNally College Publishing Co., 1977), Chapter 1.
3. Russell J. Dalton, *Citizen Politics: Public Opinion and Political Parties in Advanced Industrial Democracies*, 2nd edition (Chatham, New Jersey: Chatham House Publishers, 1996), Chapter 3.
4. Sidney Verba, Kay Lehman Schlozman, and Henry E. Brady, *Voice and Equality: Civic Voluntarism in American Politics* (Cambridge, Massachusetts: Harvard University Press, 1995).
5. See, for example, Robert E. Lane, *Political Life: Why People Get Involved in Politics* (Glencoe, Illinois: The Free Press, 1959); also see Milbrath and Goel, Chapter 4.

6. Lane, ibid.
7. Verba, Schlozman and Brady, op. cit., Chapter 11.
8. Dalton, *Citizen Politics*, Chapter 3.
9. Milbrath and Goel, ibid., Chapter 2.
10. Verba, Schlozman, and Brady, op. cit., Chapter 8.
11. See, for example, Marvin Olsen, "The Social and Political Participation of Blacks," *American Sociological Review*, Volume 35 (August 1970), pp. 682-97; Marvin Olsen, *Participatory Pluralism: Political Participation and Influence in the United States and Sweden* (Chicago: Nelson-Hall, 1982), Chapter 4.
12. On the general argument about personal resources available for political participation, see Verba, Schlozman, and Brady, op.cit., Part III.
13. Steven J. Rosenstone and John Mark Hansen, *Mobilization, Participation and Democracy in America* (New York: Macmillan Publishing Company, 1993).
14. Verba, Schlozman, and Brady observe that their emphasis on resources and civic engagement "complements Rosentone and Hansen's analysis of the role of strategic elites in generating citizen activity." Verba, Schlozman, and Brady, op. cit., p. 415.
15. For one of the best theoretical expositions of the importance of associations to sustaining democratic government, see William Kornhauser, *The Politics of Mass Society* (Glencoe, Illinois: The Free Press, 1959).
16. Robert D. Putnam, with Robert Leonardi and Raffaella Nanetti, *Making Democracy Work* (Princeton, New Jersey: Princeton University Press, 1993).
17. Robert D. Putnam, "Bowling Alone: America's Declining Social Capital," *Journal of Democracy*, Volume 6, Number 1 (January 1995), pp. 65–78.
18. Everett Carll Ladd, Jr., *The Ladd Report* (New York: The Free Press, 1999), p. 155.
19. Theda Skocpol, "Unravelling From Above," *The American Prospect*, No. 25 (March-April 1996): 20–25, at p. 22.
20. For the classic treatment of contentious politics, see Charles Tilly, *From Mobilization to Revolution* (Reading, Massachusetts: Addison-Wesley Press, 1978). For one of the best current treatments, see Sidney Tarrow, *Power in Movement: Social Movements and Contentious Politics*, 2nd edition (Cambridge, England: Cambridge University Press, 1998).
21. This is the point of view adopted in the pioneering work of William A. Gamson, *The Strategy of Social Protest*, 2nd edition (Belmont, California: Wadsworth Publishing, 1990).
22. William A. Gamson, *Power and Discontent* (Homewood, Illinois: Dorsey Press, 1968). Also see, Anthony Oberschall, *Social Conflict and Social Movements* (Englewood Cliffs, New Jersey: Prentice-Hall, 1973).
23. The hazy line between conventional and contentious politics helps to explain why one of the earliest and still most imaginative works on political sociology, by Rudolf Heberle, went by the title, *Social Movements: An Introduction to Political Sociology* (New York: Appleton-Century-Crofts, 1951).
24. For a good general discussion, see Clark McPhail, *The Myth of the Madding Crowd* (New York: Aldine de Gruyter, 1991).

25. Gustave Le Bon, *The Crowd: A Study of the Popular Mind*. Originally published as *Psychologie des foules*, 1904. (New York: Viking Press, 1960).
26. Eric Hoffer, *The True Believer: Thoughts on the Nature of Mass Movements* (New York: Harper & Row, 1951).
27. McPhail, ibid.; also, for example, see Clark McPhail and Ronald Wohlstein, "Collective Behavior As Collective Locomotion," *American Sociological Review*, Volume 51 (August 1986), pp. 447–63.
28. McPhail, *The Myth of the Madding Crowd*, Chapter 5.
29. Charles Tilly, "Repertoires of Contention in America and Britain, 1750–1830," in Mayer N. Zald and John D. McCarthy, eds., *The Dynamics of Social Movements: Resource Mobilization, Social Control and Tactics* (Cambridge, Massachusetts: Winthrop Publishers, 1979), pp. 126–55.
30. Charles Tilly, *The Contentious French* (Cambridge, Massachusetts: The Belknap Press of Harvard, 1986); and Charles Tilly, *Popular Contention in Great Britain, 1758–1834* (Cambridge, Massachusetts: Harvard University Press, 1995).
31. Tarrow, *Power in Movement*, Chapter 9.
32. Ibid., pp. 150–55.
33. William H. Whyte, Jr., *The Organization Man* (Garden City, New York: Anchor Doubleday, 1957).
34. On this period of political foment, see Todd Gitlin, *The Sixties: Years of Hope, Days of Rage* (New York: Bantam Books, 1987).
35. Anthony Oberschall, "The Decline of the 1960s Social Movements," in Louise Kriesberg, ed., *Research in Social Movements, Conflicts and Change*, Volume 1 (Greenwich, Connecticut: JAI Press, 1978), pp. 257–89.
36. See, for example, Crane Brinton, *The Anatomy of A Revolution* (New York: Prentice-Hall, 1952).
37. Theda Skocpol, *States and Social Revolutions* (New York: Cambridge University Press, 1979).
38. Jack Goldstone, *Revolution and Rebellion in the Modern World* (Berkeley, California: University of California Press, 1991).
39. Jack Goldstone and Bert Useem, "Prison Riots as Microrevolutions: An Extension of State-Centered Theories of Revolutions," *American Journal of Sociology*, Volume 104 (January 1999), pp. 985–1029.
40. Alberto Melucci, "The New Social Movements: A Theoretical Approach," *Social Science Information*, 1980, Volume 19, pp. 199–226.
41. Also see, Alberto Melucci, *Challenging Codes: Collective Action in the Information Age* (Cambridge, UK: Cambridge University Press, 1996).
42. For various illustrations of such movements, see the recent edited collections: Donatella della Porta and Hanspeter Kriesi, eds., *Social Movements in a Globalizing World* (New York: St. Martin's Press, 1999); and J. Craig Jenkins and Bert Klandermans, eds., *The Politics of Social Protest* (Minneapolis: University of Minnesota Press, 1995).
43. Ibid., p. 130.
44. Craig Calhoun, "Social Theory and the Politics of Identity," in Craig Calhoun,

ed. *Social Theory and the Politics of Identity* (Cambridge, England: Blackwell Press, 1994), pp. 9–36, at p. 22.

45. Nelson Pichardo, "New Social Movements: A Critical Review," *Annual Review of Sociology*, 1997, Volume 23, pp. 411–30.
46. Ralph H. Turner and Lewis M. Killian, *Collective Behavior*, 2nd edition (Englewood Cliffs, New Jersey: Prentice-Hall, Inc., 1972).
47. Neil J. Smelser, *Theory of Collective Behavior* (New York: Free Press, 1963).
48. See, especially, Charles Tilly, *From Mobilization to Revolution*, ibid.
49. Doug McAdam, *Political Process and the Development of Black Insurgency, 1930–1970* (Chicago: University of Chicago Press, 1982); Sidney Tarrow, *Power in Movement*, ibid.
50. Peter K. Eisinger, "The Conditions of Protest Behavior in American Cities," *American Political Science Review*, Volume 67 (January 1973), pp. 11–28.
51. See, for example, Crane Brinton, *Anatomy of A Revolution*, and Theda Skocpol, *States and Social Revolutions*.
52. See, for example, Timothy Garton Ash, *The Uses of Adversity: Essays on the Fate of Central Europe* (Random House: New York, 1989).
53. McAdam, op.cit.
54. Ibid.
55. There is such a large number it is impossible to keep track, much less record, all of them. For some such studies, however, see both Tarrow, *Power in Movement*, as well as Doug McAdam, John McCarthy, and Mayer Zald, eds., *Comparative Perspectives on Social Movements: Political Opportunities, Mobilizing Structures, and Cultural Framings* (Cambridge, UK: Cambridge University Press, 1996).
56. Tarrow, ibid., pp. 76–80.
57. For an excellent recent overview of the connections between culture and politics, see Mabel Berezin, "Politics and Culture: A Less Fissured Terrain," *Annual Review of Sociology*, 1997, Volume 23, pp. 361–83.
58. The classic cases of the new modes of explanation, absent ideology, were those of Theda Skocpol, and Mayer Zald and John McCarthy, resource mobilization. But even while ideology was being abandoned by many sociologists, there were others, such as William Sewell, who argued strongly that ideology was a very critical component for the explanation of social revolutions. See William Sewell, *Work and Revolution in France: The Language of Labor from the Old Regime to 1848* (Cambridge, England: Cambridge University Press, 1980).
59. David A. Snow, E. Burke Rochford, Jr., Steven K. Worden, and Robert D. Benford, "Frame Alignment and Mobilization," *American Sociological Review*, Volume 51 (August 1986), pp. 464–81.
60. This old debate, which had first come to public attention in the famous Scopes trial in 1925, resurfaces now and then. Most recently, the Kansas Board of Education ruled that the doctrine of evolution and the Big Bang theory for the origins of the Universe could not be mandated education for the state, but that each school board (304 altogether) was free to engage in its own interpretation. The ruling was seen as a victory for the political forces on behalf of the cre-

ationist view of the origins of mankind. See, for example, the story as it unfolded and was reported in *The New York Times* over the course of August, 1999.

61. For some additional writings on frames, see, for example, David A. Snow and Robert Benford, "Master Frames and Cycles of Protest," in Aldon Morris and Carol Mueller, eds., *Frontiers in Social Movement Theory* (New Haven, Connecticut: Yale University Press, 1992), pp. 133–55.
62. Doug McAdam, John McCarthy, and Mayer Zald, "Introduction," in McAdam, McCarthy and Zald, eds., *Comparative Perspectives on Social Movements*, at p.6.
63. David Snow et al., *American Journal of Sociology*, Fall 1999.
64. Manuel Castells, *The Information Age: Economy, Society and Culture,* Volumes I–III (Oxford, England: Blackwell Publishers, 1996–1998).
65. Melucci, *Challenging Codes*, Chapter 10.
66. Roberta Ash Garner, "Virtual Social Movements," paper delivered at the Zaldfest, Ann Arbor, Michigan, September 17, 1999.
67. See also, McAdam, McCarthy, and Zald, *Comparative Perspectives on Social Movements*, Part II.
68. LeBon, *The Crowd,* op.cit.
69. David A. Snow, Louis Zurcher, and Sheldon Ekland-Olson, "Social Networks and Social Movements: A Microstructural Approach to Differential Recruitment," *American Sociological Review*, Volume 45 (1980), pp. 787–801; also see Kenneth L. Wilson and Anthony M. Orum, "Mobilizing Individuals for Collective Political Action, *Journal of Political and Military Sociology,* Volume 4 (Fall 1976), pp. 187–202.
70. Roger Gould, "Multiple Networks and Mobilization in the Paris Commune, 1871," *American Sociological Review*, Volume 56 (December 1991), 716–29.
71. Jo Freeman, *The Politics of Women's Liberation* (London: Longman, 1975).
72. McAdam, *Political Process and the Development of Black Insurgency, 1930–1970.*
73. See the general discussion on this matter in Oberschall, *Social Conflict and Social Movements.*
74. Aldon Morris, *The Origins of the Civil Rights Movement: Black Communities Organizing for Change* (New York: Free Press, 1984).
75. Bert Klandermans, *The Social Psychology of Protest* (Oxford: Blackwell, 1997), Chapters 5 and 6.
76. Charles Tilly, *From Mobilization to Revolution.*
77. Ted Robert Gurr, "A Causal Model of Civil Strife: A Comparative Analysis Using New Indices," *American Political Science Review,* Volume 62 (December 1968), 1104–24; also see the various writings on these issues in James C. Davies, ed., *When Men Revolt and Why* (New York: Free Press, 1971).
78. Bert Useem, "Breakdown Theories of Collective Action," *Annual Review of Sociology*, Volume 24, 1998, pp. 215–38.
79. Mayer Zald and Roberta Ash, "Social Movement Organizations: Decay and Change," *Social Forces*, 44 (March 1966), 327–40.
80. John D. McCarthy and Mayer N. Zald, "Resource Mobilization and Social

Movements: A Partial Theory," *American Journal of Sociology*, Volume 82 (May 1977), pp. 1212–41; and more generally, see Mayer N. Zald and John D. McCarthy, eds., *Social Movements in An Organizational Society* (New Brunswick, New Jersey: Transaction Books, 1987).

81. For an excellent overview of this rather eclectic school of thought, see J. Craig Jenkins, "Resource Mobilization Theory and the Study of Social Movements," *Annual Review of Sociology*, Volume 9, 1983, pp. 527–53.
82. David S. Meyer and Sidney Tarrow, eds., *The Social Movement Society: Contentious Politics for a New Century* (Boulder, Colorado: Rowman & Littlefield, 1998).
83. Tarrow, *Power in Movement*, see, for example, pp. 186 ff.
84. Russell Dalton, *Citizen Politics: Public Opinion and Political Parties in Advanced Industrial Democracies.*
85. See John D. McCarthy and Clark McPhail, "The Institutionalization of Protest in the United States," in Meyer and Tarrow, eds., *The Social Movement Society*, pp. 83–110; and Jan Kubik, "Institutionalization of Protest During Democratization and Consolidation in Central Europe," pp. 131–52 in the same edited collection.
86. For the most general and systematic review of these issues, see Marco G. Guigni, "Was It Worth the Effort? The Outcomes and Consequences of Social Movements," *Annual Review of Sociology*, Volume 24, 1998, pp. 371–93.
87. Paul Burstein, Rachel L. Einwohner, and Jocelyn A. Hollander, "The Success of Political Movements: A Bargaining Perspective," in Jenkins and Klandermans, eds., *The Politics of Social Protest: Comparative Perspectives on States and Social Movements*, pp. 275–95.
88. William A. Gamson, *The Strategy of Social Protest*.(Belmont, California: Wadsworth, 1975; 1990).
89. Ibid., p. 35.
90. Ibid., p. 87.
91. See, for instance, Jack A. Goldstone, "The Weakness of Organization: A New Look at Gamson's *Strategy of Social Protest*," *American Journal of Sociology*, Volume 85 (March 1980), pp. 1017–42.
92. Frances Fox Piven and Richard Cloward, *Poor People's Movements: Why They Succeed, How They Fail* (New York: Vintage, 1979).
93. Ibid., p. 174.
94. See, for example, Tarrow, *Power in Movement*.
95. Thus, for example, in their recent book, Verba, Schlozman, and Brady actually credit Zald and McCarthy's resource mobilization perspective for helping them to come up with their own model of political participation based upon the notion of civil resources and skills.
96. Robert Alford and Roger Friedland, "Political Participation," *Annual Review of Sociology*, Volume 1, 1975, pp. 429–79.

Chapter 10

Building Nation-States in the Modern World

> We hold these truths to be self-evident, that all men are created equal, that they are endowed by their Creator with certain unalienable rights, that among these are life, liberty, and the pursuit of happiness. That to secure these rights, governments are instituted among men, deriving their just powers from the consent of the governed, that whenever any form of government becomes destructive of these ends, it is the right of the people to alter or to abolish it, and to institute new government, laying its foundation on such principles, and organizing its powers in such form, as to them shall seem most likely to effect their safety and happiness.
>
> *The Declaration of Independence*

With the collapse of so many nations in recent years, among them, the Soviet Union, Hungary, Poland, and South Africa, the attention of a growing number of social scientists has turned to the critical question of how to reconstruct new nation-states out of the old ones. For many scholars such a question had been mainly theoretical, allowing them to trace the rise of the older Western nations, such as Great Britain, France, or the United States. But now, at this very moment in history, it has turned into something more—much more. The struggling nations of Eastern Europe, among many others, are trying today to define for themselves a future that will be less troubled for their citizens and more productive for their markets. But which way shall they turn? What models exist for them to follow? And how can they balance the integrity of their own cultural traditions against the need to establish viable new states and productive new markets?

In this chapter I will focus our attention on materials that furnish some answers to these most important questions. The materials I shall cover represent a careful blend both of old discoveries and relatively new findings. There is also little doubt that, because of the very urgency of these issues, there will be reams of new materials and many new discoveries to come our way in the next few decades. This is a time and a moment when political sociologists can make a true contribution, not only to understanding our world, but also to reshaping it into a much better place in the twenty-first century.

THE ESSENTIAL ELEMENTS OF THE MODERN NATION-STATE

The nation-state is a comparatively new creation, evident in the construction of nations as different as England and India over the course of the past three centuries. Though it is somewhat artificial to speak of the common elements involved in modern nation-building, there still appear to be certain fundamental conditions associated with the emergence of the modern nation-state. Charles Tilly, for example, in a recent work argues that the creation of the modern nation-state is intimately connected to the events associated with war making (see our discussion in Chapter 3).[1] Going to war forces nations to consolidate and centralize their operations, and thus gradually to construct the bureaucratic apparatus that will take on the various tasks associated with the modern nation-state, including the levying of taxes on citizens and the creation of a modern military organization.

To date the most synthetic and persuasive treatment of the basic principles of the modern nation-state comes from the historian C.E. Black.[2] Black argues that the major feature of the modern nation-state is the consolidation of policy making—or, in other words, the centralization of political authority. Observing that this consolidation has been encouraged by the introduction of sophisticated forms of communication and transportation, Black nevertheless declares that it is "due more . . . to the desire on the part of modernizing leaders in both government and private enterprise to mobilize and rationalize the resources of society with a view to achieving greater control, efficiency and production."[3] The history of European nation-states since the Middle Ages discloses this feature to us most clearly, whereas that of the United States, since the end of the eighteenth century at least, displays a less marked trend in this direction. Another quality of the modern nation-state, Black insists, lies in the expansion of its various tasks and purposes over previous political regimes. Special tasks, involving, among other things, the provision of services to the impoverished as well as the establishment and maintenance of national defense gradually have been taken over by the modern nation-state (much as Tilly argues) and have given this institution a degree of power unforeseen by its creators. As Black observes, "modern states today collect revenues in the amount equivalent to between one-quarter and one-half of the gross national product to reimburse the costs of general administration, public enterprises, and social security, whereas in traditional societies such revenues may be as low as 5 percent or less of the wealth produced."[4]

The modern nation-state also is characterized by its proliferation of legal standards. This, in turn, has led to the growth of equally distinctive and formidable bureaucracies to which Max Weber first drew our attention (see Chapter 3). Almost everywhere in the world, political officials undertake efforts to create and expand bureaucracies; new nations often turn first to the establishment of a large civil service, while nations long underway inevitably—and to some partisans unfortunately—seem bound to keep the bureaucracy alive and well. A related and final feature of modern nation-states, according to Black, is the expansion of the citizen's role in public affairs. On this quality, of course, the differences between modern democratic and authoritarian nation-states stand out sharply. Nevertheless, as Black aptly observes, leaders of both democratic and authoritarian regimes appear to find it necessary to clothe the legitimacy of their rule in the guise of widespread popular support.[5]

A number of social scientists, especially in recent works, are interested in identifying more than these elementary features. They inquire as well into the timing and sequence of events that are characteristic of the development of modern nation-states, hoping thereby to specify ever more precisely the process of nation-building.[6] At least part of the reason behind such a concern with this process lies in the obvious differences between the creation of the older nation-states and the newer ones. While countries like England took two or three centuries to assume the outlines of their present national form, others, like Zimbabwe, have been compelled to accomplish nationhood in only a matter decades. What effects might the greater speed of nation-building have on the newer nations? Would an alternative chain of events—the establishment of large and complex political institutions before rather than after economic growth—alter the likelihood of securing a viable nation-state? These rank among some of the most compelling questions for current students of nation-building.

Hans Daalder furnishes some intriguing thoughts on these matters.[7] He claims, for example, that countries like England whose leaders gradually accepted the demands for full participation in politics from the new social classes (for instance, the working class) were better able to develop a more viable and widespread form of democracy than countries like France whose rulers continued to discourage and to resist such participation. A similar circumstance that accounts for the greater stability of British politics over French, he insists, is the earlier development of industrialization in England that permitted "many new links (to be) forged between the state and its citizens through the expansion of administration and the establishment of a great number of new political groups."[8] As we shall see later in this chapter, Daalder's insight into the timing and sequence of nation-building proves to be an important one.

MAJOR BUILDING BLOCKS IN THE CONSTRUCTION OF THE MODERN NATION-STATE

The construction of the modern nation-state often, if not always, has taken place as the result of other changes in a country. Such changes are sometimes dubbed in academic shorthand as "modernization," or "modernity," though, in recent years, that term has been consciously avoided because of its association with the development of nation-states in the West.[9] Nation-building—or sometimes as it is called state-building—represents the political aspects of these changes, while the social and economic ones go under such names as urban migration and economic development. So much have these separate events appeared to accompany one another that it has become difficult to disentangle the occurrence of one from the other. Moreover, it is impossible at times to say in general which of these several strands of development take primacy over the others. Thus, for instance, among the older nation-states, such as England, economic growth and leadership seemed to be more important to subsequent change, while among the more recent ones, as, for example, those of Africa and Southeast Asia, political leadership has provided the principal impetus for economic development. The most judicious view, especially for my general purposes here, is to consider them as concomitants of one another. In the following sections, I shall single out four such dimensions for special attention and consideration. They are: (1) nationalism; (2) political legitimacy and stability; (3) citizenship and the construction of political identity; and (4) economic development.

Nationalism

Nowhere is the significance of sheer ideas more vividly illustrated in political sociology than in the process of constructing the modern nation-state. The forming of a nation seems to depend on the capacity of leaders and their followers to discover a common set of symbols on which they can agree, and which can furnish important foundations for the edifice of the new nation-state. To some observers, in fact, the long and often circuitous struggle to locate and to sustain a common set of symbols is the very heart of nation-building. Writing of the ideology that is characteristic of nation-building, the cultural anthropologist Clifford Geertz puts the matter best: "Nationalism is not a mere byproduct but the very stuff of social change in so many new states; not its reflection, its cause, its expression, or its engine, but the thing itself."[10]

All modern nation-states appear to go through a process of attempting to forge a set of common beliefs that serve as their cornerstone. In the United States, for example, historian Louis Hartz found these common beliefs in a "liberal ethos," a congeries of ideas whose origins lay principally in the writings of John Locke and whose clearest articulation is found in the Declaration of Independence and the Bill of Rights.[11] Running as a theme throughout American history, the liberal ethos, which proclaims the freedom and equality of all individuals, is evident at one point in the significance of the frontier, and at another point in the unparalleled rate of economic expansion in the nineteenth century. In a related inquiry, Seymour Martin Lipset claims that the prevailing kind of religious institutions and beliefs in the United States—those of Protestantism, in particular—greatly contributed to the formation and maintenance of the liberal ethos by stressing, among other things, the egalitarianism of people among themselves as well as before the law.[12]

In a work of magisterial breadth and authority, the sociologist Liah Greenfeld has traced the development of nationalism in each of five countries—England, France, Russia, Germany, and the United States.[13] Greenfeld takes both ideas and nationalism seriously, so seriously that she regards them as the central feature in the construction of the modern nation-state. In this respect her argument runs counter to some popular arguments today, especially those that insist that the central dynamic of the modern nation-state is in the creation and spread of its administrative apparatus. She writes: "The focus of [my argument] is [on] a set of ideas, or rather, several sub-sets of a set of ideas, at the core of which lies the idea of the 'nation,' which I believe forms the constitution of modernity. . . . [M]odernity [in other words] is defined by nationalism."[14] Greenfeld insists that the sequence in which modern nation-states appeared—first the case of England, followed by France, Russia, Germany, and the United States—is also of central importance to the story of nationalism and modernity. The first nation in the sequence, England, had the advantage of creating itself anew, and thus became the model subsequently for all other nation-states. Even more significantly, Greenfeld argues, the later nation-states were created, in part, out of their real and imagined struggles with England, each seeking to distinguish its own symbolic configuration from the other.

England, as the first modern nation-state, was fashioned primarily during the course of the sixteenth and seventeenth centuries. Its construction into a nation involved establishing a sense of "peoplehood," the principal element underlying nationalism. There were many threads and pieces to the new fabric of nationhood. But a major piece lay in the effort to break free of the Catholic Church and to establish a separate and distinct Church of England. The Anglican Church became a kind of rallying point for English nationalism, a first break from the past. Moreover, it became a continuing struggle, one whose outlines became ever more clear through its victories over its opponents, among them, Queen Mary. A growing literature of ideas and stories came to validate the process of nationalism. The writings of Chaucer became a signpost for the new English nation, as did those of such intellectuals as Thomas Hobbes. The distinct character of English nationhood became grounded also in a set of important events. The reign of Henry VIII was critical in securing the break from Catholicism: "[t]he great importance of Henry's break from Rome consisted in that it opened the doors to Protestantism, perhaps the most significant among the features that furthered the development of the English national consciousness."[15]

Moreover, the royal authority—Henry VIII, later Elizabeth—came to represent the personification of the nation. Such personification thus grounded the nation in the actions of real, social beings. Eventually such authority would also come to be shared and distributed among the various classes of the nation. With relative ease, England managed to create itself into a corporate body in which the people identified not simply with the nation, but also with the exercise of authority. The final critical act to this thread to nationalism in England was the establishment in 1688 of Parliament, the body that, on behalf of the people, came to share in the exercise of authority with the monarch.

Nationalism, as the central, defining feature of modern England, would become embodied in a set of ideas that emphasized the individual as the seat of authority and stressed the equality of all individuals under God, including the sovereign who was bound to share his/her power with the people. In addition, because of the growth of education and the spread of literacy England's national heritage also came to emphasize the importance of science, experimental science in particular. The idea that the individual could share in power and could act as a seat of authority necessarily encouraged the development of such experimentation. The critical discoveries of Isaac Newton, coupled with the seminal writings of Francis Bacon, Greenfeld argues, were as central to the creation of modern England as the break from the Catholic Church.

Each subsequent nation-state, beginning with France, then developed, in part, in reaction to the themes and successes of England. Over the course of the seventeenth and eighteenth centuries, in particular, France struggled to fashion its own special identity, one that would form, in part, in opposition to that of England. In France, for example, the idea of the nation, rather than being grounded in the actions of the sovereign and the people, took on a highly abstract character, one that eventually became reified in the notion of "*l'etat*." In part, again, this occurred because of real critical actions on the part of French authorities. Key figures in this process, argues Greenfeld, were, among others, Cardinal Richelieu who, in the seventeenth century, played a critical role in the consolidation and centralization of authority in the apparatus of the state. Moreover, unlike in England where power would become, more or less, peacefully shared between sovereign and the representatives of the people, in France a sharp and hostile relation developed between the King and the aristocracy. The King sought to squeeze the aristocracy of resources and monies that could be used to fuel his own purposes. At the same time, other members of his Court also grew alienated from his authority. Thus, in France, Greenfeld's argument suggests, it became inevitable that the class to play the leading role in revolting against the sovereign authority would not be the bourgeoisie, but rather the aristocracy, who saw themselves as deeply humiliated and who felt sharply alienated. The themes to nationalism in France, in other words, were distinctly different from those in England.

Russia, Germany, and the United States would follow in establishing their own special threads and themes to nationalism. In Germany, for example, violence, race and the "blood of the people" would become intertwined with what it meant to be German. "Peoplehood," would come not to mean a sense of equality and a shared authority, as in England, nor a sense of being separate from the state, as in France, but rather a sense of brotherhood, of ethnic nationalism. Greenfeld writes of Germany: "[s]ince the spirit of the language reflected the race, [Germans] could retain their originality—their Ur-character—only if the blood was kept pure. . . . 'The purer the people, the better,' ruled Jahn.'"[16] In the United States, by contrast, the creation of the modern nation-state drew heavily upon its English origins, but, as the Revolution would show, also took them in new, distinct, and different directions. The notions of equality and freedom were natural to American soil, Greenfeld writes, echoing themes that date to the writings of Alexis de Tocqueville (see Chapter 4). "American society was exemplary," she writes, "in its devotion to the English ideals; it turned them into reality. Liberty and equality, for Americans, became self-evident."[17]

Today nationalism remains central to the agenda of building and creating modern nation-states. Indeed, as a body of distinctive beliefs it is those cultural traditions that single out one nation as separate and different than other nations. The course to establishing nationalism also has taken many new turns and twists. In some special instances, as in Iran, Islam, a major world religion, has become the central defining feature for nationhood, much as the Anglican Church did for England. Religious clerics have become the political authorities, raising, among other things, questions of how and whether the exercise of religious authority is distinct from that of secular political authority (though such a question must also have been raised in the reign of Henry VIII). Moreover, as Greenfeld's seminal work suggests, part of the achievement of nationhood in nations like Iran and other Muslim countries, like Indonesia, is to define themselves not only as distinct, but also as antagonists of all that is Western. In other cases, as in the republics of the former Soviet Union, struggles and clashes among different ethnic nationalities underscore the great challenge of establishing nationhood when so little common ground and so few common symbols exist. The recent establishment of the new government for Northern Ireland, bringing to a halt decades of hostility and war, might just show the way that such struggles can be brought to a peaceful and, one hopes, an enduring conclusion.

Political Legitimacy and Stability

Becoming a modern nation-state, as we have seen, is by no means a smooth and easy task. For each success there are also one or more failures. Often these interruptions are most evident in the political challenges and tensions encountered by the leaders of state. Nation-building even among the older nation-states, for instance, provides evidence of considerable political conflict. In England, major conflicts occurred in the seventeenth century and ultimately produced a fundamental change in the distribution of political power; Parliament replaced the King as the sovereign body. In France, the struggles were even more intense and widespread; they reached their peak in 1789 but continued long into the nineteenth century. German history, too, is marked by periods of political tension, though German leaders succeeded in suppressing the most extreme forms of opposition until 1848 and later in 1918, 1923, and 1932. The United States, as well, is a country whose steps in the direction of nationhood were marked in the late eighteenth century by a successful challenge to a colonial power and whose later efforts to achieve a more or less pacific nationhood were interrupted—some might even say forestalled—by a great Civil War over the issue of race. In the newly emerging nation-states of today there are equally intense and violent struggles among the inhabitants—in Asia, Africa, and Latin America.

The issue of creating a viable nation-state, one to which all citizens will subscribe, is the central issue to which Max Weber first drew attention. To Weber, as you may recall, the creation of the modern nation-state, as all states, involved the establishment of the *legitimacy* of rule and of the rulers. The nature of legitimacy is such that both the rulers and the ruled must accept the bonds of authority that tie one group to the other. In the absence of such bonds and acceptance, no form of rule or law can work effectively. Modern analysts, like Jürgen Habermas, emphasize that such bonds must be grounded in a widespread common consensus that depends, in the last instance, on the ability of both the governed and the governors to engage in sustained dialogue and communication about that consensus.[18] Other contemporary analysts have pointed to the great challenges involved in establishing such legitimacy. This is especially true for many of the newer countries that seek nationhood. Often such countries consist of feuding rival factions that seek to subdue the others. In such cases, it often seems to be less a matter of securing political legitimacy and more one of establishing the rule of force.

One might well ask: how can we explain the sporadic punctuation of nation-building with political conflicts and challenges to the reigning leaders? How, in other words, can we account for the failure to obtain legitimacy? Samuel P. Huntington, a political scientist and close student of nation-building, presents one of the older but still useful explanations. He argues that nation-building involves the unparalleled growth of political participation that is partly brought about by economic development.[19] Participation, by itself, is not a sufficient stimulus for political instability, however; it must be further joined with an inadequate number and growth of political organizations. Thus, instability is produced because there exist an insufficient number of channels and sponsors available to embrace the newly enlarged and aroused citizenry. By channels and sponsors, Huntington has in mind such groups as political parties, trade unions, and voluntary organizations that commonly dot the twentieth-century landscape of such older nations as the United States.

To prove his case Huntington provides a variety of pieces of evidence and documentation. Asserting, for example, that political instability is characteristic of the transition from a relatively peaceful traditional social order to a relatively peaceful modern one he displays evidence that shows that political violence reaches its peak among those nations midway in the level of literacy. Other research tends to support his view.[20] However, there are also analysts who have not found overwhelming evidence for Huntington's argument. For example, Paul R. Brass sought to examine the thesis among the different states of India.[21] Instead of finding that political instability comes about when the level of political institutionalization is low, as Huntington's thesis claims, Brass found that instability resulted from high levels of institutionalization. Indeed, Brass's analysis, rather than Huntington's, tends to support the most advanced thinking on the matters of instability and violence in nation-building.

Regardless of the current balance of evidence on Huntington's argument, its implication is that political legitimacy and stability exist only where political institutions are durable and strong, at least sufficiently strong to withstand the sudden numbers of newly enfranchised political participants. Huntington explores this implication and embellishes it with an exploration into the many ways in which political parties, as institutions, succeed in the control of political participation. Particular cases, like both the United States and England, come to mind that support Huntington's argument. In the United States, for example, the political parties developed at a pace that enabled them to contain and channel the growing level of political participation.

Huntington's argument about the importance of durable political organizations for political stability also reinforces analyses we have examined earlier in this book. In particular, it appears to be a direct descendant of Alexis de Tocqueville's emphasis on the crucial importance of mediating social groups, such as parties, to the creation of not only legitimate but also democratic rule. Thus, it also lies in the same tradition as that of Robert Putnam's more recent argument on the significance of social trust to the creation of viable democracies. As such, then, it should remind us of the very important role of civil institutions in the nation-building process. The real trick for the newer nations, perhaps, is not how to achieve legitimacy itself, but how to create a substantial civil order that precedes and provides firm ground to such legitimacy.

Citizenship and the Establishment of Common Political Identity

One of the major challenges involved in creating a new nation is the construction of a sense of citizenship and identity among those who are, and who will become, members of the new entity. As Liah Greenfeld, among others, has shown, this has always been regarded as an important chord to the process of building a nation, but until recent years it has been a kind of minor theme rather than the central melody. Now, in view of the worldwide spread of immigration, and the establishment of new transnational organizations such as the new European Union, the nature of citizenship has become an ever more significant part of the process of establishing new nations.

T.H. Marshall, in his classic work, helped to put sociologists on the path to a better understanding of citizenship. He claimed that "[c]itizenship is a status bestowed on those who are full members of a community . . . [making them] equal with respect to the rights and duties with which the status is endowed."[22] It helps, moreover, in his view to temper the inequalities that are associated with social class. He argued that in Great Britain citizenship evolved over time. First came the provision of civil rights, which were established in Britain in the seventeenth and eighteenth centuries. Such rights provided citizens protection from the rule of unjust authority and other abuses that might be committed by the state against them. Then, in the eighteenth and, especially, the nineteenth century, a new brand of rights came into being. These were economic rights, and they included the right to be employed and to freely engage in whatever occupational pursuit one wished. Such rights, attached to citizenship in England, permitted the growth of opportunity to an enlarged working class and, at the same time of course, helped to fill the new manufacturing plants with thousands of workers freely employed.

Finally, over the course of the latter half of the nineteenth and first half of the twentieth centuries, the rights of citizenship became fully expanded to include social rights. Now citizens of Great Britain not only would be protected against unjust authority, but their very citizenship entitled them to certain key benefits, including medical and unemployment insurance. All these rights, in the end, Marshall advised us, served to temper the inequities of harsh capitalism and to provide all citizens with universal rights, regardless of who they were. Citizenship, in other words, was a great step forward on behalf of the equality of opportunity.

Marshall's argument, though attacked for its lack of attention to agency and the ability of people to mobilize on behalf of expanding rights in a nation, nonetheless sets the benchmark for all modern discussions of citizenship. At the same time, much recent work has taken the argument in somewhat different directions. The permeable boundaries of the modern nation-state have brought about such new thinking. Citizenship now is not merely to be seen from the point of view of citizens, but from the point of view of nation-states that seek to preserve their integrity against such novel happenings as the massive mobility of people across national borders.

The pioneer in this new thinking about citizenship, and particularly immigration, is the sociologist Rogers Brubaker.[23] Brubaker argues that nation-states, besides being territorial organizations, also are bounded, or membership, associations, and that they seek, therefore, to maintain their structural integrity at all costs. But how they do so will vary from one nation to another, depending on key cultural traditions. In Germany, for example, citizenship became very closely tied to issues of race and blood (or peoplehood), whereas in France it became defined more specifically in political terms. Accordingly, if people were to become citizens of Germany, it meant that they also had to become Germans, to qualify as members of the nation. By contrast, to become a citizen in France meant that people would enjoy simply the specific rights and obligations of citizenship, such as voting rights or duties to be tax-paying members of the state. Such differences had profound implications, especially for the current period in which there has been so much movement of peoples of different national origins into and out of countries like France and Germany. Germany was more apt to relegate new immigrants to the status of noncitizens, whereas France would admit them to citizenship much more freely.

The sociologist Yasemin Soysal, by contrast, argues that there is now an emerging postnational form of citizenship.[24] With the movement of so many peoples across national borders, and the emergence of transnational communities of ethnic nationals, Soysal believes that citizenship has moved beyond the capacity of nation-states to control it. She believes further that there is an emerging form of human rights, rights that become attached to all peoples regardless of whether they belong to a particular nation-state or not. A third point of view is represented in the work of sociologist Christian

Joppke who believes, like Soysal, that citizenship is becoming transformed in the modern age.[25] In particular, he believes that many nations are now being forced to redefine what it means to be a citizen, devising specific and easy new tests of citizenship rather than relying simply on the legacy of their cultural traditions to define them. Moreover, from Joppke's point of view, such a tack makes sense for it enables nations to maintain productive economies by importing new workers—and citizens—from abroad.

There now is little question that the issues of citizenship and, by implication, national boundaries will grow in importance in coming years. Major events, like the massive flow of immigrants across nations, are apt to increase rather than to diminish with the growth in the global economy. Accordingly, nation-states will be under ever more pressure to identify precisely what it means to be a citizen within their borders. And, at the same time, the mobile and energetic groups of transnational citizens are apt to increase their demands for a set of rights fully independent of any specific nation-state.[26]

Economic Development

European nations like England vividly illustrate the close links between economic development and nation-building. In Great Britain, the gradual growth and expansion of the economy into a full-blow capitalist enterprise was paralleled by an equally gradual enlargement of the political arena. As the means and setting of production changed from simple utensils of the artisan and the comfortable location of the home or guild, so, too, the aristocracy of England ever so slowly and smoothly accommodated themselves to new circumstances in politics; for instance, in the nineteenth century the franchise was extended first to the manufacturing classes and then to the working classes. Though peaceful compared with nation-building in countries such as France, the process of development in England was nevertheless punctuated by moments of violence and upheaval.

No doubt the British case has suggested to many observers that economic development inevitably accompanies the emergence of the modern nation-state. W.W. Rostow, in a pioneering thesis, gives special significance to the importance of economic development in nation-building and suggests a multistage sequence whereby countries ultimately achieve an economic "take-off" that propels them into extensive and sustained economic growth.[27] Many economic factors appear to Rostow as part of this sequence of events. Chief among them is change in the form of agricultural techniques and market organization in a country, emergence of an economic elite that shifts its attention from traditional practices of enterprise to new forms of production, and a marked increase in the investment of a country in the technical means of production. Other observers draw upon the Rostow thesis, or one very similar to it, to claim that state administrative structures are compelled to undergo corresponding changes by, among other things, enlarging the part they play in the development of the economy and increasing their number of political personnel. The role of the state, particularly over the past three decades, has become a matter of some extended and imaginative inquiry among social scientists.

The Role of the State in Fostering Contemporary Economic Growth. By all accounts the nature of economic growth since World War II has overturned many preconceptions about the forces that can promote such growth. Perhaps the most remarkable occurrence in this period of time is not, as many point out, the very dramatic expansion (until 1990 at least) in the economy of Japan, but the tremendous growth experienced by the four Little Dragons of Asia—Korea, Taiwan, Hong Kong, and Singapore. Over the course of the past several decades, these four states have experienced greater overall growth, and higher growth-rates, than any other nations, including those in the West. What makes their growth all the more remarkable is this: They expanded their economies under authoritarian regimes that exercised tight control. Citizens possessed few rights in these regimes during their periods of rapid growth.[28] At the same time, the working class was so little mobilized that it could not pursue an aggressive agenda on behalf of expanding the rights of workers. In other words, quite unlike the European experience, capitalism grew rapidly in these countries without the aid of a democratic regime. Did this novel twist to the links between the state and the economy now mean that all conventional wisdom from the past was to be abandoned—that it was not democracy but authoritarianism that could best serve a rapidly expanding economy?

Today some of the most intriguing research on nation-building looks exactly at these kinds of questions—on what kind of state it takes to get the economy of an emerging nation to take off and develop. Naturally such a question is of immediate significance. The fate of many new nation-states hangs in the balance; their futures depend precisely on their success in attaining rapid and effective economic development. And there are, in fact, very sharp differences among both scholars and politicians over the right course to take. Some argue that a market unrestrained by government restrictions and regulations will work best, while others argue that the character of the state is absolutely vital to economic growth today. Even in late 1999 economists and other social scientists remained sharply divided over this question, particularly in light of the major economic crisis that had enveloped the Asian economies over the course of the previous several years.

Among sociologists, Peter Evans has done the most penetrating and original research on these matters.[29] Evans takes the reality of the state very seriously. In fact, for him as for a number of other analysts, the building of the modern nation-state is not a matter of nationhood, or nationalism, at all.

TABLE 10-1 Economic Growth Rates of Southeast Asian Nations, Japan, and the United States (1960–1990)

Average Annual Growth Rates of Gross Domestic Products (in Percentages)[a]			
	1960–1970	1970–1980	1980–1990
Southeast Asia[b]			
Hong Kong	9.3	9.4	6.6
Korea	8.7	8.6	9.3
Singapore	9.6	8.9	7.0
Taiwan	9.6	9.7	8.0
Japan	10.5	2.8	2.7
United States	4.3	4.3	4.1

[a]Gross domestic product measures the productivity of a country. It is defined in the *World Development Reports* as "the total gross expenditures on the final uses of the domestic supply of goods and services valued at purchasers' values less the imports of goods and services."

[b]Data for Southeast Asia actually cover the periods 1961–1970; 1971–1980; and 1981–1990; data for Japan and the United States cover the periods 1960–1970; 1970–1980; and 1980–1992.

Source: Data for Southeast Asia are from *From Trade-Driven Growth to Growth-Driven Trade: Reappraising the East Asian Development Experience* (Washington: Organization for Economic Co-Operation and Development, 1994); data for Japan and the United States are from *World Development Reports* (Washington: World Bank, 1978, 1994). Table from Anthony Orum, John W. C. Johnstone, and Stephanie Riger, *Changing Societies: Essential Sociology for Our Times* (Boulder, Colorado: Rowman & Littlefield, 1999). By permission of Rowman & Littlefield Publishers.

Instead it is the structure and character of the state administrative apparatus that matters so much to nation-building—not only the construction of the state and its allied enterprises, but also the development of the market, itself.

Evans's most significant work to date considers at length the optimal conditions for the development of the economy among the emerging nations in the late twentieth and early twenty-first century. He poses his argument on the crucial importance of the state against that of neoclassical economists who take the view that it is essentially the market, free of governmental restrictions, that will shape the economic development of modern nations. Neoclassical economists tend to the view that the economy must be nurtured and fueled, in part, through a plentiful and continuing supply of capital. Once that is done, their argument goes, entrepreneurs and their fledgling enterprises will be able to develop on their own and, depending on their particular economic niche, achieve success in the world markets. Evans questions the logic of this view.

Evans argues that the state plays a crucial role in the development of the new markets. He suggests that there are key differences among states, however. There are, he observes, such things as *predatory* states. Such states are those in which the profits produced in the market, rather than being funneled back into their respective enterprises for further development, are actually appropriated by the leaders of the state. Such leaders become the institutional representatives for the predatory state, ultimately sacrificing the interests of the nation, and the market, to their own wanton desires. The Philippines under Ferdinand Marcos and his allies was a prime example of the predatory state.

There are other emerging states, however, that actually can help to foster the growth of the economy and with it, the material development of the nation itself. The main such state is what Evans identifies as the *developmental* state. The developmental state is successful in fostering and nurturing the growth of the economy through a very subtle and delicate balance, in part, by helping provide capital and leadership to the new and emerging enterprises, but at the same time exercising a kind of loose reign over them. Evans refers to the nature of such a structural situation as that of *embedded autonomy*. By this he means that the developmental state is, as an institution, *autonomous* of other institutions in the emerging nation, grounded on its own meritocratic standards for performance, and thus not caught deeply in the web of social ties and relationships that often characterize emerging nations. At the same time, however, the developmental state and its leaders are *embedded* in the sense that its officials do share important relationships to the new entrepreneurs and corporate chieftains. Such relationships are built upon a sense of shared trust and purpose, rather than a sense of opposing loyalties and conflicts.

Evans develops his argument carefully and persuasively, examining the developing technology market in three separate countries: Korea, Brazil, and India. Korea, one of the remarkable expansionary stories of the past three decades, illustrates Evans's argument perfectly. It is an example of an effective developmental state. Evans writes:

> What separates Korea from Brazil and India is not that Brazil and India constructed greenhouses [for economic growth] while Korea did not. Nor is the difference that the Korean state intervened less than Brazil and India. The difference lies in the Korean's state blend of roles, which was in turn rooted in the structure of the state and the character of its ties to society. Internal coherence and close ties to entrepreneurial elites offered fruitful foundations from which to promote a new sector. Korea's embedded autonomy made it easier to adopt an effective combination of roles.[30]

Brazil, though effective in some respects, lacked a state that was fully autonomous from the market and hence was less able to direct concerted economic development. And India was least successful, largely because, though it helped to foster the development of the new technology companies, it was unable to create a situation in which those companies eventually took off on their own steam.

Evans has followed up his analysis in later research, arguing, among other things, that the Weberian state bureaucracy, with its emphasis on a strong civil service, meritocracy and internal careers, is precisely the kind of state that can most effectively foster economic development.[31] Moreover,

Evans's argument is allied to other recent research, including that of the economist Robert Wade who, like Evans, points to the central and significant role of the state for the new and emerging markets of new nations.[32] But there also is a strong downside to this view, and to the success of the state in these respects. And that is the matter of citizen rights under conditions in which the state exercises its autonomy. The question that the new nation-states like Korea now must struggle with is this: How can a state achieve a balance between optimal economic growth, which its citizens can enjoy, and the rights of those same citizens to freely express their opinions and views, rights guaranteed under the older democracies? The durability of these new nation-states is apt to depend precisely on the answer to this question in the future.

KEY SOCIAL AGENTS IN THE CONSTRUCTION OF THE MODERN NATION-STATE

In the creation of the modern nation-state, especially those that came to life during the course of the twentieth century, some social groups have come to play a more prominent role than others. There are three such groups to which I will draw attention in my discussion. They are: intellectuals, the military, and the peasantry. The intellectuals and the military have mainly acted as leaders of organized attempts to change societies; the peasants, by contrast, have been the major suppliers of personnel for the ultimate victories of national liberation.

Intellectuals

Some figures prominently associated with the heights of nation-building among countries of the modern world include Jefferson, Madison, and Hamilton in the United States; Lenin and Trotsky in the former Soviet Union; Mao Tse-Tung in the People's Republic of China; and Nelson Mandela in South Africa. What did all of these figures have in common? Essentially they all were people of ideas who were receptive to new knowledge and anxious to challenge the status quo in an effort to create for themselves and for their followers a new social and political order. Whatever their special motivations and talents for revolution—and often, to all outward appearances, such motivations consisted principally of an overweening ambition to secure positions of great power—the minds of these individuals were of a different cut from those of their fellow conspirators and were equally tuned to the world of ideas and that of action. They were the individuals responsible both for creating and for articulating the symbolic themes that, as we have already seen, play so crucial a part in the creation of the nation-state in the modern world. They were, in short, intellectuals.[33]

One of the twentieth century's foremost students of nation-building was the sociologist Edward Shils. Writing with great insight and wisdom, Shils maintained that intellectuals, whom he defined as possessed of "an advanced modern education," have occupied a special role in nation-building efforts in Asia and Africa.[34] In part this occurred because no other groups were available for that task. The merchants who achieve great success in the world of business, for instance, obviously have no special reason or desire to embark on an effort to sever ties with colonial nations; and other social groups that in earlier times had undertaken the effort to challenge the old orders, such as trade unions, are insufficiently organized to assume this part in the colonies. However, it is not just the absence of others that prompted the intellectuals to become revolutionaries or reformers. Often those who receive advanced educational training in their home countries, or more typically in England, France, or the United States, are unable to find sufficiently rewarding and satisfying professions in which to employ their skills and talents; hence they are open to the opportunity to engage in political activities. Their willingness to participate in protests receives added encouragement from circumstances peculiar to their role as educated individuals—their uncomfortable position vis-à-vis colonial authority. "For an intellectual in an underdeveloped country," Shils wrote, "authority is usually something into which he must be absorbed or against which he must be in opposition. It is seldom something about which he can be neutral while he goes about his business. . . . The distance of authority renders revolt against it psychologically practicable."[35]

Twentieth-century intellectuals were led to voice ideas that echo those found in earlier nation-building efforts as well. Overriding all other ideas were those of national independence and unity; these were themes that had a special attraction for the intellectuals because they seemed to reconcile the tension between the appeal of the urban life in the older nation-states, like England and the United States, and the parochial tug of ties to family and friends in the colonial country. The theme of nationalism frequently was couched in two other sets of ideas—populism and socialism. Populism possessed a particularly strong and almost natural appeal to the intellectuals because it provided a means of articulating the feeling of loyalty to home, as well as a device destined to arouse the mass of newly awakened peoples to the tactical efforts required by nation-building. These were themes, incidentally, equally as characteristic of the nation-building experience of older nation-states in Europe as those of the newer ones (on this point, also see Greenfeld).[36] Socialism, on the other hand, came to be attractive to the intellectuals for many reasons—the hatred that the intellectuals felt toward nations they perceived as engaged in imperialist expansion and rape of lesser countries; the practical political successes that communism had to its credit in the twentieth century in nations like the Soviet Union, the People's Republic of China, and Cuba; and, of course, the demonstrated ease with which socialist doctrines could accommodate the themes of nationalism and populism.

The future role of intellectuals in nation-building is somewhat unclear. Undermining whatever incentive they might possess to involve themselves in political challenges to established regimes, particularly in the newer nations, are the expansion of economic opportunities that come with economic development—once positions commensurate with their skills become available to them, then one major source of dissatisfaction will be gone. Yet, if the experience of the older nation-states is any guide, intellectuals will continue well into the twenty-first century to be a thorn in the side of established political regimes, by challenging the right of those who hold high office to continue in their positions of power.

The Military

Students of the military have often been struck by the extent to which military personnel become involved in nation-building efforts.[37] Perhaps the prototype of modern cases is that of Gamal Abdul Nasser and other members of the Egyptian army who deposed King Farouk in 1952 and assisted Egypt and later the United Arab Republic in political and economic success. There are many other examples as well, including Ahmed Ben Bella of Algeria and Mustafa Kemal in Turkey. More recently, there is the example of the role that the military forces provided to the nation-building efforts of Taiwan and Korea, and, of course, the many and various military regimes of Latin American nations over the course of the 1960s, 1970s, and 1980s. There are a number of qualities associated with the military profession and with military training that are compatible with an active and vigorous role in politics, such as aspirations for positions of power and skills useful for coping with the special nuances of politics. Moreover, military officers, like intellectuals, have often found themselves propelled to the forefront of organized efforts to change simply because there are no other groups that could assume the part.

Most modern inquiries into the part that the military plays in nation-building tend to divide over whether the military occupies a position of encouraging greater economic and political self-sufficiency or one of halting, if not reversing, such development.[38] Samuel Huntington, in a provocative analysis, resolves the seeming contradiction between equally sound investigations by suggesting that the role of the military depends not so much on features of the institution but rather on the stage of nation-building in the larger society.[39] In the first place, Huntington draws a distinction among six types of political regimes and relies on the circumstances mentioned in my earlier discussion of his analysis—namely, political participation and political institutions. Countries may be equally advanced in their development, at least in terms of the extent of political participation within them, but differ in the degree to which participation is bound within existing political organizations. Thus, Cuba today would represent an example of a society displaying high levels of participation as well as high levels of institutionalization, whereas Argentina, especially during the period of the 1960s through the early 1980s, represented a society exhibiting high levels of participation but low levels of institutionalization. The praetorian political orders are those societies in which political institutions are insufficiently developed to be strong enough to cope with the extent of citizen participation; Huntington focuses his analysis of the origins and development of military intervention in nation-building on these particular countries.

Huntington observes that the military plays its most vigorous role as a champion of nation-building in the shift from traditional to transitional political orders. In these instances, the military represents virtually the only group in the society willing and able to undertake the challenge of the existing political regime. Upon the success of its overthrow of the established political rulers—its *coup d'etat,* in other words—it initiates a large-scale effort to upgrade the economy and to replace existing political institutions with somewhat more popular and representative ones. Huntington writes:

> In these early stages of political modernization the military officers play a highly modernizing and progressive role. They challenge the oligarchy, and they promote social and economic reform, national integration, and, in some measure, the extension of political participation. They assail waste, backwardness, and corruption, and they introduce into the society highly middle-class ideas of efficiency, honesty, and national loyalty. Like the Protestant entrepreneurs of Western Europe, the soldier reformers in non-Western societies embody and promote a Puritanism, which, while not perhaps as extreme as that of the radical revolutionaries, is nonetheless a distinctive innovation in their societies.[40]

Huntington finds that change in which the military assumes a highly innovative role in nation-building was characteristic of nations such as Iraq until 1958, Egypt until 1952, and many Latin American nations in the nineteenth century.

With the transformation of a nation-state from oligarchic to radical praetorianism, and thence to mass praetorianism, the role of the military changes accordingly. In particular, as "society changes, so does the role of the military. In the world of oligarchy, the soldier is a radical; in the middle-class world he is a participant and arbiter; as the mass society looms on the horizon, he becomes the conservative guardian of the existing order."[41] Citing a number of cases in Latin America in the 1950s—Argentina, Venezuela, Colombia, and Brazil—as well as Turkey, Huntington suggests that the military at this stage tends to assume the role of a guardian of the established regime and constitution by suppressing forces aimed at the overthrow of the government and securing the reign of representatives of the middle class. Further, instead of aggressively seeking economic and other reforms, it merely serves as the agent for those middle-class groups currently the most popular and powerful, assists them in deposing recalcitrant leaders, but then withdraws from an active part in governing the new nation-state.

Whether the military will continue to play the part of a force for innovation or for conservatism in nation-building in the twenty-first century remains to be seen. At a minimum, the implication of Huntington's analysis is that the role of the military will depend on the main features of the larger society. If the more technologically advanced societies and older nation-states, like the United States, England, or France, serve as any sort of guide, then it appears that the role of the military in the developing nation-states will ultimately become subordinate to that of the civilian leaders. This is even more likely if, as seems immediately probable, the incidence and magnitude of war, itself, declines in the near future.

Peasants

While the effort to build a new nation-state must often rely (and in the past has relied) on the leadership and guidance of intellectuals and military officers, in the end it will fail unless it manages to incorporate a large and willing band of foot soldiers. Marx, of course, anticipated that the foot soldiers would come principally from the urban proletariat—individuals so stripped of their humanity that they would become willing accomplices in the effort to create a new society. To a degree Marx proved correct in his prognosis, for instance, in Russia. However, there have been a number of significant instances, particularly in the twentieth century, in which the foot soldiers for radical change in nation-building came not from the urban proletariat but from the peasant laborers—not from the city, but from the country.[42]

The story of the role of the peasants in nation-building efforts of the twentieth century has been particularly well told in a classic analysis by anthropologist Eric Wolf.[43] He studies in close detail the distant as well as the immediate histories of twentieth-century peasant wars and revolutions in six different countries—Mexico, Russia, China, Vietnam, Algeria, and Cuba—searching for both the common and unique factors of peasant rebellion. He claims that the peasant wars and revolts had their distant origins in the growth and spread of capitalism in Northern Europe; it was capitalism that succeeded in upsetting the settled and customary routine of life among peasants, as among every other social group. The meaning of land and of labor became transformed from objects of long-standing pride and respect to objects that, in the capitalist scheme of things, merely represented commodities. The spread of capitalism, moreover, had the effect of at least unleashing a chain of events that comprise the general sorts of processes to which I have previously referred, economic development among them:

> The spread of the market has torn men up by their roots, and shaken them loose from the social relationships into which they were born. Industrialization and expanded communication have given rise to new social clusters, as yet unsure of their own social positions and interests, but forced by the imbalance of their lives to seek a new adjustment.[44]

Thus aroused, people of all groups, principally peasants, became available to engage in the organized political efforts to free societies from their traditional, often debilitating forms of rule.

In all six countries studied by Wolf there ultimately resulted a political victory of more or less sustained duration that was accomplished on behalf of peasants, if not mainly by peasant forces. However, this victory neither came easily nor transpired quickly. Invariably, it was preceded by an effort to establish a dictatorship on behalf of other social forces and groups. In China the victory of the Communists on behalf and with the aid of the peasants was preceded by the dictatorship of Chiang Kai-shek; in Vietnam the victory of Ho Chi Minh and the Communists was preceded by the efforts of the French to impose an unpopular rule. Where peasant forces did not succeed in establishing a central political authority on their own behalf, as in Germany and Japan, the failure was due to the strength of the feudal barons who controlled the land.

Peasants are everywhere free or eager to engage in nation-building efforts, regardless of the ruin visited upon them by capitalism. Indeed, Wolf suggests, peasants are naturally disinclined to engage in rebellions or revolutions because of circumstances inherent in their mode of life. As all peasants tend to work alone, they come to prize the strength of their individual efforts—to view themselves, as capitalism advances, as competitors for scarce bounty rather than as collaborators. Equally true of the life of peasants is the lack of skill, not to say interest, in matters of power; life to peasants consists entirely of the workaday routine of farming the land, of harvesting the crops, and of occasionally praying for the protection of food and family.

Hence, it is in special circumstances that rebellious forces are comprised of peasants. Wolf claims, in the first place, that peasants become active in widespread rebellions only when they are led by outside agents such as military officers, political parties, and independent intellectuals:

> Poor peasants and landless laborers, therefore, are unlikely to pursue the course of rebellion unless they are able to rely on some external power to challenge the power which constrains them. Such external power is represented in the Mexican case by the Constitutionalist army in Yucatan . . . by the collapse of the Russian Army in 1917 and the reflux of the peasant soldiery, weapons in hand, into the villages; by the creation of the Chinese Red Army as an instrument designed to break up the landlord power in the villages.[45]

In the second place, Wolf argues that only the middle and the land-free peasants are the likeliest candidates for rebellions because the former are the most thoroughly caught up in the tensions of transition from a rural agrarian economy to an urban capitalist one and the latter are the least subject to the power of the landlords and the continuing attachment to the land.

Will peasants continue to play a vital part in the efforts to build nation-states in the future—either as the dominant troops or as the principal beneficiaries? Wolf suggests that the political efforts conducted in their name may prove to be limited. As societies become more complex, he observes, the consequences of peasant rebellions tend to become more narrow in scope and reduced in intensity, owing perhaps to the more minor role of peasants in the economy and society. "[A] peasant rebellion which takes place in a complex society already caught up in commercialization and industrialization," he writes, "tends to be self-limiting, and hence, anachronistic."[46]

ALTERNATIVE PATHWAYS TO NATIONHOOD: DEMOCRATIC, AUTHORITARIAN, AND TOTALITARIAN REGIMES

There are different ways in which countries can become nation-states. Some can take centuries, gradually adding on the bits and pieces of nationhood. Others must traverse the path more quickly, if only to avoid becoming a laggard. At the same time, there also are very different outcomes to the nature of nationhood. Some nations have succeeded as democratic societies, enjoying the freedom and liberty provided by democratic constitutions. Yet others have made considerable strides, even for their citizens, by exercising tight, even excessive political control, either as authoritarian or as totalitarian states.

One of the great questions of the past, and certainly one of the most pressing of the present, is this: Is there a certain constellation of events and happenings that is more likely to result in a democratic rather than an authoritarian regime? Though for many scholars this has been primarily a theoretical concern, today it obviously has much more practical importance. For, if there are certain conditions that promote democracy, rather than authoritarianism, all other things being equal most people would prefer to set into motion that chain of events that will result in democracy. But what are they? And is there any way in which people can exercise agency over such outcomes? Or is it merely predestined?

In this section I will introduce you to several key pieces of research that have tried to answer these most important questions. The latest in this line of research, I believe, provides also the best and most complete set of answers now. But to know how these scholars were able to make as much headway as they have it is important to retrace the key foundations to their work.

The Seeds of Democracy: Seymour Martin Lipset on the Structural Foundations of Modern Democratic Regimes

The story of the path that leads to democracy begins in the modern era with a seminal piece of research by the twentieth century's leading political sociologist, Seymour Martin Lipset (see also the discussion of Lipset in Chapter 4). In a 1959 publication, Lipset reported on a comparative analysis he had undertaken of several different nations.[47] They included the nations of Europe as well as those of North America and Latin America. His purpose in undertaking the research was to discover whether democratic states differed in any systematic manner from authoritarian, or dictatorial, regimes.

Lipset argued that, in theory, there should be systematic differences between the material and social conditions of democratic regimes, on the one hand, and authoritarian ones, on the other. Drawing, in part, on the ideas of such early Western philosophers as Aristotle, Lipset argued that economic development and material abundance should, in principle, be more likely to result in democratic rather than authoritarian governments. Material growth, he suggested, should be associated also with the emergence of a set of ideas and values compatible with democracy. By comparison, limited growth and development are unlikely to foster such values, in part, because they would be more consistent with the exercise of traditional, even dictatorial, authority.

To investigate his general hypothesis, Lipset relied on the most advanced use of quantitative data and statistics at the time. He established, in effect, two different sets of countries: one, those countries of Europe, North America, and Latin America that he characterized as stable democracies; the other, those countries of the same regions that he characterized as unstable democracies, or simply as dictatorial systems. The United States was an example of a stable democracy, while Spain, under the authority of Franco, was an example of a dictatorial system. Lipset then compared the two different sets of countries in terms of such basic social and economic indicators as the overall level of wealth, urbanization, literacy, and average level of education among citizens. As he predicted, the democratic nations were more apt to be characterized by, for example, higher average levels of income, higher average levels of education, and higher levels of literacy. In general, then, the democratic states appeared to enjoy certain advantages that derived from their material growth and wealth.

Having empirically verified his general thesis, Lipset went on to provide a greater detail of reasons for the conjunction between economic development and democratic states. He argued that, above and beyond the values growth furnished for citizens, it also provided a number of other important conditions. It provided, for example, opportunity for members of the lower and working classes to move up the ladder of occupational success, thus not consigning them forever to lives of poverty and insecurity at the bottom of society. He also observed:

> Increased wealth also affects the political role of the middle class by changing the shape of the stratification structure from an elongated pyramid, with a large lower-class base, to a diamond with a growing middle class. A large middle class tempers conflict by rewarding moderate and democratic parties and penalizing extremist groups.[48]

In addition, he argued, a society with great wealth provides a number of role models for members of the lower classes to emulate, thus furnishing a kind of perpetual motion for expansion and breaking the straitjacket of authority that traditional, or authoritarian, regimes sometimes furnish.

Lipset's analysis, because of the quality both of the theory and the empirical evidence, soon became a seminal piece of research. Many other students followed up on his work, seeking to test it in other circumstances, or to refine the general thesis he provided.[49] Others sought to improve on the measure of democracy itself.[50] And still others tried to disentangle the statistical association between economic development and democracy that Lipset had uncovered, seeking to determine more precisely the sequence whereby the elements of democracy came into place.[51] Yet, for all the work and research that tested Lipset's discovery, his basic thesis remained unchallenged: Democratic states were more apt to be characterized by high levels of economic development than authoritarian states.

There remained some questions that could not be answered. In particular, a number of critics pointed out that Lipset had not actually demonstrated the historical sequence that led from the growth of the economy to the development of democratic government. How, in fact, they asked, did this work? Democratic governments do not simply arise overnight with the growth of wealth. There had to be more to the story, they suggested, more to the detailed history that led from one set of circumstances, economic development, to the other, the emergence of democratic regimes. It took a few years, but soon there would be a major examination that would help to provide more details on the story.

Barrington Moore on Democracy and Oligarchy in the Modern World

Barrington Moore, Jr., like Seymour Martin Lipset, was a sociologist. At the time of the publication of what would become a seminal piece of research, Moore was best known as an analyst and student of the Soviet government. Soon he became known as the scholar who would put the thesis of the link between economic growth and democracy to a rigorous historical test by providing the kind of detailed inquiry that Lipset did not.

Moore approached the task somewhat differently than Lipset had.[52] Unlike Lipset who subjected a number of countries to a broad quantitative examination, Moore instead chose to focus on several countries in depth. They were: England, France, Russia, Germany, Japan, India, China, and the United States. By focusing only on these countries, which included the range of political regimes from democratic to fascist and authoritarian, Moore was able to address the same kinds of questions as Lipset, but also to focus more closely on the sequence and patterning of historical events. In addition, Moore brought to his examination a set of theoretical tools taken directly from the workshelf of Karl Marx. He focused intensively on the nature of the social classes of the different countries, ranging from the landed upper classes to the bourgeoisie; he also focused on the relations between the royal authority and the various social classes. And, perhaps most significantly, he took account of the coalitions and alliances that occurred between different social classes, assuming that such alliances might play a role in the eventual forms of statehood of different countries. This last was a key ingredient to his analysis.

In the course of his work, Moore soon uncovered several key conditions that promoted the growth of democracy. The first of these was the emergence of a balance of power between the principal social groups in a society, a balance that reduced the possibilities of too powerful a royal authority or too strong a landed upper class.[53] The classic illustration for this conclusion came from English history. The ascending social groups in the seventeenth century managed to make the king subordinate to parliament, and by the close of the nineteenth century, the manufacturing classes had overtaken the landed ones in both economic and political resources. French history illustrated a considerably different chain of events. The royal authority remained dominant far longer but was overthrown far more abruptly, leaving the balance among groups to be worked out through a long and difficult struggle in the nineteenth century.

A second major condition that produced democracy in the twentieth century was the development of commercial agriculture by some social groups within a country. This provided a way for promoting the growth of a class of capitalists whose power eventually counteracted that of urban manufacturing groups. That power also gradually displaced the peasants from the land, which proved to be an indispensable event in undercutting the seeds of peasant revolution, as the cases of China and the former Soviet Union show.

The third condition he uncovered, the absence of a coalition between an equally powerful landed aristocracy and capitalist class, clearly suggested why democracy first arose in France but failed to do so in Germany until much later. In France, the Revolution of 1789 and its immediate aftermath dramatically reduced the power of the landed aristocracy and left the expanding bourgeois groups, both the financial and the manufacturing capitalists, to develop unhindered by a declining aristocracy's claims to social and economic glory long past.[54] In Germany, the landed aristocracy, the Junkers, remained dominant well through the nineteenth century and succeeded in manipulating the destinies of both manufacturing classes and peasants alike.[55]

By contrast, those nation-states that produced forms of fascism or communism in the twentieth century—Germany, Italy, and Japan—took entirely different routes to their political outcomes. For example, in Germany and Japan, the landed upper classes remained a strong and vital force well through the nineteenth century and were never eclipsed by the industrial capitalists as in England. Indeed, the landed elites in these societies were sufficiently adept to have manipulated the growth of industrialism; they delayed its rise at first and later exercised considerable political control over its beneficiaries, the industrial capitalists. In so doing, they prevented a balance of power, a condition that was so crucial to the flowering of democracy in England and France.

As to the conditions that helped to promote the rise of communism in the twentieth century, Moore found that unlike those countries in which parliamentary democracy arose, the nation-states that would turn to communism entered the twentieth century still comprised of a large and significant force of peasants. Thus, such societies were compelled to deal with the peasants either through outright repression or through enlisting their aid in fundamental political change; the former route proved characteristic of fascism, the latter of communism. In Russia and China, the landed upper classes failed to become involved in commercial agriculture. This meant, among other things, that they were only able to secure their own livelihood through an increasingly harsh oppression of the peasants and that, partly in consequence, they came to appear both to those below and to those above them as a parasitic and retrogressive class. While landlords in Germany continued into the twentieth century to secure the respect of the peasants and thus contributed to the growth of fascism, those in China and Russia succeeded only in attracting their anger and thus promoting a peasant revolution. At the same time, the peasant revolutions in China and Russia were aided by the retention from an earlier period of an active solidarity and cooperation among the peasants.

Moore's work quickly became recognized as a major *tour de force*, the first of the great modern works in comparative historical sociology. Many claimed that it was a far better work of comparative sociology than that of Lipset. Still, it came in for its own set of criticisms. One of Moore's most brilliant students, Theda Skocpol (see our discussion of Skocpol in Chapter 3), had a number of penetrating criticisms of Moore's work.[56] For one thing, she argued, Moore had suggested several different routes to democratic regimes, but only one way to achieve a form of dictatorship, whether fascist or communist. Were there not also alternate routes to such regimes as well? she asked. In addition, she pointed out that Moore possessed a relatively primitive notion of political authority, as lodged in the crown or royal authority, when, in fact, there existed major bureaucratic administrations in each of the nations he examined. Such administrations, she argued, could themselves play a more decisive role in nation-building than Moore had acknowledged. Finally, and most important, Skocpol argued that Moore only had studied the internal features of nation-states, neglecting the position of the nation-state in a larger international setting. Such a setting, she insisted, could play a major role in determining the paths that countries took to nationhood, especially in determining the conditions that might unsettle emerging states. Later, in her own work, she would use that insight fruitfully, showing, in particular, how substantial losses in war preceded the revolutions that happened in such countries as Russia (see the discussion of Skocpol's work on revolutions in Chapter 4).

But other questions also remain unanswered in Moore's analysis. In particular, one was left to wonder how to square Moore's results with those of Lipset. Lipset had argued that economic growth promoted the expansion and development of a strong middle class—the bourgeoisie, in effect—that encouraged the development of democracy. But Moore had shown that economic development did not promote democracy by leading to a vigorous and strong bourgeoisie. Rather, it was a more complex chain of events that led to democracy, including especially an emerging balance of power among the various social classes. Such a balance between the major contending groups, prevented, among other things, too much power from accumulating in the hands either of the royal authority or of the landed upper classes. How could one square the results of Lipset's analysis with those of Moore? Both works were seminal. Both showed the links between economic development and the emergence of democracy, but from that point their stories went off in different directions.

Dietrich Rueschemeyer, Evelyne Huber Stephens, and John Stephens on Capitalism and the Development of Democracy

Another group of social scientists would offer the solution to the disparity. Their work would combine the breadth of Lipset's review with the depth of Moore's historical inquiry. Dietrich Rueschemeyer, a sociologist well-known for his contributions to state-centered theory, and two political science colleagues, Evelyne Huber Stephens and John Stephens, picked up the thread of the argument at the point at which Lipset and Moore seemed to disagree. They note:

> We are convinced that the main finding of the cross-national statistical work (Lipset's)—a positive, though not perfect, correlation between capitalist development and democracy—must stand as an accepted result. . . . At the same

time, such a correlation does not carry its own explanation. Nor can it account for how the same end can be reached by different routes.[57]

What the three social scientists did, then, was to try to reconcile the apparently disparate discoveries by undertaking an intensive historical analysis of the kind done by Moore, coupled with a study of a number of different countries, many of which had been previously examined by Lipset. By combining the best of both methods, they hoped finally to achieve a more complete understanding of what it might take to lay the social and economic foundations for democratic regimes, on the one hand, and authoritarian and totalitarian regimes, on the other.

They approached their project with enormous theoretical and methodological care and precision. They began by offering a clear, though conventional, definition of democracy. Democratic governments, they suggested, consisted of each of the following elements: regular, free, and fair elections in a system of universal suffrage; responsibility of the state apparatus to the parliament; and basic citizen rights such as the freedom of expression and association.[58] Authoritarian governments were those, they claimed, that lacked the first two elements, whereas totalitarian regimes lacked all three. The countries they chose to study included those of the advanced capitalist nations of Europe, such as France and Great Britain, as well as the newer nations of Latin America, the Caribbean, and Central America. As each scholar was an expert on each of these regions, in combination their expert knowledge covered a great range of the world's major countries. Finally, they developed a theoretical scheme that was very similar to that of Moore, but which also added important new elements. For instance, they included sustained attention to the development of the working class, believing that such a class could play a more important role, especially in the twentieth century, than either Lipset or Moore had believed. In addition, they gave much greater weight to the autonomy of the state, something that both Lipset and Moore had failed to do.

After extensive and detailed case-by-case analyses of the various nations, they reached a number of important conclusions—conclusions that today represent the best evidence we have on the conditions that can lead either to democratic or to nondemocratic outcomes. They confirmed one of Moore's most important discoveries, that "[l]arge landlords, particularly those who are dependent on a large supply of cheap labor, consistently emerged as the most anti-democratic force [among all forces]."[59] They also found, contrary both to Moore and to Lipset, that it was not the middle class, or bourgeoisie, that was most critical to the emergence of democratic governments, but rather the working class. The working class, as both a force of class power, and as mobilized through a range of organizations and associations, such as trades unions, proved absolutely pivotal to the creation of democratic regimes. Here, in a nutshell, is the heart of their findings:

> [C]apitalist development weakens the landed upper class and strengthens the working class as well as other subordinate classes. The respective positions of the bourgeoisie and the working class show that capitalism creates democratic pressures in spite of capitalists, not because of them. Democracy was the outcome of the contradictory nature of capitalist development, which, of necessity, created subordinate classes, particularly the working class, with the capacity for self-organization. Capitalism brings the subordinate class or classes together in factories and cities where members of those classes can associate and organize more easily; it improves the means of communication and transportation facilitating nationwide organization; in these other ways it strengthens civil society and facilitates subordinate class organization.[60]

Their major findings about the respective paths to democratic regimes, in other words, reinforce two critical theoretical lessons to which we have been drawn time and again in this book: (1) that capitalism fosters the growth of the working class and its own class organizations through a variety of devices, much as Karl Marx originally expected; and (2) that class power must be linked, at the same time, to a strong infrastructure of mediating organizations, which serve as the vehicle for grounding and channeling the political energies of the working class, a lesson on the importance of a strong civil society that emerged first in the writings both of Emile Durkheim and Alexis de Tocqueville.

Drawing the various strands of these different pieces of research together, it is clear that economic development is intimately linked to the establishment of democratic governments, much as both Lipset and Moore maintained, but for reasons different from those they suggested. The economic development of the past helped to produce an array of different social classes, among them, a strong landed upper class, a strong peasantry, and a working class. If the landed upper classes were limited in their exercise of power, and the working class were able to develop its own organizational resources, then democratic governments were likely to emerge. But if the landed upper class were able to concentrate too much power in its own hands, aided by a compliant state apparatus, and if the peasantry and working class were too weak to provide vigorous resistance, then either authoritarian or totalitarian regimes would be the end result.

It is likely that one final question might remain for you, the reader. What bearing do these results from the past have on our ability to predict the conditions necessary for democracies to emerge in the future? Historical circumstances have changed. The nature of the world's economy has become altered as we enter the twenty-first century. What social, or economic, conditions might promote, and sustain, democracies in the twenty-first century? At a minimum, it is clear that there must be a balance of power among contending social classes in the emerging nations. And it also is clear that there must be a strong civil society. But the international order is likely to have some impact on the outcomes as well. And it is to the views of that order, offered by sociologists, that we now turn.

SUCCESS AND FAILURE IN NATION-BUILDING: THE INTERDEPENDENCE OF NATION-STATES

One of the major issues in the study of nation-building is why some societies achieve great success in creating a modern nation-state whereas others accomplish next to nothing. The concern really comes down to two distinct and related matters: one, how to define the features of success, and two, how to assess the origins of success. The definition of successful nation-building presents some very difficult problems. Some observers, for instance, prefer the notion of political order, or stability, as the criterion of success and, thus, describe the successful nation-state as one in which there is no instability or violence. Others prefer the notion of change and upheaval as the criterion of success, particularly where current governments appear to be extremely oppressive of citizens' civil and political freedoms. Looking at nation-building from a slightly different angle, still other observers prefer to think of success as anything that resembles the democratic regimes of Western Europe or the United States. They, too, have their critics who believe that successful nation-building requires the erection of a socialist regime such as the People's Republic of China. These and many other issues plague the conceptual definition and empirical identification of success in nation-building.

For my purposes here, I shall define success in nation-building in the same terms I used at the outset of this chapter—the features of the modern nation-state as synthesized by Black. In particular, a successful outcome of nation-building is a nation-state in which policy making has become consolidated and routine, there is some regular means of replenishing political leadership, the interests of the citizens regularly receive recognition from political leaders, and there exists a complex and active machinery of the state. Failure, thus, means the absence of at least one of these conditions; more often, it seems, failure entails the absence of two or more of these conditions.

What is it, then, that accounts for the success of some societies in achieving the qualities of the modern nation-state as compared with the failure of others? The immediate answer might have something to do with time. Some societies, particularly those of Africa, simply have not had the benefit of several centuries during which they could erect a viable nation-state. However, as current theories and evidence inform us, the principal obstacle to success lies not in the realm of time but in a system of economic interdependence among advanced and developing nation-states. It is this system that accounts for the great political accomplishments of some societies and the tragic failures of others.

The conception of interdependence among societies actually comes in a variety of shapes and sizes, but all of them touch on practical and theoretical issues first dealt with by Karl Marx and later embellished by Max Weber. The most influential proponent of it today is Immanuel Wallerstein.[61] Wallerstein argues for the existence of a world-system. This system had its beginnings in the transformation of agriculture from that for use to that for profit in sixteenth-century Europe. This world-system is one in which some countries, the core states, are dominant over others, the peripheral and semiperipheral territories; the dominant ones receive a greater share of material and symbolic tribute in the world mainly because they contribute more than others to the survival and expansion of the system. It is a system whose foundations lie in a world-economy that had its origins in capitalist agriculture but that over time has changed in the forms of technology it employs as well as the products it creates.

Nation-states, in the world-system perspective, represent a narrower social expanse than the classes that develop from the economic mode of production; that is, the situations and interests of the classes spill over the boundaries of those entities conventionally regarded as nation-states, such as England, France, Belgium, and Italy. Those people who sit in positions of control of state machinery—the kings, the queens, the ministers—still represent major actors in the world-system, but over the long haul they are subordinate to the capitalist class that sits in positions of control in the world-economy.

As in any such system, there exists in the modern world a vast network of ties that link parts to one another and on whose continued survival the existence of the system itself depends. The network of ties is evident in specific forms of economic trade, political relations, and social exchanges that flow from one country to another. Moreover, there exists in the world-system a social division of labor in which those individuals in the labor force of a single country and those in the labor forces of other countries may perform different functions; for instance, the labor force in one country might engage principally in the production of raw materials, such as minerals, whereas labor in another might engage mainly in the manufacture of final products, such as clothing. The capitalist class resides within those countries in which the principal control of the productive enterprise is located, and garners for itself and for its nation-states the major forms and amounts of wealth.

This world-system is not a creature that remains dormant, but one that has over the past five hundred years grown ever larger. The world-economy, which represents the heart of the system, is responsible ultimately for the expansion of the world-system. As technology expands and becomes more sophisticated, for instance, the boundaries and the content of the economy incorporate more and more territories into the system as well as more and more individuals within distinct countries. Manufacture for profit represents the force that drives the economy to expand. As the system expands, its constituent units may change in the degree of their importance to the system and hence in the position they occupy in the world-system of stratification. For example, individual countries can change in their position of dominance from one century to another, representing a core state at one time and a peripheral territory at another.

From the sixteenth through the twentieth centuries, those countries that have represented the dominant positions (core states) in the world-system have been those of Northwestern Europe, particularly England and France, where capitalist agriculture first appeared. Those countries and territories that occupied the subordinate niches lay elsewhere, specifically in the Americas, in Africa, and in Asia. Over the five centuries, positions of dominance shifted, particularly within great regions, but the overall structure of dominance, the hierarchy of positions within the world division of labor, retained its original form, which was first established in the sixteenth century.

In light of this grand conception, it should be easy for the reader to answer the question about the origins of successful nation-building in the twentieth century. Why have some societies been less successful in establishing the accouterments of modern nation-states than others? They have occupied subordinate positions in the modern world-system or, more precisely, the modern world-economy. Whereas some nation-states, mainly those in Northwestern Europe, long ago established positions of dominance as core states in this system, others—now regarded as "developing" nations—at the very same time became junior members of this system, and so they remain to this very day.[62]

What are the network and hierarchy of relations that relegate some countries to the top position and others to mere followers? Concrete facts come to us from those scholars who have articulated this grand conception in whole or in part. At the turn of this century, for instance, J. A. Hobson published *Imperialism,* in which he tried to show how the nation-states of Western Europe, particularly England, had established economic dominance over those elsewhere in the world, particularly in Asia and Africa. Capitalism in Europe had worked through the auspices of the state machinery—the government—to control territories that were essential to its own success. Moreover, an important distinction existed between colonialism and imperialism:

> This recent imperial expansion stands entirely distinct from the colonization of sparsely peopled lands in temperate zones, where white colonists carry with them the modes of government, the industrial and other arts of civilization of the mother country. The "occupation" of these new territories was comprised in the presence of a small minority of white men, officials, traders, and industrial organizers, exercising political and economic sway over great hordes of

> population regarded as inferior and as incapable of exercising any considerable rights of self-government, in politics or industry.[63]

The imperialism of the Western European countries cast a wide net over the entire world and embraced lands of people that came to serve merely as the resources and as the labor force of the great capitalist machine. Most significant, at least from the perspective here, Hobson went into great historical detail to show that the domination of the imperialist countries wreaked havoc on the indigenous political structures of the subordinate territories and crippled them to such an extent as to make success at nation-building, in the terms previously outlined, an impossibility for years to come.[64]

Because colonialism insists on the political character of subordination, and imperialism insists on its economic tone, the end to colonialism in the 1950s and 1960s did not free the former colonies to become independent, not at least in this scheme of things. The network of interdependence among core states and peripheries continued to exist and to undermine the capacity of former colonies to achieve actual economic and political self-sufficiency. Harry Magdoff provides a more recent rendering of facts and analysis to support this aspect of the conception of a world-economy and world-system; his discussion echoes many of the themes first sounded by Hobson.[65] Magdoff claims that a new form of imperialism arose with the end of World War II in which the United States came to replace England as the major figure of economic and political strength, competition among capitalists quickened in pace, and corporations expanded both their size and the territorial scope of their operations.[66] Corporations in the United States as well as financial institutions enlarged the extent of their investments abroad and ultimately changed the position of the United States and England in the world-economy. Magdoff maintains, moreover, that the various programs of the United States government assist in securing the economic dominance of North American corporations abroad by establishing, among other things, a deficit in the balance of payments for foreign countries, particularly former colonies, and providing the United States with unhampered access to raw materials of the subordinate countries. Like Hobson's analysis of England, Magdoff's analysis insists that the effort of the United States to secure economic dominance over other nations has major political repercussions; the effort severely, if not entirely, reduces the likelihood that the subordinate nation can develop a viable state apparatus of the sort outlined earlier.

The conception of a world-economy has been used to special advantage to explain why particular countries and settings may fail in the creation of a viable nation-state. One such setting is Latin America. André Gunder Frank, for example, has used a conception much like the one previously presented to explain the current economic and political dependence of Latin American countries on the United States.[67] It is Frank's belief that a system of dependence originated in the sixteenth century and that this system has

TABLE 10-2 Foreign Investments of Leading Capital Exporting Countries

	1914	1930 Percent of Total	1960
United Kingdom	50.3	43.8	24.5
France	22.2	8.4	4.7[a]
Germany	17.3	2.6	1.1
Netherlands	3.1	5.5	4.2[a]
Sweden	0.3	1.3	0.9[a]
United States	6.3	35.3	59.1
Canada	0.5	3.1	5.5
Total	100	100	100

[a]The data for 1960 are estimates made solely to simplify the presentation on the relative change of the U.S. position.

Source: Adapted from Harry Magdoff, *The Age of Imperialism: The Economics of U.S. Foreign Policy* (New York: Monthly Review Press, 1969). By permission of the publisher.

been gradually modified, largely to meet the changing economic needs and interests of the dominant countries. Those countries in Latin America that display economic underdevelopment as well as atrophied politics, Frank maintains, owe their failures to the dominant nation-states. To provide some confirmation for his point of view, Frank shows that when the economic ties between the dominant and the subordinate nation-states weaken, as during the Depression of the 1930s, then the subordinate nations become considerably more successful in cultivating indigenous forms of economic production. Other support for his claims lies in evidence that reveals that even during periods when the United States proclaimed its effort to provide great financial aid to Latin America, as in the 1960s, it succeeded in extracting considerably more capital out of Latin America than it invested in it.

There are other perspectives on the success and failure of nation-building in the modern world that grew out of careful observations of the

TABLE 10-3

	(Billions of Dollars) Europe	Canada	Latin America	All Other Areas
Flow of direct investments from U.S.	$8.1	$6.8	$3.8	$5.2
Income on this capital transferred to U.S.	5.5	5.9	11.3	14.3
Net	+$2.6	+$ .9	−$7.5	−$9.1

Source: Adapted from Harry Magdoff, *The Age of Imperialism: The Economics of U.S. Foreign Policy* (New York: Monthly Review Press, 1969). By permission of the publisher.

nation-building efforts of Asian and African countries in the 1950s and 1960s. None of these views does as well in explaining successful nation-building as the general conception of a world-system. Nevertheless, this conception is not without its drawbacks. Several observers have noted that Wallerstein, its most influential proponent, does not give adequate credence to the role of nation-states in the struggles over trade and other issues in the world-system, and that his view lacks an overall understanding of the system of states in the world that predated the emergence of modern capitalism.[68] Still, his conception is, at this time, clearly the most promising, and certainly has created the largest body of adherents among contemporary students of nation-building in the world.

GLOBALISM AND NATION-BUILDING IN THE TWENTY-FIRST CENTURY

Today's world is vastly different from the one at the beginning of the twentieth century. Indeed, it is vastly different from the one of only two to three decades ago. An emerging global economy is taking shape. Though the outlines are by no means now clear, certain facts are evident. High technology goods and industries are now becoming the major items for production by a number of countries. They have displaced the older forms of production, particularly those of consumption goods and heavy machinery. Communism, as a form of exercising control over the market by the state, seems clearly to be on its last legs. But while the free market economy is booming, it is also evident that there are problems with it. Large numbers of people, even in the most productive and affluent of societies, remain on the edges of poverty. And there are deep economic problems even in some of the most successful of recent nations. Japan struggles to free itself of a decade-long deep recession. This has created many internal problems, not the least of which is a declining morale (and increasing suicide rates) among its many citizens.

How will these conditions, plus many others, bear upon the construction and development of nation-states in the future? We have seen how certain conditions are key to the development of the new democracies, conditions such as a strong and substantial civil order of groups and associations. But, at the same time, the old boundaries and barriers between nations, and thus the conditions that made one nation different from the others, seem to be disappearing. The new European Union gives cause for hope and change in Western Europe. In the making now, virtually ever since the end of World War II, it offers promise to the European nations that, as a collective group, they can remain strong and powerful players in the new global economy. But what will happen to the old nation-states that compose it? We already have addressed one such question: the matter of widespread immigration and the issue of citizenship. This will continue to be an issue, both for transnational alignments like that of the European Union and for the older nation-states. And such powerful trends as increasing migration will only make it ever more important for transnational bodies to begin to rethink the matter of citizenship, particular the matter of rights in a world that has become smaller.

The global economy has also become an ever more competitive market. It appears to take more capital, and also more nurturing from the state, to create productive domestic markets for countries. How can the laggards in this process, particularly those destitute nations in Africa, hope to catch up? It is likely that in these circumstances it will take decided new policies, both by the developed nations of the world, like the United States, and groups like the International Monetary Fund, to provide the necessary capital boost to help such countries on the way to nationhood. Many challenges now stand in their way. Among them the most pressing are those that we have not treated much in this book, save for our discussions of the welfare state. In particular, there is massive poverty throughout much of Africa right now. AIDS is a major problem for African nations. People die far too young; most infants never reach adulthood. How can new nation-states under these conditions ever hope to become productive enterprises?

There will be different answers to these questions depending on one's own point of view. World-system analysts, for example, will continue to insist that dependent relations between the core states and the peripheral states will keep such nations as those in Africa in a condition of dependency into the indefinite future. But other analysts, especially those that focus their attention on the specific conditions necessary to promote democratic governments, will furnish a different set of answers. They will point to the need to establish strong civil associations. They also will point to the need to foster a balance of power among contending social classes. Most important, they will point to the need to do what it takes to create a productive economy. Today it appears to take more than ever before. One can only hope that both farsighted elites, and the social movements that organize and assemble from below, will help to keep the world's attention on these very urgent problems.

NOTES

1. Charles Tilly, *Coercion, Capital, and European States, AD 990–1990* (Cambridge, Massachusetts: Basil Blackwell, 1990).
2. C.E. Black, *The Dynamics of Modernization* (New York: Harper & Row Publishers, Inc., 1966). For other excellent writings on these matters see also Reinhard

Bendix, *Nation-Building and Citizenship* (Berkeley: University of California Press, 1977), and Charles Tilly (editor), *The Formation of National States in Western Europe* (Princeton, New Jersey: Princeton University Press, 1975).

3. Ibid., p. 13.
4. Ibid., p. 14.
5. For good general treatments of the state, see: Bertrand Badie and Pierre Birnbaum, *The Sociology of the State,* translated by Arthur Goldhammer (Chicago: University of Chicago Press, 1983); Martin Carnoy, *The State and Political Theory* (Princeton, New Jersey: Princeton University Press, 1984); and Gianfranco Poggi, *The Development of the Modern State: A Sociological Introduction* (Stanford: Stanford University Press, 1978).
6. For example, see the following: Black, *The Dynamics of Modernization*; T.H. Marshall, Part I in T.H. Marshall and Tom Bottomore, *Citizenship and Social Class and Other Essays* (London: Pluto Press, 1992); Eric A. Nordlinger, "Political Development: Time Sequences and Rate of Change," in *Politics and Society: Studies in Comparative Political Sociology*, ed. Eric A. Nordlinger (Englewood Cliffs, New Jersey: Prentice-Hall, Inc., 1970), pp. 329–47; and Sidney Verba, "Sequences and Development," in *Crises and Sequences in Political Development*, ed. Leonard Binder et al. (Princeton, New Jersey: Princeton University Press, 1971), pp. 283–316.
7. Hans Daalder, "Parties, Elites, and Political Development in Western Europe," in *Mass Politics in Industrial Societies: A Reader in Comparative Politics*, ed. Giuseppe Di Palma (Chicago: Markham Publishing Company, 1972), pp. 4–36.
8. Ibid., p. 12.
9. For some useful critiques of the notion of modernization, or modernity, see any of the following: Joseph Gusfield, "Tradition and Modernity: Misplaced Polarities in the Study of Social Change," in *Political Development and Social Change*, 2nd edition, ed. Jason L. Finkle and Richard W. Gable (New York: John Wiley and Sons, 1971), pp. 15–26; Mark Kesselman, "Order or Movement? The Literature of Political Development as Ideology," *World Politics*, 26 (October 1973), 139–54; Alejandro Portes, "On the Sociology of National Development: Theories and Issues," *American Journal of Sociology*, 82 (July 1976), 55–85; and Lucian Pye, "The Concept of Political Development," in *Political Development and Social Change*, Finkle and Gable, pp. 83–91.
10. Clifford Geertz, *The Interpretation of Cultures* (New York: Basic Books, Inc., Publishers, 1973), pp. 251–52.
11. Louis Hartz, *The Liberal Tradition in America: An Interpretation of American Political Thought Since the Revolution* (New York: Harcourt Brace Jovanovich, Inc., 1955).
12. Seymour Martin Lipset, *The First New Nation* (Garden City, New York: Doubleday Anchor, 1967), pp. 177–80.
13. Liah Greenfeld, *Nationalism: Five Roads to Modernity* (Cambridge, Massachusetts: Harvard University Press, 1992).
14. Ibid., p. 18.
15. Ibid., p. 51.

16. Ibid., p. 369.
17. Ibid., p. 409.
18. Jurgen Habermas, *Communication and the Evolution of Society*, translated by Thomas McCarthy (Boston: Beacon Press, 1979).
19. Samuel P. Huntington, *Political Order in Changing Societies* (New Haven, Connecticut: Yale University Press, 1968).
20. Ivo K. Feierabend, Rosalind L. Feierabend, and Betty A. Nesvold, "Social Change and Political Violence: Cross-National Patterns," in *Political Development and Social Change*, Finkle and Gable, pp. 569–604.
21. Paul R. Brass, "Political Participation, Institutionalization and Stability in India," *Government and Opposition*, 4 (Winter 1969), pp. 23–53.
22. Marshall, ibid., p. 18.
23. Rogers Brubaker, *Citizenship and Nationhood in France and Germany* (Cambridge, Massachusetts; Harvard University Press, 1992).
24. Yasemin Soysal, *Limits to Citizenship* (Chicago: University of Chicago Press, 1994).
25. Christian Joppke, "How Immigration is Changing Citizenship: A Comparative View," *American Sociological Association Meetings*, Chicago, Illinois, August 1999, 43 pp.
26. For a collection of articles that provides some depth as well as variety to this discussion on citizenship in European nations, see *Citizenship, Nationality and Migration in Europe*, David Cesarani and Mary Fulbrook, eds. (London and New York: Routledge, 1996).
27. W.W. Rostow, "The Take-Off into Self-Sustained Growth," in *Political Development and Social Change*, ed. Finkle and Gable, pp. 141–61.
28. On the story of these four Asian countries, see Ezra F. Vogel, *The Four Little Dragons: The Spread of Industrialization in East Asia* (Cambridge, Massachusetts: Harvard University Press, 1991), and also Frederic C. Deyo, *Beneath the Miracle: Labor Subordination in the New Asian Industrialism* (Berkeley: University of California Press, 1989).
29. Peter Evans, *Embedded Autonomy: States & Industrial Transformation* (Princeton, New Jersey: Princeton University Press, 1995).
30. Ibid., p. 126.
31. Peter Evans and James E. Rauch, "Analysis of 'Weberian' State Structures and Economic Growth," *American Sociological Review*, 64 (October 1999), 748–65.
32. Robert Wade, *Governing the Market: Economic Theory and the Role of Government in East Asian Industrialization* (Princeton, New Jersey: Princeton University Press, 1990).
33. On various analyses of these sorts of leaders, see for instance, Black, *Dynamics of Modernization*, pp. 9–13; 62–89; and Lipset, *The First New Nation*, pp. 75–85. For slightly different perspectives on these leaders, see Reinhard Bendix, "Charismatic Leadership," in *State and Society: A Reader in Comparative Political Sociology*, ed. Reinhard Bendix et al. (Boston: Little, Brown and Co., 1969), pp. 616–29; and Reinhard Bendix, "A Case Study in Cultural and Educational

Mobility: Japan and the Protestant Ethic," in *Social Structure and Mobility in Economic Development*, ed. Neil J. Smelser and Seymour Martin Lipset (Chicago: Aldine Publishing Co., 1966), pp. 626–79.

34. Edward A. Shils, "The Intellectuals in the Political Development of the New States," in *Political Development and Social Change*, Finkle and Gable, pp. 249–76.
35. Ibid., p. 257.
36. Hannah Arendt, *The Origins of Totalitarianism* (Cleveland, Ohio: The World Publishing Co., 1958), chapter 8 especially.
37. Morris Janowitz, *The Military in the Political Development of New Nations* (Chicago: University of Chicago Press, 1964).
38. See George A. Kourvetaris and Betty A. Dobratz, "The Present State and Development of Sociology of the Military," *Journal of Political and Military Sociology*, 4 (Spring 1976), 91–92 as well as the many references cited therein.
39. Huntington, *Political Order in Changing Societies*, Chapter 4.
40. Ibid., p. 205.
41. Ibid., p. 221.
42. Ibid., pp. 279–300.
43. Eric R. Wolf, *Peasant Wars of the Twentieth Century* (New York: Harper & Row, Publishers, 1969).
44. Ibid., p. 295.
45. Ibid., pp. 290–91.
46. Ibid., p. 294.
47. Seymour Martin Lipset, "Social Requisites of Democracy," *American Political Science Review*, 53 (March 1959), 69–105; also Seymour Martin Lipset, *Political Man: The Social Bases of Politics* (Garden City, New York: Doubleday Anchor, 1959), Chapter 2.
48. Lipset, *Political Man*, p. 66.
49. For the most comprehensive recent discussions of these issues in the work of Lipset, see Gary Marks and Larry Diamond eds., *Reexamining Democracy: Essays in Honor of Seymour Martin Lipset* (Newbury Park, California: Sage Publications, 1992), especially the excellent chapter by Larry Diamond, "Economic Development and Democracy Reconsidered," pp. 93–139. This last chapter has an extensive bibliography on all the recent writings and developments that grew out of Lipset's original work.
50. Kenneth Bollen, "Issues in the Comparative Measurement of Political Democracy," *American Sociological Review*, 45 (June 1980), 370–90.
51. Kenneth Bollen, "Political Democracy and the Timing of Development," *American Sociological Review*, 44 (August 1979), 572–87.
52. Barrington Moore, Jr., *The Social Origins of Dictatorship and Democracy: Lord and Peasant in the Making of the Modern World* (Boston, Massachusetts: Beacon Press, 1966).
53. Ibid., p. 430.
54. Alexis de Tocqueville's analysis of this matter still remains among the most penetrating. See Alexis de Tocqueville, *The Old Regime and the French Revolution*,

translated by Gilbert Stuart (Garden City, New York: Doubleday Anchor, 1955), as well as our discussion of his view in Chapter 4.

55. For other details on the political significance of the Junkers, see, for instance, Reinhard Bendix, *Max Weber: An Intellectual Portrait* (Garden City, New York: Doubleday Anchor, 1960), pp. 42–45, especially; and W.N. Medlicott, *Bismarck and Modern Germany* (New York: Harper & Row, Publishers, 1965).
56. Theda Skocpol, "A Critical Review of Barrington Moore's *Social Origins of Dictatorship and Democracy*," *Politics and Society*, 12 (1973).
57. Dietrich Rueschemeyer, Evelyne Huber Stephens, and John D. Stephens, *Capitalist Development & Democracy* (Chicago: University of Chicago Press, 1992), p. 4.
58. Ibid. p. 43.
59. Ibid., p. 270.
60. Ibid., pp. 271–72.
61. Wallerstein has written many works that detail his perspective on the modern world-system. The most comprehensive view is to be obtained from his three-volume work, *The Modern World System* (Orlando, Florida: Academic Press, 1974–1989).
62. There are any number of good works that help to explain and explore the nature of the capitalist world system in greater detail. See, for instance, Thomas D. Hall, "World-System Theory," *Annual Review of Sociology*, 8 (1982), 81–106; Christopher Chase-Dunn, "Interstate System and Capitalist World-Economy: One Logic or Two?" *International Studies Quarterly*, 25 (March 1981), 19–42; Daniel Garst, "Wallerstein and His Critics," *Theory and Society*, 14 (1985), 469–95; and Theda Skocpol, "Wallerstein's World Capitalist System: A Theoretical and Historical Critique," *American Journal of Sociology*, 82 (September 1979), 1075–90.
63. J.A. Hobson, *Imperialism* (Ann Arbor, Michigan: University of Michigan Press, 1965) p. 27.
64. Ibid., Part II, Chapter 1. Incidentally, Lenin, in one of his most famous works, *Imperialism: The Highest State of Capitalism*, was greatly influenced by Hobson's analysis. See our discussion of Lenin in Chapter 2.
65. Harry Magdoff, *The Age of Imperialism: The Economics of U.S. Foreign Policy* (New York: Modern Reader Paperbacks, 1969).
66. Ibid., pp. 15–26; 34–40.
67. Andre Gunder Frank, *Capitalism and Underdevelopment in Latin America*, revised edition (New York: Monthly Review Press, 1969).
68. See, for example, Skocpol, ibid., "Wallerstein's World Capitalist System."

Credits

Page 8 epigraph: Karl Marx, *Capital,* Volume 1, translated from the Third German ed. by Samuel Moore and Edward Aveling and edited by Frederick Engels. Moscow: Foreign Languages Publishing House, 1961. Page 38 epigraph: Max Weber, "Politics as a Vocation," in H. H. Gerton and C. Wright Mills (eds.), FROM MAX WEBER: ESSAYS IN SOCIOLOGY. © 1958 Oxford University Press. Used with permission of the publisher. Page 64 epigraph: Reprinted with the permission of The Free Press, a Division of Simon & Schuster, Inc., from THE RULES OF SOCIOLOGICAL METHOD by Emile Durkheim. Translated by W. D. Halls. Edited with an Introduction by Steven Lukes. Copyright © 1982 by Steven Lukes. Translation, Copyright © 1982 by Macmillan Press Ltd. Page 91 first epigraph: Reprinted from Jean Jacques Rousseau, "The Social Contract," in *The Essential Rousseau,* trans. Lowell Bair. Copyright © 1974 New Americam Library. By permission of the publisher. Page 91 second epigraph: Reprinted from Niccolò Machiavelli, *The Prince,* trans. and ed. Thomas G. Bergin. Copyright © 1947 AHM Publishing Corp., Arlington Heights, Ill. By permission of the publisher. Page 175 epigraph: Adapted from James Madison, "Federalist Paper Number 10," in Alexander Hamilton, James Madison, and John Jay, *The Federalist Papers,* with an introduction by Clinton Rossiter. Copyright © 1961 New American Library. By permission of the publisher Page 210 epigraph: V. I. Lenin, *What Is to Be Done?* Copyright © 1943 International Publishers.

Index

A

Abortion, 201
Abramson, Paul, 197
ABSCAM, 124
Acceptance, 236–237
Activists, 212
Administration, 45–46
Adorno, Theodor, 29
Advantages, 236–237
Advertising, 204, 230–231
Affirmative action, 77, 141–142
Africa, 105, 273, 279
African Americans. *See also* Affirmative action; Ethnic groups; Race; Underclass
  and equality, 137, 139–140, 142
  political participation, 215, 222–223, 227–228, 237
  and political parties, 216
  and religion, 232
  social network, 232
Age factors, 194, 201
Agents, 34
Agriculture, 255, 268, 274. *See also* Peasants
AIDS, 279
Alexander, Jeffrey, 79
Alford, Robert, 196–197, 238
Algeria, 261
Alienation
  and bureaucracy, 41, 42
  Marcuse view, 30
  Marxian view, 12
  Weber view, 41, 42
Alliances, 268–270
Allocational policies, 153
Althusser, Louis, 25, 32
American Association of University Professors, 236
American Birth Control League, 236
American Disabilities Act, 141
Andersen, Kristi, 200–201
Arendt, Hannah, 97
Argentina, 106, 107–108, 262
Aristocracy, 35n.9, 268–269, 271, 272
Aristotle, 92–94, 108n.3, 266
Ash, Roberta, 233–234

Ash, Timothy Garton, 88
Asia, 107, 169–171, 256–257
Assembly, 219–220
Australia, 196–197
Authoritarianism, 96, 105–108, 256, 271
Authority
  Bendix view, 48–50
  and contentious politics, 234, 235
  definition, 2–3
  Durkheim view, 71
  and globalization, 61
  and nation-states, 245
  Weberian view, 42, 45–46, 48, 50
Autonomy
  embedded, 258
  of state, 33–34, 116, 271
  in totalitarian regime, 104, 169–171

B

Bacon, Francis, 249
Bakke, Allan, 141
Balance of payments, 276
Balance of power, 268, 279
Banks, 132, 134, 160
Baran, Paul, 116
Barber, Benjamin, 97
Barcelona, 169
Barnet, Richard, 121, 133, 168
Bay of Pigs, 120, 123
Beard, Charles, 113–114
Beliefs, 248
Bellah, Robert, 70, 79, 82–84
Ben Bella, Ahmed, 261
Bendix, Reinhard, 47–50
Berelson, Bernard, 98, 99–100, 197–198
Berle, Adolf, Jr., 130–131
Berlin, Isaiah, 9
Bernstein, Eduard, 23, 24
Beveridge, William, 125
Biblical individualism, 83
Bill of Rights, 248
Birth control, 236
Black, C. E., 245–246, 273
Blau, Peter, 45
Boston, 185
Bourgeoisie. *See* Middle class
Bowling, 217
Boycotts, 236
Branches, 180–181
Brass, Paul R., 252
Brazil, 106, 107, 258
Brooks, Clem, 194
Brown v. Topeka, 139, 140
Brubaker, Rogers, 254
Brzezinski, Zbigniew K., 101–102
Budget, 86, 122–123
Bull Moose Party, 236
Bureaucracy
  in challenging groups, 237
  and constitutional democracy, 100
  and economic development, 258–259
  in nation-states, 246
  in *The Organization Man,* 222
  responsiveness, 86
  in Skocpol theory, 57, 58
  in totalitarian state, 102
  Weber view, 41, 42, 43, 44, 246
Bureaucratic authoritarianism, 106–107
Burstein, Paul, 235–236
Bush, George, 122, 123
Bush, George W., Jr., 183
Business
  and cities, 149–155, 157–160, 163–164, 166
  Tocqueville view, 76, 129–130
  in the U.S., 115–116, 130–134

C

Cadre party, 182
Calculability, 43–44
Calhoun, Craig, 225
Cambodia, 108
Campaigners, 212
Campbell, Angus, 199
Canada, 196–197
Capital. *See also* Social capital
  centralization, 18
  civic, 165–167
  and globalization, 61
  and new markets, 131–132
  and the state, 33–34, 52

Capitalism. *See also* Imperialism; Monopoly capitalism
and democracy, 272
institutional, 133
Marxian view, 13, 17, 34–35
and modern democracy, 101
and nation-states, 263–264
as reigning system, 108
and the state, 16, 33–34
structures, 32
sustaining forces (Marx view), 17
and transnational corporations, 133–134
Capitalist class, 35 n.9, 157–158. *See also* Social classes
Capitalists, 13
Casey, William, 123
Castells, Manuel, 230
Caucus, 180, 181
Cells, 181–182
Central Intelligence Agency, 120, 123–124
Chambers, William Nisbet, 177
Change. *See also* Revolution
Marxian view, 10–12
military role, 262
in movement organizations, 233–234
Tilly view, 51
Chaos, 67
Charisma, 107
Charismatic personalities, 39
Charity, 84
Checks-and-balances, 118
Chicago, 185
Chile, 123
China
communism in, 269
economic zones, 148, 169–171
revolutionary conditions, 57–58, 264, 268
totalitarian state, 104–105
CIA. *See* Central Intelligence Agency
Cities. *See also* Suburbs
and business, 149–155, 157–160, 163–164, 166
declining, 159–160, 168–169
dominance, 168
finances, 161
global, 167–168
growth, 150–152, 163
industrial, 156–160
mercantilist, 156
and pluralism, 149–150
policy domains, 153
political parties, 185–187, 193
power, 150–153, 158–159, 164–165
reemerging, 165–167
regime theory, 153–155
in Sunbelt, 163–164
and welfare, 159, 186–187
Citizenship. *See also* Rank and file
and equality, 138–140
and globalism, 279
and the nation-state, 253–259
and participation, 149, 211–218, 246
Civic capital, 165–167
Civic society, 86–88, 272
Civil religion, 82–83
Civil republican individualism, 83
Civil rights
as contention example, 227–228, 232
and democracy, 100
in Great Britain, 253–254
as movement, 5
and political parties, 201
and the state, 138
Civil Rights Acts, 139–140
Civil service, 203–204, 246. *See also* Bureaucracy
Civil society, 79, 216–218
Class, ruling, 117, 134–136, 143n.6. *See also* Elite; Social classes
Class consciousness, 22–23, 36n.24
Class rule, 28–29
Class struggle, 128
Cleveland, 161
Clinton, Bill, 122, 184, 197
Cliques, 134–135, 177
Cloward, Richard, 237
Coalitions, 268–270
Cohen, Joshua, 97–98
Cohen, Michael A., 168–169
Coleman, James, 80, 84–86, 190–191, 217
Collective action, 53–55
Collective behavior, 225–226
Collective conscience, 67

Collective identity, 224
Colonialism, 275–276
Commodificaiton, 151
Communalists, 212
Communication
  Habermas view, 32
  Marxian view, 21
  and nation-states, 245
  and political parties, 178, 188
  in totalitarian state, 102, 103
Communism
  collapse, 88, 108, 121–122
  favorable conditions, 269
  Marxian view, 12, 13–14
Communist Manifesto
  on middle class, 13, 22–23
  on revolution, 18
Communist Party
  Machiavellian lessons, 28
  oligarchical nature, 189
  U.S. counterpart, 236
Community
  in cities, 156
  corporate, 131, 135
  feeling of, 84
  and institutional performance, 86–87
  societal, 79
Complete activists, 212
Comte, Auguste, 66
Conflict, 41, 64, 67, 251. *See also* Contention; War
Conscience, collective, 67
Consensus. *See* Durkheim, Emile; Tocqueville, Alexis de
Constitutional government. *See also* Beard, Charles
  and equality, 74
  in modern democracy, 100
  in the U.S., 118–119
Contention
  collective behavior, 225–226
  cultural forces, 228–230
  grievance/breakdown theory, 232–233
  and information technology, 230–231
  institutionalization, 233–235
  and political process, 226–228
  and social networks, 231–232
Contentious politics
  forms, 219–225
  historical perspective, 220–223
  identity movements, 224–225, 230
  results, 235–237
  social revolutions, 223–224
Conventional politics, 211–218
Cooperative economic ventures, 85
Co-optation, 235
Core states, 275, 279
Corporate community, 131–133
Corporations
  and imperialism, 276
  and the state, 61
  transnational, 133–134
  in the U.S., 116, 130–134, 137
  and welfare, 71
Corruption, 158–159
Coup d'etats, 262
Courts, 118–119, 139, 228
Creationists, 229, 241n.60
Crises, 82–83
Crowds, 219–220, 225–226
Cuba, 262
Culture
  basic concept, 4–5
  Bellah view, 83–84
  and contention, 228–231
  and contentious politics, 224
Cynicism, 201

D

Daalder, Hans, 246–247
Dahl, Robert A., 98, 114, 149
Daley, Richard, 185
Dalton, Russell, 195, 202, 214–215, 235
Darwin, Charles, 229
Day care centers, 86
Declaration of Independence, 248
Defense, 245–246
Defense budget, 122–123
Deliberative democracy, 97

Democracy. *See also* Dictatorships; Modern democracy; Tocqueville, Alexis de
for Aristotle, 93–95
Bendix view, 50
bottom-up *versus* top-down, 118
and capitalism, 101, 272
definition, 271
deliberative, 97
demonstration effect, 50
essential components, 80, 81, 86–88, 97–98
favorable factors, 266–272
Lenin view, 26
Lipset analysis, 80, 81
parliamentary *versus* presidential, 110n.21
in political parties, 191
and Putnam, 88
Weber view, 43, 44–45
Democrats
Jacksonian, 187
New Deal, 192, 193
and professions, 194
Demonstration effect, 50
Desegregation, 139–140, 227–228
Determinism, 11, 32
Developing countries. *See also* Colonialism
and authoritarianism, 105–107
economy, 105–106, 247, 257–259
nation-building, 246, 251–252
Developmental policies, 153
Developmental state, 258
Dewey, John, 96, 97
Dialectical materialism, 10
Dialectics, 30
Dictatorships, 56–58, 105–106
Disabled persons, 141
Disruption, 237
Dissent, 100, 103. *See also* Contention
Distribution. *See* Allocational policies
Diversity
and modern democracy, 100
and totalitarian regimes, 103
Division of labor
Durkheim view, 12, 66–67, 70, 71–72
in world-system, 274
Dogma, 104
Domhoff, G. William
on institutional elite, 117, 131, 134, 142
on Social Security, 128
Dominant class, 117, 134–136, 143n.6
Dulles, Allen, 123
Dulles, John Foster, 120
Durkheim, Emile
antecedents, 65–66
and Bellah, 82
on division of labor, 12, 66–67, 70, 71–72
and Parsons, 77
significance, 5–6
on society, 67–70, 216, 272
on suicide, 66
Duverger, Maurice, 179–183, 202

E

Eastern Europe
civil society, 88
contentious politics, 235
economy, 107
future trends, 88, 107
nationalism, 251
political parties, 182
welfare expenditures, 126
Economic development, 255–259, 266–267, 272
Economic rights, 138
Economics
neoclassical, 257
Poulantzas view, 32
Economism, 34
Economy
average income, 266
of developing countries, 105–106, 247, 257–259
global, 278–279
of Japan, 256, 257, 278
Marxian view, 12–14
and nation-building, 252, 255
and political partisanship, 201
as revolution antecedent, 18–21
in totalitarian state, 102, 104–105

Economy *(con't.)*
and totalitarianism *versus* democracy, 107
U.S., 205
and world-system, 274–275
Edge cities, 162
Education
affirmative action, 141
and democracy, 266
desegregation, 139, 140
Durkheim view, 67
in England, 249
Parsons view, 79
and political participation, 214
and values, 79
and voting behavior, 201
Efficiency, 43–44
Egypt, 261, 262
Eisenhower, Dwight, 122, 192
Eisenhower–Stevenson election, 199–200
Eisinger, Peter, 227
Eldersveld, Samuel, 189–190
Elections
and advertising, 204
direct primary, 203
partisanship *versus* issues, 198–202
representation types, 183–185
in totalitarian regime, 102–103
Elite, 188–189, 255, 279. *See also* Institutional elite; Power elite
Elitists, 113–117, 148, 150
Elizabeth I, 249
Elkin, Stephen, 153–154
Embedded autonomy, 258
Employment, 137, 159, 162, 167–168. *See also* Patronage
Engagement. *See* Citizenship
Engels, Friedrich, 9, 13
England. *See* Great Britain
Environmental concern, 5, 184, 195, 201. *See also* Green Party
Equal Rights Amendment, 140
Equality. *See also* Inequality
in England, 249
and family, 79
and modern democracy, 100
as moral vision, 96
of opportunity, 77
Tocqueville analysis, 73–76, 129–130
in the U.S., 136–142, 248
Weber view, 41
Esping-Andersen, Gosta, 125
Ethics, 41
Ethnic groups, 185, 193, 215
Europe. *See also* Eastern Europe; Western Europe
electoral laws, 183–184
Lipset study, 266
political parties, 176–177, 180–181, 182, 187–190
social movements, 224
European Union, 278
Evans, Peter, 256–257
Evolution theory, 229, 241n.60
Exchange value, 151
Expressive individualism, 83

F

Factions, 175–176
Fainstein, Susan, 152
Family
Parsons view, 79
and political affiliation, 197–198
and social capital, 85
Fanaticism, 99
Fascism, 269
Feagin, Joe, 152, 163
February Revolution, 25
Federal Bureau of Investigation, 124
Federal system, 73, 100, 118
Feminism. *See also* Women
and contention, 231–232
and culture, 5
Festinger, Leon, 208n.62
Feuer, Lewis, 11
Financial institutions, 132, 134, 160
Fogelson, Robert, 163–164
Force
Durkheim view, 71
Neo-Marxist views, 28
and state-making, 52–53
Weberian view, 38
Foreign investment, 276–277

Frame analysis, 229–230
France. *See also* Western Europe
citizenship, 254
collective action types, 54–55
contention, 221, 231
democracy, 268
Marxian view, 15–16
nationalism, 249–250
and political participation, 246
power, 118
revolutionary factors, 57–58, 72–73
voting, 213
Franco, Francisco, 106
Frank, André Gunder, 276
Frankfurt School, 29–34
Free Economic Zones, 170
Freedom, 74, 75
Freeman, Jo, 231
Freud, Sigmund, 29–30
Friedland, Roger, 238
Friedrich, Carl J., 101–102
Friends, and political affiliation, 197–198
Fukayama, Francis, 108

G

Gamson, William, 236–237
Garreau, Joel, 162
Geertz, Clifford, 85, 247–248
Gender, 60, 215. *See also* Women
General will, 66, 67, 70
Geopolitics, 53
Germany. *See also* Western Europe
citizenship, 254
democracy *versus* fascism, 268–269
Green Party, 233
nationalism, 250
and peasants, 264
political parties, 187–190
submissiveness, 207n.33
Third Reich example, 102–103, 104
voting, 213
welfare system, 125
Giddens, Anthony, 67
Glenn, Norval, 197
Globalization
and business, 133–134
and cities, 167–168
and the state, 61
Goal transformation, 233
Goffman, Erving, 229
Goldstone, Jack, 223
Gottdiener, Mark, 152
Gould, Roger, 231
Government
Aristotle view, 92–93
constitutional, 74, 100, 118–119
federal, 73–74, 201, 204
regional, 86
representative, 97
separate branches, 100
urban, 158, 163
Gramlich, James, 165–167
Gramsci, Antonio, 28–29, 31
Granovetter, Mark, 86
Great Britain. *See also* Western Europe
balance of power, 268
citizenship, 253–254
economic development, 255
Marxian view, 16
nationalism, 248–249
and partisanship, 195, 196–197
and political participation, 246–247
political parties, 187
power locus, 117–118, 148
voting, 213
welfare system, 125–127
Great Depression, 221–222, 233
Greeks, ancient, 30, 92–95
Green Party, 184, 233
Greenfeld, Liah, 248–251, 253
Grievance/breakdown theory, 232–233
Growth machine, 150–151, 163
Guatemala, 123
Gurr, Ted Robert, 232–233

H

Habermas, Jürgen
on debate, 97
on legitimacy, 3, 251
and Parsons, 79
and reason, 30
Habits of the heart, 83

Haig, Alexander, 122
Hansen, John Mark, 216
Hartz, Louis, 73, 74, 248
Harvey, David, 151
Hate groups, 230–231
Hawley, Amos, 164–165
Hegel, G. W. F., 31, 56
Hegemony, 28–29, 108
Henry VIII, 249
Highlander School, 232
Hilferding, Rudolph, 27, 131–132
Hintze, Otto, 56–57
Hispanic Americans, 140, 142, 159–160
History
  and contention, 220
  French, 54–55
  Hegelian view, 56
  leaders, 39, 44–45
  Lenin view, 25
  Marxian view, 10–12
  Weber view, 39, 44–45
Hitler, Adolf. *See* Third Reich
Hobson, J. A., 27, 275–276
Hoffer, Eric, 220
Hong Kong, 107, 256, 257
Horkheimer, Max, 29
Housing, 86
Huckfeldt, Robert, 198
Human rights, 254
Huntington, Henry, Jr., 164
Huntington, Samuel P., 252, 261–263
Hussein, Saddam, 105

I

IBM, 133
Identification, political, 192, 199–200, 202, 253–259
Identity, 253
Identity politics, 54, 224–225, 230
Ideology. *See also* Nationalism
  and capitalism, 17, 32
  and contention, 228–229, 241n.58
  of managerialism, 49
  of modern democracy, 100
  and political parties, 177, 184
  in totalitarian state, 101–102, 103, 104
  in the United States, 199
Immigration, 142, 254–255, 279
Imperial Presidency, 120–121
Imperialism
  and intellectuals, 260
  Lenin view, 26–27
  and nation-building, 275–276
Income, average, 266
Independents, 192, 194, 200, 201
India, 101, 252, 258
Individual rights, 32
Individualism
  in England, 249
  and peasants, 264
  and punishments, 68
  types, 83
  in the U. S., 58–59, 83–84
Individuals. *See also* Citizenship
  and bureaucracy, 41–42
  and choices, 41–42
  equality, 41
  in groups, 49
  and history, 39, 44–45
  in modern democracy, 96–97, 98–99
Individuation, 67
Indonesia, 250
Industrialization, 76, 119, 156–160
Industry, 48–49
Inequality, 34–35, 115, 136–138, 167–168. *See also* Equality
Information technology, 167, 230–231
Informers, 124
Inglehart, Ronald, 195
Injustice, 34–35
Innovation, 86
Instability, political, 252–253
Institutional capitalism, 133
Institutional elite, 117, 131, 134, 142
Institutions. *See also* Social institutions; Voluntary associations
  antecedents, 1–2
  basic concept, 4
  for contention, 233–235
  Durkheim view, 66–67, 68–69, 272
  effectiveness factors, 87

financial, 132, 134, 160
Marxian view, 67
as power loci, 117
religious, 68–69
and stability, 252
Weber view, 39–40, 42, 44
Integration, and political parties, 178
Intellectuals
and authority, 50
and nation-states, 259–261, 264
Intelligence, 66. *See also* Central Intelligence Agency; Federal Bureau of Investigation
Interdependence, 274–276
Interests, 54
International Monetary Fund, 279
International relations, 27–28
International Typographical Union (ITU), 190
Internet, 230–231
Investment, foreign, 276–277
Iran, 250
Iran-Contra affair, 123
Iraq, 105, 262
Iron cage metaphor, 42
Iron curtain, 114
Iron law of oligarchy, 187–189
Islam, 250
Italy, 86, 221, 269. *See also* Gramsci, Antonio

J

Jackson, Kenneth, 160
Japan
economy, 256, 257, 278
and fascism, 269
and peasants, 264
and revolution, 57
Jensen, Richard, 202, 204
Johnson, Lyndon, 120, 121, 141
Johnson–Goldwater election, 200
Joppke, Christian, 254–255
Judiciary, 118–119, 139, 228

K

Kansas Board of Education, 241n.60
Kant, Immanuel, 66
Kaufman, Herbert, 149–150
Kemal, Mustafa, 261
Kennedy, John F., 120
Kerensky, Alexander, 25–26
Key, V.O., Jr., 183, 193, 194
Khadaffi, Mommar, 105
Killian, Lewis, 225–226
King, Martin Luther, Jr., 124, 222, 232
Kings, 49–50
Klandermans, Bert, 232
Korea, 107, 256, 257, 258–259

L

Labor. *See* Division of labor; Trade unions; Workers
Ladd, Everett Carll, Jr., 194, 217
LaFollette, Robert, 184
Land, 35n.9, 151–152, 157, 163
Landlords, 35n.9, 268–269, 271, 272
LaPalombara, Joseph, 178–179
Latin America
and authoritarianism, 106
democracy study, 266
military role, 261, 262
and U. S., 120, 123, 276–277
welfare expenditures, 126
Law(s)
for Aristotle, 92–93
Durkheim view, 68, 70
and modern democracy, 100
Poulantzas view, 32
Weber view, 43–44, 45
Lawyers, 43
Lazarsfeld, 197–198
Le Bon, Gustav, 219–220, 231
Leaders
Aristotle view, 92–93
Bendix view, 48
and citizens, 149, 212
of corporations, 132–136

Leaders *(con't.)*
of developing countries, 105–107, 257–258
in modern democracy, 98–99
office *versus* occupant, 116
of political parties, 185, 188–190
of predatory states, 257–258
of social movements, 234
state-centered, 128–129
of trade unions, 191
Weber view, 39, 44–46
Legislation, 86
Legitimacy
Durkheim view, 70–71
Habermas view, 3, 31–32
and nation-states, 251–253
and political parties, 178
Weber view, 29, 46
Lenin, V. I., 22, 23–27, 187–188, 237
Leonardi, Robert, 86
Liberal ethos, 248
Libya, 105
Linz, Juan, 106, 110n.21
Lipset, Seymour Martin, 80–81, 190–191, 248, 266–267
Literacy, 252. *See also* Education
Locke, John, 248
Logan, John, 151
London, 167
Loners, 231
Los Angeles, 163–164
Loury, Glenn, 85
Loyalty. *See* Political partisanship
Lukács, Georg, 25, 31

M

Machiavelli, Niccolo, 28, 91
Madison, James, 175–176
Madsen, Richard, 83
Magdoff, Harry, 276
Majority, tyranny of, 76, 129
Managerialism, 49
Manufacturing, 76, 275
Manza, Jeff, 194
Marcuse, Herbert, 29–31
Markets, 132, 257–258, 279
Marshall, T. H., 138, 253
Marshall, Thurgood, 228
Marx, Karl
on alienation, 12
on economics, 13–14
and interdependence, 274
and Lipset, 81
on politics, 14, 15–16, 41
and revolution, 10–11, 17–23
on role of people, 34
significance, 5, 34–35, 117
on social classes, 12–13, 35n.9, 272
on the state, 16, 33, 34
Weber on, 39
Mass party, 182
Materialism, 10
Materialist values, 195–196
Mayntz, Renate, 189
McAdam, Doug, 223, 227–228, 230, 232
McCarthy, John, 230, 234
McCarthyism, 114, 222
McDonalds, 133
McPhail, Clark, 220
McPhee, 197–198
Meaning, 230
Means, Gardiner, 130–131
Media
and election campaigns, 204
and social movements, 224
Tocqueville view, 75
and totalitarianism, 102, 103
Meek, Ronald L., 19
Melucci, Alberto, 224–225, 230, 235
Meyer, David, 234–235
Michels, Robert, 187, 233
Middle class
Aristotle view, 94
in authoritarian state, 106
and democracy, 80, 267, 270
in France, 250
Lenin view, 27
Lipset view, 80
Marxian view, 13, 16, 21
political affiliation, 197
Progressive movement, 203
and social capital, 217–218
Milbrath, Lester, 211
Miliband, Ralph, 33–34, 116

Military
and nation-states, 245, 261–263, 264
and totalitarian state, 102
in the U.S., 115, 122, 139
Milling behavior, 220
Mills, C. Wright, 79, 115, 122, 152
Milwaukee, 161, 166–167
Minneapolis–St. Paul, 166
Mintz, Beth, 132
Misery, increased, 19
Mizruchi, Mark, 135
Mobilization, 54, 79, 225, 231–232. *See also* Resource mobilization
Mobs, 219–220, 221, 225–226
Modern democracy
empirical view, 98–100
foundations, 100–101
moral vision, 96–98
Modernity, 247, 248
Molotch, Harvey, 150–151
Mommsen, Wolfgang, 39, 44–45
Monopoly capitalism, 27
Moore, Barrington, Jr., 55, 56–57, 267–270
Moore, Gwen, 134–135
Moral order, 66–67
Moral vision, 96–98
Morris, Aldon, 232
MPO ratio, 165
Müller, Ronald, 132, 168
Myrdal, Gunnar, 139, 143

N

Nanetti, Raffaella, 86
Nasser, Gamal Abdul, 261
National Association for the Advancement of Colored People (NAACP), 228, 234
National Organization for Women (NOW), 216, 222
Nationalism, 5, 247–251, 260
Nation-states. *See also* Democracy
characteristics, 245–247
economic development, 255–259
and intellectuals, 259–261, 264
legitimacy, 251–253
and the military, 261–263, 264
and nationalism, 247–251
and peasants, 263–265
and political identity, 253–259
success factors, 273–278
Native Americans, 129, 140
Neighborhood organizations, 165
Neo-consensualists. *See* Bellah, Robert; Coleman, James; Lipset, Seymour; Parsons, Talcott; Putnam, Robert
Neo-Marxists. *See* Frankfurt School; Gramsci, Antonio; Lenin, V. I.
Neo-Weberians. *See* Bendix, Reinhard; Skocpol, Theda; Tilly, Charles
Networks. *See also* World system
and contention, 231–232
and dominant class, 134–135
and political affiliation, 197–198
and political parties, 178–179
and social movements, 225
New York, 161, 167, 169, 185–186
Newspapers, 75
Newton, Isaac, 249
Nie, Norman, 200–201, 211–212
Nietzsche, Friedrich, 39, 44
Nihilism, 84
Nineteenth Amendment, 139
Nixon, Richard, 120, 121, 122, 192
Norms
for Durkheim, 68, 70, 75
for Parsons, 77–79
North, Oliver, 123
North Carolina Manumission Society, 236

O

Oberschall, Anthony, 54
Occupation, 46–47
O'Donnell, Guillermo, 106
Oligarchy, 93, 105–106
iron law of, 187–189
Opportunity, 54, 227–228
Opposition, 71. *See also* Contention; Protest movements
Orators, 188

Orfield, Myron, 162
The Organization Man, 222
Organization of American States (OAS), 120
Organizations. *See* Institutions; Voluntary associations; *specific organizations*
Orum, Anthony M., 165–167
Ostrogorski, Moise, 187, 202

P

Pareto, Vilfredo, 188
Paris Commune of 1871, 26
Parks, Rosa, 227, 232
Parliamentary democracy, 110n.21
Parochial participants, 212
Parsons, Talcott, 77–79
Participation. *See* Citizenship
Partisanship. *See* Political partisanship
Passivity, 188, 190
Patronage, 203–204
Peace Corps, 120
Peasants
  and Communism, 269
  Lenin view, 25
  Marx view, 21, 25
  and nation-building, 263–265, 268
Pedagogical approach, 6–7
Pennsylvania, 137
Pensions, 59, 71, 128
People. *See* Agents; Individuals
Peripheral states, 275, 279
Peron, Juan, 106
Perot, Ross, 184
Peterson, Paul, 152–153, 154
Philippines, 258
Pittsburgh, 166
Piven, Frances Fox, 237
Plato, 93
Plessy v. Ferguson, 139–140
Plunkitt, George Washington, 186
Pluralism
  in cities, 149–150
  and modern democracy, 97–98, 100–101
  and totalitarianism, 102–103
  and U.S., 114, 149–152
Pluralists, 113–117, 148, 149–150
Pol Pot, 108
Poland, 227
Political action committees, 135
Political machines, 185–187
Political opportunities, 227–228
Political participation
  and civil society, 216–218
  contentious forms, 219–225
  and education, 214
  effectiveness, 238
  gender factor, 215–216
  identity movements, 224–225, 230
  institutionalization, 262
  and nation-building, 252
  polity-centered view, 216
  race factor, 215
  society-centered view, 215–216
  and socioeconomic class, 213–215
  Tocqueville view, 157, 216
Political parties
  and African Americans, 216
  candidate campaigns, 183, 203, 204
  characteristics, 176–177
  in Europe, 176–177, 180–181, 182, 187–190, 252
  and loyalty, 199–202
  membership types, 182–183
  in modern democracy, 98, 100–101
  organizational units, 180–182
  origins, 177–179
  patronage, 203–204
  and peasants, 264
  and power, 47, 187–191
  in suburbs, 162
  in totalitarian state, 102, 104
  in the U.S., 128, 176–177, 183, 202–205, 252
  and welfare, 186, 204
Political partisanship
  Independents, 192, 194
  and issues, 198–202
  realignment theory, 192–193
  and social context, 196–198
  and values, 195
Political process, 226–228
Political stability, 252–253

Politicization, of working class, 21
Politics. *See also* Cities; Contentious politics; Political participation
  Bellah view, 82–83
  Bendix view, 48–49
  and corporate community, 135
  gender effect, 60
  issue orientation, 200
  Marxian view, 14, 15–16, 41
  mobilization, 53–55
  Parsons view, 79
  Poulantzas view, 32
  and status groups, 46–47
  voluntary associations, 74–75
  Weber view, 39, 41, 46–47
  and welfare, 127–128, 153, 186–187
Polity, 92–94
Population density, 70, 223
Populism, 260
Post-materialist values, 195–196
Potter, David, 130
Poulantzas, Nicos, 25, 32–34, 116
Poverty, 101, 152, 167–168, 278
Powell, Colin, 122
Power
  balance of, 268, 279
  of bureaucracy, 43
  of business, 129–136
  and cities, 150–153, 158–159, 164–165, 185–187
  concentration, 164–165, 237
  in contentious politics, 237
  definition, 2–3
  demonstration effect, 50
  and economic progress, 108
  executive branch, 119–122
  of groups of officials, 43
  local, 149–150
  of military, 122–123
  in movement organizations, 233–234
  of nation-states, 245–246
  and political participation, 237, 238
  and political parties, 47, 187–191
  of state, 16, 29, 43, 129
  in the U.S., 117–119, 134–136
  in war-making state, 119–121
Power elite, 115
Praetorianism, 262
Precinct captains, 180
Predatory states, 257–258
Presidential democracy, 110n.21
Press, 75
Primary elections, 203
Primogeniture, 73
Priorities, 217–218
Prison riots, 223
Private realm, 104
Production
  Marxian view, 12, 14
  and nation-states, 255
  Poulantzas view, 32
  and technology, 278
Professionalism, 41, 46–47
Progressive movement, 203
Proletariat. *See also* Workers
  Marxian view, 13, 35 n.9
  politicization, 21–22
  relative misery, 19
Proletarization, 18
Propaganda, 188
Property
  ownership, 13
  valuation, 151–152
Proportional representation, 183–184
Prosperity, 130–131, 137
Protest movements, 53–55. *See also* Contentious politics; Opposition
Protestant Ethic, 44
Protestantism, 39, 42, 248
Protests, 210
Prussia, 57
Public, appeal to, 229–230
Public assemblies, 219–220, 221
Punishments, 68
Putnam, Robert, 86–87, 205, 217, 253

Q

Quadagno, Jill, 128

R

Race. *See also* Ethnic groups
  and equality, 139–140

Race *(con't.)*
  and political participation, 215
  Tocqueville view, 75–76, 129
Racism, 83
Rank and file, 188–189, 190
Ratcliff, Richard, 132
Rationality
  Marcuse view, 30–32
  and political protest, 219–220
  and voting, 198–202
  Weber view, 30, 41, 43–44
Reagan, Ronald, 121, 122, 123
Real estate, 151–152, 157, 163–164, 167
Realignment theory, 193–194
Rebellions. *See* Revolution
Redistributive policies, 153
Regime theory, 153–155
Regional governments, 86
Regionalism, 162, 166
Regions, geographical, 53
Religion
  and African Americans, 232
  Bellah view, 82–83
  civic, 82–83
  Durkheim view, 68–69
  in England, 248–249
  and evolution theory, 229
  in Iran, 250
  Marxian view, 14
  Parsons view, 79
  and Progressive movement, 203
  and social norms, 79
  in totalitarian regime, 103
  in the U. S., 82–83, 248
  Weberian view, 42
Repertoire, of collective action, 54
Representation, proportional, 183–184, 206n.20
Representative government, 97, 100
Repression, 29
Republican Party, 162, 193
Resource mobilization, 234, 245
Resources
  and authority, 122
  and nation-states, 245
  and politics, 41
  and U.S. corporations, 130–131
Revolution. *See also* Coup d'etats
  Lenin view, 23–25
  Marxian view, 10–11, 17–23, *20*
  by peasants, 263–264, 269
  Skocpol view, 57
  social, 223–224
  Tillyian view, 55
Richelieu, Cardinal, 249–250
Rights, 138–141. *See also* Civil rights; Human rights
Riots, 223. *See also* Contention
Rituals
  Bellah view, 82–83
  Durkheim view, 69
Roads, 161, 162–163
Roosevelt, Franklin D., 56, 119–120, 125, 192
Roosevelt, Theodore, 184, 236
Rosenstone, Steven, 216
Ross, Thomas, 124
Rostow, W. W., 255
Rotating credit association, 85
Rousseau, Jean Jacques
  on democracy, 91
  general will, 65–66, 67, 70
Roy, William, 130
Royko, Mike, 185
Rubin, Robert, 129
Rueschemeyer, Dietrich, 106, 270–272
Ruling class, 117, 134–136, 143n.6. *See also* Elite; Social classes
Rural areas, 193. *See also* Peasants
Rusk, David, 161–162
Russia. *See also* Soviet Union
  Bolshevik Revolution, 227
  future prospects, 107
  and ideology, 49
  nationalism, 251
  pre-Communist, 25–26
  revolutionary conditions, 57–58

S

St. Louis, 161
Sanctions, 68. *See also* Boycotts
Santiago de Chile, 169
Sartori, Giovanni, 98
Sassen, Saskia, 167, 169

Sayre, Wallace, 149–150
Scandinavia, 125, 127. *See also* Sweden
Schlesinger, Arthur, Jr., 120
Scholars. *See also* Intellectuals
  Marx view, 10
  Weber view, 40
Schudson, Michael, 138
Schumpeter, Joseph, 81, 98
Schwartz, Michael, 132
Science, 249
Secularization, 178
Segregation, 139–140, 227–228
Self-concept, 31
Self-governance, 96–97
Semantics, 230
Separate but equal, 140
Sewell, William, 241n.58
Sexual harassment, 141
Shils, Edward, 105, 260
Singapore, 107, 256, 257
Skocpol, Theda, 55–60
  on nation-states, 269–270
  on political participation, 217–218
  on social revolution, 223
  on state power, 117, 142
  on welfare policy, 127–128
Skowronek, Stephen, 118–119
Slavery, 75–76, 236
Smelser, Neil, 226
Snow, David, 229–230, 231
Social capital, 216–218
Social classes. *See also* Capitalist class; Division of labor; Peasants; Ruling class; Workers
  alliances, 268–270
  and citizenship, 253
  and democracy, 266–269, 271–272
  Durkheim view, 71
  and hegemony, 29
  Marxian view, 9–12, 12–13, 15, 35n.9
  and political affiliation, 193, 196–198
  political participation, 213–215, 238
  and the state, 33, 53
  and suburbs, 161
  Tilly view, 53
  Weberian view, 46–47
  world-system perspective, 274
Social cliques, 134–135
Social institutions, 4, 12
Social movements, 5, 224–225, 229, 279
Social networks, 4, 231–232, 234
Social rights, 138
Social Security Act of 1935, 125, 128
Social trust, 85–86, 97
Socialism
  in Canada, 80
  as ideology, 228–229
  and intellectuals, 260–261
Socialist parties, 182, 187–189
Societal community, 79
Society
  civil, 79, 216–218
  Durkheim view, 67–70
  Parsons view, 77–79, *78*
  rights-based, 138
Sociology
  basic premise, 2–3
  conflict *versus* consensus, 64–65
  Durkheim definition, 66
  in the U.S., 127–129
Solidarity, 88
Solidarity movement, 227
Sombart, Werner, 58
South Korea. *See* Korea
Southern Christian Leadership Conference, 222
Soviet Union. *See also* Russia
  and authority *versus* power, 3
  Communism rise, 269
  and Marxism, 10
  and peasants, 268, 269
  and Reagan, 121
  soviets, 26
  as totalitarian state, 101, 104
Soysal, Yasemin, 254
Spain, 106, 107
Sparta, 93–94
Special Economic Zones, 170
Speech, freedom of, 75
Spencer, Herbert, 70
Sprague, John, 198
Sprawl, 163–164
Stability, 252–253
Stalin, Josef. *See* Soviet Union
State(s). *See also* Bureaucracy; Developing countries; Nation-states

State(s) *(con't.)*
autonomy, 33–34
and class struggle, 33
core and peripheral, 275, 279
and corporations, 61
crises, 82–83
developmental, 258
diversity, 53, 56–57
Durkheim view, 70–71
and economic growth, 256–259
globalization impact, 61
Gramsci view, 29
Lenin view, 25–26
Marxian view, 16, 33, 34
maternalistic, 59–60
Miliband view, 33–34
origins, 51–53
Poulantzas view, 33–34
and power, 16, 29, 43, 129 (*see also* United States)
predatory, 258
Skocpol view, 56–60
Tilly view, 51–53
Weber view, 38, 43–44, 56
Status, 208n.62, 217–218
Status groups, 46–47
Stephens, Evelyne, 106, 270–272
Stephens, John, 106, 270–272
Stone, Clarence, 153–154
Strikes, 236
Structures
for Marx, 13–14
for Poulantzas, 32–33
Student Non-Violent Coordinating Committee (SNCC), 222, 234
Students for a Democratic Society (SDS), 222
Sublimation, 29
Submissiveness, 188, 207n.33
Suburbs, 160–162
Suffrage, 73, 182
Suggestibility, 188
Suicide, 66, 71
Sullivan, William, 83
Sweden, 101. *See also* Scandinavia
Sweezy, Paul, 116
Swidler, Ann, 83
Symbols
Bellah view, 82
and contentious politics, 224
Durkheim view, 69

T

Taiwan, 107, 170, 256, 257
Tammany Machine, 186
Tarrow, Sidney
on contention, 221, 223, 226
on opportunity, 228
on protest cycles, 234–235
Taxation, 223, 245–246
Taylor, Frederick, 49
Taylor, Maxwell, 122
Technology
and authoritarian state, 106
and cities, 167
and contention, 230–231
Marxian view, 18–19
and production, 278
and totalitarian state, 102
and values, 195
Television, 204
Terror, 102, 103
Terrorism. *See* Hate groups
Thatcher, Margaret, 126–127
Third party candidates, 184, 204
Third Reich, 102–103, 104
Thurmond, Strom, 184
Tilly, Charles, 50–55
on contention, 220, 223, 226
on grievance, 232–233
on nation-states, 245
Tipton, Stephen, 83
Tocqueville, Alexis de, 72–77
and Bellah, 83
on equality in U.S., 129–130, 139, 143
and Lipset, 80–81
on political participation, 157, 216, 253
and Putnam, 87
significance, 5–6
Toennies, Ferdinand, 156
Tokyo, 167
Tolerance, 79

Totalitarianism, 95–96, 101–105
Trade, 278
Trade unions. *See also* Strikes
  and cities, 165
  leadership, 190–191
  Lenin view, 22
  Lipset work, 80–81
  and Marxism, 22–23
  and strikes, 236–237
Transportation
  and nation-states, 245
  and political parties, 178
  and suburbs, 161, 162–163
  and Sunbelt, 164
Tribal councils, 105
Trow, Martin, 80, 190
True believers, 220, 231
Truman, Harry, 120
Trust
  and contention, 234
  and democracy, 97
  and economic growth, 258
  and social capital, 85–86
Turkey, 261, 262
Turner, Ralph, 225–226
Tyranny, 92–94
Tyranny of the majority, 76, 99, 129

U

Underclass, 137, 159–160, 162, 167–168. *See also* Social classes
Unemployment, 137
United States. *See also* Civil rights; Political parties; Political partisanship
  bureaucracy, 100
  business, 115–116, 130–136
  Civil War, 82
  class struggle, 128
  common beliefs, 248
  Congress, 119, 121, 134, 140–141
  contentious politics, 221–222, 235, 236–237
  culture, 5
  as democracy, 97–98, 99
  dominant class, 134–136
  economic growth, 257
  elections, 184
  equality and inequality, 136–142
  executive branch, 16, 119–122
  and imperialism, 276
  intelligence agencies, 123–125
  and Latin America, 276–277
  Lipset view, 81
  local governments, 118
  Marcuse view, 30
  nationalism, 250
  New Deal, 56
  pluralist *versus* elitist views, 113–117, 148–150
  political participation, 213, 217, 252
  power, 117–119, 134–136
  reaction to liberalism, 141–142
  religion, 82–83, 248
  and socialism, 80
  sociological perspectives, 127–129
  Tocqueville analysis, 74–76
  trends, 84
  values and norms, 77
  welfare, 58–60, 122, 124–128, 137
  women, 60, 137, 140
Universal pragmatics, 31
Urban development, 86
Urban League, 234
Urban migration, 247
Urban sprawl, 163–164
Urbanization, 21. *See also* Cities
Use value, 151
Useem, Michael, 132–133, 135, 223, 233
Utilitarian individualism, 83
U-2 incident, 123

V

Valuation, of cities, 151
Value judgments, 40
Values
  and partisanship, 195
  and religion, 69, 79
  and society, 77
Ventura, Jesse, 184
Verba, Sidney, 211–212
Verelendung, 19

Vietnam, 264
Vietnam War, 120–121, 123, 201, 222
Violence, 236, 251, 252. *See also* Hate groups
Voluntary associations
  Bellah view, 84
  and cities, 165
  Lipset view, 81
  and modern democracy, 100–101, 272
  and political parties, 178
  Tocqueville view, 74–75, 272
  trends, 205, 213, 279
Volunteerism, 217
Voting. *See also* Elections
  decision-making process, 198–202
  and modern democracy, 98
  party identification, 192–194, 196–197
  in totalitarian regime, 102–103
  turnout, 84, 202, 213, 217
  women's suffrage, 139

W

Wade, Robert, 259
Wallace, George, 200
Wallerstein, Immanuel, 274, 278
War. *See also* Vietnam War
  and power, 119–122
  and state-making, 52–53, 245
  Tilly view, 52
Warner, Sam Bass, Jr., 156
Warren, Earl, 139, 228
Wealth
  and democracy, 80–81, 87, 101, 267
  and institutions, 87
  Lipset view, 80, 266–267
  in postindustrial economy, 167–168
  Putnam view, 87
  Tocqueville view, 76
  in the U.S., 130, 136–137
Weapons, 102
Weber, Max
  on authority, 42, 45–46, 48, 50
  dualism, 46
  and Frankfurt School, 30, 31
  and institutions, 4
  and interdependence, 274
  on Marx, 39
  and Parsons, 77
  on rationality, 30, 41, 43–44
  on scholars, 10
  significance, 5
  and Skocpol, 56
  and the state, 38, 43–44, 56, 251
  on theory, 40
Weiner, Myron, 178–179
Welfare. *See also* Citizenship; Redistributive policies
  and cities, 159, 186–187
  Durkheim view, 71
  and globalization, 61
  in modern democracies, 101
  and nation-states, 245–246
  and political parties, 186, 204
  Poulantzas view, 33
  in the U. S., 58–60, 122, 125, 127–128, 204
  in Western Europe, 125–127
West
  values, 195
  and work ideology, 49
Western Europe, 125–127, 147–148, 176–177. *See also* Imperialism; *specific countries*
Whibley, Leonard, 94–95
Whyte, William H., 222
Wisconsin, 137
Wise, David, 124
Wolf, Eric, 263
Wolff, Edward N., 137–138
Women, 60, 137, 140. *See also* Feminism; Sexual harassment
Workers. *See also* Proletariat; Trade unions
  and democracy, 271–272
  and ideology, 49
  political affiliation, 194, 196–197
  political participation, 217–218
  politization, 21–22
World system, 274–278, 279
Wu, Weiping, 169

Y

Young Republicans, 222
Youth, 194, 201, 225

Z

Zald, Mayer, 230, 233–234